D1766552

7 8.13
29.8 13

His

JOSEPH GOEBBELS

A biography by

CURT RIESS

FONTHILL

Fonthill Media Limited
Fonthill Media LLC
www.fonthillmedia.com
office@fonthillmedia.com

First published in 1949
This revised edition first published 2013

British Library Cataloguing in Publication Data:
A catalogue record for this book is available from the British Library

ISBN 978-1-78155-122-6

Typeset in Sabon 10/13.5
Printed and bound in England

Connect with us
 facebook.com/fonthillmedia twitter.com/fonthillmedia

PREFACE
by
LOUIS P. LOCHNER
Editor of 'The Goebbels Diaries'

When I ran into Curt Riess in the American Press Camp at Berlin sometime in the latter part of 1945, I noticed that he seemed less interested than previously in the daily news of occupied Germany. He was rather irregular in attendance at the official press conferences, frequently absent from the correspondents' mess, away from his billet for hours in his automobile and considerably preoccupied when in our midst.

In short, he was different from the Curt Riess I had hitherto known. The alert war correspondent had—so it appeared to me—become somewhat of an absent-minded recluse.

Then, however, one day he revealed himself to me. 'I am working day and night and all the time on a biography of Joseph Goebbels,' he confided. 'Goebbels to me is the most outstanding man of the Nazi regime, not even barring Adolf Hitler himself.' Now I knew why Curt Riess seemed changed.

Little did I imagine then that, two years later, I should be occupying myself almost as intensively with 'Unser Doktor' as did Curt Riess. Late in 1946 the Goebbels Diaries had been found. In May 1947 I was asked to edit, annotate and translate a one-volume version of the diminutive Propaganda Minister's voluminous output. From 1 July 1947 my mind, too, was on Joseph Goebbels to the exclusion of many matters with which I should have preferred to fill my cranium. I do not hesitate to say, however, that Goebbels captivated me in a weird sort of way.

Curt Riess has rendered us all a real service by meticulously putting together, in a readable and graphic way, the story of one of the most fascinating, albeit vilest, characters of our time. Goebbels is bound to have his permanent place in history, even as Mephisto has his in mythology.

I do not rate Joseph Goebbels as highly as my colleague Curt Riess does. I believe Hitler himself out-classed all the men under him. I do not think it

3

likely, for instance, that he used Goebbels to draft his last will. But that is a matter of opinion and Riess may be right and I wrong. Also, I have seen no evidence that Goebbels wrote two diaries, one intended for publication, the other revealing his innermost thoughts. On this divergence historical research will in due time pronounce judgment.

In having candidly made these two reservations I do not in any way desire to detract from the monumental task performed by Curt Riess. He has spared no pains to study Goebbels personally and from such sources as are already available, to saturate himself with the literature bearing upon the Third Reich of Adolf Hitler, and to interview scores of people who were associated by professional, personal or blood ties.

Curt Riess has assembled a wealth of detailed and intimate facts about Joseph Goebbels that enables us the better to understand how a man handicapped by nature, frustrated in his dreams of leading a heroic life, rebuffed by his own family, and tormented by a consuming jealousy of his rivals, could rise to the second position in Hitler's Reich and even be designated as German Chancellor to take over the reins of government after Der Fuehrer's self-destruction.

For Goebbels' rise to the top was not an easy one, as Riess shows us. I recall meeting Ernst Roehm, the only man in the Nazi hierarchy who addressed Adolf Hitler with the familiar German 'Du', in 1930 and discussing the Nazi leaders with him in the course of my professional duties. When the name of Goebbels was mentioned, Roehm pointed out that the 'little Doctor' often gave Hitler a headache because of his gutter-snipe methods and coarse language.

'Goebbels is a special case,' Roehm said, 'and our Fuehrer at first did not know what to do with him. He finally decided that, since Berlin was so "red", that would be a good city in which Goebbels might work off his energies.'

Although the dynamic new Gauleiter for the metropolis acquitted himself well of the task of 'nazifying' Berlin, he was not, like Goering and Frick, given a cabinet post immediately upon Hitler's assumption of power on 30 January 1933. The new Ministry of National Enlightenment and Propaganda was not established until a few months later.

Curt Riess traces Goebbels' rise with scrupulous care and at the same time in a colourful and easily readable manner. In so doing he has not failed to introduce one element into the story of his 'Devil's Advocate' for which one looks in vain in the Goebbels Diaries for 1942–1943 which I had the honour of publishing. That element is Goebbels' insatiable passion for sensuous sex life. One cannot understand Goebbels fully without taking into account his penchant for philandering. Curt Riess exposes the promiscuity of Goebbels' private life with utter candour.

PREFACE

Curt Riess was well along with his book before announcement was made of the finding of the 'Goebbels Diaries'. It therefore does him special credit that the picture he has drawn of the Midget Teuton corresponds so accurately to Goebbels' own self-revelation in the day-by-day record of his busy life (omitting, of course, the amours just referred to!).

Much as we must detest Joseph Goebbels, it cannot be denied that he injected many new ideas into the art of influencing the masses. In no country, for instance, was the radio used as effectively for moulding public opinion as in Nazi Germany. No democracy, of course, would think of imitating his method by which all work was stopped throughout the Reich for an hour and longer whenever Der Fuehrer chose to harangue the nation, and loud-speakers were placed in every factory, in every public building, and at every important city and village square. But there is much one can learn from his basic insistence upon the efficacy of constant repetition of slogans and telling facts.

Goebbels, moreover, has shown us what a dictatorship does to re-make the thinking processes of an entire people. A study of his means and methods can help us to evaluate and estimate other dictatorships more easily. Knowing how authoritarian governments work, we of the democracies should be in a better position to meet their challenge after reading Curt Riess' biography of Joseph Goebbels.

NEW YORK, SEPTEMBER 4, 1948.

CONTENTS

Biographical Note on Curt Riess   9
Introduction   11

Part One: The Battle

    I   The Road to Hitler   17
   II   The Sorcerer's Apprentice   30
  III   The Streets of Berlin   49
  IV   The Landslide   70
   V   The Last Lap   89

Part Two: The Power...

   VI   The Dictator   105
  VII   Tomorrow the World   122
VIII   Interlude   143
  IX   The Muffled Sound of the Drums   162

Part Three: ...And the Glory

    X   Victories and Silence   181
   XI   The War of Many Fronts   203
  XII   World War   223
XIII   The Catastrophe   241

Part Four: Goetterdaemmerung

  XIV   Fortress Propaganda   263
   XV   The Death of God   283
  XVI   The Time Bomb   301
XVII   The Birth of the Hitler Legend   320
XVIII   Finita Comoedia   335

End Notes   355
Index   359

PUBLISHERS' NOTE
TO THE 2013 EDITION

Curt Riess interviewed many people during 1946 and 1947 who were prominent in the Third Reich, in the Propaganda Ministry, in German cultural society and in Goebbels' own family. In some instances various degrees of circumspection were exercised by Riess, most prominently in the case of Lida Baarová, Goebbels' mistress, who is referred to as 'Miss X' throughout the text. No attempt has been made in this edition to add in names, and the text is almost entirely as Riess produced it. Minor changes have been made in the presentation of dates and other points of consistency, otherwise it is unchanged.

The 1948 American edition and 1949 British edition were not illustrated. This new edition contains a section of 96 photographs in approximate chronological sequence.

BIOGRAPHICAL NOTE ON CURT RIESS

Curt Riess, originally Curt Martin Steinam, was born of Jewish-German origin on 21 June 1902 in Wurzburg, Germany, the son of Bernhard Steinam, proprietor of a clothes shop, and his wife Jenny Straus. As a young man, Riess studied in Paris, Munich, and Heidelberg, and spent time working as a merchant in both New York and Berlin. On a business trip to the USA he discovered his talent for journalism and decided to pursue a career in the industry. Riess' first journalistic position was for a liberal 12 o'clock worksheet in Berlin, for which he also edited the sports section.

Throughout the 1920s, Riess toured Europe as a reporter and film and theatre critic. The breadth of subjects that he encountered and wrote about in these early years give an indication of the prolific and wide-ranging author he was to become.

In 1933, Riess was forced into exile and emigrated to Paris via Prague and Vienna. A year later, he became the European correspondent for the French newspaper *Paris-Soir*, a position that entailed travelling between New York, Paris, London, and Los Angeles, which enabled him to forge close friendships in Britain and the USA.

Having officially become a US citizen in 1938, Riess settled in Manhattan in 1941 at the age of thirty-nine. From there he wrote for the *Saturday Evening Post*, and contributed articles for *Collier's Weekly* and H. L. Mencken's *American Mercury*. Throughout the Second World War, he was heavily engaged in anti-Nazi activity, serving as a spy, and then, once the USA had joined the Allies, as a specialist in the United States Navy. His final military job was as a war correspondent for the Army, and as such he became well known for his exposure of the moral depravity of Adolf Hitler's regime. Other than his biography of Goebbels, another of Riess' great works inspired by the war is *The Nazis Go Underground* (also published by Fonthill), which describes German espionage and the plans the Nazis made for their conquered territories after the war.

At the end of the war in 1945, Riess returned to Germany and began work on his biography of Joseph Goebbels, minister of Nazi propaganda; it would consume him for three years. The discovery, in late 1946, of Goebbels' diaries from 1942-43 was of significant benefit to Riess, whose biography is based chiefly on detailed first-hand information. The diaries were edited by Riess' friend Louis Lochner, who wrote the original preface for this book.

Riess' prolificacy has rarely been matched among twentieth century authors. In addition to his biography on Goebbels, he also wrote acclaimed books and articles on various prominent contemporaries, including composers Rolf Liebermann and Wilhelm Furtwängler, comic actor and director Charlie Chaplin, and Austrian actress Romy Schneider. Then there were his many journalistic articles and an extensive body of novels, screenplays, and plays. He wrote some of his published work under the pseudonym Peter Brandes.

In 1952, he settled down in Switzerland and married the Austrian actress Heather Marie Hathaway. On 13 May 1993, at the age of ninety, Curt Riess died at Maur, a hamlet outside Zurich. He is buried with his wife in Enzenbuhl cemetery.

INTRODUCTION

It may be decades, perhaps even half a century, before every inch of that grim picture, the Nazi Interlude, is revealed. Moreover, many of us will not live long enough to witness its unveiling. Nor will there be anyone to explain the incomprehensible realities to our descendants: gas chambers for the organized slaughter of numberless human beings; the enslavement of entire peoples; the attempted extermination of whole nations; the destruction of complete cities.

Coming generations will ask themselves how it was possible that millions of people, victims of an artificially induced enthusiasm, could be moved to do the very things which led to their own ruin. The answer could be given in hundreds of thousands of words, but, if it were expressed in one word alone, that word would be: Goebbels.

Without the growth of an amoral nihilism such as the world has not witnessed for hundreds of years, and of which Goebbels was the most outstanding exponent, Hitler would never have achieved world notoriety. Without Goebbels' propaganda magic, Hitler certainly would not have become a world menace. Without the tremendous power conferred upon him, Goebbels never could have carried out his utterly depraved propagandistic experiments on the living body of the people—experiments which can be compared only to the horrors performed by Nazi doctors in the concentration camps. Goebbels created a new reality woven entirely out of lies.

There could be no doubt that he did not belong to the category of the crazed, chauvinistic petty bourgeoisie as did Hitler and Himmler, or that of the great gangsters, such as Goering, or of the little gangsters, such as Sauckel. In terms of the law he was neither a criminal such as Streicher, nor mad as Hess, or perverse and oversexed as Roehm and Heines. He was in a class by himself.

The former French Ambassador in Berlin, André François-Poncet, once declared, with some justification, that Goebbels was the most dangerous man of the Hitler regime. He said that his style was far superior to that of all other Nazis, in fact, he had high praise for his polemic arts, which, he said, were permeated with overpowering irony. 'He was probably too intelligent to harbour any illusions about the moral stature of most of his Party comrades,' the Frenchman wrote.

This alone would be a fascinating phenomenon to contemplate: a Propaganda Chief who despised most of the things he propagandized and who made no bones about his contempt—and who still did a brilliant job. A cripple as the principal exponent of the Master Race theory! A man who invented one slogan after the other and finally accustomed a whole nation to live by them. A man who refused to make war propaganda when the war was going well for Germany; a man who invested his whole talent only when the war was being lost, and then to tell the people that catastrophe was upon them. A man who fulfilled his task one hundred per cent: he was ordered to keep up public morale, and he did. The struggle in Germany lasted until there was not a square foot left on which the fighting could have been carried on. In a manner of speaking, Goebbels was perhaps the only general of World War II who was not in the end defeated.

When his work was done he stepped down from the stage he had held so long. Goebbels could have no interest in conversing with the Allies at Nuremberg.

To write a Goebbels biography appeared simple enough in the beginning. Goebbels had made so many speeches, written so many articles and books that my work apparently consisted of research on this published material. However, when I revisited Germany shortly after the end of the war and talked to people who had known Goebbels, who had lived and worked with him, I began to realize that research of the aforementioned kind could not suffice: Goebbels lied about himself as extensively as he lied about the Nazi state.

Thereupon I decided to start from scratch: to discard the ground-work which had taken several years to prepare and to throw out whatever I could not substantiate through the testimony of those who knew the Nazi propagandist. Hence this book is essentially based on the conversations with persons who were in close touch with Goebbels for one reason or another. The most important eyewitnesses are:

Goebbels' mother, Maria Katharina,
Goebbels' sister, Maria Kimmich,
Goebbels' brother-in-law, Herr Axel Kimmich,
Goebbels' mother-in-law, Frau Augusta Behrendt,
Dr Hans Fritzsche, number-two man in the Propaganda Ministry and
    Goebbels' closest associate,
Frau Ilse Freybe, Magda Goebbels' private secretary,

Fraeulein Elli Guenther, Magda Goebbels' nurse and for many years
  employed in the Goebbels household,
Karl Mehlis, superintendent in the Propaganda Ministry,
Willi Wernitz, chief of the secret printing office of the Propaganda
  Ministry,
Frau Inge Haberzettel, liaison employee of the German News Agency in
  the Propaganda Ministry (for many months she worked exclusively for
  me),
Wilhelm Rohrsen, Goebbels' butler,
Gustav Froehlich, German film actor,
Eberhard Taubert, chief of the Anti-Comintern Office and friend of
  Goebbels,
Frau Hauser, wife of the superintendent of Goebbels' house at
  Schwanenwerder,
Fraeulein Inge Hildebrand, for a brief time Goebbels' private secretary,
Otto Jacobs, Goebbels' personal stenographer.

Furthermore, I interviewed many actors and actresses who had known
Goebbels; women who had close relations with him and asked me not to
divulge their names; approximately twenty employees of the Propaganda
Ministry; physicians who examined him; photographers who took pictures of
him; tailors who made suits for him; manicurists.

Naturally, not everything I learned from these witnesses could be taken
at face value. It was clear from the beginning that his family would try to
exonerate him; that his colleagues would try to indict him. In the minds of
some of the people the chronology of events had become confused. Hence, in
many instances, it was necessary to check and double check. Generally it may
be said that I refused to accept evidence at its face value, especially if it was
given to me by persons who, for one reason or another, wished to absolve
themselves. Whenever I was forced to make use of such information, I have
indicated that it should be viewed with scepticism.

Less than two weeks before Goebbels' suicide, his mother fled from Berlin
together with her daughter and son-in-law. Concealing themselves in a
Bavarian village, they lived for more than a year under an assumed name.
When I finally located the old woman, I had many talks with her about her
son. In fact, she was my main source for the chapter on Goebbels' youth, the
past which moulded his attitude towards religion; the questions of his health.

Interestingly enough, Goebbels' sister (who, like her mother, was never a
Nazi) spoke to me with caution and avoided statements which might hurt the
memory of the former Reich Minister. On the other hand, the mother showed
remarkable honesty and did not try to conceal anything.

I obtained most of the material on Magda Goebbels, her life before she met Goebbels, her first and second marriages, as well as her death, from her mother, Frau Augusta Behrendt, from Frau Ilse Freybe—the friend of Magda's youth who later became her secretary—and lastly from Elli Guenther, the nurse who, during the last few years, was almost constantly in the employ of the Goebbels family.

I found Frau Behrendt destitute, living in a cheap, sparsely-furnished room whose windows had no panes. She talked to me for several days and everything she said was noted by a stenographer. It must, however, not be taken as absolute truth for Frau Behrendt naturally tried to eclipse the facts that might show Magda in an unfavourable light. In addition, she passionately hated her son-in-law; she blamed him exclusively for whatever mishaps overtook herself and her family. The secretary was more detached and just; so was the nurse who, gifted with a keen memory, supplied the numberless incidental details on this family's life—to its very last days.

For the insights into Goebbels' work at the Propaganda Ministry, his ideas and his methods, my main informant was Hans Fritzsche, number-two man of the Ministry. When he was still on trial in Nuremberg I contacted him through his attorney; it was then, while still in his cell, that he composed and sent me his first handwritten report. I met him personally the day after his acquittal and for the next two or three days I barraged him with innumerable questions covering the entire activity of the Propaganda Ministry. A stenographer was present and noted the more important answers, thus amassing roughly twenty thousand words. Again and again Fritzsche declared that only in Nuremberg did he realize the extent of Goebbels' duplicity. This may or may not be so, but most of Fritzsche's factual statements left the impression of being truthful and, in so far as I could test them, they were correct.

The other principal sources for Goebbels the propagandist were his stenographer, Otto Jacobs, and Frau Inge Haberzettel. Goebbels employed two stenographers and kept them constantly occupied with the recording of his diary, his speeches, his articles or, in fact, whatever Goebbels said on any particular subject during any particular day. Jacobs was one of them. He volunteered to work for me and, partly from memory, partly from old note-books, wrote forty thousand words, some of which were based upon the dictation for the diary. Although I am convinced that the actual journals were transcribed from Jacobs' notes, I have not used his material as quotations from these diaries but indicated that, according to the stenographer, they were Goebbels' thoughts on this or that subject.

Frau Inge Haberzettel, an employee of the Deutsche Nachrichten Bureau (the official German News Agency), serving first at the Propaganda Ministry and then in Goebbels' house, worked for me from August 1945 to March

1946. She compiled, in these months, memoranda of about twenty thousand words, searched together with me or by herself the ruins of the Propaganda Ministry and succeeded in excavating some rather illuminating files which have been of valuable assistance to this book. In addition, she introduced me to other employees of the Ministry, thus broadening my area of reference.

There was nothing clandestine about Goebbels' so-called private life. More material, more witnesses were available than I could possibly exploit in this book.

As to the other attestants useful to clarify specific questions, there is no need to name them here. I wish, however, to stress that wherever, in this book, an actual scene is described—that is, Goebbels' conversations with other people—it has been related to me by the person or persons who had been there. There is not one scene in the book which took place between people whom I could not interview; I have, for instance, not given the dialogues between Hitler and Goebbels but only what Goebbels said of them to third persons.

It is not necessary to discuss the books and brochures which I have read and partly quoted; a bibliography is listed at the end of this volume.

There should, however, be a word about Goebbels' diaries. Goebbels kept diaries most of his life. His novel, *Michael*, composed in diary form, is based upon early diaries since destroyed, therefore I included occasional excerpts of the novel in this biography.

The journals of Goebbels, the young Nazi agitator, covering the year 1925–6 were found by Allied Intelligence. I was permitted to read and quote them at length. The notebook for 1932, the year in which Hitler made his final bid for power, was published by Goebbels in 1934 under the title *Vom Kaiserhof zur Reichskanzlei*. Since there is every indication that Goebbels refurbished and suppressed quite a few entries I referred to it only sparingly. In addition, I consulted the journals dictated to stenographers between 1933 and 1935. Then there were the entries for the years 1933–45 which Goebbels ordered to be cremated; fortunately those for 1942 and 1943 were saved. My good friend Louis Lochner edited them and was kind enough to lend them to me.

I have tried to write the life of Goebbels without lifting a warning forefinger and pointing to what was good and what was bad, what was false and what was right. Some readers may feel that I have created too much sympathy for my hero and that I even have fallen under his spell. Nothing would be farther from the truth. But in answer to such possible criticism, I say this:

It is impossible to write about Goebbels (or any other Nazi leader, for that matter) by supposing that he can be judged by any moral standard. Morally and ethically speaking, all of them are non-existent. And no gallows is high enough to equal the enormity of their crimes. It is pointless to indicate what was evil about Goebbels because everything about him was evil. Therefore his life and his work must be viewed as completely detached from all moral considerations, in the manner of looking upon an athlete or a prize-fighter for the exclusive purpose of finding out whether he has achieved what he set out to do, whether he has established a world record, or whether he has failed. But this is still an open question. What he injected in his retorts has not perished amid the debris of the Third Reich. Goebbels hoped it would survive and, as this book explains, worked during the last few months for this hope alone: almost everything he wrote then must be interpreted as time-bomb propaganda, planted in the minds of men, not for its immediate effect but to be remembered five, ten and twenty years later.

But even this is only part of the whole problem of which Goebbels was the living embodiment. Goebbels has not only planted propaganda time bombs so that Germany, or the world, might call back Hitler in ten or twenty years; his own specific creation of propaganda itself may become a time bomb. If Goebbels' example is copied; if propaganda can fake and thus create reality; if all barriers between the living reality and the wishful thinking of a few demented individuals are collapsing; if human beings can become robots, building up and tearing down, according to the dictator of a handful of men, dancing to the tune of a propaganda which is no longer recognizable as such—then Goebbels' time bomb has exploded. Then it will be high time for the atomic bombs to sweep all of us away in a terrifying but cleansing cataclysm.

Curt Riess,
Hemlock Hague,
Christmas 1947

PART I: THE BATTLE

CHAPTER I

THE ROAD TO HITLER

I

During one of the all-out bombings of Berlin in the spring of 1945, a few weeks before the end of the Third Reich, the Propaganda Minister opened a safe in the air-raid shelter of his home and took out a faded photograph which he showed to his assistants: Paul Joseph Goebbels at the age of five, dressed in a dark velvet suit with a white lace collar. A thin little boy with a head too big for his body, with large, serious eyes: a pathetic-looking creature, who seemed far from being a happy, well-adjusted child—that was the impression of those who saw the photograph.

But up to that time Goebbels had supposedly been a healthy, normal boy. It was only when he reached the age of seven that something happened. He fell sick with osteomyelitis (inflammation of the bone marrow). His left thigh had to be operated on. As a result, his left leg, which became four inches shorter than his right, remained thin and without strength. The doctor told the parents their son would limp all his life, he would forever wear special shoes, braces and bandages.

In later years this operation gave birth to the idea that Goebbels was born with a club foot. The theory became more or less 'official'. There are many reasons to believe that even his closest associates never knew the truth, since many of them at one time or another attacked him for his physical deformity—when it was still safe to attack Goebbels.

Gregor Strasser, for many years second only to Hitler in the Nazi Party, went so far as to say that Goebbels had Jewish blood in his veins, citing the club foot as 'proof' of it. Erich Koch, another prominent Nazi, once compared Goebbels to Talleyrand, who also limped and who in the course of his diplomatic career betrayed all his sovereigns; the implication being that Goebbels too would betray, or was already betraying, his masters. Max Amann, the powerful Nazi publisher, had the habit of referring to Goebbels as Mephistopheles, synonym for the Devil, who in German mythology is pictured with a horse's hoof.

As Minister of Propaganda, Goebbels could have forced German papers to publish the real story. It would have rendered him less objectionable to the German people, to whom he remained a 'marked man'. By allowing the truth to be known Goebbels might have earned their compassion. By cleverly using his propaganda magic he might even have won their sympathy. He never did. He was interested in manipulating the thoughts and feelings of other people only within the political sphere. Whether he himself was popular or not was a matter of supreme indifference. In the last analysis he held only contempt for the people.

Not even with his closest colleagues did he discuss the infirmity of his childhood. Some of them had worked with him for more than a decade but knew little, if anything, about his formative years. They were indeed surprised when Goebbels showed them the picture taken in his youth.

II

Yet Goebbels had nothing to hide: he had never been destitute as Hitler; never a dope fiend like Goering, prosecuted for criminal offences like so many other Nazi leaders. His youth was quiet, middle-class and protected.

Goebbels was born on 29 October 1897, in Rheydt, an industrial town in the Rhineland with a population then of 30,000 inhabitants. His father, Fritz Goebbels, was the manager of a small textile plant. His mother, Maria Katharina, bore three sons: Konrad, Hans and Paul Joseph. Seventeen years after Paul Joseph was born, there was finally a daughter, Maria. The family was relatively poor, although they owned the two-storied house in which they lived. It was situated in the Prinz Eugen Strasse, later renamed the Paul Joseph Goebbels Strasse. Both his parents were orthodox Catholics. He was a lonely boy, withdrawn from his brothers, avoiding the company of neighbourhood children, of classmates, in whose games he could not participate. Since he was physically inferior he had to prove to them, as well as to himself, that he was more intelligent: he jumped at the chance to make sport of them, to criticize them, to scorn them. His constant and malignant remarks earned him the reputation of being arrogant, quarrelsome and difficult.

Nor was he popular with adults. He hated their whispering as he passed by, their patting him on the back, their muttering: 'Poor boy!' or 'Too bad!' He loathed their patronizing glances. He could not tolerate people being sorry for him. He ran away, hid himself. If he could, he would have run away from the town; he hated its streets, its houses. It was all so small, so crowded, so prying;

depressing. He longed for the freedom of the countryside which, at that point, spelt escape with every letter of the word.

Most of his predecessors came from industrial towns. (His grandfather, Conrad Goebbels, a carpenter, married Gertrude Margaret, née Rosskamm, the daughter of a farmer from Beckrath, near Duesseldorf. His maternal grandfather, Michael Odenhausen, was a blacksmith, who married Johanna Maria Coervers, the daughter of a worker.) But later, while studying at universities, he proudly told his friends that he was of peasant stock. The hero of his autobiographical novel, *Michael*, claimed: 'My peasant blood is mounting slowly and healthily in my veins.' Still later, as Minister of Propaganda, he made his official biographer turn him into a descendant of old agrarian families.

The mother was the only person this stranger in his home town, in his own family, felt attracted to. He loved her, he idolized her. He was overwhelmed by her simplicity and modesty and diligence. But what moved him most was her unshakable faith. Time and again, until the very end, he would relate an experience of his childhood which left a deep impression upon him: his father was stricken with pneumonia and the doctors had forsworn him. The mother called in all her children and asked them to hold each other by the hand and sing and pray, and, lo and behold!—his father miraculously recovered.

Perhaps this story was not entirely true, but even if Goebbels invented it later such a fabrication was characteristic of him. He boundlessly admired and envied all those who had the true faith.

His mother watched him with constant anxiety. She prayed for him, she took him to church and they prayed together. If he had been physically capable he might eventually have become a worker in the factory his father managed. As it was, such a possibility did not exist for little Joseph. Frau Goebbels, however, firmly believed that God had ordained his deformity: her son was much too intelligent to be a common worker; he buried himself in the study of Latin and Greek, avidly read Cicero and Virgil, happily escaped into the fascinating beauty of foreign languages, into the grandiose adventures of heroes who enacted deeds of physical prowess, feats from which he, a cripple, would forever be barred. To the mother this strong predilection for books meant that Joseph should become a priest, and, since he was so intelligent, why not one day a bishop?

Through friends she was able to approach one of the men who directed the Albertus Magnus Catholic Society. Two years before Goebbels finished *Gymnasium* he was granted an interview which was to decide the future course of his life. The priest with whom he spoke soon realized that he was facing one of the most intelligent boys he had ever met. Goebbels, eager to make a good impression, won the sympathies of the gentle old man. After a few hours' talk, however, the priest knew more of Goebbels than the young man had hitherto known himself.

'My young friend,' said the priest, perhaps a trifle saddened, 'you do not believe in God.' Goebbels saw his brilliant plans for the future shattered. Somehow, a compromise was reached. The Society granted him a scholarship for the first two years of his studies, with no strings attached.

III

The boy's impediment which, according to his mother, should have drawn him towards God, made him sceptical and cynical: since fate treated him so unjustly, he could not believe in the existence of a higher justice. The war proved to him again that there was no 'justice' for him.

The war broke out on 1 August 1914. For many days and nights before that day, and for many weeks afterwards, troop trains passed through the Rhineland and the town of Rheydt, headed for the Belgian frontier; trains full of soldiers preparing to celebrate victory in Paris by Christmas.

Soon the German armies were standing deep in enemy territory; one victory succeeded the other. Those who felt that a war waged against a numerically-superior enemy must be lost were in the minority. Such notions were unpopular. The school-teachers in particular surpassed themselves in their outbursts of 'patriotism'. The Kaiser and his generals were presented to the students as heroes of antiquity; it was an honour to live in such a 'heroic era', and an even greater honour to die—of course for the Fatherland.

Schoolboys of sixteen and seventeen volunteered for the front, among them some of Goebbels' classmates, and Goebbels limped after them to the recruiting centre. There he was told to undress. The doctor went through the motions of examining him—perhaps feeling sorry for the maimed boy, so eager to do his duty. The inevitable verdict was returned: Goebbels was *kriegsuntauglich*—unfit for military service.

He went home, locked himself up in his room and wept. His mother tried to reason with him, but he refused to open the door. He cried all night, as though he had experienced the most tragic of life's disillusionments. And yet, he must have known all along he would be rejected. Was he afraid of facing reality? Did he prefer to submerge himself in tragedy? Later he elaborated upon this fantasy for the benefit of others. During the university years, whenever students or professors noticed his slight limp, he volunteered the information that he was a war casualty.

The five university years were no happier than his childhood at Rheydt. They were spent at eight different universities. He went to Bonn, then to Freiburg, then to Heidelberg, from there to Wuerzburg, Cologne, Frankfurt and Berlin, back to Heidelberg, on to Munich and lastly once more to Heidelberg.

It is a German custom to study at several universities, but to switch from one to the other every six months was most unusual even in Germany. This constant desire for change is indicative of Goebbels' early pattern of retreat and uncertainty. He began to study philosophy, history, literature and art history—a large programme, and at the same time no programme at all. 'What exactly do I study?' he wrote. 'Everything and nothing. I'm too lazy and, I believe, too stupid for any particular science. I want to become a man. I want to become a great personality!'[1]

At the front, boys he had gone to school with were fast becoming men and personalities and, above all, heroes—but suddenly the war ended. As late as the autumn of 1918 the twenty-one-year-old Goebbels had written to his mother that the 'great German victory' would 'be won before Christmas'. Now he and millions of other disillusioned, frightened Germans were confronted with defeat. The Kaiser, idol of the German youth, fled, and a revolution swept the country. The 'great, heroic era' was at an end. The insignias were torn off the uniforms of home-coming officers; overnight, they ceased to be heroes, but imperialists, war criminals and reactionaries.

Soon the universities were invaded by young men walking on crutches, their sleeves hanging empty, their faces mutilated. Defeat became an ever-growing reality. Millions of young Germans were torn and hopeless. The universities became political incubators. The students split. The nationalists and reactionaries dreamed of a restored monarchy, of starting another war, of avenging Germany's 'honour'; the minority of radical leftists tensely observed and applauded the communist experiment in the Soviet Union. But few were interested in the young Republic. It had nothing to offer, its leaders had neither talent, nor passion, nor ideas. The German Social Democratic Party betrayed the workers, they thought. Conditions throughout the country rapidly deteriorated. People starved. The staggering sacrifices of four war years seemed to have been in vain. There was no hope—at least not from those in power.

Still another condition invaded Goebbels' life; inflation. Mysteriously, the German mark began to lose its value. Wealthy people found themselves suddenly penniless, selling their valuables to buy food. Foreigners flocked to Germany and with their exchange bought up whole blocks of real estate for a pittance.

Goebbels, poor to start with, was now almost destitute. He owned but one suit of clothes and could afford no more than one meal a day—despite the fact that his mother sent him every penny she could spare.

IV

'He looked so fanatical! The very image of Savonarola!' remarked a woman who had known Goebbels at Heidelberg. He was very slim, and his face with its large, dark eyes was almost ascetic. His dark brown hair was combed back from his forehead. Everyone agreed that he was well-mannered and always polite; women said he possessed a certain wistful charm. They found it pleasant to listen to his Rhenish dialect which had a definite musical quality about it.

In contrast to most students Goebbels declared that he was not interested in politics. He would quote Goethe's words on the American Revolution: 'In our little circle we took no notice of news and newspapers: our object was to know Man, as for men we left them to do as they chose.'

He was retreating again, this time into literature: 'What exactly do I study?' He studied the German Romantics. His favourite teacher was Friedrich Gundolf, professor of literature at the University of Heidelberg. Gundolf had written on Goethe and Shakespeare, especially on the latter's influence on the German classics. He was tall, good-looking in an ascetic fashion, but few students succeeded in striking up a personal acquaintance, let alone friendship, with him. At that time he was the guiding spirit of the so-called George Circle, named after Stefan George, one of the greatest poets of that period. The George Circle consisted of literati and aesthetes, somewhat anaemic young men who were more passionately interested in good verse than in the urgent questions of the day.

Goebbels longed to become a member of the George Circle, but although Gundolf was to a certain degree impressed by the young student (as he told the writer), he did not like him, and eventually rejected him.

Goebbels, attending Gundolf's lectures on the German Romantics, was completely captivated by the strange spell which emanated from the works of the Schlegel brothers, of Tieck, Novatis and Schelling. He became submerged in a world a hundred years ago, and in 1922 wrote his doctor's thesis on the Romantic era, *Wilhelm von Schuetz: Ein Beitrag zur Geschichte des Dramas der Romantischen Schule (Wilhelm von Schuetz: A Contribution to the History of the Romantic Drama)*. Professor von Waldberg, with whom he graduated, received from young Goebbels an enthusiastic letter in which he reiterated how much he owed to his teacher. Professor von Waldberg was half Jewish, while Gundolf was a Jew.

Goebbels later realized that his preoccupation with the German Romantics was a flight. When he became Minister of Propaganda, he not only removed his doctor's thesis from the library of Heidelberg University but in his official biographies had its theme changed to *The Spiritual Political Currents of Early Romantics (Die geistig politischen Stroemungen der Fruehromantik)*, thus giving his literary studies political colour in retrospect.

V

Even before his doctor's thesis was written, Goebbels had experienced the first great love affair of his life. When he left home he had had no knowledge of women. Rheydt was too small a town and too Catholic to countenance promiscuous relationships. It was during the second semester in Freiburg that Goebbels fell in love.

'... In front of me sits a young student. What a wonderful woman! Her blond hair, soft as silk, rests in a heavy bun on her lovely neck which seems sculptured from whitish marble. Dreamily she gazes out of the window, while a timid ray of sunshine plays around her head.... I listen to her rapid breathing, I feel the warmth of her body, I inhale the fragrance of her hair. Casually her hand rests on the table. Long, narrow and white as freshly fallen snow. ...'

And:

'For hours I wander through the night bright with stars. Deep in my soul I hear beautiful melodies. Everything around me has awakened to new life....'[2]

It was one of the three times in his life that he became deeply involved with a woman. Her name was Anka Helhorn. She was tall—taller than Goebbels—and was fairly good-looking.

Although their idyll lasted only four months, Goebbels could not forget Anka. More than ten years later, shortly after he became Minister of Propaganda, he told a friend about his first love affair. His revelations were typical of his cynicism and vanity.

'She betrayed me because the other fellow had more money and could afford to take her out to dinner and to shows,' Goebbels said. 'How foolish of her! Of course, eventually I would have finished with her anyway, but since I was her first lover I would have married her. Imagine, today she would be the wife of the Minister of Propaganda! How frustrated she must feel!'

Whatever feelings Anka may have had, they did not stop her from approaching Goebbels in 1934. In the meantime she had been married and divorced and had to make a living. Goebbels got her a job on one of the largest magazines in the country, *Die Dame*. After the magazine closed down he provided her with another job.

Anka, making no secret of her former friendship with Goebbels, often showed her friends a book with his personal inscription on it. It was the *Buch der Lieder*, by Heinrich Heine.

VI

The unhappy ending of this first love affair strongly influenced Goebbels' whole life. During the next twenty years he was to possess many women and to be forever tormented; forever suspicious of their motives, of their love; to be forever disillusioned, forever throwing himself into a new adventure in order to find the woman who could love him for himself.

When Anka left him, however, he turned away from women for a while. He tried to bind himself to the one friend of his student years, Richard Flisges, whom he also met in Freiburg. Flisges, a badly-wounded war veteran, was the recipient of many decorations for bravery. His intelligence was questionable. He evaded the University's entrance examinations which had been specially devised for the returning soldiers.

His only interest was politics, but at least he knew his own mind. Politics, he explained to Goebbels, was a natural phenomenon. 'Every father who begets children thereby makes politics.'³ Flisges hated war, which he called imperialistic; hated the Kaiser for driving Germany to war; hated the present socialist and liberal masters who let the country starve. He was a communist.

He lent Goebbels the works of Marx and Engels, among them *The Civil War in France* and *The Eighteenth Brumaire of Louis Bonaparte*. An internationalist and pacifist, Flisges, introduced Goebbels to the works of Walther Rathenau, German industrialist, statesman and philosopher who, in contempt of the German militarists, coined the phrase: 'Never will the moment come when the Kaiser, as victor over the world, together with his paladins will ride on white horses through the Brandenburg Gate (Berlin's Arc de Triomphe). On this day world history would have lost its meaning, not one of the great ones who are going into this war will outlast it.'⁴

Goebbels buried himself in Rathenau's books. He became an enthusiastic reader of the liberal German daily, the *Berliner Tageblatt*, which had opposed the war and now sided with the Weimar Republic. Goebbels submitted fifty articles to this paper, among them: 'Christian Thought and Socialism', 'On Socialization', and 'Sociology and Psychology'. Its editor-in-chief, Theodor Wolff, turned them all down.

Flisges, partial to the Russians, introduced Goebbels to the works of Dostoevsky. The great Russian both fascinated and disturbed him. In many of Dostoevsky's characters Goebbels recognized the young intellectuals around him, recognized Flisges, recognized himself. He learnt that Dostoevsky thought little of intellectuals, doubted the salvation of reading and thinking: 'You must have faith,' he proclaimed.'⁵

Faith—in what? in whom? Reactionary and leftist students insulted and denounced each other as traitors, lunatics. Whenever Goebbels scrutinized them closely, he discovered a bunch of unstable, disoriented youngsters. Before his dissecting analytical mind all their words became meaningless phrases, their promises empty pretences. There was nothing to hold on to: there was a vacuum. He wanted to be inspired; he wanted to be like the others; he wanted to believe. He needed to be positive.

Flisges, simpler, clearer, less agitated, was positive, or so it seemed to Goebbels. Flisges believed, had faith. Goebbels followed him—as his first Fuehrer. Perhaps it is better to say that he was afraid that, by himself, dependent upon his own intelligence, he would find the flaw in everybody and everything, discover life was not worth living; fall into the abyss of nihilism. His was the problem of Peter Stepanovitch Verchovansky of Dostoevsky's *Possessed* who cried out in despair: 'Stavrogin ... I am a nihilist, but I love beauty. Are nihilists incapable of loving beauty? It is only idols they dislike, but I love an idol. You are my idol ... it is just such a man as you that I need. I know no one but you. You are the leader, you are the sun and I am your worm.... Why do you look at me? I need you. Without you, I am nothing. Without you, I am a fly, a bottled idea, Columbus without America.'

VII

But Goebbels did not submit to the unconditional guidance of Flisges for very long. The second year of their friendship brought nothing but endless intellectual struggles. Goebbels began to understand that Flisges, seemingly so positive, was really like himself; on the verge of being sucked into the nihilistic whirlpool. He was bitter, he was demoralized; charged with hate for everything German. Sometimes it seemed that Flisges' communism was but another expression of that deep-rooted all-pervading hatred.

Were the Germans really as stupid, devoid of instinct, wanting in civilization as Flisges asserted? Had not Dostoevsky himself called them a 'great, proud and peculiar nation'—peculiar in a sense which commanded respect? Peculiar in the sense of being special, apart? According to Dostoevsky, faith in the Germans was justified. According to Dostoevsky, England was a nation of businessmen and France was but a lukewarm democracy, an unsavoury melange of people of mixed races.

In any case, Dostoevsky was first and foremost a Russian. Why, then, should he, Goebbels, not be first and foremost a German? Here was not only one man to lean on: here was a whole country, millions of people to uphold him.

Goebbels' nationalism did not stem from a knowledge of Germany's genuine interests, of which he understood nothing. Nor was it a love for the German people. Whenever he rubbed shoulders with them, he abhorred and despised them. He wanted something to identify himself with. He wanted a Germany, great and glorious.

Neither was his nationalism an organic development nourished by his love of home, family, friends: in other words, a larger and finer family attachment. On the contrary it was the result of flight from everything that had surrounded him so far: away from his family and his native city which did not let him forget his deformity; away from the leftist intellectuals; away from Professor Gundolf, from the editors of the *Berliner Tageblatt* who rejected him; away from Flisges who wanted to convert him to Communism. Away from the aesthetics of life, from the comforting wisdom of the philosophers and poets; away from Goethe whom he revered (and later mocked), from Goethe who said: 'Let us leave politics to the diplomats and soldiers.'

When he became a nationalist, Goebbels, in a certain sense, betrayed everything he previously aspired and lived for. Mysticism pervaded his chauvinism. Dostoevsky believed Russia had a special mission, Goebbels now believed Germany had a special mark to leave on history—on contemporary history. Or better, he needed to believe this. From this point the rest of his rationalization unravelled itself simply: A non-German was *a priori* inferior, did not count. 'I'm spending a good deal of time in the cafés these days,' he wrote in *Michael*. 'I meet many people from different countries. This makes me love all things German all the more. Alas, it has become rare in our Fatherland.'

Because he was a cripple he felt inferior to most people. Yet in spite of this he managed to feel, at times, better than the average, due to his superior intellect. But ever since he left school he was rejected by some who, from an intellectual standpoint were undoubtedly his superiors: Professor Gundolf and Theodor Wolff (editor of the *Berliner Tageblatt*), both Jews; so was Walther Rathenau, whose books he once so fervently read; Karl Marx.

Until then Goebbels had not been anti-Semitic, although in the universities where he studied anti-Semitism was steadily growing and it became increasingly fashionable to blame the Jews for every misfortune, including Germany's defeat. Goebbels knew many Jews, some were, at times, close to him; now he broke off relations. He decided that Germans were superior to non-Germans and that Jews were non-Germans. Therefore, at last he could feel superior to all Jews, no matter how enthusiastically he once admired them, how warmly he once sued for their friendship, how ardently he tried to write articles for them.

When Goebbels accepted this philosophy, he accepted its uniform, its buttons: 'The Jew is to me physically repugnant. When I see one I feel like vomiting.'[6]

His type of nationalism spelt enthusiasm for war. If one nation, a race, was better than the others, then the others must be subdued and, if possible, eliminated. It spelt war for war's sake: only through war would the heroic qualities of the German nation be fully expressed. The pacifism of many Jews (the editor of the *Berliner Tageblatt*) made all of them doubly hateful.

When someone ventured the opinion that the four war years had been meaningless, Goebbels answered: 'Meaningless? Oh, no. It only seems so on the surface. The war was a great manifestation of our will to live, and although we did not reach our goal, the task is still before us ... one day millions of voices will cry out: The disgrace is ended ... the Fatherland belongs to those who make it free, where are our guns?'[7]

He who never handled a gun, and never expected to, now donned the cloak of the militarist with such supreme conviction that it became his second skin. He lived vicariously, spun the wildest yarns about war experiences he never had: identified himself with a 'heroic era' he never knew; became one of its war heroes. He wrote and talked about this role so much that, in the end, he believed his own words. He began to have reservations about Richard Flisges, who really had been a war hero and who now rejected war. The two friends drifted farther and farther apart. Eventually Flisges became a labourer and died in a mining accident, July 1923.

Ten months before this happened Goebbels had discovered the man who from now on was to be what Flisges failed in being: The man to lead him; to lead not only him but all German 'patriots'.

VIII

In those days Munich was the undisputed centre of all nationalist movements and conspiracies. Here numerous parties of the extreme Right maintained offices. Here countless groups and clubs with ambiguous names and with anything but harmless intentions, convened. Here the so-called Free Corps—units of young mercenaries, former soldiers and officers who yearned for more and more wars, were recruited, conscripted and indoctrinated. Here the illegal German army, the Black Reichswehr, had its headquarters and its key officers. Here secret organizations mushroomed with the avowed purpose of overthrowing the German Republic.

Goebbels had spent one term at the University of Munich. Then, the beautiful old city delighted him; he loved its architectural beauty; he loved its restaurants, cafés, little nightclubs. He loved Schwabing, the favourite meeting-grounds of artists and literati whose company he once sought. He loved its theatres and its concerts, but when he returned to Munich, in 1922, he did not return to sit in its cafés, listen to its concerts. He went to meet the conspirators, he went to become one of them.

He was thrilled by the boys of the Free Corps. They were strong, husky; they were veterans; afraid of nothing but a normal peaceful life; they hated capitalists as much as workers. They were rowdies and often homosexuals; they boasted about their exploits, slandered the Republic; indulged in endless drinking bouts. They were like wild animals, insensitive and inaccessible to any civilizing influences. Yet, in a sense, they represented a whole generation of young Germans disillusioned by war and revolution, on the verge of sinking into cynicism and crime. Although they were inferior, Goebbels envied them. They knew no inhibitions, they did things while Goebbels exhausted himself in frustration. He saw through their bravado and their noisy, false patriotism, but he yielded to their spell.

In June of 1922 Walther Rathenau, then Germany's Foreign Minister, was murdered by close friends of the very men with whom Goebbels now associated. They spoke of the crime as of a glorious act of patriotism. What Goebbels really felt about the murder of the man he once admired we shall never know. Years later he published a series of articles glorifying the murderers, but by that time he was, of course, one of them.

That same week Goebbels went to a meeting which had been organized by one of the numerous nationalistic parties. The enormous posters announcing the rally had attracted his attention. He was amazed to see that Munich's largest assembly hall, the Circus Krone, was filled to capacity: 8,000 people was a tremendous response for a city which had only half a million inhabitants.

A man stood on the speaker's platform. Goebbels could not recognize his features because the floodlights were arranged to blur his identity. He did not even know whether the man was dark or blond, whether he had a beard, whether he was clean-shaven. According to the programme, the speaker was a 'Herr Adolf Hitler'. Goebbels had heard he was a gifted politician. Now he listened to him. Now he would find out.

'I hardly realized that suddenly someone was standing up there and had begun to talk, hesitatingly and shyly at first, as though groping for words adequate enough to express the thoughts whose greatness would not fit into the narrow confines of ordinary language. Then, suddenly, the speech gathered momentum. I was caught, I was listening....

'The crowd began to stir. The haggard, grey faces were reflecting hope. Over there, someone got up shaking his fist. His neighbour opened his collar, wiping the sweat from his forehead. Two seats farther to my left an old officer was crying like a child. I felt alternately hot and cold. I didn't know what was happening. It was as though guns were thundering ... I was beside myself. I was shouting hurrah! Nobody seemed surprised. The man up there looked at me for one moment. His blue eyes met my glance like a flame. This was a command! At that moment I was reborn.... Now I know which road to take....'

Hitler had spoken; Goebbels had taken his words as a command. Hitler had spoken; all doubts fell from Goebbels. A command. Goebbels, floundering for years, now knew which road to take. Hitler left no room for scepticism, opposition. He spoke and the crowd cheered. To ask questions, to start a discussion was unthinkable. Storm-troopers, stationed all around the hall, silenced whoever tried to contradict the Fuehrer. The Fuehrer! Even in those early days Hitler had conferred this title upon himself. It meant that all decisions were his, he dictated; his followers applauded, obeyed, had no responsibilities.

No responsibilities, no questions, no discussions. Is it possible for adults to be led like children? Could a man like Goebbels, whose analytical mind saw the flaw in all things, be capable of the complete submission Hitler demanded?

That first evening gave the answer. In the person of Hitler Goebbels found what he had been unconsciously searching for all these years: freedom from any form of responsibility, freedom from the troublesome necessity of making decisions. The final escape from himself. But why Hitler? What was there in Hitler which predestined him as Goebbels' master?

It was this: Hitler himself had no doubts. Hitler had faith in his preachings. Never since Goebbels left his mother's house had he found such unconditional belief in any one person. 'This man is dangerous because he believes in what he says,' Goebbels wrote of Hitler.[8]

'The secret of his strength is his fanatical belief in the movement and therefore in Germany.' One almost experiences Goebbels' astonishment in these lines: astonishment at a person actually believing in everything and anything he said. Goebbels had never done so and never would. That was the difference between Goebbels and Hitler. Hence, no matter how great was the superiority of Goebbels, the Fuehrer would always be the man to save him from himself; from the danger of nihilism. Beyond all critical considerations and beyond all doubts, he recognized his master that first night; knew he would always be bound to him with the same chains that tied the nihilist, Verchovansky to his idol, Stavrogin: 'I need you ... without you I am nothing. Without you, I am a fly, a bottled idea, Columbus without America.'

That is why Goebbels stepped up to a table near the exit and obeyed the sign reading: 'Application for membership to the National Socialist German Workers Party may be signed here.' He filled out a blank and was given the membership number of 8762.

A moment later he left the building just in time to see Hitler enter a car and drive away.

CHAPTER II

THE SORCERER'S APPRENTICE

I

On 11 January 1923, French and Belgian troops occupied the Ruhr because, according to Premier Poincaré, the German Government was not even trying to live up to the obligations imposed upon it by the Versailles Treaty. It hit Germany like a bombshell. The Social Democratic Reich President, Friedrich Ebert, issued an appeal to the population calling for bloodless, passive resistance. People responded immediately. Trains stood still, mail was no longer delivered, work in the factories ceased. This cost money, and Berlin printed it freely. Within the first four weeks of the Ruhr occupation the dollar climbed to 50,000 marks.

There were a few incidents of violence perpetrated by French troops: theft and rape and murder were committed; in short, things happened that always happen during a military occupation. German propaganda played it up for all it was worth. The population in the non-occupied part of Germany was told that French generals and their mistresses were behaving scandalously; that French officers were whipping German citizens in the streets; that Germans were not allowed to use the sidewalks; and, above all, that French coloured troops from Africa were defiling blond German girls. This kind of thing was called 'the black infamy', and soon everyone in Germany picked up the phrase.

Members of the Free Corps and anti-Republican elements in Germany seized an opportunity not to be by-passed; they switched from passive to active resistance. Many of the men Goebbels had met in Munich, among them the Free Corps leaders, Heinz Hauenstein and Hans Hayn, came to Elberfeld, a city just outside the occupied territory, to organize sabotage. They worked closely together with two men who were born in these parts: Karl Kaufmann and Erich Koch, both of whom were soon to become prominent members of the Nazi Party.

Goebbels had returned to Rheydt and lived again in the little room of his boyhood. He had to, he did not have money to go elsewhere. Most of the time he brooded, rarely speaking a word to his brothers or his young sister, Maria. They were openly antagonistic. After all, had they not scraped together every penny to enable him to study? To their dismay Goebbels showed no intentions of taking up any profession whatsoever and eventually repaying them. They thought he was lazy.

He was, during the day. At night he sat in his little room and wrote for hours on end, often until dawn. Then he would throw himself on his bed, exhausted and sleep late into the morning.

When he learnt about the disturbances in the occupied Ruhr nothing could keep him in Rheydt. He had a long talk with his mother who willingly gave him the little money she had. He took a train to Elberfeld, only a few miles away, to volunteer for whatever assignment they could give him. He was ready to brave any danger. The others only smiled at him. He was a cripple: he could not even run away in an emergency.

II

In Elberfeld, the conspirators planned the underground warfare to be waged in the occupied zone. The idea was to hit the enemy hard and often. This was not to be a clean fight. The men around Hauenstein and Hayn worked as saboteurs, engaged in the dangerous business of blowing up bridges and trains and of killing French officers and German collaborators.

One of the most active among them was Albert Leo Schlageter, a young man in charge of a small unit stationed at Essen. On 14 March 1923, he blew up the railroad tracks between Duesseldorf and Duisburg, thus dislocating traffic in the zone. The French tracked him down and arrested him. Hoping for amnesty he told the French court-martial about the entire subversive organization (as he admitted in a letter to Hauenstein which was smuggled out of prison). It did not help. On 26 May he was shot.

Schlageter had confessed that the industrialists Gustav Krupp and Fritz Thyssen were implicated in the conspiracy. They had contributed large sums of money to pay for the salaries of such 'idealists' as Hauenstein, Hayn, Kaufmann, Koch and Goebbels, yes, Goebbels, too. Equally compromised was the German Government. It had to resign and the new Cabinet called off passive resistance.

Nearby, Goebbels watched the Ruhr fight to the bitter end; as a spectator, however, not a participant. All he could do was organize Nazi cells in the non-occupied part of the Rhineland. He managed to start quite a few such cells among the students. He addressed groups of ten or twenty assembled in the back room of a beer-garden. They listened to him and liked it.

The situation in which Goebbels found himself was to be the one that would forever repeat itself: he could not do things but he could talk about them. Now that the fighting was over he, the cripple, could step to the fore; now that the danger was past he could—talk. Since he was not permitted to be a hero he became a propagandist.

He talked about Schlageter. He did not admit that Schlageter had been a paid agent and a traitor, guilty of the lowest and most dishonourable act, that of squealing: far from it. While talking he subtly transformed reality and put a legend in its place; he turned an informer into a hero, into an unselfish patriot, a martyr who preferred to go to his death rather than betray his cause.

And Goebbels talked. Every evening he addressed another meeting. He spoke with pathos and ever increasing emotion, as though his very life depended upon his ability to convince his listeners, as though he was forever trying to convince himself. To convince himself—perhaps this is why he was so fiery, so persuasive a propagandist even at this early date.

Schlageter then was a hero. And what about him, Goebbels? He talked— and suddenly he, too, became a hero. He told his listeners strange and exciting stories; that he had been working under different names in the occupied zone; that he had founded a great many branches of the Nazi Party, branches which fronted as harmless clubs; that he had been able to operate them for many weeks; that he finally had been betrayed—of course by a Jew. He described in detail his encounter with the French general—in some versions it was a Belgian general. He said he had been brutally beaten. The story went on that he was forced to leave the occupied zone, but, as he triumphantly informed his audiences, the Nazi units remained there still in existence. (Prominent Nazis never swallowed the story and openly challenged Goebbels for proof.)

Thus the mysterious ruse of the fearless warrior, who limped because he had been badly wounded, lived on as an underground fighter against the French occupation forces.

III

After the fight was over Goebbels could not go home. He was unable to face the quizzical glances of the family, their silent reproach. He remained with friends in Duesseldorf. He would sleep on a sofa in the living-room and if given to understand that he was no longer welcome he moved to another friend. When he was invited, he ate. Often he did not. He had no money whatsoever.

The year 1923 brought hunger, misery and unemployment for the whole of Germany. Although these conditions helped Goebbels recruit new party followers, although enthusiasm for his speeches grew in relation to the growing misery, he could not live on enthusiasm and new members.

He decided to give up politics. He would write again, he would become a *freier schriftsteller*—a freelance writer.

He wrote a play called *The Wanderer*, and his autobiographical novel, *Michael*. The play, written in verse, was never published. It dealt with the life of Jesus Christ. Two years later he wrote another play, *The Lonesome Guest*, also in verse, but neither was accepted by any German producer.[1]

Michael was published in 1929 and later, when Goebbels was Minister of Propaganda, it became quite a success. To Goebbels, *Michael* was more than just a novel. He thought it was a lyrical song in prose. Later he used to say that he would have written many such books, if he had not gone into politics. However, to discerning critics it was plain trash, poorly written and full of half-digested ideas. Large sections consisted of aphorisms of an unbelievable banality, for instance:

'All a man needs is a mother.'

'I'm searching for the teacher who is simple enough to be great enough to be simple.'

'I have no more money. Money is dirt, but dirt is not money.'

Aside from such pearls of wisdom the book contained a good deal of free verse, which was influenced by the German expressionists of the early 'Twenties. Neither the verse nor the story made much sense, and the synthesis of the book was even of dubious value to Goebbels himself. He reached the conclusion that a young man must not search for salvation through his intellect; his salvation lay in physical labour. The only difficulty was that Goebbels could not live by his own recipe. He had given up the struggle for intellectual salvation, but what was he to put in place of it? He had to face it: he was a failure.

Hitler too had been a failure, but had made a spectacular comeback. The unsuccessful painter who had fallen to the lowest depths was now the leader of a political party and—on 9 November 1923—Hitler took one more step forward. He attempted a putsch. It could not succeed because of inadequate means and because the whole undertaking was premature. After a spectacular beginning the putsch collapsed, Hitler fled, was tracked down, arrested and made to stand trial.

Feverishly Goebbels followed the events in Munich as reported in the newspapers. He was frustrated and desperate. Would fate never let him be in the midst of battle? Everyone else had been present in Munich: Himmler, Streicher, Hess, Roehm, Goering—Goebbels alone had not shared the historic experience.

The miserable outcome of the putsch shook him deeply. But when Hitler stood up in court Goebbels began to breathe easier. Unlike Schlageter, the Fuehrer did not try to better his lot by putting the blame on others. In fact, he did not even try to defend himself. He gave a perfect demonstration of the truism that attack is the best defence and—more significant—that any defence can be turned to good propaganda. A court room was transformed into a stage for a one-man show and millions of people who had never heard of Hitler and the Nazi movement were suddenly made aware of it.

'The army which we have formed is growing from day to day, from hour to hour, faster and faster,' Hitler said in his sensational final speech. 'Especially in these days I nourish the proud hope that the stormy units will soon become battalions, that the battalions will become regiments, that the regiments will become divisions.... Then the voice of the only court that has a right to try us will speak from our graves. For not you, my judges, will judge us. Judgment will be made by the eternal jury of History alone. You may pronounce us a thousand times guilty, but the Goddess presiding over the Eternal Court of History will smilingly tear up the accusations of the prosecution as well as the verdict of the court: she will acquit us!'

Goebbels was only at the beginning of his career as a propagandist, but he realized instantaneously that Hitler had accomplished a propagandistic masterpiece. In the heat of his first enthusiasm he sat down and wrote Hitler a letter.

'Like a rising star you appeared before our wondering eyes, you performed miracles to clear our minds and, in a world of scepticism and desperation, gave us faith. You towered above the masses, full of faith and certain of the future, and possessed by the will to free those masses with your unlimited love for all those who believe in the new Reich. For the first time we saw with shining eyes a man who tore off the mask from the faces distorted by greed, the faces of mediocre parliamentary busybodies. We saw a man who showed us how shamelessly corrupt and base is the system which chooses leaders according to their party affiliations and their ability to make a speech....

'In the Munich Court you grew before us to the greatness of the Fuehrer. What you said are the greatest words spoken in Germany since Bismarck. You expressed more than your own pain and your own fight. You named the need of a whole generation, searching in confused longing for men and tasks. What you said is the Catechism of the new political belief, born out of the despair of a collapsing, Godless world.... We thank you. One day, Germany will thank you....'

This was the most genuine enthusiasm Goebbels was ever capable of; not the enthusiasm of the disciple for the Fuehrer; not the enthusiasm of the young man for his idol, but rather the enthusiasm of the amateur propagandist for the master propagandist. But since Goebbels was nevertheless an authentic propagandist himself, he was not content merely to write a letter: he also kept a copy of it. And two years later, prompted by a suitable occasion, he had it printed. That was sound propaganda, both for Hitler and for himself.

IV

Conditions in Germany had improved, the mark had been stabilized at 4 trillion, 200 billion to one dollar. Credited with having achieved this minor miracle was the new president of the Reichsbank, Hjalmar Schacht, then a man with progressive tendencies.

The majority of the German people believed that the Republic should be given a chance. Parties of the extreme Right and the extreme Left suffered greatly from the upward trend. The Nazi Party was losing followers rapidly. In addition, the wind had been taken out of Nazi sails by the election of the former Chief of the German General Staff, Field-Marshal Paul von Hindenburg, a monarchist and nationalist of the old-fashioned variety. In the 1924 Reichstag elections the Nazis won only nine seats.

Goebbels looked for a job. The Nazi Party, split since Hitler's imprisonment, disintegrating from day to day, could offer him nothing. Finally he was hired by Franz Wiegershaus, of Elberfeld, to be his private secretary for a salary of 100 marks a month. Wiegershaus was Reichstag deputy for a small nationalist splinter group, the *Voelkische Freiheitspartei* (People's Freedom Party). Together with his friends he published a minuscule weekly in Elberfeld, the *Voelkische Freiheit* (*People's Freedom*). Goebbels was assigned to editing this paper. Furthermore, he had to make speeches for the *Voelkische Freiheitspartei*, whose existence depended more or less on the death of the other nationalist groups and their subsequent amalgamation. It followed that Goebbels was obliged to attack the other parties and to prove to his listeners that these parties had no future. Among the parties 'without a future' were the Nazis.

One hundred marks was not much money. Furthermore, the work was highly unsatisfactory. The paper was without influence and on a low level. The people to whom Goebbels addressed his speeches were stupid and could be aroused with a few slogans. Goebbels realized, however, that agitators of the opposition could just as easily persuade them to change their minds. He felt disgusted and out of place, like a 'good actor with a provincial troupe', he wrote home. He was wasting his time. Again he dreamt of devoting himself to writing books.

One evening a tall, slightly corpulent man listened to his speech: Gregor Strasser of Landshut, Bavaria. Goebbels, of course, knew who Strasser was.

After Hitler had been sentenced to jail, the man from Landshut, an old Party member, had taken over the political direction of the Party. His provincial, bourgeois appearance was deceptive. This man, who seemed so placid and composed, possessed tremendous energy and was willing to use it all for the benefit of the Party. Besides, he was an excellent organizer, and, in a sense, more efficient than Hitler. He had greater patience with Party functionaries, he was not given to nervous breakdowns, like Hitler, and he seldom raised his voice. This quiet façade, however, concealed a personality of much more revolutionary character than Hitler's.

Goebbels was by no means happy that as important a personality as Strasser should see him in such unfavourable circumstances; but Strasser had a sense of humour, he did not get angry, instead, he visited Goebbels after the meeting, introduced himself and remarked: 'You are a fine speaker. Maybe one day we can work together.'

The day came sooner than either of them expected. About a week after that meeting, just before Christmas 1924, Hitler was pardoned. He immediately set out to consolidate the remnants of his Party and as early as February, 1925, he was again chosen to be its Fuehrer. Strasser gave his consent, on condition that he would have a free hand in building the movement in the west and north of Germany. He sold his drug-store and, together with his younger brother, Otto, founded a Nazi publishing house in Berlin, the *Kampfverlag*. He needed a new private secretary, as Heinrich Himmler, who had held this job previously, no longer believed in the future of the Nazis and had invested all his money in a chicken farm.

Then Strasser remembered Goebbels. He later stated that 'it was not hard to bribe Goebbels.' He offered him the position of private secretary, made him business manager of the Rheinland-Nord *Gau* (District) and proposed a monthly salary of 200 marks. Goebbels accepted at once, resigned his job with Franz Wiegershaus—without a word of explanation. Later he complained about the members of the *Voelkische Freiheitspartei*, 'with whom I went part of the road, and who hardly seem to recognize me now.... Not a word, not a glance, not a handshake.' He was highly indignant that the others drew their own conclusions on his about-face.

Soon he was Strasser's private secretary in name only. His principal activity was that of making speeches and of organizing meetings—it kept him busy almost every night of the week.

Rhineland-Westphalia is a densely populated industrial region. One city practically overlaps the next, and communication between most of them is maintained by electrically-driven tramways. Goebbels was always on the road. Essen, Cologne, Duesseldorf, Elberfeld, Duisburg, Krefeld, Dortmund.... He seldom slept in the same bed twice.

He became a forceful agitator; necessity developed him. He learned every trick of the trade. His talent for repartee was strengthened by the tremendous routine required of him. If he ever had stage-fright, he had it no longer; if he was ever shy, his public found no trace of it. He was able to step on to the platform and deliver a speech to a public loudly proclaiming its distrust. And oddly enough, even with an openly hostile audience he created some impression, won over a few to the Nazi cause. He was much too busy, too tired to invent new slogans. But he soon realized that this was by no means necessary, that indeed the very same words said over and over again had the effect of a sledge-hammer (a truth which Hitler also discovered). When he was cynical—and often he was—he admitted to himself that the more banal, the more stupid his arguments, the stronger the effect.

He also found that personal contact was of the essence. 'Revolutionary movements are not made by great writers but by great orators,' he commented later.[2] 'It is a fallacy to believe that the written word is more effective because the daily press is read by a larger number of people. Even if the speaker can reach at best a few thousand—while the political writer reaches ten or even a hundred thousand readers—the spoken word not only influences those who hear it but will be passed on a hundred and a thousand times. And an effective speech is infinitely more suggestive than a good editorial.

'Therefore, during the first phase of the battle in the Rhineland and in the Ruhr we were almost exclusively agitators. This mass propaganda was our only weapon and we were forced to use it all the more as we did not yet have an editorial weapon.'

Together with the Strassers, Goebbels now proceeded to forge such an editorial weapon. Jointly they issued a fortnightly news-letter, the official organ of several combined *Gaue*. Beyond that, they hoped it would become the ideological mouthpiece of the Nazi Party.

On 1 October 1925, the first issue of the news-letter appeared. It was edited by Goebbels under the title *Nationalsozialistische Briefe* (*National Socialist Letters*).

V

After the first few issues appeared most of its readers were convinced that Joseph Goebbels was a communist in disguise. In Rheydt, people had thought so for years. There was indeed very little difference between the language of Goebbels and the language of the communists. The Party 'big shots' became apprehensive. Those in Munich—the clique around Max Amann, publisher of the *Voelkischer Beobachter*; Alfred Rosenberg, its editor; Gottfried Feder, Hitler's economic expert—were openly suspicious. The more 'revolutionary' Nazis of northern and western Germany were just as openly in support of Goebbels.

It is true that in the *National Socialist Letters*, Goebbels put the accent on Socialism rather than on Nationalism, to such an extent that he sponsored an alliance between a Nazi Germany and Soviet Russia; he also flirted with an ideological alliance with other rebellious 'have not' countries such as India and China.

'We will never get anywhere,' Goebbels wrote, perhaps remembering his discussions with Flisges, 'if we lean on the interests of the cultured and propertied classes. Everything will come to us if we appeal to the hunger and despair of the masses.' He specialized in articles on Bolshevism of a decidedly pro-Russian tone. He worked on a speech, 'Lenin or Hitler?' In this comparative study he came to the conclusion that Hitler's ideas were superior. Nevertheless, the comparison was not necessarily unflattering to the Russian.

In a number of contributions published in the *Voelkischer Beobachter* he celebrated Lenin as the national liberator of his country. 'The Soviet system does not endure because it is Bolshevist or Marxist or international but because it is national—because it is Russian,' he wrote to a 'leftist friend'. 'No Czar has ever aroused the national passion of the Russian people as Lenin did.'

Another time he wrote: 'When Russia awakes, the world will witness a national miracle.' He also declared that Germany should never fight 'in the pay of Capitalism—perhaps, in all likelihood, in the "Holy War against Moscow",' and added, 'Could there be a greater political infamy?'

Goebbels' sympathies were to some extent reciprocated by the Russians. On 20 June 1923, Karl Radek had made a speech in the Executive Committee in which he praised, of all people, Schlageter, hailing him as a 'courageous soldier of the counter-revolution'—the implication being that Schlageter had been victimized by western Capitalism.

But Goebbels was not a communist in any sense of the word, and he took pains to say so. 'Communism is nothing but a grotesque distortion of true Socialist thought,' he wrote to Count Reventlow, a politician of the Right. 'We and we alone could become the genuine socialists in Germany, or for that matter, in Europe.' His socialist ideas were hazy, to say the least. 'I believe in the determination of the proletariat to make sacrifices, the determination that is now slumbering but will one day awake.... I believe in the rhythm of the masses, I believe in the future of history....' Which means precisely nothing.

'We are living in the era of the masses,' he wrote to Albrecht von Graefe, minor nationalist leader and Reichstag deputy. 'However, the future does not belong to the masses but ... to him who drives them; to him who organizes them. The new century belongs to the king of the masses. The mass movements of our time will end in a dictatorship.'

VI

According to his mother, Joseph Goebbels had kept a diary since his twelfth birthday. There he presumably recorded what he thought of the world in general and of his own little world in particular.... In short, he confided to his diary what he might have told a close friend if he had had one. Thus the entries of 1925 and 1926 are more conclusive proof than testimony from anyone who knew Goebbels personally, how confused and torn a man he was—although in his articles and speeches he knew all the answers. Indeed, he was not at all certain of anything, least of all of himself. Again and again he tried to find time to think things over and decide what he was going to make of his life: but there was no time, there was too much work. 'Between 1 October 1924, and 1 October 1925, I spoke 189 times,' he wrote. 'You can drop dead from this kind of work.'

29 October 1925: 'Birthday! My twenty-eighth! I'm getting old. I shudder at the thought of it. I'm losing my hair. I'm going to go bald!'

8 March 1926: 'I weigh one hundred pounds. Less than a feather-weight. They use me for the most strenuous jobs. That is what I call ruining a man systematically.'

19 June 1926: 'I should like to get rid of the whole mess. It is disgusting. Nonsense! Intrigues! Filth!'

30 August 1926: 'My back hurts continually. I hope I won't get sick. Tuberculosis! That would be too horrible for words.'

Time and again he asked himself whether the tremendous investment of energy was really worth while. He was undermining his health—and for what? Did the Party have a future? Were not his co-workers little gangsters and intriguers, incapable of representing a great idea?

23 October 1925: 'Sometimes I think our fight is hopeless.' 10 November: 'I am in a terribly pessimistic frame of mind. My faith in the spiritual powers of the German people begins to fail.'

20 January 1926: 'I am fed up with our organization.' 12 June 1926 (referring to his closest associates): 'I am sick and tired of this organization. To think that these are the people with whom we want to liberate Germany!' Overworked and nervous, haunted by his scepticism, frantically shuttling back and forth between the cities of the Rhineland (in fulfilment of his propagandistic duties), Goebbels still had the time for a very promiscuous sex life.

15 August 1925: 'Elslein, when shall I see you again? Alma, you happy-go-lucky character! Anka, I shall never forget you. And yet, I'm all alone now.'

He was eternally trying to find the woman who would love him and 'understand him'—in whom he could trust. For instance, 27 August 1925: 'On Tuesday Elslein will come to Elberfeld. A great love. I could sacrifice my life to her.'

28 October 1925: 'What a sweet night. She's a darling, and so good to me. Sometimes I hurt her so much.... I'm being loved! So why do I complain?'

20 December 'Else is here. Full of tears and grief. We are going to break up. She implores me not to leave her. Hours of deep anguish, until we find each other again.... She is extremely happy. And I? I don't want to speak about myself. It seems it must be like this: there is a curse on me, as far as women are concerned.....'

12 June 1926: 'Else writes me a short note to call it quits. What shall I do? She is right in everything she says. We cannot even be friends. A world is between us. We have refused too long to recognize it.... And yet, I love this poor, sweet child.' But there were many other women....

VII

However, in the last analysis it did not matter to Goebbels if he overworked and fell ill; if he despised his associates; if he was in love or not. His whole emotional balance depended on his feelings toward Hitler. Hitler was his God. As long as he could believe in Hitler all was well.

14 October 1925: 'I just finished reading Hitler's book. Am most enthusiastic. Who is this man? Half-plebeian, half-God? Christ or John?'

2 November 1925: 'Wednesday I shall speak at a joint meeting with Hitler in Brunswick. I rejoice in anticipation of it. Perhaps I shall succeed in talking to Hitler longer than usual.'

6 November 1925: 'We drive to Hitler's house.... This man has everything to be a king. The dictator of the future....' And then he began to have his first moments of doubt. Despite his determination to exclude all criticism, where Hitler was concerned, his analytical mind started functioning. At first Goebbels was able to maintain the illusion that Hitler himself was without fault, that it was only his entourage which was incompetent, dishonest, devoid of 'true socialist' ideas.

21 August 1925: 'Strasser ... reports many dreadful things about Munich, the inefficient and corrupt management ... Hitler is surrounded by the wrong kind of people.'

26 September 1925: 'The movement in Munich stinks. I am absolutely disgusted with the Munich clique.'

11 February 1926: 'No one any longer believes in Munich. Elberfeld shall become the Mecca of German Socialism.'

But in the entry of 22 February 1926, his reasoning got the upperhand: 'I no longer entirely believe in Hitler himself.'

Many things had to happen before he could bring himself to make such a confession. At the beginning of 1926 the German Communists and the Social Democrats demanded a plebiscite. They wanted to expropriate the German ex-monarchs and their families who had kept their enormous estates and fortunes, despite the revolution of 1918. Both the Strassers and Goebbels proposed that the Nazi Party officially endorse the plebiscite.

This was too much for Hitler. Since several ex-monarchs and princes had contributed handsomely to his treasury, he was in no position to antagonize them. In addition, his other financial backers, a number of German industrialists, would indeed be upset to find the movement in consort with Communists and Socialists. This must have been anathema to Goebbels who only recently had written, 'We will never get anywhere if we lean on the interests of the cultured and propertied classes....' Now Hitler was doing just that.

It was mainly to prevent this that Goebbels, in conjunction with the Strasser brothers, drew up a plan to change the Party's constitution.

The political centre of gravity was to be shifted to the north, away from the realm of the 'reactionary' clique of the Rosenbergs, Feders and Amanns. If Hitler refused to consent, he would have to abdicate as active leader of the Party, and become an honorary chairman, while Gregor Strasser would take the helm. Goebbels visualized Hitler reposing in his house above Berchtesgaden, living on a pension. Graciously he promised, 'We will visit him once a year and we will be very nice to him.'

In order to discuss this new plan, Strasser invited the Gauleiters of northern and western Germany to a conference in Hanover on 22 November 1925.[2]

The men sitting around the long table at the Hannoverscher Hof—all of them more or less Strasser's disciples—were not exactly the cream of German manhood. They were adventurers without means of subsistence and unable or unwilling to lead a normal life. They had followed Gregor Strasser because they had nothing better to do; now wanted to try their hand at politics. Lack of money was their ever-present problem. Funds were secured in various shady ways; they blackmailed persons who had something on their conscience, perhaps an extra-marital affair or a sexual perversion. Middle-aged women who had fallen for the youthful charm of some of these Gauleiters had to pay dearly for the discretion of their lovers. Some of the money supposedly for the Party treasury was sometimes sidetracked into their own pockets.

There were twenty-four Gauleiters and important officials when the meeting started at 10 o'clock sharp. Only one of them was against the proposed constitution: Robert Ley, leader of the Rheinland-Sued Gau, who was operating from Cologne. Hitler was not present but he had sent a representative, Gottfried Feder. Now Ley insisted that Feder be admitted.

Goebbels was beside himself. 'We don't want any stool-pigeons,' he shouted.

But Strasser did not want to offend Hitler. Therefore, Ley's proposal was accepted by a majority of one vote and Feder had to listen to some very strange speeches.

Most of them were made by Goebbels. It was he who introduced the recommendations for the new constitution which was subsequently accepted unanimously. When Dr Ley said that nothing could be done without the Fuehrer, some of the Gauleiters shouted that they could very well do without a 'Pope'. Goebbels was outraged. 'I move that the petty bourgeois Adolf Hitler be excluded from the National Socialist German Workers' Party!' he screamed.

To call Hitler a petty bourgeois was the greatest insult Goebbels could think of. Obviously he was through with Hitler. Pandemonium broke loose. Goebbels had said what no one in the Party had yet dared to say. This was a case of revolt, of *lèse-majesté*, of blasphemy! Still, although this unprecedented motion was never voted upon, spontaneous hand-clapping showed that at least some of the others sided with the heretic.

It had happened then: despite all his efforts Goebbels could no longer believe in Hitler with unconditional loyalty. He could no longer silence his critical mind; he could no longer accept empty phrases for absolute truth. And above all, he could no longer be reconciled to Hitler's throwing the socialistic doctrine overboard. Goebbels, who four years ago had elected Adolf Hitler to be his hero, nay, his God, was now ready to desert him.

VIII

On 22 January 1926, a vigorous and passionate appeal composed by the Strassers and Goebbels announced that the National Socialists—at least in the north—would vote for expropriation. In order to stop his 'revolutionaries', Hitler called a meeting at Bamberg, a small Bavarian town, for 14 February 1926.

Goebbels knew that a fight was in the offing. On 6 February 1926, he had written: 'Next Sunday to Bamberg. Hitler has invited us. We must stand up and fight. The time of decision approaches.'

12 February 1926: 'Tomorrow to Bamberg. Hitler will address the Gaufuehrers.... Our campaign is all mapped out.... We want to arouse the people and we want to riot.....

Goebbels arrived in Bamberg on the morning of 12 February. Heinrich Himmler, again active in the Party, was waiting for him at the station and drove him to his hotel in a large, black, expensive-looking limousine. Goebbels was impressed. He was even more impressed when he saw quite a few cars in front of the hotel. They belonged to the leading men of the Party in Munich, the Bavarian Gauleiters, and some even to their immediate subordinates, the *Kreisleiters*.

It was evident that the southern Party leaders were living in vastly better circumstances than the men around Strasser. They seemed to have no money troubles: they had taken the best suites at the hotel, they sat around in the lobby and the bar, smoking big cigars, looking well fed and well-to-do and very much at ease.

In view of what he had written about them, Goebbels was quite prepared to be snubbed. Oddly enough, Alfred Rosenberg, Gottfried Feder, Max Amann and others he had insulted, shook hands with him, slapped his back, acted as though he were one of them. He realized in a flash that to them he was *somebody*.

The meeting opened with a long speech by Hitler, explaining why the delegates could not vote for expropriation. He used the old and shop-worn argument: a National Socialist must not aid Communist-inspired movements, and that expropriation would not stop at the princes.

'Hitler makes a two-hour speech,' Goebbels wrote in his diary. 'I feel completely exhausted. What a Hitler! A reactionary? Extremely awkward and unsteady. Completely wrong on the Russian question. Italy and England are our natural allies! Horrible! Our task is to wreck Bolshevism! Bolshevism is a Jewish creation! We must annihilate Russia! ... Compensation for the noblemen. Justice must remain justice. Furthermore, the question of the private property of the nobility must not even be touched upon. Horrible! The programme (of Hitler) is satisfactory to the Munich clique. Feder nods. Ley nods. Streicher nods. Esser nods. "It hurts to see you in this company." (Quotation from Goethe's *Faust*.) Brief discussion follows. Strasser speaks. He stammers, he is trembling, he is awkward. Good, honest Strasser.... I cannot utter a word. I feel as though I've been hit over the head. We're driving to the station. Strasser is completely confused. More quarrels, more disputes. All this hurts a lot. I say goodbye to Strasser. The day after tomorrow we'll meet again in Berlin.'[4]

On 23 February Goebbels noted: 'Long conference (with Strasser). Result: We must not begrudge the Munich crowd their Pyrrhic victory. We must work and gain strength and then begin again our fight for Socialism.'

Hitler himself must have well realized that his was a Pyrrhic victory. He must also have felt—which proves his flair for people—that he could win Goebbels over to his side and that an attempt was worth while.

The fight for Goebbels' soul began by the end of March: 'This morning a letter from Hitler,' Goebbels noted on 29 March. 'I shall make a speech on 8 April at Munich.' The prospect of going to Munich excited him considerably.

On 7 April he left for Munich. 'Hitler's car is waiting. To the hotel. What a royal reception! Another hour's drive through the city.... There are giant posters everywhere. I will speak at the historic Buergerbraeu (where Hitler started his putsch).'

'Thursday (8 April). Hitler 'phones. He wants to say hello to us. He will be with us in fifteen minutes. Tall, healthy, full of pep. I'm fond of him. His kindness in spite of Bamberg makes us feel ashamed. He is lending us his car for the afternoon.'

'At 2 o'clock we drive to the Buergerbraeu. Hitler is already there. My heart is beating so wildly it feels about to burst. I enter the hall. Roaring welcome....'

Goebbels could well appreciate what it meant to speak with Hitler from the same platform. Hitler wanted to honour him. 'And then I talk for two-and-a-half hours. I put my heart and soul into my speech. People roar and shout. At the end Hitler embraces me. There are tears in his eyes. Somehow, I feel happy. Through the crowd, to the car.... Hitler is always by my side.'

Some time before, Strasser had remarked that it was 'easy to bribe Goebbels.' Now Hitler made the same discovery. He showed Goebbels what success meant: speedy motor-cars, expensive suites in first-class hotels; thousands at the Buergerbraeu, delirious with enthusiasm. But Hitler's trump card was and remained, Hitler himself. 'He talks to me for three hours,' Goebbels wrote in his diary. 'Wonderful! Could drive you wild with enthusiasm.' Goebbels was soon convinced. 'I bow to the greater, the political genius.'

But he bowed first and foremost to Hitler's genius for propaganda. This genius, Goebbels realized, was primarily responsible for the Party's success. In *Mein Kampf*, Hitler had outlined his principal ideas on the subject of propaganda, and Goebbels had read the book six months before. Now Hitler showed him the galley-proofs of the second volume that would contain a chapter on 'Propaganda and Organization'. Goebbels was fascinated. Most of what Hitler said about propaganda, about posters, about the need to influence the great mass of people, had been said before by psychologists better equipped to deal with such matters. However, it was Hitler's merit to have rediscovered these truths, as it were, by intuition. Goebbels read with growing interest that Hitler considered the job of Propaganda Chief the most important function in building up a political party. For the time being, Hitler was still his own Propaganda Chief but he confided to Goebbels that very soon he would have to appoint someone else since his own time was taken up with shaping the Party's general policy.

Hitler and Goebbels also argued at length about Russia and the Fuehrer made it unequivocally clear that Goebbels was no longer to indulge in praising Lenin as a 'national liberator' nor to draw any parallels between the Bolshevists and the Nazis. On 16 April, Goebbels noted: 'His arguments are convincing, but I think he has not quite recognized the Russian problem. Still, I may have to reconsider some of its aspects.'

On 17 April he left Munich. Hitler had won him over. Goebbels once more believed in the Fuehrer—and, in a birthday letter, pledged undying allegiance:

'Dear and revered Adolf Hitler! I have learned so much from you! In your comradely fashion you have shown me fundamentally new ways which have finally made me see the light.... The day may come when everything will go to pieces, when the mob around you will foam and grumble and roar, "Crucify him!" Then we shall stand firmly and unshakably and we will shout and sing, "Hosanna!"'

On the same day (20 April) he confided to his diary: 'He is thirty-seven years old ... Adolf Hitler, I love you because you are both great and simple. These are the characteristics of a genius.'

On 16 June, when Hitler came to Cologne, Goebbels again went overboard with enthusiasm: 'He has discovered the final form of German Socialism. Such a man will be able to turn the world upside down.'

In July he went to Berchtesgaden. He did not stay at Hitler's house, Wachenfels, but at a 'wonderful boarding-house'. As usual, Hitler talked and talked. 'Ideas which he had developed in Munich, but now presented in a fresh and forceful manner, illustrated with striking examples. Yes, one must work for such a man. This is the creator of the Third Reich.... The chief discusses the racial question. His brilliance is unequalled. It is a great privilege to listen to him. He is a genius.'

Goebbels was always at his worst when he became lyrical. He jotted down: 'Up in the sky a cloud takes the shape of a swastika. A flickering light shines in the heavens. It cannot be a star. Perhaps a signal of Fate?' And on the night of 25 July: 'These days have shown me the way and the direction.... I feel at peace with myself. Now my last doubts have vanished. Germany shall live. Heil Hitler!' It was the first time he had used this salute—and, of all places, in his own diary.

The fight for Goebbels' soul had ended. Hitler had won it; or, in the last analysis, it was not so much Hitler that convinced Goebbels, but Goebbels who convinced himself.

He wanted so much to believe in Hitler, now he really believed in Hitler.

IX

The Goebbels who had saluted Hitler in his diary no longer hesitated to make his new position clear to the world at large. This meant a necessary revision of his attitude towards the Strassers and the conspirators of Hanover. Therefore in an article published in the *Voelkischer Beobachter*, August 1926, he professed to have nothing in common with his former clan. In fact, he acted as though he never led them at Hanover. 'Only now do I recognize you for what you are: revolutionaries in speech but not in deed.... Don't talk so much about ideals and don't fool yourselves into believing that you are the inventors and protectors of these ideals. Learn, have confidence! Have faith in the victory of our ideals! What I said then I am repeating now: we are not doing penance by standing solidly behind the Fuehrer. We do not bow to him in the manner of the Byzantines before the throne of an Asiatic emperor, but with the manly, unbroken pride of the ancient Norsemen, who stand upright before their Germanic feudal lord. We feel that he is greater than all of us, greater than you and I. He is the instrument of Divine Will that shapes history with fresh, creative passion.'

And from now on his diary showed a growing coolness towards Strasser.

4 August 1926: 'Letter from Strasser, and letter to him. First break in our relationship. But we will mend it up.' 20 September 1926: 'Strasser envies me a lot. That is how I explain his awkward and thoughtless action against me. I'm going to be decent to the very last, even if I should kick the bucket on account of it.'

The result of the plebiscite was exactly as was to be expected. According to the Weimar Constitution, half of all eligible voters, or 20 million, were required to vote. If 20 million had voted, with 10 million and one votes in favour of expropriation, the princes would have lost. As it happened, 15.5 million people voted for expropriation on 20 July, and practically no one voted against it. Not all who stayed away from the polls wanted to defeat the expropriation issue. Only a minority was out to sabotage the plebiscite. Among them were the Nazis.

The business world greeted this outcome with considerable relief. Germany was looked upon with increasing confidence and foreign money began to flow back. While the administration of President Coolidge steadfastly refused to alleviate British and French war debts, Germany got all the loans she wanted. German princes, bankers and industrialists, afraid of the Socialists and Communists who might some day make another try at expropriation, began to listen to Hitler. And listening to Hitler meant paying him.

X

In the middle of October 1926 Goebbels experienced a great disappointment. Hitler made Gregor Strasser Propaganda Chief of the Nazi Party, the post Goebbels coveted. He was astonished that Hitler could promote the man who had lately so often opposed him.

Little did he know his Fuehrer, who had no intentions of doing without talented Gregor Strasser. Furthermore, Hitler liked his sub-leaders to quarrel among themselves. The more resentment between them, the less chance of their conspiring against their Fuehrer.

A few days later Goebbels learned that Hitler had not forgotten him. On 26 October he received a warm and cordial letter appointing him Gauleiter of Berlin. Goebbels would have extraordinary powers, even the Berlin S.A. was under his command; he would be responsible to no one except the Fuehrer.

Gauleiter of Berlin! The young man who had boasted of his peasant origin, for whom the town of Rheydt was too much of a city, the recluse and lover of nature, was to go to Berlin. Berlin, the biggest city on the European continent though undoubtedly one of the ugliest. At first, it seemed as though Hitler could have chosen among all his sub-leaders none less fitted for this post. Goebbels' diaries record his misgivings. He called Berlin a 'sinful Babylon', a 'pool of sin'. The idea of going there horrified him. But Hitler knew him better than he knew himself. Hitler knew that the young writer and agitator, Joseph Goebbels, would have died from sheer boredom if exposed to the freedom of nature which he so blatantly yearned for; he knew that he really belonged to the crowded streets of a city where there was the most noise, the most turbulence: Berlin.

Goebbels' reservations had also a practical slant to them. The Party membership of Berlin was corrupt and divided. Some higher-ups among the storm-troopers used their position to terrorize the other Party members and to extort money from them. The worst of these rowdies was the former Free Corps leader, Heinz Hauenstein, friend of Leo Schlageter and once deeply admired by Goebbels. He had been thrown out of the Party by Goebbels' predecessor, but both Hauenstein and Kurt Daluege, chief of the Berlin storm-troopers, had ignored the order. This situation was symptomatic of the conditions prevailing in the Berlin Gau. Worst of all, Berlin had only a handful of Nazis; it was a city in which Social Democrats and Communists held the majority. Nobody in his right mind would have given the Nazi movement a chance in 'Red Berlin'.

Goebbels was aware of this. Sitting in a third-class railway compartment, on his way to his new field of activity, he was deep in thought. He had only a small suitcase with him, containing a few shirts, two suits, some books and manuscripts. He wore a black alpaca jacket and over it a light, tan-coloured raincoat, which was to become his sartorial trademark through the years.

'What is awaiting me in Berlin?' he wondered.[5] 'Three years ago, in Munich, machine-guns rattled near the Feldherrenhalle and the marching columns of Young Germany were mown down by the reaction. Was this meant to be the end? Will not our own strength and determination, hope and assurance be enough for Germany to rise again in spite of all, that she will have a new political face moulded by us?

'The grey November evening hangs heavily over Berlin, while the express train is racing towards the city....'

He got off the train and pushed his way out of the station. People were rushing past; taxis raced down the streets, their horns tooting into the night; trolleys drove along, clanging. The streets were teeming with noisy crowds. The night was bright with hundreds of electrically-lighted advertisements. No one paid any attention to Joseph Goebbels.

This, then, was Berlin.

CHAPTER III

THE STREETS OF BERLIN

I

'Only two hours later I stood on the platform which was to become so important for our political development, and spoke to the Party of Berlin,' Goebbels wrote about his first evening in the German capital. 'A Jewish gazette, which was soon to smother us with violent abuse, was the only paper which noted my first speech. It said, "A certain Herr Goebbels, supposedly from the Ruhr, made a spectacle of himself by dishing up the shop-worn old slogans".'[1]

Later Goebbels told a close friend about his first glimpse of Berlin: 'I had an hour's time before the meeting started. I climbed on the open deck of a bus, not caring where I was going. Just anywhere. I sat among strangers, holding on to my suitcase, driving through the town. It suddenly occurred to me how big Berlin was, how immense. It seemed like a gigantic, sprawling animal, and I felt instinctively, "This monster will swallow me".'

This was Berlin: an enormous desert of cement, with ugly, though modern buildings, with four million people who seemed to be in a perpetual hurry, driven by an inexplicable urge to be still more efficient, still faster, consumed with the ambition to make Berlin the most 'American' city on the continent. This was Berlin: the city with the finest theatres in the world; the city with the most diverse and perverse amusements; the city where anything was possible.

Now he had been flung right into the turmoil, a meek-looking young man of short stature, who might have been taken for a provincial travelling salesman. He was scared, but even greater than his fear was the sense of adventure that dominated him in that hour. For Berlin was great adventure. Of all the cities in Germany, Berlin was the hardest place for a Nazi to succeed.

Goebbels had almost nothing to start with. 'Headquarters,' he wrote, 'housed in the filthy basement of a building in Potsdamerstrasse, were extremely primitive. There resided a so-called business manager; he had a ledger in which, guided solely by his memory, he made entries of incoming and outgoing moneys. All corners of the place were stuffed with heaps of old newspapers. In the front room you would see lingering groups of debating Party members, out of work.

'We called our headquarters the "Opium Den", and the name was very fitting. The rays of the sun never penetrated down there and the electric light was left burning day and night. As soon as you opened the door the smell of stale cigarette smoke overwhelmed your nostrils. It was impossible to do any systematic work in such surroundings.... There was complete confusion. The finances were in a mess. The Berlin Gau then possessed nothing but debts.'

There were roughly a thousand members, most of whom were fed up with the Party and about to revolt—that is, to join other parties. Practically no one paid his dues. Goebbels, undaunted, combed the membership lists and expelled 400 members, which left him with exactly 600. His friends were dismayed: even a thousand had been little enough for a city of more than four million, they said. But Goebbels remained firm. He preferred a small but dependable membership. Among those who had to go were the once-admired Heinz Hauenstein and his gang. As for the Berlin S.A. Chief, Kurt Daluege, who was not much better than the rest, Goebbels was finally persuaded to put him on probation: Goebbels needed a *saalschutz*—a guard to protect Nazi meetings against troublesome intruders—and Daluege was the man to organize it.

'We must break through the wall of anonymity,' he told his Party comrades on 1 January 1927. 'The Berliners may insult us, slander us, fight us, beat us up, but they must *talk* about us.

Today we are six hundred. In six years we must be six hundred thousand!'

He kept his vow.

II

When he expelled 400 members, Goebbels had only carried out Hitler's directives formulated in his second volume of *Mein Kampf*.

'The task of propaganda is to attract followers. The task of the organization is to win new members. A follower of a movement is one who declares himself in agreement with its aims. A member is one who fights for it.... There will be ten followers for every one or two members, at the most.... Membership requires an active mind and thus applies only to a minority among men. Therefore, propaganda will have to see to it untiringly that an idea wins followers, while the organization has to watch most sharply that of the followers only the most valuable ones are made members .... When propaganda has imbued a whole people with an idea, the organization, with the help of a handful of people, can reap the benefits.' Only the most valuable.... A handful of people....

But Hitler had also written: 'Propaganda has to precede far in advance of the organization and to win for it the human material to be utilized.'

Propaganda, publicity—how was Goebbels to go about getting it in Berlin? Here was a city of a million interests, a city with a dozen daily papers and barely enough space to print important news. Why should they be interested in a party of 600 members?

Berlin was then interested in a great many other things. The six-day bicycle race at the Sportpalast made headlines. Italian Fascists were staging demonstrations against France. In Britain a seven-month coal strike, which had enabled Germany to intensify her coal exports, was nearing its end. A Reichstag deputy had introduced a law against trash and vice—a kind of literary censorship. In Rumania raged a controversy about who was to succeed the dying King Ferdinand on the throne. In France, the painter Claude Monet had died. Gustav Stresemann, Aristide Briand and Austen Chamberlain—the foreign ministers of the great European powers—and Charles G. Dawes, Vice-President of the United States, had received the Nobel Prize for Peace. The largest German motion-picture company, UFA, was facing an unprecedented financial crisis. A certain Harry Domela, posing as a Hohenzollern prince, had swindled hotels and store owners throughout Germany out of large sums of money, before he was finally arrested. There were so many things going on in the world, and Berlin was interested in all of them. How could Goebbels succeed in catching the eye of the capital?

He had a plan. For 11 February 1927, he rented a hall called Pharus-Saele, in the Wedding district, where the Communists usually held their meetings. He had posters printed on dark-red paper. 'The Bourgeois State is approaching its end!' they screamed. 'We must forge a new State. Workers, in your hands lies the fate of the German nation!' They looked precisely like Communist posters.

He could easily have chosen another hall for his first mass meeting, but he wanted to provoke the Berlin workers. To push things farther he arranged for a parade to precede the meeting. 600 Nazis—every single member had been forced to participate—marching with their swastika flags through the north of Berlin. 600 Nazis, blackjacks in their pockets.

'The Pharus-Saele was the uncontested domain of the Communists.... This was an open challenge,' Goebbels later admitted. 'It was meant that way by us. It was understood that way by the opponent.... The Communist press surpassed itself in blood-curdling threats. They said they would give us a hearty welcome, so hearty that we would have no desire to return. We were not even conscious, then, of the actual danger.'[2]

Although Daluege had picked his best men to act as 'guards', the situation was far from being comfortable for the Nazis. There were quite a few Socialists and Communists in the hall, and outside, in the neighbouring streets, were thousands of them. Daluege, the chairman of the meeting, had hardly begun to speak when a worker at the back stood up and shouted: 'I want to clarify a point on the agenda!'

Daluege acted as though he had not heard. The man repeated his request and the next moment he was surrounded by six storm-troopers who kicked him out. Some of his friends came to his help. Daluege picked up a beer glass from the speaker's table and hurled it in their direction. It hit one of them on the head and he collapsed.

In a matter of seconds, all the people had jumped from their seats, screaming wildly, and in the infernal noise there was no further room for arguments. Soon hundreds of beer glasses were flying through the air.

The workers slowly realized that the whole scene was a premeditated and cleverly engineered Nazi manoeuvre. Suddenly all the side entrances opened and scores of stormtroopers—every single one available in Berlin—burst in, and a regular battle was in full swing.

When the police finally turned up, they counted twelve wounded storm-troopers and seventy-five wounded anti-Nazis. Throughout the uproar Goebbels had calmly stood on the platform, unflinching, his arms folded. The storm-troopers had watched him closely. He had not tried to seek cover, he had not paled, his knees had not trembled. They were impressed and they had to admire him: the meek, little cripple had shown courage. He had won their respect, and from this day on they called him 'The Doctor'. 'The Doctor is okay,' they would say.

Gradually order was restored. At Goebbels' request the stretchers with the wounded S.A. men remained on the platform, in full view of the public, and their moaning could be heard.

Goebbels spontaneously turned around, grabbed their hands and then addressed the audience: 'I had to shake hands with these brave people,' he said. In a voice trembling with emotion he continued: 'You will understand that I can no longer speak about this evening's topic (which was to be, 'The Collapse of the Bourgeois State'). I shall now talk to you about the "Unknown S.A. Man".'

And Goebbels spoke. After a few minutes the first of the wounded S.A. men was carried out. At ten-minute intervals the others were removed. Thus, every ten minutes, the audience was roused to deep anger or overcome with compassion—whichever way Goebbels wanted it.

And Goebbels spoke. His speech was delivered in staccato manner. He had learned a great deal; through the years, when he was obliged to speak almost daily, he had become a fully-fledged orator. He had long outgrown the awkwardness of the beginner and had added many effective tricks to his oratorical repertory. The stream of his speech flowed smoothly and his voice, formerly brittle and without warmth, had acquired new nuances and could express anything he wanted: contempt, rage, indignation, pain and sadness.

And Goebbels spoke. His speech was different from Hitler's and other Nazis'. It was streamlined. His sentences were shorter. What took Hitler a hundred words to say, Goebbels could say in ten. He was at his best when he was ironical and contemptuous; then his words were like a whip lashing out at his listeners. Perhaps he could not carry the people to the same pitch of delirium as Hitler, perhaps there always remained a touch of level-headedness in their enthusiasm for Goebbels—but he did convince them.

Did Goebbels improvise his speech at the Pharus-Saele, or had he prepared it beforehand? Many years later, in a primer for Nazi speakers, he stipulated: 'Every speech must first be written down. However, it should give the impression of being spontaneous ... otherwise, the confidence of the audience might be shaken.'

Press comments the following day were not flattering, to put it mildly. But the story of the 'battle' figured on every front page—and that was what Goebbels had hoped for.

Three days later, Party headquarters received 2,600 membership applications and 500 additional applications to join the S.A. Goebbels then knew he had used the right tactics. He continued to use them.

III

Goebbels organized other meetings in the workers' districts of Berlin. There was, for instance, the one on 4 May. Thousands of posters announced, 'A people in distress! Who will save us? Jakob Goldschmidt?'

Jakob Goldschmidt was a Jew and one of the leading German bankers, the head of the Darmstaedter und National-bank. He had every intention of listening to the speech himself. His hastily-summoned board of directors thought he was exposing himself to a rather unnecessary risk. Therefore, Goldschmidt's private secretary was sent in his stead.

Goebbels, in the best of humour, greeted the assembly with the following words: 'Welcome, workers of Berlin! Welcome also to a charming young lady, the secretary of Jakob Goldschmidt. And please don't bother to take down every word I say. Your boss will read it all in tomorrow's papers.'

The whole speech was delivered in this ironic vein. Goebbels apparently did not wish to provoke another incident. But one man in the crowd kept interrupting him until Goebbels motioned to some storm-troopers to kick him out. He was an elderly pastor named Fritz Stucke. He repaired to a hospital, where a doctor certified that he had been beaten-up.

Again Goebbels had made the front pages. But this time he had gone too far—or so it seemed. Forty-eight hours afterwards the Police Commissioner suspended the National Socialist Party in the area of Greater Berlin.

More headlines. The following morning, a man dashed into the office of the Police Commissioner, walked up to his desk, slapped down the official notice of the suspension, shouted, 'We National Socialists do not recognize the decree!' and disappeared.

Still more headlines.

A few days later it was found that Pastor Stucke had not been officiating for some time; he had been compelled to resign because he was a chronic drunkard. All of Berlin laughed. More headlines.

This is what happened to the fervent democrat, Stucke, after Hitler came to power: in 1934 he became head of the Labour Office in the little town of Koeslin, and for some time prior to that appointment he had been *amtsleiter* (minor Nazi bureaucrat) of the National Socialist Party in that town.

IV

Goebbels knew only too well why the Party had been suspended. Since his arrival in Berlin not a single night had passed without incidents, without storm-troopers molesting and beating-up innocent passers-by. Every meeting had ended in a fist fight, to say nothing of a series of political murders which the police had been compelled to investigate, without being able to track down the guilty party.

All this was reason enough to suspend the Nazi Party, but Goebbels' readers heard a different story. He told them that the suspension was due to the Party's increasing strength, and that fear was the real motive behind the measure. In an article, 'We will not Capitulate!' he traced the developments of the recent past.

'Soon they stopped laughing. They began to smear us and to drag us in the mud.... When persecution and slander failed they sicked the Red Terror on us. It found us upright and fighting. Now the opponent was foaming at the mouth. Now ... he resorted to lawlessness and arbitrary action. Acting against his own (democratic) convictions he prohibited our Party.

'Now we no longer exist.... A stroke of the pen has eliminated us from the list of realities. We have become anonymous. The mere mention of our name and the mere sight of the swastika are shaking the foundations of the

Republic. Who among us would have thought that we are as strong as that?'

Hitler's financial backers did not take the measure of the Berlin police too seriously. Prominent among the backers was Prince August Wilhelm von Hohenzollern, brother of the ex-Crown Prince. He could well afford such a gesture: the Kaiser alone had received 180 million gold marks—roughly 8½ million pounds—in settlement of his confiscated estates. Other regular donors were Prince Christian von Schaumburg—Lippe, the Grand Duke of Mecklenburg and Hesse, Duke Ernst August of Brunswick and dozens of minor ex-potentates, as well as a dozen of the more powerful industrialists. They all seemed to believe in the future of the Nazi Party.

In May 1927—at the time when Goebbels' slim organization was put out of existence—a Black Friday hit the Berlin Stock Exchange and all German stocks and bonds took a terrific dive. Goebbels' knowledge of economic problems was negligible. And while Hitler, who knew but little more, took private lessons in order to enlighten himself, Goebbels never bothered to understand the intricacies of international finance. But he did know that an extremist party like the Nazis could grow only in a climate of permanent insecurity. Hence he lost no time in informing the Germans that the situation was very bad indeed. 'Believe me, the collapse is at our doorstep ...' he shouted.

The Party went underground, and Goebbels began to create substitute organizations. He founded seemingly harmless clubs supposedly devoted to athletics or other outdoor sports, with such edifying names as *Zum Ruhigen See* (The Quiet Lake), *Zur Schoenen Eichel* (The Beautiful Acorn), or *Wandervogel 1927* (Hikers of 1927). These new organizations were intended to provide him with a platform for his political activities. Then the Police Department informed him that he was now placed under *redeverbot* (a ban on speech-making) because the Government considered his speeches highly seditious. The decree was enforced throughout the territory of Prussia, i.e. the greater part of Germany. This was a severe blow to Goebbels. It deprived him of his strongest, if not his only, weapon of propaganda.

V

In one of the issues of the Munich *Voelkischer Beobachter* there appeared a picture of Goebbels in handcuffs, indignantly captioned, 'Our Doctor is handcuffed!'

Although it was true that Goebbels had been called to the Police Department for questioning, he had never been put under arrest, let alone handcuffed. The publication of the picture was the prelude to a new chapter in Goebbels' career: he had decided to become a martyr.

The readers of National-Socialist newspapers soon learned that the Gauleiter of Berlin was living 'dangerously'. Goebbels wrote some stirring articles in which he referred to himself in the third person, for instance:

'Suddenly, Dr Goebbels jumps up from his seat. Stop, comrade driver, stop! The car stops. What is the matter, Doctor? Don't know, but we're in danger! We reach for our guns and rush out. Everything is quiet, there's no one to be seen. We inspect the car, but the tyres are all right. But there, what's that? Four bolts are missing on the left rear wheel, four bolts out of five! What a disgusting, low-down trick!... This is how the Jews and their hirelings are fighting us!'

Berlin, so Geobbels' readers were informed, was a 'Communistic' city, a hotbed of subversive action. Once he visited a sick friend in a hospital and suddenly found it surrounded by communists who threatened to stone him. This, in the very heart of Berlin!

There was a straight line from the young Goebbels who wished to be taken for a war veteran, to the alleged saboteur who had risked his life during the Ruhr occupation, to the Nazi propagandist who was facing 'mortal danger' in wicked Berlin. Goebbels again presented himself as a hero. Possibly this impressed his storm-troopers, but it definitely left the Berliners cold. To them, his heroic pose was a joke and they made fun of him.

The average Berliner was too realistic to be taken in by a few meaningless phrases and Goebbels knew it. 'Berlin is a city where people are tougher than anywhere else in Germany. The breath-taking tempo of this monster of cement has made men hard and soulless and devoid of compassion. Here, the fight for the daily bread is waged with greater cruelty than in the provinces.'[3]

By these words he betrayed the small-town boy's fear of the big city. But his fear was superseded by his desire to conquer Berlin, and even while he insulted and slandered it, he was fascinated. 'Only after you've lived there for years do you begin to know Berlin. Then, suddenly, you understand its mysterious, sphinx-like quality. Berlin and the Berliners have a worse reputation than they deserve.... Berlin has incomparable intellectual flexibility. Berlin is alive and active, industrious and courageous; it has less sentimentality and more reasoning power, more wit and less humour. The Berliner loves to work and loves to play.... A hundred different forces are constantly tearing at the city's vitals and it is very difficult to find a secure hold and to maintain one's intellectual integrity.... Berlin judges politics with a clear mind, not with its heart... but the mind is subject to a thousand temptations, while the heart continues to beat in the same rhythm.'

VI

'One day, some of the closer collaborators of the Gauleiter were gathered at his apartment,' Goebbels' friend Julius Lippert wrote. 'We talked of this and that, we had a modest supper and then Dr Goebbels sat down at the piano to play a few battle songs that no one in Berlin had yet heard. Suddenly the Gauleiter broke off, jumped up from his chair, and said, "I've just had a splendid idea. We're going to start a weekly which will permit us to say in print what we can no longer say from the platform."

'We all knew that the material prerequisites for such an undertaking were non-existent. How were we to win the battle against the Berlin press without expensive publicity, without paying the news-stands, without lucrative ads.?'

There was no particular necessity for another newspaper. The principal organ of the Nazi movement, the *Voelkischer Beobachter*, was published daily in Munich and reached its Berlin subscribers with only twelve hours' delay. The Strasser brothers published their daily, the *Berliner Abendzeitung*. But Goebbels insisted on having his own mouthpiece—an independent paper, in which he could write as he pleased.

That first evening Dr Julius Lippert was named editor-in-chief of the new paper. 'Up to this day I remember how we searched for a suitable name,' Goebbels wrote later. 'Suddenly, I had an inspiration. Our paper could only have one title, one name: *Der Angriff (The Assault)*! The name in itself was effective propaganda, and covered everything we aimed for.' *Der Angriff* would be subtitled, 'For the Oppressed against the Oppressors!'

As Lippert had anticipated, there was no money, no printer, no paper, no editorial staff. Except for Goebbels, the only man who knew anything about publishing a newspaper was Lippert himself. He contracted for a printer whom he talked into giving him credit. He found a party willing to supply paper on credit, he made a number of other important arrangements—and then he was arrested. (He was due to serve a sentence for assault and battery.)

The advance publicity for Angriff was handled by Goebbels himself. On 1 July, thousands of posters screamed these two words at gaping Berliners: 'Der Angriff!' The next day there were new posters, saying: '*Der Angriff erfolgt am 4 Juli!*' (The assault will take place on 4 July!). While all of Berlin began to wonder about these battle cries, the next posters read: '*Der Angriff—das deutsche Montagsblatt!*' (*Angriff* will appear every Monday).

The following day the first issue of *Angriff* was published in an edition of 2,000 copies. They could not be found on many news-stands. Specially hired news-dealers tried to sell them, with little success. *Angriff* seemed to be a failure.

Even Goebbels was horrified when he saw the paper. 'I was overcome by a feeling of shame and despair beyond consolation, when I compared this makeshift to what I had planned. What a miserable provincial sheet! Piffle in print! That was how I felt about the first issue. There was a lot of goodwill on the part of the staff, but very little competence.'[4]

With the assistance of Dr Lippert, who eventually was released from jail, Goebbels gradually managed to transform *Angriff* into something resembling a newspaper. They copied the make-up from the Communist evening paper, *Welt am Abend*, and slanted its contents to appeal to the workers. In the fourth issue Goebbels addressed himself exclusively to the workers, ending with the words: 'We demand that the system of exploitation be abolished! We demand the German workers' state!' The paper was crammed with crusading articles for the workers' benefit, and against their employers: 'We demand apartments for German soldiers and workers!'—'We challenge our Capitalist torturers!'

The industrialists and ex-potentates who provided Hitler with funds were far from delighted. When they complained, Hitler shrugged his shoulders and declared *Angriff* was Goebbels' private business in which he could not interfere. Gregor Strasser, who feared Goebbels would become his competitor in the newspaper field, pointed out that there were not enough Nazis in Berlin to justify the existence of two newspapers. He received a similar reply.

A kind of gang warfare soon started between the newsdealers of Goebbels and Strasser. Goebbels' men took the initiative. Storm-troopers in civilian clothes followed Strasser's news-dealers on their way home and beat them up in quiet side streets. On several occasions Strasser brought these incidents to Goebbels' attention. Goebbels suggested that the culprits must have been Communists, and regretted there was nothing he could do about it.

In spite of these strong-arm tactics, *Angriff* was anything but a success. 'Our entire time was taken up with money troubles,' Goebbels wrote. 'Money, money and again money! We couldn't pay the printer. Salaries were paid only in small instalments. We were behind with the rent and the telephone bill....'

However, on 29 October 1927—Goebbels' thirtieth birthday—the worst was over. The Police Department let him know that he was again permitted to speak in public—a decision reflecting the Government's lack of firmness towards the Nazis. The Party members presented Goebbels with a cheque for 2,000 marks to pay his most pressing debts. But the most beautiful birthday present to him was 2,550 new subscriptions for *Angriff*, solicited during the previous weeks. 2,550! What an enormous figure!

There was no record of *Angriff*'s circulation figures during that period. A circulation of 100,000 was then considered pretty good in Berlin. At least one daily printed more than half a million copies, and several others printed between 200,000 and 300,000. Five years later, when Goebbels became Propaganda Minister, he decreed that all newspapers should publish their circulation figures. Ironically enough, *Angriff* was then forced to reveal that by May, 1933, it was selling a mere 60,000 copies, although every Nazi paper increased its circulation considerably during the first year of the Nazi regime.

Whatever influence *Angriff* had was due mainly to the editorial in the right-hand column of the front page. It was 'a written poster, a soap-box speech in print. It was short and concise, its style was such that no reader could overlook it." It was signed: 'DR. G.'

VII

For years Goebbels had ranted against the evil doings of the Jews, the harm they were inflicting on the German nation, the catastrophes they had precipitated. But he had always remained in the realm of generalities. For since 1922 there had not been a single Jewish cabinet member. No Jew had held any important post in the state-owned railways, the state-owned mails, or in the Reichsbank. There were no Jewish mayors and no Jewish police commissioners. There was only one major Jewish official in the city of Berlin: Deputy Police Commissioner Bernhard Weiss.

He was a typical Prussian functionary, who had risen high in the bureaucracy because he was very conscientious, of more than average intelligence, and a hard worker. During the war he had been an officer and was awarded the Iron Cross First Class. As Deputy Police Chief he often had to step in when Nazi meetings got out of hand. Once in a while a letter Goebbels received from the Berlin Police Department was signed by Bernhard Weiss.

It occurred to Goebbels that the man's name sounded Jewish. Furthermore, Weiss was short and had a large nose, and looked Jewish or, at least, like the average person's conception of a Jew.

Goebbels started attacking him. Goebbels, who himself had never been in battle, attacked Weiss for having stayed at home, while the others died for the Fatherland. Goebbels, the cripple, attacked Weiss for being short and for having a large nose. Arbitrarily he changed Weiss's first name to Isidor, knowing that to the average prejudiced German this name had an anti-Semitic connotation.

'You hit the wrong guy,' someone argued with Goebbels. 'Weiss is a decent fellow and was a courageous officer.' Goebbels replied: 'I have no interest whatsoever in the man. But let's talk about him again three months from now. You'll be astounded to see what I will have made of Weiss.'

To Hans Fritzsche he was even more outspoken when he reviewed his campaign against Weiss almost ten years later. 'It was too good an opportunity to be missed. Imagine! A Jew, short, with a large nose in such a job! Our cartoonists could always fall back on him.'

'Dr Weiss was soon an inflammatory slogan,' Goebbels wrote. 'Every National Socialist knew his face from thousands of cartoons and photographs.... Weiss was made responsible for every wrong done to us by the Police Department.'[5]

He was *made* responsible—without actually having any responsibility. Goebbels made the cynical statement (though of course years later) that it was not the Jewish Police Commissioner but his own propaganda that had aroused popular resentment. When he lost a libel suit to Bernhard Weiss and was forbidden to refer to him as Isidor, he immediately sat down to write an article entitled, 'Isidor'.

It told the story of a German called Hase (Rabbit), who went to China but did not like to be regarded as a German by the Chinese. Therefore, he grew a pig-tail, called himself Wukiutschu and acted as though he had always lived in Shanghai. Somehow he became Police Commissioner and issued a number of decrees, one of them saying, 'It is forbidden to be discontented,' another saying, 'Whoever calls me Rabbit, incites to class struggle and will be imprisoned.' The article ended: 'But this is all make-believe. For the Chinese would be really too stupid if they believed this Wukiutschu business and made me Police Commissioner. People are not that stupid. Such things happen only in fairy tales.'

There seemed to be no reason for calling the story 'Isidor', but by now 'Isidor' was a symbol and a public menace; Isidor—not in connection with the name of Weiss just Isidor. 'Isidor remains Isidor. A nose remains a nose. There are many kinds of noses.... This particular nose is known to everyone, there's no need to identify it.'

Or: 'Isidor: this is no particular individual, no person in the sense of the law. Isidor: this is no particular individual, no person in the sense of physical appearance. Isidor is the face of our so-called democracy, blackened and distorted by cowardice and hypocrisy.'

Eventually Goebbels managed to convince a great many people by such tactics. While on an inspection tour, Bernhard Weiss was suddenly seized by some of his own men and beaten-up with rubber truncheons. Later they claimed that they had not recognized him. But it was more likely that they were Nazis who had long been waiting for such an opportunity.

Overjoyed, Goebbels published an open letter addressed to Weiss. 'I'm no Aristophanes, to write a satire about this brawl. But before such overwhelming manifestation of Destiny the blind man recovers his sight, the deaf-mute sings a *Te Deum*, the most prosaic person becomes Homer, and the doorman of a theatre starts writing comedies....'

But pretend as he might that he was laughing at Dr Weiss, in reality he was furious at him and his hate grew all the time. And fifteen months later he ended one of his articles with these words: 'Now I have but one desire: I wish to see the day when we drive up to the Police Department, knock at the door and say: "Herr Weiss, your day has come".'

VIII

Angriff could hardly be described as a newspaper. At best it was a pamphlet, a poster. It had no news coverage and published only such items as gave Goebbels an opportunity to display his polemical talent. A war could have broken out in China, and Goebbels might not have written a line about it, according to Fritzsche.

Angriff was full of lies, all of which could have been easily refuted. After all, Berlin had a powerful liberal and democratic press, and there were many progressive and talented newspaper-men. But none of them rose to fight Goebbels. Perhaps none of them dared, or perhaps none of them wished to stoop so low.

Never before had German journalism fallen to such depths in morals and manners. But at the same time these arguments proved effective. Goebbels was hitting low, but he was hitting hard. He did not bother to offer proof for his contentions; he simply said it was so. He was not interested in readers of taste and culture—he wanted to arouse the rabble.

During the few years Goebbels had lived in Berlin he had changed in more ways than one. There was nothing provincial about him any longer, he was tough and smart and slick, scrutinizing people through half-closed eyes, barely concealing his irony and scorn. He had adapted himself to the typical brand of Berlin humour, he had picked up Berlin slang and Berlin sarcasm, and his writings and speeches were full of it.

He no longer attempted to dramatize himself. When one of his opponents called him *oberbandit* (super-gangster), Goebbels, unlike Weiss, did not sue. Instead, he adopted the name. From then on Nazi posters would proclaim: 'Tonight's speaker will be *Oberbandit* Dr Goebbels.'

IX

Oberbandit....

Yet, after all, he had studied at various universities and he did have a doctor's degree. After all, he had edited the *Nationalsozialistische Briefe*, considered a fairly sophisticated publication. He was conquering the streets of Berlin—an assignment which admittedly had nothing to do with matters of the intellect—but at the same time he wanted to prove that he could be as 'profound' as Alfred Rosenberg, of the *Myth of the Twentieth Century* fame. He had fraternized with the roughnecks of the S.A. and their attentions had flattered his vanity. Now, sitting in his office at headquarters, joking with his assistants and seeking to win their admiration by all sorts of cheap little tricks, he wished to prove that he was 'something better'.

It was for this reason that he decided from time to time to make speeches or, what he hoped would be a higher intellectual level, with no regard for their immediate propaganda effect. The first of this series was called, 'What is Politics?' (5 October 1927). 'The individual develops into a nation', Goebbels stated. 'The nation is a part of humanity. Humanity is not the thing-in-itself, and neither is the individual. The nation alone is the thing-in-itself. The individual is only useful in so far as he develops and perfects the nation....'

'The nation is creative. The nation achieves cultural deeds.'

'Politics must concern itself with space, liberty and bread. Space needs a nation, and a nation needs space.... Without liberty, space is worthless to a nation.'

For a man of Goebbels' talents it was an amazingly dreary and muddled dissertation. He never explained why the nation was the thing-in-itself—*das Ding an sich*, a phrase he had borrowed from Immanuel Kant—or why the individual was not, and the German philosopher would have turned in his grave if he had been obliged to listen to such 'philosophy'.

When it came to stating the fundamentals of the Nazi *credo*, Goebbels' limitations became apparent. He tried to be 'highbrow' and 'deep', but managed to be neither. Nevertheless, being more intelligent than the other leading Nazis, he made an attempt to cover up what they did not see: that there was no fundamental idea behind National Socialism, that there was no philosophical outlook, no *weltanschauung*.

The *weltanschauung* which he needed for his articles and 'lectures' was borrowed from others. Plagiarism of ideas was nothing new to the Nazis. The term 'National Socialism' itself was plagiarized. It had been coined by the economist Max Weber, a progressive democrat and one of the great German scientists of the pre-Hitler era teaching at the universities of Heidelberg and Munich. (To Weber, National Socialism meant a Socialism which would conform itself to the conditions peculiar to the respective countries. Weber did not live to see the Nazis adopt the term that he had created for an entirely different political philosophy.) Goebbels himself stole many ideas from Alfred Rosenberg's books—much as he hated their author—from the old anti-Semitic stand-by, Houston Stewart Chamberlain, from Hitler's friend Dietrich

Eckart, and from the philosophers Arthur Moeller van den Bruck and Oswald Spengler.

From one of Eckart's early poems he lifted the phrase, '*Deutschland, erwache!*' (Germany, awake!) which became the battle-cry of the Nazi movement. From Moeller van den Bruck he took the title of his most important book, *Das Dritte Reich* (*The Third Reich*).

Moeller van den Bruck was in many respects an interesting personality. Long before Hitler, Eckart or Feder, he had written about Germany's rebirth and Germany's mission. 'A war can be lost, but a revolution must be won,' he wrote. He firmly believed that Germany had enough inherent strength to recover from the defeat of 1918 and to become a stronger and more powerful country than she had been under the Hohenzollern (Second Reich) or under the emperors of the Middle Ages (First Reich). This new and powerful state he called the Third Reich and he predicted that one day it would dominate the world.

As distinguished from that of other Nazi philosophers, his thinking was clear. He also translated and edited the complete works of Dostoevsky. On 30 May 1925, he committed suicide because he no longer believed that Germany would make the sort of revival he had hoped for.

Goebbels had read Moeller van den Bruck. On 18 December 1925, he entered into his diary: 'He writes like a prophet. He puts into words all that we young men instinctively have known for a long time. He writes clearly and calmly, but with passionate emotion.'

But Goebbels saw that Moeller's conception of Germany's future clearly differed from Hitler's. 'Why did not Moeller van den Bruck draw the final conclusions and proclaim his intention to fight together with us?' he wrote. 'Spiritual redemption? No fight to the last drop of blood?'

On 30 December again: 'Why did he not join our ranks?' He realized that the vast majority of Nazi followers was incapable of reading one page of Moeller's writings, let alone understanding them. As far as he was concerned, the philosopher had done his duty by coining the phrase of the Third Reich. He exploited the term to the utmost. Moeller van den Bruck's name was never mentioned in this context and by the time the Nazis came to power only a few of the more literate Germans remembered its origin.

Another German philosopher who inadvertently provided Goebbels with background for *weltanschauung* was Oswald Spengler. His book, *The Decline of the West*, had established his international reputation. Hitler had read the famous work. No doubt there were some parallels between Hitler's and Spengler's philosophy. But Spengler was predominantly a pessimist—and, like Nietzsche, a philosopher of the Decadence. The very base of Hitler's movement was optimism, the shallow optimism of a patent medicine salesman. Therefore, he did not care for Spengler's book.

Spengler even then clearly disapproved not only of the Nazis but of the entire extreme Right. He wrote in *Neubau des deutschen Reiches* (*Reconstruction of the German Reich*): 'In the beginning of June, 1795, Paris daily expected the establishment of the monarchy.... The *jeunesse dorée* made its appearance: determined young men who were sick and tired of the Jacobins and who, with their fists and their sticks, ... wished to introduce a new era. The extremists of the Right are the *jeunesse dorée* of today.... They are carried away by the same easily inflamed enthusiasm.... They are just as honest and just as narrow-minded. Neither the one nor the other had any inkling of the gravity of the political tasks in a thoroughly devastated country.... How small and flat and unworthy is the German slogan, "Down with the Jews!" when compared to the famous American saying, "... Our country, right or wrong!" Members of one's own race are always more dangerous than those of a foreign race, who as a minority must prefer assimilation if compelled to make a choice.'

Goebbels studied the essay carefully and on the assumption that his listeners would neither read nor understand Spengler he appropriated many of his ideas. Some passages he even quoted literally—of course without mentioning the source. The parallels between Goebbels and Spengler—in other words, Goebbels' plagiarism of Spengler—can be shown in some fifty articles and as many speeches written by Goebbels. Only when the Nazis became so prominent that Goebbels' utterances were reprinted in the entire German press did he become more cautious.

But then, Goebbels might have argued that he had a legitimate reason for stealing ideas from others. He had too little time to develop some of his own, he was altogether too busy. As Gauleiter he had to attend to many administrative tasks. He was the most important speaker of the Party, outside of Hitler. He was publisher of *Angriff* and its chief editorial writer. In addition, he wrote various pamphlets, such as the *Little A B C of the National Socialist*, *Those damned Swastika Men*, *The Nazi-Sozi*, *Roads into the Third Reich*. He also published his collected articles under the titles *The Book of Isidor*, and *Knorke*.

He was working eighteen hours a day, tireless and as in a fever.

X

On 9 January 1928, Goebbels gave a rather 'important' lecture on *Erkenntnis und Propaganda* (Perception and Propaganda), in which he made some shrewd comments on the art he was practising.

'There is no theoretical way of determining what kind of propaganda is more effective and what kind is less effective. The propaganda which produces the desired results is good and all other propaganda is bad, no matter how entertaining it may be, because it is not the task of propaganda to entertain but to produce results.... Therefore, it is beside the point to say your propaganda is too crude, too mean, or too brutal, or too unfair, for all this does not matter.'

What did matter? 'Ideas are in the air, so to speak. And if someone comes along and expresses what all others feel in their hearts, then everybody says: "Yes, this is what I have always wanted and hoped for."'

'The moment I have recognized some truth or other and begin to speak about it in the tram—I am making propaganda. This is the moment when I begin to search for others who, like myself, have recognized the same truth. Thus, propaganda is nothing but the predecessor of an organization. Once there is an organization, it becomes the predecessor of the state. Propaganda is always a means to an end.'

He repeatedly underlined the fact that propaganda was but a means to an end. He would say: 'If our propaganda had not resulted in our being suspended by the Jewish police, something would have been wrong with it because it would not have been considered dangerous. Our suspension is the best proof of the fact that we are dangerous.'

A means to an end. Nevertheless, throughout his speech Goebbels seemed to be gripped by fear that the listeners might look upon propaganda as a second-rate profession. Therefore he made it amply clear that, in his opinion, propaganda was an art. 'You either are a propagandist, or you are not. Propaganda is an art which can be taught to the average person, like playing the violin. But then there comes a point when you say: "This is where you stop. What remains to be learned can only be achieved by a genius...."'

And then he made a final persuasive effort: 'If they say, "But you are only propagandists," you should answer them: "And what else was Jesus Christ? Did he not make propaganda? Did he write books or did he preach? And what about Mohammed? Did he write sophisticated essays or did he go out to the people and tell them what he wanted? Were not Buddha and Zoroaster propagandists?... Look at our own century. Was Mussolini a scribbler, or was he a great speaker? When Lenin went from Zurich to St Petersburg, did he rush from the station into his study to write a book, or did he speak before a multitude?" Only the great speakers, the great creators of words have made Bolshevism and Fascism. There is no difference between the speaker and the politician.'

Goebbels refused to be taken for a 'means to an end', he wanted to be taken for one of the important philosophers or, at least, for a politician.

XI

A few weeks later, on 31 March 1928, the Prussian Government lifted the ban on the Party. New Reichstag elections were scheduled for 20 May.

The so-called radical wing of the Party, under Goebbels' leadership, had been opposed to taking part in the elections. In numerous articles, Goebbels had ridiculed the Reichstag and its deputies. 'We enter through large portals into the holy halls,' he once wrote. 'Over the front entrance you can read a good joke, "Dedicated to the German Nation!" There's irony for you....

'There are large lobbies to facilitate digestion. They are flanked by long rows of upholstered chairs which provide ample opportunity to take a short nap. To say a short nap is putting it mildly. If you come here in the afternoon, you can hear the blissfully soothing collective snores of all the deputies. The representatives of the German people are resting from their strenuous duties performed for the Fatherland.'

Now Goebbels changed his mind about the Reichstag. He strongly favoured putting up Nazi candidates for the coming elections. This looked like sheer opportunism. But it would be unfair (if such a word can be used in connection with Goebbels) to attribute Goebbels' change of mind to such matters as the additional income of a Reichstag member and the immunity he enjoyed. Goebbels saw farther. He believed that the Reichstag would provide an excellent propaganda platform.

'We will move into the Reichstag to supply ourselves at the Arsenal of Democracy with its own weapons,' he declared. 'We will become deputies of the Reichstag to paralyze the Weimar way of thinking with the support of Weimar.... If we succeed in planting in parliament sixty or seventy of our own agitators and organizers, then the state itself will equip and pay for our fighting machine. Whoever is elected to parliament is finished, but only if he plans to become a parliamentarian. But if, with his inborn recklessness, he continues his merciless fight against the increasing scoundrelizations of our public life, then he will not become a parliamentarian but he will remain what he is: a revolutionary. Mussolini also was a member of parliament. In spite of that, not long afterwards, he marched on Rome with his blackshirts.... The agitators of our Party are spending between six hundred and eight hundred marks a month on train fares in order to strengthen the Republic. Is it then not just and fair that the Republic should reimburse their travelling expenses by giving them free railway passes?... Is that the beginning of a compromise? Do you believe that we would lay down our arms for free railway passes? We, who have stood in front of you a hundred and a thousand times in order to bring you faith in a new Germany?... We do not beg for votes. We demand conviction, devotion, passion. The vote is only an expedient, for ourselves as well as for you.... We do not care a damn about co-operation for building up a stinking dung-heap. We come to clean out the dung.... We do not come as friends or as neutrals: We come as enemies.'

He engaged in some cynical campaigning for his own candidacy. In an article entitled, 'Do you really want to vote for me?' he enumerated the countless libel suits and other legal proceedings in which he had been involved. He then explained at length why he had been convicted, fined or sentenced to various prison terms (which he never served). This offered him a wonderful opportunity to repeat previous libellous statements such as those against Bernhard Weiss. He wound up by saying: 'Under the system which has prevailed since 1918 I have no chance whatsoever of getting elected. Do you seriously intend to vote for me?'

But in reality he very much wanted the people to vote for him. He campaigned until he was exhausted.

'I can hardly see or think. For eight weeks now I have been all over Germany. Sometimes I have travelled by car as much as five hundred miles a day. In the evening I have spoken before thousands of people, who applauded or booed me. After the meeting, in the middle of the night, I got a few hours' sleep. Then up at six or seven, and more driving until five in the afternoon. Berlin! Heaps of mail, newspapers, complaints, demands, telephone calls, no money, nothing but troubles, conferences, a poster, a pamphlet, a few words to someone who is discouraged, a few words of thanks to a brave comrade; home, change clothes, the telephone rings. It is high time for me to leave, they are waiting for me, the hall is already crowded....'

The leftist parties won the elections. The Nazis received only 800,000 votes out of a total of thirty million. This gave them twelve seats in a Reichstag composed of 500 deputies, as compared to their previous nine. In Berlin, 50,000 people had voted for the National Socialists. This was not an overwhelming victory, but nevertheless a far cry from the meagre beginnings of two years before.

Gregor Strasser, Hermann Goering (recently returned from abroad, where he had fled after the putsch of 1923), Gottfried Feder, Wilhelm Frick and General Ritter von Epp—and, of course, Goebbels himself—were among those who represented the Party in the Reichstag. If Goebbels had been highly sarcastic about the election campaign he was no less so about his success.

'Maybe the representatives of the other parties regard themselves as representatives,' he wrote. 'I am not a member of the Reichstag. I am an I.D.I. and an I.D.F. *Inhaber der Immunitaet* (possessor of immunity) and *Inhaber der Freifahrkarte* (possessor of a free railway pass).... The I.D.I. is a man who may speak the truth from time to time even in this democratic Republic. He distinguishes himself from other mortals by being permitted to think aloud.

He can call a dung-heap a dung-heap and needn't beat about the bush by calling it a state.'

The article ended with the words: 'This is but a prelude. You're going to have a lot of fun with us. The show can begin.'

XII

This was the year 1928. Calvin Coolidge was still President of the United States. Prosperity was reigning, Wall Street was in high spirits, stocks were soaring.... The Secretary of State, Frank Billings Kellogg, was busy arranging for a new international treaty to outlaw war. Representatives of all great countries signed the Briand-Kellogg Pact, as it was finally called. Everyone knew that if a country decided to disregard its stipulations, nothing much could be done about it. Nevertheless, Mr Kellogg received the Nobel Prize for his efforts to safeguard the peace.

One of the first points on the agenda of the new Reichstag was to vote on the funds for a new battle cruiser. Even the Social Democrats, by far the strongest party and usually given to much talk about international disarmament, voted in favour of building the cruiser.

The American lawyer, Seymour Parker Gilbert, came to Germany to investigate the state of German finances and to look into the problems of reparations. He wrote several reports in which he stated that, in his opinion, German official figures were to some degree falsified and that German big business was doing everything to conceal its real wealth; he also said that much capital had been moved abroad for reasons of tax evasion. He declared that the once-famed honesty of the German businessman no longer existed—at least it was no longer safe to depend on it.

Mussolini had brought 'order' to Italy and was looked upon with great respect by the ruling classes in numerous countries. Many people wondered if it would not be a good thing to have a Mussolini in other countries as well.

In Soviet Russia things were not going smoothly. Stalin had exiled Trotsky and sent Kamenev, Zinoviev, Rakovski, Radek and others to Siberia, and there were those who predicted that the collapse of the Soviet Union was but a question of weeks.

Then on the evening of 20 May, something very strange happened in Germany's second-largest city, Hamburg: greenish vapours floated in the streets and penetrated into the houses. Hundreds of peaceful citizens fainted and had to be taken to hospital; many died.

It was found that these vapours had escaped from a certain factory. There was no doubt that there they were conducting experiments in poison gas. Was it not against all international agreements, against the Treaty of Versailles? A thoroughgoing investigation somehow never materialized. Even the progressive papers soon stopped writing about the incident, which had occurred the same evening that the Nazis increased their seats in the Reichstag from nine to twelve.

This was the state of world affairs when Goebbels took another important step forward. On 9 January 1929, Hitler reshuffled his set-up. Gregor Strasser was made head of the Organization Department, thus becoming second only to Hitler. Goebbels was appointed Reich Propaganda Chief. Now he was among the handful of men determining the future course of the movement. The Party was as yet small. He was to make it bigger and bigger.

CHAPTER IV

THE LANDSLIDE

I

It was Goebbels' first job to make the masses accept Hitler as their God.

When Hitler appointed himself Fuehrer of the Nazi Party he did so mainly to be above the intrigues of his sub-leaders. Most of them agreed to this arrangement because they had no choice. Now Goebbels tried to imbue them with genuine faith. He proposed that Hitler's speeches, writings and actions should be declared 'infallible', and that nothing Hitler did or said could be doubted or even discussed. Goebbels' propaganda was out to promote the superstition that, without Hitler, his followers would be lost.

Since everything depended upon Hitler it was only logical that Goebbels should build his new propaganda machine with the Fuehrer as its central figure. It was bigger, more streamlined and more efficient than the organization he had inherited from Gregor Strasser. He introduced modern propaganda methods to make it flexible and responsive to the slightest outside stimulus; he wanted to be able to swing the whole apparatus into action by a flick of the wrist.

The Amanns, Rosenbergs, Feders were impressed with Goebbels' temperamental personality, they admired the speed with which he acted and the countless ideas that sprang up in his mind. They were even a little in awe of him, but they did not like him. Somehow they felt that he did not belong. To them, he was not a dyed-in-the-wool Nazi. They never accepted him as one of their own.

During the next few years Goebbels concentrated on political meetings as his chief propagandistic weapon. Until then, meetings had an informative character; people attended to listen to the political programme of one or the other party. Goebbels thought that such an approach was too time-consuming. 'What a waste of energy to let a speaker talk for half an hour to establish contact with the audience,' he exclaimed. 'We don't speak for the sake of speaking but for the sake of creating an effect.'

Having nothing but contempt for the average human being, he did not stop for one minute to consider what the people might think or whether they did any thinking at all; nor did he believe that it would be difficult to sway whatever opinions they had. All that was needed was to 'prepare the audience'. Every single person must be prejudiced in favour of the Nazi cause before the speaker ever opened his mouth. Goebbels staged political meetings in the manner of a pageant. He developed new formulas. He 'invented' the 'Guard of the Speaker'—tall, good-looking boys in uniform, standing stalwart on the platform. He invented the 'solemn entrance of the flag-bearers.' He laid down rules for the speaker to welcome the audience. The entire meeting became a ritual in which flags, music, special groupings and parading were assigned definite roles. In other words, instead of clearing the heads of his listeners he further obscured their already hazy notions. Upon leaving a Nazi rally, the people knew less than before, but they were impressed, carried away.

The centre of attraction was, of course, the speaker himself. Since Goebbels was preparing for a flood of meetings, the like of which had never been known in Germany, he needed a vast number of speakers. Within the Department of Propaganda he created a special section for speakers whom he divided into groups. Only the best were allowed to 'perform' in Berlin, Munich, Hamburg and other large cities. For smaller audiences lesser talents would do.

Lest they should say things he did not wish them to say, Goebbels furnished them with material and created a control office to make sure that his orders were carried out.

Goebbels' star performer was Hitler himself. In the autumn of 1928 the Prussian Government had revoked the ban on Hitler as a public speaker. On 16 September Goebbels had rented Berlin's Madison Square Garden, the Sportpalast, and filled it with more than ten thousand people. He introduced the Fuehrer, who then spoke for two hours and fifty-five minutes, ranting against the Republic, the Versailles Treaty and the existing order. There were many flags, much singing and much parading, and the audience was in a frenzy of enthusiasm.

Such meetings were to be repeated frequently during the following years, with Hitler making the main speech and Goebbels introducing him, staging the whole show but remaining more or less in the background. He did not resent this anonymity; as a matter of fact, he seemed to like it. Perhaps this, too, could be explained by his deep contempt for the masses. Perhaps he really did not care for their applause (certain remarks he made many years later seem to bear this out). He may have thought his triumph was all the greater because he enjoyed it from the wings, because, in a way, it was his secret. Thousands of people were carried away—but none of them knew that he, Goebbels, had planned it all, and carefully and shrewdly had lifted them into this state of delirium. Wherever he staged meetings people began to react as he wanted them to; people began to believe what he wanted them to. It was, as Goebbels often admitted to his own astonishment, unbelievably easy.

It was so easy that Goebbels sometimes wondered whether it was worth going to all that trouble to impress the public. There were more primitive ways of doing it, for instance, by bashing in other people's skulls. As a student, Goebbels had felt frustrated because he could not keep up with the rowdies of the Free Corps. Now he was in a position to order them around and his feelings of frustration dissolved before the sense of power that got hold of him. Perhaps this was the reason why Goebbels the propagandist so often substituted brute force for political magic. While he was converting Germans into Nazis, he allowed his storm-troopers to roam the streets and to beat-up and kill those who were not eager to be converted.

II

The storm-troopers were the scum of the earth. Schlageter had been no better; yet, Goebbels had been capable of making him the hero of the movement. The average German, emotional and sentimental, has always been more impressed by the spectacular exploits of 'heroic' individuals than by the rational approach to a given problem. Therefore, what Goebbels needed now were new and more Schlageters, other young men he could build up into 'heroes'. In fact, with his first speech in Berlin, with his first article in *Angriff*, all his efforts were concentrated on persuading the public that all Nazis were heroes because they were living under the constant threat of death—at least in Berlin.

'On a Saturday or Sunday afternoon we took an hour or two off to visit the hospitals,' he wrote in an article entitled 'Heroes' (October, 1929). 'Here was one who had been shot through the head. He had not been a member long. But now his comrades regarded him as their equal. Gathered around his bed were his young wife and half-a-dozen storm-troopers. They had brought him flowers and fruit.... I visited a man whose arm had been stabbed three times. The whole family, the mother and three sons, were all National Socialists: one a worker, the second an apprentice, the third a tram conductor. And yet, the fat Jews running the Communist press have the nerve to call us mercenaries of Capitalism!... Here was a man with a severe abdominal wound. For six days after the bullet struck him his life had been in danger. With their last pennies his comrades bought him flowers; he was not allowed to eat anything.... That's how they are! Not all of them, but many, many. Hundreds and thousands of them, heroes full of courage and a spirit of sacrifice. They have nothing to lose but their wretched lives....'

Alas, these were only generalities. What Goebbels needed was not a dozen anonymous storm-troopers but one man he could describe down to the last detail, whose name he could hammer into the heads of his followers, day after day and week after week. While frantically looking for a potential martyr, his eyes fell on Hans Georg Kuetemeyer.

Kuetemeyer had been wounded in the war. Since his release from the army he had been out of work except for occasional odd jobs. He had become a Nazi sympathizer and, living on the dole, put in his spare time as a voluntary worker for the Party. One evening after Hitler had spoken in the Sportpalast, he had celebrated with other Party members and got very drunk. The next morning his body was found in the Landwehr Canal. He had left a letter saying he was tired of living in poverty, without hope of getting a job, and the police were reasonably sure he had committed suicide.

Goebbels saw an opportunity. He wrote an article called 'Kuetemeyer', which he followed up with several other pieces about the man. According to Goebbels, Kuetemeyer had not been in the least disgruntled with the Nazis (as he had said to friends before his death). On the contrary, he loved the Party, he lived only for it. He revered Hitler. During the night of his death he had been fortunate enough to listen to the Fuehrer's speech 'with a beating heart ... and when at the end he arose with sixteen thousand others he sang, his eyes full of tears, "*Deutschland, Deutschland ueber alles!*"'

Did someone mention that he had got drunk that night? Goebbels had an answer. 'Who would quarrel with him on that account? After having experienced such great emotional tension he could not immediately go back to his drab, everyday existence. For two hours he sat with his comrades, in joyous and excited debate.'

Then Kuetemeyer went home. But he never got there because—along the way the dreaded Communists turned up. Goebbels, of course, was not on the spot to see what had happened; in fact there were no witnesses and the police could never get a shred of evidence to prove that Kuetemeyer had got into a fight. But this did not prevent Goebbels from describing the ensuing struggle down to the smallest detail. A taxi crowded with Communists stopped Kuetemeyer in the street. He was beaten-up with, iron bars until he became unconscious, and then was thrown into the canal. 'Shouts for help could be heard while the taxi raced off.'

No one ever volunteered this information to the Berlin police. But Goebbels knew even the exact time at which the murder had occurred. 'At four in the morning his wife awakened. She was sure she had heard her husband call, "Mother, Mother!" That was the hour when he died.' Goebbels did his utmost to build up the dead Kuetemeyer. He proclaimed that Kuetemeyer's name would be carried on the honour roll of Party members who had died for the cause. He would be remembered along with the victims of Hitler's putsch in 1923, and along with Schlageter. But it was in vain. The Kuetemeyer story just did not come off. Soon he was completely forgotten.

Then finally Goebbels found his man. His name was Horst Wessel.

III

Goebbels first heard of Horst Wessel at the end of 1926, when the latter joined the Party. In those days the Party was so small that the Gauleiter knew practically every member by name, and Horst Wessel, tall, strong and good-looking in a brutish way, was definitely a personality. Born in 1907 as the son of a Lutheran pastor, he had been too young to enlist in the army, but he made up for it by joining the Free Corps.

Goebbels put him in charge of the notorious storm unit 5. Wessel soon made a name for himself by his constant street brawls with Socialists and Communists. Goebbels kept his eyes on the promising young man. He sent him to Vienna to study the organization of the Austrian Hitler Youth and he used him as a speaker in Berlin, where he soon became extremely popular. Then, suddenly, he seemed to lose interest. Goebbels was told that Wessel even neglected his own storm unit, and soon afterwards he completely disappeared from the scene.

Upon further investigation Goebbels learned that Horst Wessel had met a prostitute by the name of Erna Jaenicke, and had gone to live in her furnished room at Frankfurterstrasse No. 62. Goebbels sent some of Wessel's friends to look him up but they reported that the young man no longer cared for the Party or his storm-troopers—he only cared for Fraeulein Jaenicke.

Since Wessel made no money whatsoever, she continued to exercise her profession, delivering the proceeds to her lover. This irritated a man called Ali Hoehler, who had started Fraeulein Jaenicke along her road and who had been her procurer until Wessel turned up. On 14 January 1930, Frau Salm, Fraeulein Jaenicke's landlady, went to the saloon where Hoehler spent his days and suggested that he should do something about getting his girl friend back. Hoehler returned with her and opened Erna's door with the landlady's key. When Wessel saw him enter he reached for his gun. But Hoehler was faster. He shot Wessel, grabbed the girl and was gone. The bullet had passed through Wessel's mouth. He was taken to hospital in a critical condition.

From then on, Goebbels took over. The next day he published his first article on Horst Wessel. He reported how he had learned about Wessel being wounded. 'Dead?—No, but it's hopeless. The walls close in on me, the ceiling threatens to come down. No, no, it cannot be!'

Goebbels went to see Wessel at the hospital and every single detail of these visits was published in *Angriff*; but there was not a word about Fraeulein Jaenicke or Hoehler. As far as Goebbels was concerned, Wessel had belonged only to the Party and to the storm-troopers. 'The storm-troopers—that is Horst Wessel. Wherever there is a Germany, you will be, too, Horst Wessel!'

For days Goebbels continued to eulogize the young pimp. On the morning of 23 February Horst Wessel died. His funeral turned into a Nazi demonstration of tremendous proportions. Small wonder, since Goebbels had staged it. Before thousands of mourners Goebbels made the funeral oration. Then they all sang the Horst Wessel song.

This was a little poem of sixteen lines written by Wessel five months before and published in *Angriff*. It was a rather ingenious and effective mixture of several Nazi slogans which struck the listeners as familiar. Someone discovered that the verse could be sung to an old tune, which was done on several private occasions without causing too much of a stir. At Wessel's funeral, however, it was first sung in public. From that time on it was to be the anthem of the Nazis.

After the song was over Goebbels called into the crowd, 'Horst Wessel!' As though he expected his storm-troopers to report for duty, all of them shouted back, 'Present!' This symbolic ritual was to become a regular feature of future Nazi demonstrations.

A short time afterwards, Ali Hoehler was tried, convicted of manslaughter and sentenced to six years in prison. Throughout the trial Goebbels filled the National Socialist newspapers with his cries of despair and anger, but all that concerned him was how much would leak out. As was to be expected, the hearings revealed the whole truth, with all the unsavoury details, and the story made sensational headlines.

Goebbels found himself in quite a predicament. How could he perpetuate the legend of the martyr Horst Wessel when the real story was being circulated throughout the country's press? It looked like an impossible task and, yet, Goebbels did it, despite the fact that he had no illusions about the real Horst Wessel.

'That didn't bother him in the least,' was Hans Fritzsche's comment on that phase. By the time the Nazis came to power Hoehler had served three years. The Nazis then killed both him and Frau Salm, in addition to murdering all other witnesses who might have threatened the Horst Wessel legend.

IV

This was Goebbels' propagandistic substitute for reality: Horst Wessel had been murdered because he was a Nazi. All Nazis were in constant danger of being murdered or maltreated. The Republic oppressed them, through the wicked officials in its pay, and, above all, there was the most powerful enemy—'Jewish international capital.' 'The Isidor of the year 1929 is called John Pierpont Morgan,' Goebbels wrote, thus proving his rather limited knowledge of international finance.

'The Allies who demanded reparations were out to "enslave" Germany,' Goebbels declared. In 1924, the Dawes Plan, named after the American Vice-President, Charles G. Dawes, had been adopted. It would have been hard on Germany's economy had it not been for the fact that the foreign loans granted to her simultaneously far exceeded any reparations she was required to pay under the plan. Goebbels had hardly become Propaganda Chief when he drew up a poster showing the name D A W E S spread out in large letters. Underneath was the sentence, 'Deutschlands Armut Wird Ewig Sein' (Germany's poverty will last for ever).

When one of his colleagues asked him what line the Nazis should take if reparations were eased, Goebbels replied darkly, 'Whatever plan is proposed, we shall say it cannot be carried out.'

Such an opportunity presented itself in May, 1929, when the American banker, Owen D. Young, worked out a new plan of reparations which lessened Germany's burden considerably. The Germans had every reason to be pleased with the arrangement. Eventually, after a few payments, the whole problem of reparations might have been liquidated.

A commission of German experts headed by the Reichsbank President, Hjalmar Schacht, had started negotiations in Paris. Everything was proceeding smoothly and eventually Schacht declared himself willing to accept Mr Young's proposals.

The Young Plan might have enhanced the prestige of the German Republic[1] and, consequently, of its Government which then was controlled by the Social Democrats. This alone was intolerable to most nationalists and, of course, to the Nazis. It was for this reason that one of the negotiators, the industrialist Albert Voegler, walked out of the conference at the first opportunity. It was for this reason that another industrialist of great power, Alfred Hugenberg, came to the fore.

Hugenberg, a small, wiry, white-haired man, was then sixty-five years old. He had been general manager of the Krupp works and played a leading part in German heavy industry. He was the leader of the *Deutschnationale Volkspartei*, largest rightist party in the early 'Twenties. He had bought up several Berlin newspapers, reorganized them, added a news service, was constantly acquiring stock in large provincial papers and in this way had built up a formidable machine to influence public opinion. Finally, he had purchased Germany's largest motion-picture company, the UFA.

Now Hugenberg saw an opportunity to make himself and his party heard. He wrote three thousand letters to important industrialists in Germany and abroad, pointing out that the Young Plan would ruin Germany, and that its signatories knew it could not be carried out. Although these letters openly discredited the German Government nothing was done about the matter.

Hugenberg was not cut out to be a leader of the masses. His friends were industrialists and Junkers, former officers and aristocrats, and his party lacked mass appeal. Hugenberg knew that he could not upset the Young Plan, nor, ultimately, bring about the fall of the Republic unless he acquired a broader following. He needed an ally and he thought Hitler might be the right man.

The Nazis had attacked the Young Plan even more violently than Hugenberg. 'For us it is not binding what you have signed,' Goebbels wrote on 1 July 1929. 'Solemnly we raise our hands, pure and untainted, before history and swear that we will not relax ... until these hands tear up the shameful treaties.'

But this did not mean that Goebbels wanted to be in the same boat with Hugenberg. He despised Hugenberg and his friends and constantly denounced them as a 'reactionary crowd'. Hitler, however, felt that it might be financially advantageous to walk part of the way with Hugenberg. Without notifying Goebbels, he came to Berlin and spoke before Hugenberg and other industrialists and bankers. It was only by chance that Goebbels heard about it and went to the meeting. Hitler was just about to conclude his speech when he walked in. Hitler and Hugenberg decided that they would jointly promote a plebiscite against acceptance of the Young Plan.

Goebbels was not happy about this alliance and made no secret of it. 'If we resort to a plebiscite, we will use it only as a tactical means to get nearer to our goal. The means for reaching a goal can change. The goal itself never changes. The fact that certain groups are employing the same means—groups which are separated from us by a deep gulf both from a socialistic and nationalist point of view—does not prove that the goal is wrong,' he wrote rather petulantly.

On the other hand, there were certain aspects of the alliance that pleased him. Hitler had laid down the condition that Goebbels was to direct the propaganda machine during the forthcoming campaign. This was the first time he did not have to labour under all sorts of restrictions; he could operate through a group of large and powerful newspapers; he had a news syndicate at his disposal; he could use the news-reels and the movie houses. But above all, there was enough money. No longer did he have to work in dark, smoke-filled rooms; no longer did he have to be afraid of being presented with a summons, to economize with every step he took. This time he could go to the limit.

He was extremely generous with Hugenberg's money although he knew long before the day of the plebiscite that the whole undertaking would be a failure. But he also had figured out that the Nazi Party was getting several millions worth of free publicity. Twenty million votes were required to carry through the plebiscite, but only 5.8 million voted against the Young Plan on 22 December 1929.

V

In October 1929 the New York stock market had crashed, billions of dollars were lost, prosperity in the land of unlimited opportunities was abruptly halted. Millions of people who had believed in their financial security found that they had nothing left. Businesses closed, people lost their jobs. All over the world the army of the unemployed grew.

It is unlikely that the Nazi leaders, knowing as little as they did about the intricacies of world economy, had any inkling of the significance of this collapse of world markets, but Hjalmar Schacht knew what it meant. On 23 June he had wired to Reich Chancellor Hermann Mueller his willingness to assume responsibility for the Young Plan. In November Goering met Schacht and learned that the banker considered throwing in his lot with the Nazis. (Several months later Schacht resigned, explaining that he no longer believed the provisions of the Young Plan could be carried out.)

The man who thought that the Young Plan could be carried out was Germany's Foreign Minister, Gustav Stresemann, the main villain in Goebbels' propaganda scenario. Originally, Stresemann had come from the Right. During the war he had favoured a policy of annexations. After the defeat he realized that Germany could recover from the war only by co-operating with the Allies.

It was Stresemann's Government that called off the ill-fated policy of passive resistance during the Ruhr occupation in September, 1923. It was he who in 1925 signed the Treaty of Locarno which was actually just another pledge to adhere to the Treaty of Versailles.[2] (Even at Locarno Stresemann made it clear that he did not feel bound to respect the status quo in the East, meaning the Polish-German border.) It was he who, in September 1926, succeeded in getting Germany admitted to the League of Nations, thanks to his close collaboration and friendship with the French Foreign Minister, Aristide Briand.

To Goebbels, even the pretence of a policy of fulfilment was a crime. 'Stresemann is really not an individuality but the incarnation of everything rotten in Germany,' he wrote, and continued: 'His entire foreign policy is one enormous field of ruins, strewn with questions tackled but never solved....'

In the municipal elections of 17 November 1929, the Nazis won more than twenty per cent of the seats in the newly-elected City Council. This was a personal success for Goebbels, who had conducted the entire campaign, speaking night after night and writing many articles, posters and pamphlets. He had made a definite step forward towards the 'conquest of Berlin.' *Angriff* now appeared twice a week.

During the year 1930 Goebbels was to win another important victory. The publishing house of the Strassers went out of business. The brothers had been quarrelling for some time among themselves, and Hitler thought that Otto had become by far too radical. He bought the stock Gregor owned in the publishing company, closed the firm, discontinued the newspapers published by the Strassers and left Otto holding the bag.

Hitler ordered Goebbels to expel Otto Strasser and his friends from the Party. At the time of the Hanover resolution these same men had been close to Goebbels, but he showed no qualms over carrying out the Fuehrer's instructions. A while later, when Captain Stennes, head of the Berlin S.A. and one of Goebbels' intimates, staged a strike of his storm-troopers to win higher pay and greater political influence for his men, Goebbels purged him too.

This occurred while he was in the middle of a new campaign. The Reichstag had been dissolved once more and new elections were scheduled for 14 September 1930. Goebbels was optimistic over the chances of the Party. He publicly predicted that the Nazis would occupy forty seats in the new Reichstag, instead of their previous twelve. Newspaper comment was heavily ironical and it was said that soon Goebbels would have to eat his words because no party had ever trebled its votes from one election to the next. But Goebbels had not made empty campaign promises. Those who smiled incredulously at his bold prophecy failed to take into account the formidable machine he had built up during the past eighteen months.

Now he set it in motion. His speakers covered the whole of Germany, the big cities and the smallest village. All the Nazi leaders, from Hitler down, had to make speeches till they were hoarse.

It was a campaign the like of which had never been seen in Germany. Goebbels had worked out a regular deployment plan for his speakers, so that none of them would have a moment's idleness. He organized 6,000 meetings. He had tents erected to hold thousands of people, he staged open-air meetings at night, lighted by torches. Millions of posters were stuck on the walls of every city. The entire Nazi press was unified under Goebbels' command. He himself supervised the news coverage on the meetings and the next morning identical reports would appear in all Nazi papers throughout Germany. Whatever copies were not bought by the public were given away free. Nazi papers which previously had had a circulation of 50,000 now printed half-a-million copies.

On 14 September more people than ever before cast their votes in Germany. For hours they queued up in front of the voting booths. It was obvious that a good many were voting for the first time in their lives.

In the evening the first election returns came in. They were, of course, not conclusive but showed a certain increase of Nazi votes. Nobody seemed surprised. By then the Bruening Government was convinced that Goebbels' original prediction—forty seats in the new Reichstag—would come true. During the night further returns poured in. Suddenly the people listening at their radios, the cabinet members in the Wilhelmstrasse and the Nazi leaders gathered around Goebbels realized that the Nazi victory amounted to a landslide.

In 1928, in East Prussia the Nazis had polled 8,000 votes; now they counted 253,000. In Frankfurt-on-the-Oder they leaped from 8,200 to 204,000 votes; in Pomerania from 13,500 to 236,000; in Breslau from 9,300 to 259,000; in Thuringia from 20,700 to 243,000; in Cologne from 10,600 to 169,000; in Leipzig from 14,000 to 160,000; in Hamburg from 17,800 to 144,000. And in greater Berlin they climbed from 50,000 to 550,000.

Everyone was stunned. Time and again the officials went over the figures to see if by any chance there had been some error. At Government quarters some of the higher-ups were so depressed that they got drunk and made rather unwise statements to interviewing newspaper-men. But the figures were correct. Eighteen per cent of all voters—all in all 6,400,000—had cast their ballot for the Nazis. Hitler's Party had become the second largest in the Reich (the Social Democrats were still leading), and it would be represented by 107 deputies in the new Reichstag. It was an unprecedented success. Nowhere in the world had a political party increased its following tenfold within two years.

The next morning reporters from all newspapers rushed to Berlin Gau headquarters. They wished to interview the Propaganda Chief of the Party, the man whom they rightly believed to be responsible for the landslide. It was the first time that the non-Nazi press was interested in what Goebbels had to say. He made a few brief statements and indicated that he had little time for the newspaper-men. 'The battle has just begun,' he snapped. 'In fact, it has not even begun. I have just given directives for the coming struggle.'

Then he left them to dictate a triumphant article entitled '107'.

VI

On that day many people believed Hitler would make another putsch. The Government was so stunned over the outcome of the elections that he might well have succeeded. However, Hitler did nothing of the sort and ten days later—during the trial of three army officers before the Leipzig Supreme Court—he testified under oath that he had every intention to remain within the limits of legality.

Goebbels interpreted Hitler's 'legality' in his own way. 'The Constitution does not dictate the goal of a political development but only the means by which it can be achieved,' he wrote. 'Within the framework of these limits any political goal is attainable.... And it is the goal which is revolutionary—not the method. A man can fight on the barricades and still be a reactionary, but it is possible for him to fight within the constitutional limits of the law, while his goal remains revolutionary.'

Outwardly success had changed Goebbels' life in numerous ways. He moved the office of the Berlin Gau to better quarters at No. 10 Hedemannstrasse. To visitors he would explain that during the war his present office had been occupied—by Walther Rathenau; yes, the same Rathenau whose works he had once admired and whose murderers he later glorified; one of the outstanding German statesman of the post-war era. In a way, Rathenau's office was a historical shrine and Goebbels savoured the ironical coincidence that he, of all people, should be sitting in it.

The Party's success made itself felt everywhere. The sales of *Mein Kampf* went up. Important American and British correspondents came to interview Hitler. *Angriff* became a daily. If Goebbels needed funds, all he had to do was to call up the Party treasurer and a cheque would be forthcoming: there were many industrialists eager to pay their way into the Party before it was too late.

Goebbels' offices at the Braun Haus in Munich were still more luxurious than his quarters in Berlin. But even now he did not become one of the Munich clique. He remained as untamably aggressive as he had been before. No big cigars for him, and no drinking bouts. If there was anything he resented it was being described as a man of comfort and leisure. When a small-town newspaper-man wrote an article about Goebbels the bourgeois leading a life of ease Goebbels responded furiously. 'They're lying! They're lying!' he wrote, reprinting the reporter's story in full and adding his own parenthetical comments.

'Goebbels' private life.... He lives in an elegant apartment in Charlottenburg. (The apartment is neither elegant nor in Charlottenburg, but in Steglitz.) He is still single (this is the only true statement in the whole article), although stubborn rumours have it that he will become the son-in-law of Party member Kunze. (Well, well! Kunze has no daughters!) The great little Doctor's interest in the fair sex is largely platonic. (Hear, hear!) The noise of the street does not penetrate the peaceful realm of his fancy six-room apartment. (The apartment is not fancy and, alas, has only two rooms.)' And so on. Obviously the reporter had hit a vulnerable spot....

On 13 October the Reichstag convened. Goebbels thought that a day on which the eyes of the country were turned towards Berlin was ideally suited for a publicity stunt. He mapped out a plan with the new chief of the Berlin storm-troopers, Count Wolf von Helldorf, the black sheep of a good family, a blackmailer and gambler. At the very moment when the 107 Nazi deputies made their entrance in the Reichstag, thousands of storm-troopers in civilian clothes broke the windows of Jewish-owned department stores and other Jewish-owned enterprises. When Goebbels was asked if he had inspired this vandalism, he indignantly denied any knowledge of it. Three years later he cynically boasted in public that he had in truth been the instigator.

Another opportunity for making headlines presented itself when a leading theatre in the west end of Berlin showed the American-made movie, *All Quiet on the Western Front*. The film was based on the book by Erich Maria Remarque. Goebbels had attacked Remarque for a long time: he was a pacifist, his book was published by a Jewish-owned firm, but most important of all, it was a best-seller and by attacking it he automatically gained publicity. The same reason prompted Goebbels to do something about the motion-picture.

Here is what happened, as reported by one of Goebbels' friends:[3]

'The day after the première of the movie we were sitting in Goebbels' office at Hedemannstrasse. Dr Goebbels gave directives. Within a few minutes he had outlined the project which was to cause a sensation far beyond Berlin.

'"How do we get so many tickets for tonight's performance?" someone asked. Goebbels got up, snapped his fingers. A few telephone calls, and we had the tickets. Half an hour later they had been distributed. That evening the theatre was full of Nazis....

'You know the rest. A few white mice caused considerable unpleasantness, stink-bombs smelled up the place. Suddenly, an inexplicable panic broke out among the audience. Police were summoned. They searched around, not knowing what to do next. There was no one that could be arrested for disturbing the peace. Everyone present demanded to see the picture.'

But what with white mice running wild and stink-bombs exploding the performance had to be stopped. Goebbels himself dictated the story for next morning's *Angriff*. He had been in the theatre and remembered every detail. Result: the film was banned throughout Germany.

All of Berlin laughed and Goebbels thought he had the last laugh. A few months later he found he was mistaken. In March 1931 a short story centring around trench warfare in the First World War was published in *Angriff*. An unknown contributor had sent it in, the editor explained, predicting that his name was bound to become famous.

The next day several liberal Berlin papers revealed that this story by an 'unknown contributor' had been lifted word for word from Remarque's famed book. For once Goebbels had no answer.

But usually the Propaganda Chief was not tongue-tied. In those days he needed his eloquence more than ever. On 10 February 1931, the Nazi deputies had walked out of the Reichstag, Goebbels had lost his parliamentary immunity and was immediately involved in a dozen lawsuits. Among other things he also had to defend himself against the accusation of having instigated the anti-Semitic outrages of 13 October. He was placed under oath.

'I was in a pretty bad spot,' he said when he related the story later. 'I could not very well perjure myself—there were too many witnesses who might have spilled the truth. On the other hand, I could not admit my role in the events and go to prison. I chose the only way out.'

The only way out for Goebbels was to behave like a lunatic. He shouted at the judge, at the prosecutor, he made libellous statements. He staged a terrific scene which left everybody speechless. Finally the judge fined him 200 marks for contempt of court. But Goebbels had got what he wanted: he was not required to testify under oath. And in addition, he got a great deal of publicity in the press.

VII

In March 1930 Heinrich Bruening had succeeded the Social Democrat Hermann Mueller as Reich Chancellor. He was fond of reminiscences about the war, in which he had fought as a captain, and he pointed with a certain pride to his active opposition during the revolution of 1918. He was honest and kind but he had no idea whatsoever of how to stop the growing economic depression and the political radicalization of the masses. His only concern was to balance the budget. To that effect he had to cut down expenses, which meant the dismissal of officials, the stoppage of subsidies—which in turn resulted in further dismissals, more people out of work, and more reasons for joining the Nazis or the Communists. Capitalists became seriously worried and transferred their money abroad, which brought about the closing of more businesses and increased unemployment.

The economic crisis was assuming wider proportions everywhere. In May 1931 the *Oesterreichische Kreditanstalt*, one of the largest banks in Europe controlled by the Vienna Rothschilds, collapsed. Panic spread through Austria and Germany. Foreign loans were withdrawn by troubled investors, a run on the banks began. Hindenburg appealed to President Hoover, who proposed to the French and British Governments to grant Germany a moratorium for one year. Nevertheless, the depression was going from bad to worse. On 13 July, Jakob Goldschmidt's bank had to close, and twenty-four hours later all other German banks followed suit. So did the Berlin stock exchange. Germany's economic leaders were at their wit's end.

Despair flooded the country. People feared that a new inflation would wipe out their last savings. Again, all Bruening could think of were further economies. He was worried over the coming winter which, he openly admitted, would be the 'worst winter of the last hundred years'. In the middle of September it was evident that at least six million Germans would soon be out of work. From the United States came news that the number of unemployed was expected to exceed ten million. The Bank of England had gone off the gold standard.

Humanity trembled. Goebbels was optimistic. He sensed his great chance. During the summer he had declared that he would double the membership of the Party and he had kept his promise. Now the Party counted one million members, with applications pouring in hourly. The worse things fared under Bruening, the easier it would be to make the people vote for Hitler. The gloomier the predictions, the more fervently the masses would search for a way out.

One liberal Berlin paper, the *Boersenkurier* saw clearly what Goebbels was up to. 'You misjudge Goebbels entirely if you believe that his motive is governed by the slogan, "After us the deluge." He reverses the sentence. For him it reads, "After the deluge: We!"'

Goebbels hammered into the people's heads that they had nothing to hope for if Bruening stayed in power. 'They gave you stones instead of bread,' he wrote. 'Five million are already out of work—and this coming winter, according to the statement of Chancellor Dr Bruening, there will be seven million. (For good measure Goebbels added one million to Bruening's estimate.) ... You men and women without work and without hope, you have fallen prey to the blackest despair....'

All that Nazi propaganda had to do at this time of extreme crisis was to make promises. And Goebbels made promises—to all classes, to all professions. Many of his promises contradicted each other. He would tell real estate owners that the rents would rise, and people living in apartment houses learned that rents would drop. He would tell the peasants that they would get higher prices for their grain, and the workers were assured that bread would become cheaper. But the people paid no attention to these contradictions. They were happy to have something to hope for.

Was Germany ripe to fall into the hands of the Nazis? Had matters gone far enough? In October, Reich President Paul von Hindenburg received Adolf Hitler in audience. He was not impressed by the Fuehrer. He thought the man talked too much. At best Hitler might be suited for the job of postmaster-general, he said.

The people's fear subsided, they relaxed again. Hitler would not get anywhere, many hoped. Hjalmar Schacht, however, strengthened his ties with Goering and Goebbels, and told them they had no cause for pessimism. Time was working for them, he said.

And so if was. From day to day the situation grew steadily worse, the starving masses were desperate.

It was in those days, laden with tension and gloom, that Goebbels got married.

VIII

Magda—tall, blond, slim and very beautiful—was the child of an unhappy marriage. Her father, Herr Rietschel, was a man of considerable learning, his principal interest being Buddhism and oriental languages. He sent his daughter to be educated in a Belgian convent, where she learned to speak fluent French and English. Magda's mother, a very good-looking woman, came from a typical middle-class family and was mainly concerned with financial security. She divorced Rietschel to marry a Berlin businessman named Friedlaender, a Jew with whom Magda was on very friendly terms. Her second marriage was not a success either, whereupon she divorced Friedlaender to marry a certain Herr Behrendt, whom she ultimately also divorced.

In 1917 she owned and managed a small perfume and soap store which Friedlaender had settled on her. While on a brief vacation, mother and daughter met Guenther Quandt, a wealthy industrialist in his forties but well preserved for his age. Occasionally he would invite them for a drive in his car. He fell in love with eighteen-year-old Magda and eventually proposed to her. Her mother had certain misgivings on account of their difference in age. But Magda accepted. She was intrigued by his social position and the riches she would possess as Quandt's wife. She was nineteen when they were married.

She moved into his twenty-two-room villa at Babelsberg, a fashionable suburb of Berlin.[4] The Quandts lived in grand style. They saw only 'the best people'. After the war they travelled widely: to the United States, to the French Riviera, to Paris. Through her husband, Magda became interested in politics. He was a reactionary and an anti-Semite within limits. Provided they had enough money, Jews were acceptable to him.

Quandt had two sons from his first marriage, Herbert and Helmut, and Magda was very fond of the two boys. On 1 November 1921, she gave birth to a son, Harald. Shortly afterwards Quandt's older son, Herbert, then twenty, made a trip to New York. Passing through Paris on his return he was stricken with appendicitis. Magda rushed to his bedside and he died in her arms. Later there were rumours that their relationship had not been entirely innocent.

Whatever the truth, Magda was not happy in her marriage. As her mother had predicted, the difference in age was too great. Quandt found his wife with a young student in a compromising position. He told her bluntly that he would divorce her and that she would not get a cent of his fortune.

Magda did not lose her head. In her predicament she remembered certain documents that Quandt was keeping at home. She returned to Babelsberg, searched the house and found the papers which proved that her husband was guilty of income-tax evasion. The ensuing conversation between the couple gave her the upper hand. Quandt agreed to pay her a lump sum of 50,000 marks, a monthly allowance of 4,000 marks until such time as she would remarry, and to furnish an apartment for her.[5]

The Quandts divorced in 1929. Magda took an apartment in the west end of Berlin and led the life of a beautiful, elegant and wealthy divorcee. She was soon bored with this kind of existence. Among the people she had met through Quandt were some of Hitler's financial backers. By that time the Nazi Party had become fashionable. The aristocratic reactionary set of Berlin thought that some of the Nazis were really 'quite interesting'. They were 'so tough'. This Dr Goebbels, for instance, what an extraordinary character!

A friend suggested to Magda that it might amuse her to work for the Nazis. She need not take it too seriously, of course, but just volunteer for a few hours a week. Magda thought it was a fine idea, and she went to headquarters, where they were glad to have her. On her first day she met Goebbels.

He aroused her interest. She had never met anyone like him before. She wanted to know more about him. She went to the Sportpalast to hear him speak. It was a fascinating experience. Here was a man with terrific driving power, courageous, tough and yet of subtle irony. She found him far more entertaining than the rich industrialists or the decadent aristocrats she had met through Quandt. Here was a man who was still young, with an almost boyish charm and a superior intellect. Goebbels' scintillating, demoniacal personality captured her imagination and, as so many women after her, she sensed that he would dominate her.

Goebbels, contrary to the average person's conception of him, had become an *homme à femmes*. He was not handsome in the accepted sense of the word. But women were attracted by his sharp, ascetic features, his expressive eyes, his shiny, brown hair, his slender, nervous hands. Above all, his voice was an instrument with which he could play many tunes. It could sound soft as a caress, or sharp as a whip. His limp—hardly noticeable—was almost an added attraction; women found it made him 'interesting'.

At first Goebbels paid little attention to Magda. But almost everyone else at headquarters had noticed her and there was a lot of gossip about her. She was young, beautiful and rich—in contrast to the other women working there. One of the minor officials had made advances to her and—was slapped in the face. Magda then decided it would be best to stop working for the movement.

Goebbels heard about the incident and asked her to his office. He obviously enjoyed her embarrassment and made her relate every detail of the unpleasant encounter. Finally he persuaded her to stay on, transferring her to the archives, where work was more interesting.

He made it a point to appear occasionally in her office. They talked, first about Party politics, soon about more personal matters. She felt that he was getting interested and was trying to impress her. She would have become his mistress at once, she later said, if only he had asked her. But he did not. On the contrary, he would suddenly start an argument, leave the room and not come back for days. Then the same game would begin all over again. But at the last moment Goebbels would always run away.

The truth was that he was afraid of Magda. She represented something he had never known: society, wealth, glamour. He who had no fear of speaking in front of thousands of people, was afraid to take her out to dinner because he was not certain of what kind of clothes to wear in the places she frequented, nor how to behave there. With her he felt as insecure as in his boyhood days. Once, in a restaurant, she chose lobster, while he ordered a Viennese schnitzel. Years afterwards he admitted that he had not known how to eat lobster and had wanted to be on the safe side.

He decided that the situation was getting out of hand. Not since the days of Freiburg and Heidelberg had he met a woman who made him feel inferior, and he rebelled against it. With Magda he was on the defensive and his only way of fighting his sense of inferiority was to treat her with abrupt sharpness and even insolence. Magda misinterpreted his conduct, she was hurt. Therefore, in the summer of 1931, she took her little son and left for the seashore, trying to get away from what she felt was a deliberate attempt to humiliate her.

Ten days later Goebbels joined her. He wanted to explain his curious attitude. She ought to understand that he was much too involved in politics to have any time left for a private life. He ended up by confessing that he could not live without her.

It was the first time since his unhappy experience with Anka Helhorn that he felt certain of a woman's love. With her wealth and her position in society she could have made a more profitable choice than marrying a man who had neither. There was no opportunism in Magda's love for him. When he finally proposed to her he came out with a strange and puzzling statement: he told her that he loved her, that he wanted to marry her, that he wanted her to be the mother of his children, that he wanted to make her the 'Queen of his life'—but that he could not promise always to be faithful to her. Could she understand and appreciate his frankness?

Magda was not entirely sure whether she understood him well and whether his last words were to be taken seriously. But nothing mattered to her in that moment except Goebbels, her man.

Her mother was dismayed when she learned of Magda's intentions. If her daughter married Goebbels, she would lose her monthly allowance. Goebbels made only 900 marks a month (400 marks as Gauleiter and 500 marks as Reichstag deputy). But the rent of Magda's west-end apartment alone was 500 marks. When she could not be persuaded to reconsider her decision, old Herr

Rietschel was called in. He was brutally frank: in his opinion, Goebbels was a good-for-nothing agitator and no suitable match for his daughter.

Magda showed her father the door and told him never to come back. Even in later years, when he asked to see his grandchildren, she remained deaf to his pleas. To her mother she explained: 'I know what I'm doing. If the Nazis come to power, I'll be sitting pretty. If not, the Communists will take over and then I'll lose my allowance any way.'

They were married towards the end of 1931. The ceremony took place on an estate in Mecklenburg owned by Guenther Quandt. Hitler was Goebbels' best man. Goebbels' mother had asked that he be married by the Catholic Church. This was somewhat difficult as Magda was a divorced woman. Goebbels wrote to the Bishop of Berlin asking for a special dispensation, but the offensive tone of his letter made the granting of this request almost impossible. Three days later, when he had received no reply, Goebbels informed the Bishop that he would marry without the blessing of the Church, as, indeed, he had lived all his life.

CHAPTER V

THE LAST LAP

I

When the year 1931 ended, nothing had happened which was likely to turn the Nazi victory at the polls into practical results. Goebbels wondered how long they would have to wait. Once again the Party was in money troubles. Now, however, it was no longer a question of getting hold of a few thousand marks. Goebbels' enormous propaganda machine consumed hundreds of thousands, the storm-troopers millions of marks. *Angriff* continued to be suspended at irregular intervals. Up to then Goebbels had not cared, because the ensuing publicity was worth it. Now he was worried. 'The Berlin police have suspended *Angriff* ten times in less than a year.... In other words, it is possible today to push a daily to the verge of bankruptcy, while the publication has no way of countering such unjustified and untenable procedure.....

Then Goebbels saw what he believed to be an excellent opening. According to the Constitution, the President of the Reich was elected every eight years. Hindenburg's time was almost up. Chancellor Bruening hoped to get Hindenburg re-elected by an overwhelming vote arranged beforehand. Hitler and most of his lieutenants believed no one had a chance against Hindenburg. By throwing their weight on the side of the old President, the Nazis could ask for certain favours in return. The deal was almost concluded when Goebbels interfered. He saw no reason why Hitler should not campaign for himself. The Nazis must not pass up the opportunity of showing their increasing strength, he argued. Single-handed, he persuaded Hitler that he must run against Hindenburg. Single-handed, he convinced the Munich clique that a victory over the old Marshal was in the realm of possibility.

For several weeks Hitler was incapable of coming to a decision. It was not until 19 February that he made it. Hitler gave Goebbels permission to announce his candidacy at the next mass meeting in the Sportpalast on 22 February. 'For one hour I prepared the audience. Then I proclaimed that the

Fuehrer would be a candidate for the Presidency. For ten full minutes the crowd was delirious with enthusiasm. Wild demonstrations for the Fuehrer. They all rose from their seats, jubilant and crying. The roof threatened to come down.' The following day Goebbels became incensed with the press. 'They assert that it was I who nominated the Fuehrer or rather, "forced" him to be a candidate. How poorly informed they are!' In reality, the newspapers were not poorly informed at all. Goebbels alone had pushed Hitler into this campaign, and Hitler knew it too. Perhaps Goebbels was worried about what the Fuehrer would do if things turned out badly.

II

Head over heels Goebbels plunged into the campaign. Glancing over his book, *From the Kaiserhof to the Reich Chancellery,* one gains the impression that he was campaigning not so much for Hitler's election but rather for the purpose of showing off his propaganda machine. 'I had the ambition to make this year's campaigns masterpieces of propaganda,' he wrote on 20 February. And later: 'Our posters turned out wonderfully. Our propaganda was coming through magnificently. The whole country would sit up and listen.'

Posters were of the utmost importance. 'I explained our propaganda plans to the Fuehrer in detail,' he wrote on 29 February. 'The election war would be fought mainly with posters and speeches. Our funds were limited....' He took great pains in preparing the posters. He told the American newspaperman, Edgar Ansel Mowrer, that sometimes it took him three days to find two words of text for an effective poster.

There were four presidential candidates, but the head of the Communist Party as well as a leader of the Right were running for the record only. From the beginning the race was between Hindenburg and Hitler. The Constitution required that the winner receive the absolute majority, otherwise new elections would have to be held.

As so often before, Goebbels depended mainly on the Party speakers. During the last two weeks of the campaign he spoke at three different places every night. His main competitor was Chancellor Bruening, who had fallen into a kind of religious trance about Hindenburg. 'It only happens once in a century that a nation is fortunate enough to have a God-sent man like Hindenburg,' he declared, knowing all the while that Hindenburg was a mental ruin.

On election day—13 March—Goebbels noted: 'Everybody believed in our victory, I alone was sceptical.' If this had been true, he certainly would not have invited so many people to his home to celebrate the Party's victory. But by 10 o'clock in the evening, no further doubt was possible: 'We were beaten.

What a terrible perspective! We had not been wrong in estimating our own votes so much as in misjudging the chance of the opposite side. They only needed another 100,000 votes for an absolute majority. We had gained 86 per cent since September 1930—but what was the use? The Party members were deeply upset and discouraged....'

The truth was that no one was so upset as Goebbels himself. He became almost panicky. If it had not been for him, the Fuehrer would never have run. If Hitler held him responsible for his loss of prestige—then what? At first he did not even dare telephone to Munich to learn of Hitler's reaction. Instead, he got in touch with one of Bruening's associates to find out if it was not too late for an understanding.

Midnight was approaching. Hindenburg had received 18,661,000 votes, Hitler 11,338,000; and the Communists almost five million, the extreme Right 2,500,000. Finally, Goebbels put a call through to Munich. He had decided to advise the Fuehrer to concede Hindenburg's victory. Since Hindenburg had not achieved the absolute majority there would have to be a second election, but in Goebbels' opinion that would be only a matter of form. So why not withdraw with dignity?

This was one of the occasions when Hitler proved he was truly the Fuehrer of his Party; he alone did not lose his nerve, and declared he would not give up the fight. Goebbels, listening to the Fuehrer's voice, regained his composure.

While he was getting ready for the second campaign he took account of the flaws in his propaganda machine, he recognized the mistakes committed by his underlings and voiced concern over the performance of his own press. He controlled only 120 out of 976 German dailies and no one knew better than Goebbels that his newspapers left much to be desired. ('We need a reorganization of the press as badly as our daily bread,' he had noted on 13 January.)

He called a conference of the men working under him and urged them that they must improve their output. 'We must have the courage to learn from our mistakes,' he noted on 19 March. 'No one wanted to admit errors, but that would get us nowhere. I was determined to take them in hand. They simply had to co-operate.'

Again, a few weeks later: 'The main burden of our work in the coming months was placed on propaganda. Our entire technique had to be refined to the last possible degree. Only the most up-to-date methods could lead us to victory.'

The best among his new ideas was to charter a plane for Hitler, thus enabling him to 'speak three or four times a day in public squares or in stadiums ... to make himself heard by one and a half million people, in spite of the lack of time.' He worked out a schedule, arranged for the most important Nazi journalists to go along, and ordered them to report on the tour in the fashion of war correspondents.

Goebbels fought until the last moment. Although Hindenburg won again, with more than nineteen million votes, Hitler succeeded in amassing 13,417,000, thus proving that his star was still in the ascendant.

The next morning Goebbels was already engaged in a new campaign, this time for the Diets of several states (among them Prussia and Bavaria) which were coming up for election two weeks later. Goebbels was now speaking three times a night while at the same time directing hundreds of other speakers. In order to make the front pages he challenged Reich Chancellor Bruening to a public debate. When Bruening refused to appear on the same platform with Goebbels, the Nazi Propaganda Chief played back 'a record of a radio speech which Bruening had made in Koenigsberg.' Again and again Goebbels would stop the record to answer his invisible opponent. 'The public went wild with enthusiasm. It was a fantastic success,' he wrote. And the following day: 'The press was full of our speech duel in the Sportpalast. The Jews are really stupid! Instead of killing me by silence they protested that I had stolen Bruening's intellectual property, and that the Government planned to sue me!'

From a purely technical point of view, these propaganda campaigns were brilliantly executed. There was a steady crescendo from one campaign to the next, and in retrospect one may say that they all were but parts of one over-all campaign. Goebbels had a thousand new ideas—but they applied only to the execution of propaganda themes; they only tried to make a better and bigger impression on the people, to fill them with still greater enthusiasm. Goebbels made a terrific noise—but he had little to say. The vehemence of his machine easily drowned out all others, and the racket was such that no one could understand what anyone else was saying. In all fairness it must be said that Goebbels knew his audiences. The unbelievably low level of his campaigns may well reflect his opinion of their intelligence.

What, then, did Goebbels say in those months? He said that the Government was no good. He said that it could not restore order, let alone prosperity. He was right on both counts, but to make doubly sure the storm-troopers saw to it that whatever order there had been would now crumble.

More speeches. During the last week before the Diet elections Goebbels spoke four times a night. 'I could only say a few words, but the people were satisfied.' In the last days he suffered from an attack of influenza but carried on in spite of a high fever.

More victories for the Nazis. In the Bavarian Diet they now held 43 seats, as compared to their previous 9; in Wurtemberg 23 seats as against 1; in Prussia 162 as against 9. More people had voted for the Nazis than in September 1930, during the landslide.

III

For Goebbels the end of the election campaigns was not even a respite to catch his breath. The fight continued without pause. The National Socialist representatives in the Reichstag started a brawl, the Deputy Police Commissioner, Bernhard Weiss, appeared at the head of his men to restore order. At the sight of him Goebbels became hysterical. 'Get out, Isidor!' he screamed in a high-pitched voice.

In the Prussian Diet 160 Nazi deputies fought 80 Communists, with both parties using chairs, desks, inkwells. 'We sang the Horst Wessel song,' Goebbels commented triumphantly. 'This was just a warning. It was the only way to make them respect us. The auditorium presented a spectacle of grandiose devastation. We were the winners.'

He was so proud of the achievement that he telephoned Hitler to tell him the good news. 'He was enchanted!' Goebbels wrote, so much so that he had to tell the Fuehrer the story all over again when they met the following day. 'I had to report every detail and joyfully he rubbed his hands. Politically speaking, the incident was of inestimable advantage.'

For some time the S.A. had been banned in Berlin and Goebbels hoped that this would cause some incidents. He did his best to provoke them. 'In the evening I entered a large café on Potsdamerplatz, followed by some fifty S.A. leaders. In spite of the ban, they were in full uniform, hoping to cause trouble. Nothing would have pleased us more than if the police had arrested us.... Unfortunately, they wouldn't oblige. Slowly we walked across Potsdamerplatz and down Potsdamerstrasse. Policemen gave us an amazed stare and then, shamefacedly, averted their eyes.'

Goebbels had more luck with the students of Berlin University. They started to riot, demanding that all Jewish students be kicked out. Berlin was shocked. Nothing like it had ever happened before.

In the meantime the fight against Bruening continued with unabated fury. 'He must fall, no matter what the cost.' And fall he did, although it was not Goebbels who caused his doom; it was the man for whom Bruening had fought unselfishly, in his ceaseless effort to have him elected President of the Reich—Field-Marshal von Hindenburg. The old man, covering up for his Junker friends whom the Chancellor intended to prosecute for mismanagement of public funds, told him that he no longer had his confidence. Bruening resigned.

Four hours later Hitler and Goering were received by Hindenburg to learn what they already knew—that Bruening was out. The old President let Hitler know that he had chosen Franz von Papen as his new Chancellor, and he hoped that Hitler would co-operate with Papen. Hitler mumbled something unintelligible and Hindenburg, misunderstanding him, nodded: he was pleased to learn the Fuehrer acquiesced.

Franz von Papen was almost completely unknown. Although a member of the Catholic Centre Party he had never played any role in it. Politically, he was further to the Right than Bruening. A wealthy industrialist, he had excellent connections with the Ruhr magnates and had some influence with those in control of the steel cartels. As a former officer he was close to the Hindenburg clique, and the President was especially fond of him.

Only one incident in his career had received a good deal of publicity: during the First World War he had been an attaché of the German Embassy in Washington and in this capacity had engaged in espionage and sabotage in the United States. When he lost his briefcase in the New York subway, US authorities got hold of the names and addresses of all his sub-agents, enough evidence against him to demand his recall. This alone would have ruined his political chances in any country except Germany.

Goebbels was furious over Papen's nomination. Again they had been cheated. Again they would have to wait. Time was running out. The economic crisis which had helped the Nazis along was beginning to hurt them because it inconvenienced their financial backers. Some of the firms which subsidized the movement had gone into bankruptcy. I. G. Farben was forced to halve its dividends.

IV

On 13 June 1932, the Reichstag was dissolved once more, and new elections were set for 31 July. Goebbels had to start his propaganda machine rolling again, not a minute was to be lost. 'We had to do our work standing, walking, driving, and flying,' he noted on 1 July. 'All-important discussions were held in stairways, in a lobby, in a doorway, or while driving to a station. There was never a minute's rest. We were carried through Germany in all directions by railway, car and plane. We would arrive half an hour before the meeting started, sometimes later, we stepped on the platform, we began to speak.

'The public little knew what the speaker had gone through before he opened his mouth. They were annoyed if he was not in good form, that he was not at the peak of his wit and that his words lacked preciseness. All the while he suffered from the heat, trying to gather his thoughts; the acoustics were bad, the air was stuffy, and his voice became hoarser and hoarser. The next day a learned newspaper scribe would point out that, the speaker unfortunately had been "less lively than usual"....

'When the speech was finished, you felt as though emerging from a hot bath, fully dressed. You got into a car, drove for another two hours over bad roads ... arrived at two in the morning, discussed pressing Party matters until four, and at six you took the train to Berlin. Sometimes a talkative passenger wanted to dispel your fatigue by keeping you awake with friendly conversation....'

Back in Berlin.... 'For two days I dictated posters, pamphlets, articles.... Was almost knocked out with tiredness. Also wrote a speech for the radio.'

It sometimes happened that popular enthusiasm, welcome as it was, would get on his overwrought nerves. Returning from a strenuous meeting and tired to death, he would hopefully settle down for a few hours' sleep. 'Instead, at 8 a.m., a girls' choir posted itself in front of the hotel and started singing ballads with great abandon. I can't say I was exactly delighted.'

However, the Nazis were not always welcomed with unqualified enthusiasm. One evening Goebbels passed through his home town, Rheydt. 'The mob was blocking the roads. But it was so dark that we could slip through without being recognized. The communists had put up posters threatening we would not get away alive.'

The next morning 'the mob was clamouring for us in front of the hotel. The police refused to interfere, declaring it was not their business to protect oppositional politicians. That was how they were running things in Germany.... We finally had to call on storm-troopers and S.S. reinforcements to clear the streets. Naturally they didn't treat the crowd with kid gloves. Our men were wild with fury. I had to leave my birthplace like a criminal, followed by curses and scorn. They were throwing stones after me.'

On 9 July 1932, speaking before a crowd of some hundred thousand people in Berlin's largest public square, the Lustgarten, Goebbels finally decided to attack Papen. 'I want the German people to sit in judgment on the past fourteen years of shame and disgrace, of decadence, of political humiliations.... Have there been any changes in the last few weeks? None whatever! Except that those who govern now have different faces. The economic situation is as bad as ever. No public works programme has been tackled by the new Government. Misery is growing and the hungry no longer know where their next meal is coming from....

On 31 July, the elections took place. The Nazis won their biggest victory by more than doubling the landslide of two years before. In the new Reichstag they would have 230 deputies, more than any party had ever had. The Social Democrats were second with 133 delegates; third, the Communists with 89.

Even Goebbels believed that this was the limit of what he could achieve. 'Now we must take over,' he wrote on 1 August in his diary. 'A short breathing spell to consolidate our position, and then we must rule and show what we can do.' And a few days later he added ominously: 'Once we hold power we will never relinquish it, except if we are carried out of our offices as dead bodies.'

V

After his marriage Goebbels moved into Magda's apartment in the west end of Berlin. Throughout 1932 this apartment was the unofficial headquarters of the Party. Hitler, who stayed at the Hotel Kaiserhof, just off the Wilhelmstrasse, whenever he came to Berlin, used to spend his evenings with the Goebbels, and Magda prepared special vegetarian meals for him. Hitler would bring along his friend, Putzi Hanfstaengl, and his adjutants, Brueckner and Schaub. Goering and Count Helldorf dropped in almost every evening, while their chauffeurs would eat with the servants in the kitchen. Goebbels had a special guard of six storm-troopers who constantly hovered in the lobby.

To keep up this kind of household cost a lot of money. Goebbels gave his wife 700 marks every month. When she told him she needed at least 1,200 marks, he had a fit. He repeatedly explained that as a student he had lived on 90 marks a month; therefore, surely she ought to be able to manage on 700 marks. He knew quite well that she could not. But he wanted to make her suffer because she had been better off than he.

She never argued with him. She simply began to use up her capital of 50,000 marks. But from then on she saved pennies wherever she could. All her servants were unanimous in saying she was extremely stingy and would spend no more on food than was necessary to keep alive.

Even after the great victory at the polls it was by no means certain whether Magda had acted wisely in throwing in her lot with the Nazis, at least from a financial point of view. In a way, the Party was in a more precarious situation than before. Everything depended on avoiding major errors during the next few months. Goebbels constantly reiterated this warning and the more intelligent leadership understood. But the storm-troopers did not: they went berserk.

For years Goebbels and other Nazi leaders had harangued the storm-troopers in inflammatory speeches. This was necessary to heighten their nuisance value and to embarrass the Government in every possible way. The storm-troopers would cover the walls of every city with Nazi slogans and tear down the posters of rival parties. At the slightest provocation they would scream, 'Germany, awake!' or, 'Down with the Jews!' Sometimes they would spray a special liquid on opposition billboards which caused them to go up in flames a few hours later. These small fires attracted hundreds of passers-by, baffled the police and proved to the public in general that the police were incapable of maintaining order. Goebbels originally conceived the idea of this stunt, although Party scientists had developed the technical end of it.

If the S.A. had confined themselves to this type of 'innocent fun', Goebbels would have approved heartily. But they got out of hand. Harmless persons who looked Jewish, but were not, were molested and severely beaten-up. Rash murders which could not be covered up eventually began to antagonize the public.

Goebbels was fully aware that it was impossible to keep the Nazi rank and file under control after they had been aroused to their present pitch of frenzy. He himself had done his utmost to put them into this violent frame of mind. Like the Sorcerer's Apprentice, he could not stop what he had started, and there was no telling what they would do next.

'If this opportunity is missed a catastrophe of unpredictable proportions will occur,' Goebbels wrote in his diary the day Hitler arrived in Berlin. 'The Fuehrer was facing a difficult decision. Without supreme powers he could not master the situation. Unless they were granted, he had to refuse to take over. If he refused, a mighty depression within the ranks of the movement and among the voters would be the consequence.'

Papen offered Hitler the post of Vice-Chancellor in the Government. Hitler had, of course, to decline. Did they not know that he had no other course? Did they not know that a man who had been so widely publicized as a demi-God and a Saviour could not accept second best? In the afternoon Hitler was ordered to appear before Hindenburg. The Marshal did not even offer him a seat. He barked that Hitler had broken his word to support the Papen Government. He accused him of demanding all power. And without giving Hitler a chance to reply he dismissed him as one dismisses a disloyal servant. What angered Goebbels even more was that he had been beaten in his own special field, publicity. All leading papers published the hand-out of the Reich Chancellery on the Hindenburg-Hitler meeting. Hitler was made to look like a fool, a man whose face had got slapped. Too late did Goebbels write a sharp rebuttal. The damage was done.

On 30 August the new Reichstag convened for the first time. The Nazis were now the largest party. According to German parliamentary tradition, the President of the Reichstag would be elected from their ranks. Their choice fell on Hermann Goering.

Once in his new post, Goering moved into a small palace opposite the Reichstag building. In order to go from his house to the Reichstag he did not have to cross the street; there was a tunnel connecting the two buildings.

VI

Goebbels continued his attacks on Papen and his government. 'In my editorials I hammered away at the "upper classes". If we wanted to keep the Party intact, we had to appeal again to the most primitive mass instincts,' he wrote on 4 September. Three days later, he made a speech. 'The hall was overcrowded. My slogan was, "Down with the Barons!"'

But Goebbels also had plenty of trouble. Many Germans began to suspect that the Nazis were perhaps 'too radical'. On the other hand, the leaders of the storm-troopers felt that the Party was not radical enough. Their men became restless. Most of them were either unemployed or had given up their jobs, believing that soon they would be in control of Germany, enjoying all the privileges this entailed. Some of the S.A. leaders dropped out of the Party, formed new organizations and declared that Hitler had 'betrayed' them. Goebbels commented gloomily: 'Where will it all end?'

Papen's own position was far from enviable. The most incompetent chancellor Germany ever possessed had no popular support whatever. His following was composed exclusively of Hugenberg's industrialists and Junkers. His dilemma became painfully obvious when 512 votes were cast against him in the Reichstag, and only 42 for him. 'The most terrible parliamentary defeat ever,' Goebbels commented. 'The Fuehrer is beside himself with joy.'

Goebbels was not. He was faced with a new election campaign, and it had become increasingly obvious that the Nazis were running into difficulties. 'This campaign is going to be harder because the Party chest is empty. Recent campaigns have eaten up all our funds,' he admitted on 16 September. But there were other troublesome angles to consider. 'The excessive speech-making is numbing the people.... Our opponents are hoping we will lose our breath.'

As far as the financial situation was concerned, the Party had already lost its breath. It needed between 70 and 90 million marks to balance its annual budget. By election day it would be in debt to the extent of 15 million marks, and that was a conservative estimate.

Goebbels' newspapers still were not up to par. 'Present performances are not sufficient to master our enormous task,' he wailed on 1 October. Three days later: 'It is difficult to integrate the various newspaper staffs into the campaign. They are over-conscientious and work too slowly.'

No matter what he thought of 'excessive speech-making' he had to fall back on mass meetings and speakers. 'Our propagandists were much better. Day by day, and night by night they were in immediate contact with the broad masses.'

Goebbels himself challenged the leaders of all other political parties to a public debate. Most of them knew what was good for them and turned him down. Only Hugenberg's *Deutschnationale Volkspartei* had the heart to invite Goebbels to one of its meetings. On 19 October he and two of Hugenberg's men were to speak from the same platform, and then there would be a discussion. Here was his big opportunity—and he made the most of it.

'In the afternoon I was working and then I was waiting excitedly for the big battle of the speakers.... At 6.30 the phone rang and I was told there was bedlam in front of the meeting place. The German nationalists were not up to the situation. They had proved themselves incapable of keeping the masses under control. Thousands of our people were crowding the streets....

'Hundreds had already squeezed their way into the hall, God alone knows how. The German nationalist followers were queuing up at the entrance, waving their perfectly good tickets, but could not get in. The chairman was frantic. Had he really believed that there would be only those Nazis for whom he had generously consented to provide tickets?... Before the meeting opened, I was carried inside on the shoulders of wildly enthusiastic S.A. men. Our members were jubilant beyond description. The meeting was won before it started.'

The chairman was much too scared he might be lynched by the mob to interfere with Goebbels. The two speakers who were supposed to debate with him were unable to make themselves heard above the noise. Finally the chairman begged Goebbels to calm the audience, and 'I had to stand next to the speaker in order to enable him to continue his speech.'

Immediately afterwards he went over to the office of *Angriff*. 'We printed one million copies because we feared that the German nationalists would use the overwhelming power of their press to change their defeat into victory. At 3 o'clock we had composed the stories. At 6 o'clock our paper was on the news-stands.'

More speeches. 'I spoke, spoke, spoke. I could no longer remember when and where and how.' But he knew despite his efforts that the Party would lose ground—perhaps to the extent of millions of votes.

'The National Socialist movement found itself in a very bad tactical position,' he later wrote about that period. 'In the last elections it attracted a large number of voters who believed that with the Party coming to power they would soon be rewarded. However, the Party seemed further removed from power than ever and the fellow-travellers were turning away.'

VII

He was right. The Nazis lost more than two million votes, or 34 representatives in the Reichstag. Although they were still by far the largest party, the spell of invincibility was broken. Goebbels did not try to fool himself or his followers. 'We have been licked,' he stated on 6 November. A catastrophe was imminent. 'The report of our financial situation ... looked absolutely hopeless,' he wrote on 11 November. 'Only debts and obligations, and the impossibility of getting important sums of money after this defeat.'

More than six million Germans had voted for the Communists. In order to appeal to these voters Goebbels continued his battle against the 'aristocrats' around Papen. At the same time he played up the Communist danger for all it was worth. Hardly a day passed that Hitler's well-to-do backers were not given to understand that, unless the Nazis soon came to power, Germany would go Communist.

Such predictions did not fail to leave their impression upon the men around Hindenburg. Papen had to go. Yet, once more the aged Marshal asserted his dislike for the corporal upstart and snubbed the Fuehrer. The man who succeeded Papen was General Kurt von Schleicher, who had long been a powerful manipulator behind the scenes, who had conspired in turn with Hitler against Bruening and Papen, and with Bruening and Papen against Hitler, whichever was more advantageous for his own scheming. Now, at Hindenburg's call, he had to step into the limelight to keep Hitler out.

Goebbels, himself a man who often preferred to wield his power behind the scenes and in this respect felt akin to Schleicher, could appreciate the general's predicament better than anyone else. He wrote in *Angriff*: 'Now General von Schleicher, the man always in the shadow, has advanced into the floodlight of public opinion. We do not think that this will do him any good. Because it is well known that the shadow of a man is always larger than the man himself.'

However, this was small consolation for the Nazis. The trend was against them. In the elections in Thuringia, twenty-four hours after Schleicher's appointment, they lost almost forty per cent of their votes. 'The situation is catastrophical,' Goebbels commented.

Gregor Strasser, Principal Organizer (*Organisationsleiter*) and still the second most important man in the Party, was convinced that the Nazis had passed the peak of their power. Now or never was the time to make some kind of deal with other parties, he said. This precipitated the final break between him and Goebbels.

Nine years before, Strasser had 'discovered' Goebbels. He gave him his first chance. There had been a certain rivalry between the two men after Goebbels became Gauleiter of Berlin. It was intensified when *Angriff* forced Strasser's papers off the Berlin news-stands. Still, there was no open hostility, and there is nothing to prove that Goebbels resented Strasser to any appreciable degree.[1]

Now Strasser entered into negotiations with General von Schleicher. Beforehand, he had tried to convince Hitler that it was necessary to reach a compromise. What happened afterwards has never been clarified. In any case, Hitler was on his way to Berlin and Strasser waited for him at the station. He waited in vain because Goebbels and Goering had gone to meet the Fuehrer *en route*, and had talked him into leaving the train before it arrived in the capital. For Goebbels and, perhaps to a lesser degree, Goering realized that in spite of the prevailing anti-Nazi trend there was still a good chance for the Party to reach its goal; primarily because there was no other party which could fill the bill.

Then things began to happen fast. Hitler declared he would have no part in the bargain, whereupon Strasser divested himself of all his Party offices, packed his bags and disappeared from Berlin. Hitler had not expected him to go that far. He was worried. 'If the Party splits up, I'm going to end it all with a revolver shot,' Hitler shouted.

The next three days were decisive. If Strasser had mobilized his friends in the Party, it might have been the end of Hitler and Goebbels, and of the whole movement. But strangely enough, Strasser did nothing of the sort. This gave Hitler valuable time to assure himself of the loyalty of the men around him, while Goebbels told everyone who cared to listen that Strasser 'had engaged in sabotage for years'. After a few days the crisis had passed. It had been established that the Party could carry on without its No. 2 man. Strasser's offices were closed and some of his duties were taken over by Goebbels. 'His "legacy" was being apportioned,' he commented cynically.

Christmas was approaching. The economic crisis was at its height. The number of jobless had reached the staggering figure of seven million. While women could still find employment, because they worked for lower salaries, some of the men had been idle for two, three and four years. Beggars roamed the streets.

Magda Goebbels fell sick and had to be taken to hospital. Goebbels spent a depressing Christmas Eve at her bedside. On Christmas Day he left for Berchtesgaden. Magda was to join him on New Year's Eve, but she never did. Instead, a telephone call from Berlin informed him that her condition was very grave. When he tried to call back, all telephonic communication between Berchtesgaden and Berlin was interrupted owing to a snowstorm. It was impossible to charter a plane. It was thirty-six hours before Goebbels could reach Berlin, where he was told that his wife had not improved.

But in those thirty-six hours he had conceived the idea which was to save the Party.

VIII

The following days were perhaps the most hectic in Goebbels' life. He dared not leave the hospital for more than a few hours at a time. Yet he had to continue working night and day if the new plan was to succeed. This new plan was simply to win the election campaign for the Diet of Lippe, smallest state within the German federation, with less than 150,000 inhabitants and a territory covering about 450 square miles. It made very little difference who ruled in Lippe. There was not one city of importance, only villages and small towns.

But Goebbels figured this way: no other party was very much interested in the Lippe elections. No leader of any other party would even make a speech there. Therefore, it might be relatively easy for the Nazis to achieve a smashing victory in Lippe, thus showing the people that the anti-Nazi trend had stopped. 'We are going to concentrate all our strength on this small country to gain a prestige success,' Goebbels candidly admitted on 3 January. 'The Party would show once more that it could win.'

It was an obvious idea but at the same time a stroke of genius. Nevertheless, it proved very difficult even to finance this small campaign. 'I borrowed all of 20,000 marks to start the campaign,' Goebbels later admitted. A few weeks before he had spent millions.

The influential Berlin papers made fun of the Nazis. Goebbels did not care. 'On the first evening I spoke three times, mostly in small villages. All meetings were overcrowded.... All this was so beautifully satisfactory that I could not wish for anything better. I was again in contact with the people.... I was speaking plainly and simply, and I was convincing.'

The others, too, had to do their share. Goering, Frick, even Hitler himself, addressed the peasants and small-town citizens of Lippe. The same men who had spoken to tremendous crowds, sometimes numbering as much as a hundred thousand, 'now stood on a platform in a small village inn and appealed to fifty, sixty or seventy people.'

During the two weeks of the campaign Goebbels was mostly out of town. He telephoned the hospital two and three times a day to inquire about Magda. He was told that she was not doing very well, but they concealed from him that the doctors had given her up. Hitler alone knew how badly things stood for her. However, eventually she made a miraculous recovery and a few days before the campaign was over she was pronounced out of danger. It was only then that Hitler disclosed the truth to his friend Goebbels. Goebbels noted the fact in his diary but made no further comment. 'Politically everything was still in flux,' his next sentence read.

And then the Nazis achieved another overwhelming victory. 'The Party is marching again,' Goebbels noted. More important even than the election results was the task of telling the German people that the 'Party was marching again.' 'The decision of the citizens of Lippe is not a local affair,' Goebbels commented in *Angriff* on 20 January. 'It corresponds to the sentiment prevailing throughout the country. Again the great masses of the people are on the move—in our direction.'

In the meantime a very important meeting had taken place. In the home of the Cologne banker, Baron Kurt von Schroeder, Hitler met Papen—the man whom until recently he had detested—and a number of industrialists, among them Fritz Thyssen. He was assured of enough money to pay the most pressing debts of his Party and was promised aid in his fight against the Schleicher Government. The 'barons', the 'upper-class people', whom Goebbels had attacked so mercilessly, were putting themselves at the disposal of the Fuehrer. Did they not know that his star was waning, that the trend was against him? It was precisely for that reason that they rescued him. Because, who knows, in six or eight months the Nazi Party would fall apart and then the industrialists and the Junkers would have no popular movement which would fight their battles. It was now or never. The gentlemen in Cologne decided it was to be now.

'The Government has lost all prestige,' Goebbels wrote, gloating. 'One may well ask in the Reichstag: Does the Schleicher Government still exist, and if so, what does it intend to do about it?'

Schleicher resigned on 28 January. On 30 January 1933, Hindenburg received Hitler once more. Goebbels remained sceptical to the last. Anything might happen to upset their plans, he felt. A few hours later he knew nothing could happen any more. 'It is almost like a dream,' he jotted down. 'The Wilhelmstrasse is ours.'

The evening came and hundreds of thousands of people marched past the Chancellery, singing the Horst Wessel song, greeting the Fuehrer in the approved Nazi fashion. 'The new Reich was born,' Goebbels commented proudly. 'Fourteen years of work had been crowned by victory. We had reached our goal. The German revolution had begun.'

The monster parade lasted until long after midnight. The gleam of torches carried by the marchers could be seen far into the dark night, and their voices rang out. Hitler was beside himself with happiness, and so were all other Nazi leaders. Only Goebbels, standing behind the Fuehrer, seemed calm. He was watching the parade almost with detachment. He had staged so many parades in his life that, in a way, this was just another. He saw no reason for exuberance. It was so typical for him that even now he did not fool himself. Looking down at the jubilant masses, this is what he thought:[2] 'Now everything has changed. Now none of them ever doubted we would achieve victory. Now it would be impossible to find the two million voters who deserted us two months before.'

Even in this hour of supreme triumph Goebbels did not forget, even now he had nothing but contempt for his fellow men.

They marched for hours and hours. There stood Hitler, smiling at them, saluting them. There, behind him, stood Goebbels, in the shadow, unseen....

Issues of *Angriff* at the time of the 1936 Olympic Games.

PART II: THE POWER...

CHAPTER VI

THE DICTATOR

I

'For a long time I have pondered over the idea of starting a fire. A fire is so popular, it appeals to the people's imagination... But I have always saved it for the critical time, for the great moment when we would all rise.' These are the words of the nihilist Peter Stepanovitch Verchovenski in Dostoevsky's novel *The Possessed*, a book which had greatly influenced young Goebbels; Verchovenski, who in many ways was so much like Goebbels that at times the young propagandist seemed to be falling into the same pattern of thinking and acting.

'At 9 the Fuehrer came for supper,' Goebbels wrote in his diary on 27 February 1933. 'We had a little music and talked. Suddenly the telephone rang. The Reichstag is burning! I thought the news was pure fantasy and wouldn't even tell the Fuehrer about it. After a few more calls I got the terrible confirmation that it was true. The flames were rising from the cupola of the Reichstag. Arson!

'I informed the Fuehrer and we raced downtown at 70 miles an hour. The whole building was in flames ... Goering met us, and soon von Papen arrived. It had already been established that the conflagration was due to arson. There was no doubt that the Communists had made a final attempt to usurp the power by creating an atmosphere of panic and terror ...

'Goering at once banned the entire Communist and Social Democratic press. The Communist Party officials were arrested during the same night. The storm-troopers were warned to be ready for any eventuality... I drove with the Fuehrer to the editorial offices of the *Voelkischer Beobachter*. Without delay we began to compose editorials and appeals.'

Not merely the Communists but thousands of other opponents of the Nazi regime were arrested during that night. It was obvious from the start that the Nazis had prepared the coup long in advance. In many cases storm-troopers or policemen produced lists to verify the identity of their victims; nor could it be a coincidence that, with election day being just a week off, 27 February was the only evening on which none of the prominent Nazis—neither Hitler nor Goering, Goebbels, Frick, and so on—were out of Berlin on campaign tours.

All kinds of rumours were spreading throughout Germany. The name of Hermann Goering loomed large wherever the Reichstag fire was mentioned. But Goebbels, and not Goering, was the man behind the whole plan. Members of the Berlin police department learned the truth only a few months afterwards. In the middle of February, Brigadefuehrer Karl Ernst, right-hand man of Berlin S.A. leader, Count Helldorf, had asked a few of his men to a secret conference at his home and told them that they would be expected to bring off a coup to finish the Marxists once and for all, namely to set fire to the Reichstag, a place which had been the scene of 'too much talk anyway.' Later, the Communists were to be blamed, Ernst said, and he promised that the police would not interfere.[1]

'For a long time I have pondered over the idea of starting a fire....' Goebbels was the man who conceived the idea of the Reichstag fire. It was Goebbels who had the initial conversation with Karl Ernst on 18 February; it was Goebbels who had supervised the selection of the men destined to carry out the operation; it was Goebbels who had pointed out the rooms in the Reichstag which would burn fastest. Most important of all, it was Goebbels who had assured Ernst that there was no danger of the police investigating the subterranean passage between the Reichstag and Goering's palace.

'A fire is so popular, it appeals to the people's imagination....' Goebbels was the first to understand that the Reichstag fire would have far-reaching repercussions. He had been able to convince Hitler that 'something striking' had to happen. He had even rehearsed Hitler's outburst of rage upon seeing the burning Reichstag.

Inside the burning building the Dutch Communist, Marinus van der Lubbe, was arrested, and he confessed being guilty of the crime. This provided Goebbels with the necessary link to the Communist Party, for obviously one man alone could not have done the damage. Since others must have helped him, it was logical enough that they too were Communists.

'Now we have to put a radical stop to the Communist threat,' Goebbels roared in next day's Angriff: 'What are we waiting for, when a twenty-four-year-old foreign Communist hired by Russian and German functionaries of this world pestilence can set fire to the Reichstag! Must not these terrorists be judged as criminals only, and must we not proceed accordingly? And do not the statesmen who are liberating Germany from this scourge deserve to be rewarded by the Almighty?'

Goebbels did not wait for the Almighty to express an opinion. He wished to act without delay. He implored Hitler to order van der Lubbe to be hanged in front of the Reichstag. So convinced was he that this was the only fitting punishment that later he publicly stated this had been his original plan.[2] However, there must have been another reason for Goebbels' urgent desire to get rid of van der Lubbe: Goebbels himself had arranged for the Dutchman to gain entrance to the Reichstag, where he was allowed to start his own little fireworks, while the S.A. men attended to the real job.[3]

But Goebbels did not have his way because old Hindenburg refused to have the German Government compromised by so rash an action. Van der Lubbe was to have a fair trial before a German court, together with others who had been arrested in the meantime; Ernst Torgler, chairman of the Communist Reichstag faction; the Bulgarian Georgi Dimitroff, leader of the Central European section of the Communist Internationale, as well as two other Bulgarian communists, Popoff and Taneff.

II

Goebbels, full of dark forebodings, decided to leave nothing to chance. He called upon a certain Dr Eberhard Taubert, a shifty-eyed individual in charge of anti-Communist propaganda in the *Party* Propaganda Department to prepare the necessary evidence. Taubert consulted with the examining magistrate of the Supreme Court who declared that the deed could be labelled an 'official communist crime' only if the culpability of Torgler or Dimitroff could be established; this, he believed, was next to impossible. At that point, Goebbels, according to Dr Taubert, suggested that he and Goering should be called as witnesses to prove that the Communist Party had been planning an armed revolt for a long time.

In preparation of the forthcoming cross-examination a long list of suitable questions was handed to the president of the court, the public prosecutor, as well as to Goebbels and Goering. Goebbels' scheme would contain a special 'sensation'. He wanted the public prosecutor to ask Torgler whether he had ever advocated violence in his political struggle, for he was reasonably certain Torgler would deny this. Then Goebbels would intervene and make a sworn statement complete with exact dates and places establishing the truth of the accusation against the Communist leader.

The well-conceived plan miscarried owing to the unbelievable negligence of the public prosecutor who remembered the scheme only after Goebbels had left the witness stand.

But by the time Goebbels testified in Leipzig the trial was already lost for the Nazis. During his cross-examination three days earlier, Goering lost his temper; he threatened the defendants, and behaved altogether foolishly.

Moreover, he gave Dimitroff a hundred opportunities to use the trial as a platform for anti-Nazi propaganda.

The Bulgarian communist acted with great courage; but then, he knew that little could happen to him since Stalin had made it clear he would not sacrifice this valuable agent. Dimitroff's testimony in the Leipzig Supreme Court must have been a strange experience for Goebbels. If anyone knew the publicity value of a trial it was he. Ten years before he had watched Hitler turn his own trial into a propaganda campaign for the Nazi cause. During the past decade Goebbels himself had stood in court countless times for libel or slander, and had always been able to profit in some measure from his court appearances. Now Dimitroff proved that he could beat the Nazis with their own weapons. He received wonderful publicity abroad. Even before the trial started, world public opinion was convinced that the Nazis, and they alone, were guilty of burning down the Reichstag.

III

'The Party has won a great victory', Goebbels had written three days after Hitler came to power. 'But this victory does not suffice. We have a government, we have a programme, we have a will to reconstruction; what is missing is the great and overwhelming confidence of the German nation.'

What Goebbels meant was that the Nazis had not yet the majority, even in Hitler's own cabinet. Aside from the Fuehrer, Frick who became Minister of the Interior, and Goering, the other members were conservative nationalists, as for instance Vice-Chancellor von Papen, Foreign Minister Konstantin von Neurath, Finance Minister Count Schwerin von Krosigk, and Alfred Hugenberg who held the ministries of agriculture and economics. This preponderance of the so-called non-Nazis could be broken by dissolving the Reichstag and holding another election, which meant perhaps the final campaign for Joseph Goebbels. 'In a discussion with the Fuehrer it was decided that I should be free from cabinet rank in order to devote myself entirely to the campaign,' he wrote in his diary. Later: 'The Gauleiters were assembled in Berlin. I lectured them on the technique and tactics of the forthcoming campaign. Our goal must be to obtain the absolute majority...' This campaign was different from all previous ones, Goebbels admitted. It was easy because we could use the entire machinery of the state for our purposes,' he wrote on 3 February. 'Press and radio were at our disposal. We were going to produce a masterpiece of political agitation. Money was abundant.'

The German radio had always been state-controlled; the parties of the opposition were not supposed to plead their case before the microphone.

Therefore, Goebbels had made only one radio speech, and Hitler none at all during the struggle for power. Now Goebbels set out to transform the radio into an instrument of Nazi propaganda. Overnight he replaced the managers of the broadcasting stations by dependable Party members. Hitler would speak only in the larger cities with powerful transmitters so that his message would reach every home in the surrounding towns and villages. In order to convey to the listeners what was happening in the hall where Hitler was speaking, Goebbels always introduced the Fuehrer.

The campaign started in Berlin's Sportpalast. Hitler, as usual, drove his audience into a frenzy of enthusiasm, but the radio listeners remained cold. To them, Hitler sounded colourless, uninteresting, and at the same time over-excited. As soon as the meeting was over, Goebbels and Hitler had the records played back. Hitler wistfully remarked, 'It seems to me I am not exactly a radio personality (*radio-schoenheit*):

Goebbels, too, thought there was room for improvement. He worked all night with a staff of radio engineers and experts, trying out different ways of changing the timbre of the Fuehrer's voice, of making him sound softer, more pliable, or more determined and concise. In this way, Goebbels made him a radio personality. After that first speech in the Sportpalast, Hitler's radio audience became just as deliriously excited (or disgusted, as the case may be) as those who saw and heard him in the flesh.

5 March was election day. 'A glorious triumph has been achieved,' Goebbels commented on the outcome. 'It is far more overwhelming than we had dared to hope. But what do figures mean now? We are the masters in the Reich and in Prussia; all the others have been beaten.'

What did figures mean? In the Reichstag the Nazis controlled only 44 per cent and—together with the party of Hugenberg—barely 51 per cent of all votes. That was hardly enough to carry through Hitler's plans. Now the real meaning of the Reichstag fire became apparent. Obviously a party (the Communists) which had almost 'started an armed revolt' could not be permitted to send deputies into parliament. It was equally obvious that a few dozen Social Democrats could be sufficiently implicated in the Reichstag fire to justify their arrest. As for the remaining deputies, the Nazis would control a comfortable majority.

From that point on, things went fast. Within a few months not only the Communist and Social Democratic Parties were dissolved but all other parties as well, including the German National People's Party of Hugenberg. Hugenberg himself resigned in a huff. Some of his friends stayed on and eventually joined the Nazis.

IV

On 13 March 1933, while the first editor of *Angriff* Julius Lippert, was appointed Mayor of Berlin, Hitler informed his cabinet that he wished to create a Ministry for National Enlightenment and Propaganda. The next day Hindenburg swore in the new cabinet member, Dr Joseph Goebbels. At this point the old President was so senile that he probably had forgotten about the edict he was led to sign during the night of the Reichstag fire decreeing, among other things, that 'Restrictions on personal liberty and on freedom of speech and of the press are permissible beyond the limitations placed upon them by law ...' These few words formed the basis of the Propaganda Ministry.

But why a Propaganda Ministry? Why propaganda for the Nazis? Overnight the German people—not 40 per cent but apparently 90 per cent—seemed to have been seized with drunken happiness. They put out their flags and decorated their streets, they sent enthusiastic telegrams to Hitler and other Nazi leaders, they changed the names of their streets and public squares so that every small village had at least one Hitlerstrasse or Hitlerplatz. Everybody was happy because somehow everybody believed that now all problems were solved, and that there would be enough food and work for all. It was like a spell, like a mass hypnosis, it was contagious. Not an evening passed without a torch parade. Every day the German anthem and the Horst Wessel song were sung in public. The whole of Germany appeared to have fallen into a kind of semi-religious paroxysm.

Perhaps this sudden change of heart and mood had something to do with Goebbels' propaganda after all, with the formulas for public meetings he had developed over the years, the use of music, flags and young men in uniform. Now all Germany seemed to be united in one single monster meeting, staged by Goebbels.

It was not a pretty picture of the German character that presented itself in those days. Goebbels, for one, could scarcely hide his contempt. During a visit to his mother in Rheydt he wrote: 'The entire little town which only a few months ago expelled and cursed me is now in an unbelievable turmoil of enthusiasm ...'

Propaganda was no longer necessary: since the Reichstag fire almost every German wanted to be a Nazi. In any event, he was afraid that, unless he made up his mind soon, it would be too late. Nobody wished to be the last to join up. Everybody sought contact with higher-ups in the Party; also, for practical reasons, with storm-troopers. The storm-troopers had the disconcerting habit of beating up all those who were not their personal friends, which meant the people who did not pay them.

In those days most Germans paid for a variety of reasons: to be accepted by the Party, to be given a faked lower membership number, to be protected by the S.A., to be protected by the S.S., to join any of the numerous other units of the Party. Despite the general optimism most people were afraid, some with reason. Nobody could be sure he had not offended a member of the Party at one time or another. After all, any worker or employee dismissed during the last few years might have joined the Party to become an influential member. There was only one protection: to be a Party comrade, too. Was it really necessary to have a Propaganda Ministry?

Nobody knew better than Goebbels that a Propaganda Ministry was almost a contradiction in terms. Propaganda is the more effective, the less people know that they are supposed to be influenced, and vice versa. It was to be expected that the very announcement of a Ministry of Propaganda (or, as it was officially called, Ministry of National Enlightenment and Propaganda) would create resentment among the people and increase whatever determination they had left not to be 'enlightened or influenced.' Goebbels, according to Fritzsche, was fully aware of this. But officially he voiced the contrary opinion. 'There ought to be nothing mystifying about propaganda,' he said. 'We openly admit that we want to influence the people. This is the proper way to do it.'

In a speech on 16 March 1933, Goebbels stated it with almost passionate emphasis: 'A government such as ours which has to take such far-reaching measures ... must make propagandistic preparations in order to draw the people on its side ... Public enlightenment is essentially passive; propaganda is active ... We are determined to work on the masses until they have fallen to us.' He could not have put it more plainly.

He was still obsessed with the idea that he had to defend the intrinsic value of propaganda and he used his speech to expound once more his views on the subject. 'Propaganda is a term which has been much-maligned and frequently misunderstood. In the mind of the layman it is something inferior or contemptible. The word *propaganda* has a bad connotation.'

Despite this 'bad connotation' Goebbels never disavowed the word *propaganda*. On the contrary, in June, 1937, he instructed the advertising group of the Organization for National Economy to issue the following order: 'The use of the term *propaganda* in conjunction with any commercial products cannot be permitted ... The term *propaganda* must be reserved for political activity. The politician who wished to impose an idea or to prepare the people for certain legislation uses propaganda. The merchant who wants to sell goods or services *advertises*.'

Presumably the principal reason for creating the Propaganda Ministry was Goebbels himself. There can be no doubt that Hitler wanted to make him a member of the Government, and on the basis of his past performance he had a right to be rewarded. But he was no specialist in any accepted field, like Goering in aviation; he was no career bureaucrat, like Frick. We may disregard diary entries according to which Hitler promised him a Propaganda Ministry a year before it was actually founded. As previously mentioned, there is ample evidence to show that these entries were interpolated at a later date. Shortly before Hitler came to power Goebbels had hoped that the Fuehrer would appoint him Minister of the Interior. Hitler talked him out of it, according to Frau Behrendt, saying that the position was without real power; the reason for Hitler's refusal was that he already had committed himself to Frick. Then Goebbels wanted to become *Kultusminister* (Minister for Cultural Affairs), but unexpectedly old Hindenburg protested because he did not trust Goebbels and did not wish him to have a voice in running schools or supervising church activities. Hitler then proposed to create a Press Ministry for Goebbels, but Fritzsche believes that Goebbels refused because it was 'too limited a field' for him. In addition to the press, he wanted control over radio, motion-pictures and theatres. This eventually led to the conception of the Propaganda Ministry, probably in the early days of February, 1933.

V

The Propaganda Ministry was to move into the Leopold Palast on Wilhelmsplatz, opposite the Chancellery and the Hotel Kaiserhof. It was a beautiful old building devised by Schinkel, one of the few great Prussian architects of the nineteenth century. Goebbels liked the building but not the interior. 'The masons will have to cut the stucco from the walls and tear down the stuffy plush curtains and let in the sunshine.' When he could not get the bureaucrats to co-operate with him, he ordered a few dozen storm-troopers to start the necessary work. Several old officials came running along, tearing their hair. 'Sir, do you know that you may get prison for this?' Goebbels laughed and saw to it that these men were soon removed from the Government payroll.

The old palace was speedily remodelled and furnished in modern, quiet taste. Goebbels was proud of his new Ministry.

Years later, when a Hollywood-produced anti-Nazi picture, *I Was a Nazi Spy*, showed Goebbels' office adorned with enormous swastika emblems on the walls and rugs, he was outraged and complained to an American correspondent that his Ministry should be slandered in that way.

More important than the physical layout was the departmental organization. Originally Goebbels planned to have five different departments, 'covering radio, press, motion-pictures, propaganda and theatre,' he noted on 8 March.

'All these departments were of deep concern to me and I would devote myself to them with all my heart.'

But most of the things he wanted to control from now on had in the past been under the jurisdiction of one Government branch or another. Before he could become Propaganda Minister, Goebbels had to pry loose his would-be empire from the grip of other cabinet members.

From the Ministry of the Interior he obtained the supervisory powers over press and radio as well as the right to proclaim and regulate national holidays, in addition to the then existing censorship of books, plays, and movies. From the Ministry of Economics he took over all commercial activities, including the Leipzig and Koenigsberg fairs. The Postmaster-General let him have the network of agencies advertising the German railways and airlines as well as the entire propaganda outfit concerned with *fremdenverkehr* (foreign tourism). Furthermore, Goebbels took over, or rather established, complete control over all German theatres (with the exception of the Prussian state theatres, which, to his disgust, remained under Goering's wing). Most important: the Ministry for Foreign Affairs handed Goebbels all foreign publicity and the right to enlighten foreign countries about Germany by whatever means he considered suitable.

Those who observed the little Doctor at the time he took over his new functions were astonished at his apparently insatiable appetite for power. It was true that during these first few months all Nazi leaders were grabbing whatever big jobs they could get their hands on. But Goebbels seemed to use his elbows more recklessly than the others. He was suspected of being motivated by vanity and revenge, and it was remembered that he had more or less failed in some of the fields he was now going to control.

However, upon opening his Ministry, Goebbels made his motives quite clear. 'There are two ways of fomenting a revolution,' he explained. 'You can mow down your opponent with machine-guns until he admits the superiority of the party in possession of the machine-guns. That is a simple way of doing it. You can also remake a nation by a spiritual revolution and thus you do not destroy your opponent but win him over....'

Opponent? Who had to be won over? Was not the entire nation behind Hitler, as Goebbels constantly proclaimed? The majority of Germans *were* all for Hitler. But how long would they follow the Fuehrer with unwavering loyalty? There must be ways and means to keep the people in line and at the same time in good humour. That was the real reason for the existence of the Propaganda Ministry, the first of its kind created not for the duration of a war but for the duration of a regime, then estimated to last for a thousand years.

Therefore, Goebbels had to have complete control over every means of influencing and moulding the minds of the people. One scene in a motion-picture, a few lines in a poem, the portrait of a girl, a violin concerto—nothing must be overlooked, and that was why Goebbels demanded dictatorial authority over so many different fields. It would assure him the monopoly over news and news commentary, the monopoly over play and fun, relaxation and escape; it would enable him to eliminate any kind of influence or information which might prove detrimental to his purpose. It gave him the perfect strategic position from which to direct the average German's feeling and thinking.

Soon after Goebbels had set up his Propaganda Ministry, the average German was like an animal trapped in a small cage. The prisoner was, perhaps, not a 100 per cent Nazi in the beginning. Yet, being fed nothing but the Nazi propaganda diet, how could he help becoming a Nazi? Even if he did not believe everything Goebbels told him, he had no way of finding out the lies or distortions presented to him. He had to swallow what Goebbels fed him. He swallowed it whole.

This seemed strange to observers abroad: there were so many contradictions in Goebbels propaganda. Experts therefore surmised that Goebbels would eventually lose the confidence of the masses. But since no one inside Germany could point out to the people that the official propaganda machine was contradicting itself, few realized it. Goebbels could always depend on the poor memory of the masses.

On one occasion Goebbels himself described the effects of such propaganda methods on the unfortunate victims:

It is of course a matter of taste to admire the accomplishment of a propaganda which, by sealing them off hermetically from the outside world and by reiterating its empty phrases about salvation, universal happiness and so on, has succeeded in bamboozling the peasants and workers into believing that this state of affairs constitutes paradise on earth. One can arrive at independent judgment only by means of comparison. Here, such possibilities of comparison are totally lacking. The peasant, or the worker, resembles a man who has been imprisoned in a dark cellar; after many years of captivity he can easily be convinced that a burning kerosene lamp is the sun ... A national intelligence which might fight against this system no longer exists. The system itself possesses every means to smother such intelligence from its very inception. The whole country is penetrated with a network of informers, abusing children against their own parents ...

There exists no better description of the purpose and effect of German propaganda. However, Goebbels did not write this article until 19 July 1942, when he commented on 'The So-Called Russian Soul.'

VI

When Goebbels opened the Propaganda Ministry he prided himself on being in charge of the smallest German ministry. He envisaged a modern, streamlined machine working with speed and efficiency. It did just that, but it was never as small as Goebbels tried to make out.

In the beginning there were nine departments (instead of the five Goebbels originally planned); later they were increased to twelve, and finally to sixteen. Among them were Administration, Propaganda, Press, Radio, Film, Theatre, Art, Music, Literature, etc. By the middle of 1933 there were already 300 officials and 500 employees.

Foremost among the officials were Leopold Gutterer and his adjutant, Hugo Fischer, in charge of the Party propaganda machine. Gutterer had been with the Free Corps; Hugo Fischer had been close to the murderers of Rathenau, an active S.A. man and later one of Himmler's prominent staff officers. Another man of great value to Goebbels was his first adjutant, Karl Hanke, officer of the S.S., a tall, good-looking but somewhat melancholy man who later resigned from the Propaganda Ministry under rather dramatic circumstances.

Hans Hinkel had been one of the early Nazis, who joined the Party even before Goebbels did. He was among those who participated in the Munich beer cellar putsch in 1923. Afterwards he published a number of small Nazi papers. He came to Berlin about the same time as Goebbels and helped the Strassers edit their *Nationalsozialistische Briefe*. Goebbels now used him mainly to control the movies and theatres. Hinkel, who looked like a matinee idol, achieved notoriety by his countless affairs with motion-picture stars and actresses, which provoked the wrath of his boss, Goebbels. Hinkel was discharged and reinstated over and over again. Goebbels was not above petty niggling and petty jealousy. Eugen Hadamovsky was a discovery of Goebbels; a young, lively reporter and, next to Goebbels, the most talented theoretician on propaganda. Goebbels put him in charge of radio, where he did an excellent job.

Goebbels, who had always believed the spoken word to be more effective than the printed word, rightly recognized the radio as propaganda weapon No. 1. 'What the press has been for the nineteenth century, radio will be for the twentieth century,' he proclaimed on 18 August 1933. As early as March, 1933, Goebbels issued a decree announcing that all the shares of the German Broadcasting Company had been acquired by the Propaganda Ministry. Thus he obtained a monopoly on German broadcasting. On 16 August, Hadamovsky, in charge of the entire system, said in a speech: 'We National Socialists must show enough dynamism and enthusiasm coupled with lightning speed to impress Germany and the whole world ... Party comrade Dr Goebbels ordered me on 13 July to purge the German radio of influences opposed to our cause. I can now report that the work has been done thoroughly.'

Taking over the radio from the Postmaster-General was sound business for Goebbels. Every radio listener had to pay two marks per month for a licence. It was on this income that Goebbels based his pronouncement that the Propaganda Ministry would be self-supporting. This proved to be an illusion. The German radio listeners might have supported the small, streamlined machine Goebbels originally intended to run, but not the blown-up colossus into which the Propaganda Ministry soon developed.

The domestic Press division supervised more than 2,300 newspapers and periodicals. Notwithstanding the definite courage displayed by many newspapers before Hitler came to power; notwithstanding the fact that some of the largest newspapers were Jewish-owned and about half a dozen belonged by all standards among the finest papers in the world, the Propaganda Ministry had no trouble in bringing the German press into line.

This was achieved mainly by the *Schriftleitergesetz*, a law which permitted the state to do with journalists whatever it liked. If a journalist was not a Nazi or not considered 'dependable'; if by any chance he had a Jewish grandmother, he was finished; if he wrote an article which someone in the Propaganda Ministry did not approve of; if he wrote a sentence which somebody did not like, or if he cut a sentence which somebody did like—he was out.

There was no one who could protect him, least of all the owner of the newspaper. Anyway, most of them were no longer the owners. Pressure was being brought upon them to sell out. If they did not do so right away their papers were banned, for a day, for a few days, for a week. Thus, step by step brought to the verge of ruin, they finally sold.

Many newspapers were acquired by Max Amann, head of the Eher-Verlag, whose silent partner was Adolf Hitler. Some of them were bought by Goering. Goebbels himself did not acquire any of the lot, although in his position nothing would have been easier. That much must be said for him. Outwardly there were very few changes. The names of the papers and their make-up remained the same, their millions of readers realized only gradually that they were reading a Nazi product instead of an independent newspaper. A few papers, among them the well-known *Frankfurter Zeitung*, were permitted a certain measure of independence, mainly to impress upon foreigners that there was no censorship in Germany.

Head of the news section of the Press division in the Propaganda Ministry was Hans Fritzsche, by far the most competent man Goebbels hired. Then in his middle thirties, Fritzsche was tall and good-looking, a smooth and efficient newspaperman. For many years he had held leading positions in various news services. He was a nationalist of the Hugenberg variety. In 1937, he became Chief of the Home Press division (*Chef der Abteilung Deutsche Presse*). He held this job until 1942. Then for a few months he went to the eastern front as a soldier and upon his return became head of the Radio division.

Fritzsche knew everything about the newspaper business, about news services and about radio. He never harboured any illusions about the low standard of the German press under Hitler. More important still, he never concealed his low opinion of Nazi editors. All those who attended the press conferences were astonished, and sometimes shocked, at his ironical remarks about the *Voelkischer Beobachter* and its publisher, Alfred Rosenberg, who after all was one of the intimates of the Fuehrer. There is no doubt that Fritzsche knew his job and that without him Goebbels would have had a more difficult time in building up the Propaganda Ministry. It is equally true that Fritzsche never believed for one moment in Nazism, although he served his masters ably.

Fritzsche could even permit himself an occasional word of criticism to Goebbels. The only other person who enjoyed this privilege was Walter Funk, a short, ugly man given to hard drinking and homosexual debauchery, but extremely amusing and often brilliant. He had been editor of the *Berliner Boersenzeitung* and, being an expert in economics and finance, had been Hitler's private tutor. Goebbels had selected him to be his under-secretary in charge of the Press Department, a position he kept until 1937, when he resigned to become Minister of Economy.

His talent was a great asset to Goebbels, but he also created many embarrassing situations for his employer on account of his relations with well-known male prostitutes. However, Goebbels never lost his temper with him. The reason was that Funk 'belonged.' Funk knew the 'right people,' Funk was on excellent terms with Berlin society, Funk was a man of the world. The very fact that the 'right people' did not seem to mind his eccentricities made Goebbels feel that he, too, should not mind. For this was the kind of snobbery he now went in for.

VII

Now Goebbels had power.

Not the power to shape the over-all policy of the Third Reich, as did Hitler. Not the power to build up Germany's economy, as did Schacht; nor to arrest people and to send them to concentration camp, as did Himmler. His was the power to decide what people should read, what people should know, what people should think. It was a vast assignment, but an assignment superbly suited to Goebbels' talents to persuade and to convince others, to drive a point home.

For years he had complained that the Weimar Republic cramped his style and hindered him in every possible way. Now there was no one who could hinder him any longer. Hardly a year before he had condemned a state and a police which banned his newspaper for political reasons and brought it to the verge of financial ruin. Now he was in charge, and it would have been up to him to demonstrate that there were other, more intelligent ways to combat oppositional newspapers rather than brutal suppression. 'Now we could proceed against the press and we banned the oppositional papers to our heart's delight. All the Jewish papers which caused so much bitterness suddenly disappeared from the streets. This had an immensely calming effect,' he wrote in his diary on 15 February 1933.

Goebbels was no longer the same. The past year had changed him. Somehow he seemed to have lost interest in using his natural gifts of persuasion, in debating an issue, in fighting with his most effective weapons, which were his pen and his mouth. Somehow he had become complacent in the few weeks since Hitler's rise to power. When driving through the towns in which he had spent his university years he made sentimental notes in his diary, as though he were reminiscing about events thirty and forty years back. 'How old Heidelberg brought back memories! It made me nostalgic to think of them.... And wonderful Freiburg! For fifteen years I had not seen that city, and it was still exactly as it had always been.'

Apparently Goebbels the demagogue had abdicated. Why should he waste his time being more intelligent, wittier and faster than his opponents, when he could silence them by force? There was no one who could contradict him now, because there was no one who had the physical ability to do so. Goering stole and built chateaux; Himmler built himself a private army; and Goebbels held an endless monologue, while all others had to listen.

Goebbels had failed as a writer. Now he could watch the flames devour the works of those who had been more successful than he—the books of Thomas Mann, Sigmund Freud, Maxim Gorky, Henri Barbusse, Lion Feuchtwanger, and many other great writers. On that occasion he made a speech, but it was short and immediately afterwards the Propaganda Ministry instructed all German newspapers that the burning of the books should be played down. Was his conscience bothering him?

Another of Goebbels' 'cultural achievements' was his quarrel with the great German conductor, Wilhelm Furtwaengler, who protested courageously against the ban on Jewish musicians. Goebbels wrote a sharp letter in which he explained to Furtwaengler precisely what was German culture and what was not. To Goebbels culture had become nothing but an enormous poster advertising the Third Reich. One incident is symptomatic in this respect:

Some time during the early part of 1933 Goebbels staged a mass demonstration in Cologne. He demanded from the Archbishop that the bells of the cathedral should chime at a given moment. The Archbishop declined, knowing well that Goebbels' request was strictly for reasons of propaganda. Goebbels wasted no time arguing. He had the Cologne broadcasting station make recordings of the chiming of the bells. 'I could have played them back in the studio,' he told a Berlin actress a few days later. 'Thus millions of radio listeners would have believed that the bells were really ringing. But what about the 100,000 people of Cologne crowding the square in front of the cathedral? Therefore, I had a number of loudspeakers placed around the cathedral. When the records were played and the sound amplified through the loudspeakers, even those in front of the cathedral believed that they were listening to the real thing.'

VIII

Many signs pointed to the fact that there were still Germans left who for one reason or another were opposed to the Nazis. Hundreds of new jokes were making the rounds, criticizing the regime and making fun of Hitler, Goering, Goebbels and others. Goebbels was infuriated. He blamed the Jews for it all, and said so to his associates on more than one occasion. Fritzsche once asked Goebbels why he believed that only the Jews were opposed to the Nazis. Would not the French or the Russians, to name but a few, be equally antagonistic to Nazi doctrine? 'I think that the French and even the Russians could be influenced by our propaganda,' Goebbels replied, 'but not the Jews, never the Jews.'[4]

The Jews had of course every reason to be immune to Goebbels' propaganda: Hitler had made it painfully clear that they had nothing to hope for in the Third Reich, and those who left Germany did their utmost to tell the world what was going on in their former homeland: the arrests and tortures, the concentration camps, the indiscriminate killings. Goebbels labelled their reports 'atrocity stories devoid of all foundation.' Nevertheless, something had to be done about them.

For this purpose he conceived the idea of a gigantic blackmail. 'We will be able to stop the liars abroad,' he decided after a talk with Hitler, 'only if we can lay hands on the originators or at least the beneficiaries, namely the Jews living in Germany, who so far have been left alone. We must stage a huge boycott against all Jewish business enterprises in Germany. Perhaps, if the Jews abroad see that we mean business with their German brethren, they will change their tune.'

While Hitler, and especially Julius Streicher, enthusiastically endorsed the idea of the boycott, Hjalmar Schacht, Walter Funk, and even Goering, who knew something about economics, were dismayed. They realized that if the boycott lasted for even as long as a week, thousands of enterprises would be ruined, hundreds of thousands of people would lose their jobs and the entire German economy might totter. But it was too late to call off the boycott. Preparations had already been made. Furthermore, Hitler refused to disavow Goebbels publicly. Goebbels himself knew a way out. He would 'interrupt' the boycott after the first day—1 April 1933. He would give 'World Jewry' a chance to behave. If it rose to the occasion, the boycott would not be resumed, which he knew could not be done under any circumstances. But the world fell for his bluff. Many Jews sent letters and telegrams to their relatives and friends abroad imploring them to stop spreading anti-Nazi propaganda. Thus Goebbels won his first war of nerves. He had tried out and found useful a technique which he and the Nazis were to use on many occasions—and almost always with success.

The boycott was stopped but anti-Semitic measures continued, although for the time being in a less spectacular fashion. Since it was not practical to ruin Jewish business enterprises, the Nazis first concentrated on eliminating Jewish officials and lawyers, physicians and university professors, teachers and journalists, actors and musicians. A week after the boycott had been 'interrupted' the first anti-Jewish decree was published, stipulating that all German officials (including, for instance, postmen or guards in museums) had to be 'pure Aryans.' This was less dramatic than a boycott. It went on for the better part of the next year. What on 1 April 1933, had been considered everywhere an outrage against civilization was slowly becoming routine.

But Goebbels never succeeded in throttling criticism of the Nazis abroad. The irony of it all was that this was mainly the work of a few men whom Goebbels had driven out of the country, courageous writers and editors, some of them 'non-Aryans,' who had escaped arrest after the Reichstag fire.

There were only a handful of these men. They went to Paris, Prague, London, New York and Amsterdam. They were not too well received. They had no money to live on and most of them could not write in a foreign language, which made it difficult for them to pursue their former profession in their country of exile. Nevertheless they insisted on spreading the truth of what was going on inside Germany; stubbornly they warned a world which did not wish to be warned; they continued to appeal to the conscience of humanity, which played deaf and dumb.

They starved but they managed to publish magazines and small daily newspapers in which they exposed the truth. They were often treated like unwelcome intruders because they 'abused hospitality' by denouncing a 'friendly power.' They were subjected to countless indignities. But it was impossible to silence them.

Compared to Goebbels, they wielded little influence. But Goebbels hated them because they were the first to interfere with his cherished monopoly on the dissemination of German news. In a few cases Nazi agents abroad sought them out and beat them up; in one case an anti-Nazi writer was murdered, another was kidnapped from neutral territory and taken back to Germany.

But the small group of devoted anti-Nazi writers continued raising their voices in spite of all handicaps. They were the first to stand up against Goebbels. Few listened to them.

'The Fascist Lie-Gun', a Russian cartoon from 1942.

CHAPTER VII

TOMORROW THE WORLD

I

A good many of Goebbels' speeches during the first year of the Hitler régime ended with the words of Ullrich von Hutten: 'It's a joy to be alive.' He had every reason to be pleased. It was his job to make the rest of the nation feel the same. In this spirit, and for this purpose he set out to create, or invent, a number of national holidays.

It started with the First of May. For more than fifty years this had been the holiday of the Socialist workers all over the world. After the revolution of 1918 the Social Democrats had tried in vain to have it declared a national holiday in Germany. Now Goebbels succeeded where his predecessors had failed. By stealing an idea which was not his own (a method he practised often and in many fields) he accomplished several things at the same time: he demonstrated to the workers that their leaders had been ineffectual; and he won the sympathy of large numbers who, falling for his propaganda tricks, began to wonder if the National Socialist Party was not, after all, a workers' party.

In every German town parades and mass meetings were staged. The biggest affair of course took place in Berlin, where a million and a half people assembled on the Tempelhofer feld, the site of Berlin's airport. Though a few hundred thousand people might have attended anyway, Goebbels was taking no chances. He saw to it that the workers of every plant, the employees of every place of business, even the actors of every theatre and the teachers of every school would witness the spectacle. And since the weather was fine (most of the time Goebbels' festivities were favoured by the weather, and in those days a clement day in Germany was called 'Hitler weather') a good time was had by all.

The very next morning, police raided and shut down the headquarters of the numerous trade unions. They were banned, their leaders arrested and their considerable funds confiscated by the state. Now the German workers were without organizations, without leadership, without their traditional rights. All they were left with was Dr Robert Ley, who organized them into the Labour Front and gave them 'Strength through joy.'

In September there was the Nuremberg Party Rally. These rallies had grown bigger and bigger as the years went by. Yet, even in September, 1932, when it seemed certain that Hitler would take over, it had been no more than the annual congress of a party which was wary of the police. In 1933 Goebbels did not have to restrain himself: he could stage the biggest convention ever seen in Germany or, one may well say, in the whole world.

Nuremberg was transformed into a city of tents. Two or three days before the convention opened, 750,000 people arrived there—roughly twice the population of Nuremberg—and they took over. Those who could not afford regular meals, subsisted on soup which was constantly cooking in 800 huge pots, containing about 125 gallons each, established on every street corner. Within a few days the crowds had consumed the following amounts of food:

About 1,200,000 lbs of bread; more than 100,000 lbs of butter; 150,000 lbs of cheese; 220,000 lbs of sauerkraut; 20,000 lbs of pork fat; 110,000 lbs of coffee; 280,000 lbs of sausage; 330,000 lbs of canned meat; 380,000 lbs of fresh meat; furthermore, 2,500,000 cigarettes and 450,000 cigars were smoked.

No statistics were published on the amounts of beer and wine that were drunk. But the Nurembergers, who were themselves far from abstemious, testified that the drinking beat all world records. This and all subsequent Party rallies were accompanied by minor crime waves, and several thousand traffic accidents. Another holiday built up into national prominence by Goebbels was the *erntedankfest* (harvest thanksgiving), celebrated in the first week of October in the town of Bueckeburg. It offered a good opportunity to make speeches about the common cause of the peasant and the workers, about the inseparable bonds between town and country.

Needless to say, Hitler's birthday became a national holiday, too. It always started with a long radio speech by Goebbels, celebrating the Fuehrer, hammering away at the theme that every German must be grateful to serve under such a unique man.

Goebbels knew national holidays were nothing but another type of the mass meetings, pageants and torch parades he had created in the late 'twenties—transposed to a national scale; monster rallies for which stadiums and ordinary halls were not big enough, and which therefore were overflowing into all the streets, all the squares, while all the loudspeakers of the Third Reich amplified the people's happiness. Following his own dictum to prejudice the masses in favour of the Nazi cause 'before the speaker ever opened his mouth,' Goebbels established a body of Nazi tradition. After two or three years had passed it seemed to many Germans that they had been celebrating the new holidays all their lives, as though the Nazis had been on the scene for ever. But, more important, these celebrations served to make them forget that some of Hitler's promises had not been fulfilled. It was the old Roman recipe; let them have *panem et circenses*.

At the same time the holidays were designed to create an impression of stability and integrity abroad. The world, not yet used to Hitler's tactics, could not believe that a government would be so intent on celebrating if the gory tales of the concentration camps, of people beaten up in the cellars of S.A. headquarters, were true. The number of national holidays was taken to mean that the Nazi leaders had a clear conscience.

II

From the outset Goebbels realized that it was important to create this impression of harmlessness abroad. Therefore, during the first years his radio propaganda consisted above all in short-wave transmissions of operatic performances in Berlin, Dresden and Munich, of philharmonic concerts in Leipzig. Goebbels and Eugen Hadamovsky worked out what amounted to a five-year plan for German broadcasting. This plan provided for a constantly increasing output of foreign radio propaganda. It was easy enough to swamp Germany's neighbours with German programmes. From Stuttgart, Freiburg, Frankfurt and Trier, Alsace-Lorraine was covered. The Cologne transmitter was beamed towards Belgium; Hamburg, Bremen and Stettin concentrated on Denmark. Breslau and Gleiwitz broadcast to Czechoslovakia, and Munich to Austria. The rest of the world had to be covered from Zeesen, near Berlin.

Goebbels possessed twelve short-wave stations in Zeesen operating on 100,000 kilowatts. Britain had sixteen stations, but they only operated on 50,000 kilowatts. (Italy had four short-wave transmitters, Russia six, the US eleven, Japan and France three each.)

Goebbels started transmissions in six languages. As early as 1933 he began broadcasting to the United States; in 1934 South Africa, South America and East Asia were included in the programmes; in 1935 he added South Asia and Central America.

In 1933 not more than 1-hour-and-45-minutes' radio time daily was allotted to foreign broadcasts; a year later it had increased to 21 hours 15 minutes; in 1935 to 29 hours 45 minutes; in 1936 to 43 hours 35 minutes and in 1937 to 47 hours per day. This meant that in 1937 throughout every minute of the day at least two German transmitters were broadcasting to foreign countries.

III

Between 1933 and 1936 the Nazi regime was passing through a difficult and dangerous period. 'The western European plutocracies,' Goebbels wrote when reviewing that particular period,[1] 'were faced with the choice of destroying this new Germany immediately and completely, or attempting to arrive at a lasting peace. In those days the former alternative was still possible.'

It was Goebbels' job to prevent such an alternative. The world must be lulled into some kind of trance lest it realized that Hitler was rearming, and until such time, when it was too late to prevent him from re-arming. His difficult task was not facilitated by the untimely boasts of such leaders as Vice-Chancellor von Papen, who made a speech scorning the idea of peaceful death and claiming that death on the battlefield was alone worthy of man. In order to counteract the impression created by such talk, Hitler himself had to tell Reichstag deputies that 'No European war would enable us to exchange the unsatisfactory circumstances of today for better times ... The outbreak of such complete madness would lead to the collapse of our existing social order.'

What was merely pretence on Hitler's part, was the sincere hope of the League of Nations, and the reason why the League had put the problem of disarmament on its agenda. This move in itself was a danger to the Nazis. For as long as Germany was a League member it would be difficult for her to re-arm without leaving herself open to embarrassing questions and investigations. Discussions in Geneva were certain to disclose the very fact which the German Government wished to hide behind a veil of secrecy. On the other hand, leaving the League might arouse world-wide suspicion. In order to determine which of these procedures was preferable Hitler sent Joseph Goebbels to Geneva.

By rights the Foreign Minister should have been entrusted with this mission. However, Goebbels had taken over from the Ministry for Foreign Affairs 'the right and the duty to enlighten foreign nations about Germany.' A few old-timers at the Foreign Office had protested against this usurpation of power, but Konstantin von Neurath, a tired man and no match for dynamic Goebbels, had handed over everything the Propaganda Minister desired.

Late in September, 1933, Goebbels arrived in Geneva. Except for a short trip to Rome he had never been abroad. He was enchanted with the old Swiss city, its crooked, winding narrow streets, its old houses, its beautiful churches and the gorgeous lake framed by towering, snow-covered mountain peaks. The particular charm of Geneva and the reason why it could have been the home of a real League of Nations was its informality. Geneva was no stage set for important statesmen to show off in all their splendour. Geneva was a place where influential politicians could become private, or almost private, citizens, and discuss state affairs over a casual apéritif. But Goebbels was no longer a private citizen. He arrived in Geneva accompanied by six S.S. men, tall, husky fellows who hovered about him constantly and who made it impossible for anything like an intimate atmosphere to develop in the presence of foreign diplomats. His companions went sightseeing with him, they followed him to the Assembly of the League of Nations and were present when he gave his press conference. They left their unfavourable impression through the entire sojourn.

Geneva was horrified by their very presence. None of the other important personalities had ever brought a bodyguard along. Goebbels was equally disgusted with Geneva. The democratic principles of the League nauseated him. The minute Chancellor of Austria, Herr Engelbert Dollfuss, would make a long speech at the Assembly, while everybody listened respectfully, although they should have known that Austria was nothing compared to Germany. Why, there were even coloured deputies in the League! Goebbels was baffled. He returned to Berlin and sixteen days afterwards Germany left the League of Nations.

The official reason for this step was that the League did not grant Germany equal rights with other great powers....

IV

On his arrival in Berlin he advised his propaganda agents attached to the embassies and legations abroad that soon they would receive important instructions. These so-called propaganda attachés were a Goebbels innovation. Most of them had never been in the foreign service, they had no experience abroad and knew nothing about foreign mentality. They were rather clumsy agitators who expounded the Nazi doctrines whenever they had a chance, and made a thorough nuisance of themselves.

During the autumn of 1933 Goebbels sent his attachés more than 20,000 words of secret instructions.[2] 'It can be confidentially confirmed,' he wrote, commenting on Germany's exit from the League, 'that the development which has just taken place aids German interests in some respects and will bring about a faster and more radical change in questions of armament than would lengthy negotiations in Geneva. But all publications or personal statements made within the framework of our propaganda abroad under all circumstances must avoid the impression that Germany had wished for this development.'

He also wrote: 'To the outside world all our propaganda must underline impressively that Germany does not wish for anything but a peaceful settlement of all pending problems ... In a skilful way all those who have refused to accede to Germany's rightful demands must be blamed for the failure of a peaceful understanding ... This must be done unobtrusively and in a constantly varying manner ... We must persuade at least part of public opinion abroad that Germany has no other way than to take what is absolutely coming to her....'

Finally: 'Everything in the way of strengthening the defence of Germany—to say nothing of preparations for an aggressive war—which would have taken place under the eyes of international control would have been insufficient....'

There were numerous other instructions. 'Developments in our foreign policy which have already taken place as well as those which are about to take place make it imperative that the offices charged with propaganda and enlightenment concentrate their work in the immediate future more strongly on foreign countries,' the directives said. 'It has been decided, at least for the time being, to relegate the question of expenses to the background ... Wherever small newspapers abroad subscribing to a German news service cannot afford to pay, it is possible to reimburse their expenses.'

Another passage mentioned the possibility of 'well disguised financial commitments, which German propagandists may make to willing editors.' The *leitmotiv* of the directive was that news supplied to foreign papers should be disguised as coming from neutral sources; if features by well-known 'special correspondents' were written, every precaution should be taken lest the clients learn that the correspondents were in any way connected with the Propaganda Ministry.

In other cases newspapers were bought outright by Goebbels or his agents, or subsidized on such a large scale that they could not have existed a day without Berlin money. According to several private estimates (there were never any official estimates) more than 350 papers throughout the world, not including the 300 German-language papers, were either owned or subsidized by the German Propaganda Ministry. Most of them, however, were of little importance and could hardly sway public opinion. All this cost tremendous sums of money, which were out of proportion to Goebbels' regular budget. In 1934 alone, 262 million marks were spent for propaganda abroad. Part of the money was paid by members of German clubs and associations in various countries, all of whom were organized in the *Auslands-Organisation* (Association of Germans Abroad).

Nevertheless, Goebbels spent too much money, at least in the opinion of Reichsbank President Hjalmar Schacht, who became worried about the large amounts going abroad. In November, 1935,[3] he marked certain bank notes which he handed over to Rosenberg, Himmler and Goebbels for use in Germany proper. Soon they were discovered abroad, which meant that the aforementioned Nazi leaders had sent them to their agents. Foreign Minister von Neurath later told the American Ambassador in France, William C. Bullitt, that Goebbels, the most indiscriminate of the offenders, had spent millions for propaganda abroad, with almost no success whatever.

V

German propaganda abroad was a failure largely because Goebbels, the expert moulder of the German mind, was completely ignorant when he had to deal with foreign mentality. In this one respect he was probably a typical German. He knew no more about handling foreigners than his agents abroad. Proof of this was his first talk to the foreign press (7 April 1933) in which he proceeded to enlighten the newspapermen about journalism—in their own countries. 'In England and France it is a matter of course that, regardless of the different views of political parties on any particular subject, public opinion is directed and moulded in a unified manner in all important questions concerning the nation.' Goebbels had rarely shown himself less informed than on that occasion; he could scarcely have committed a graver *faux pas*.

Whenever possible, Goebbels tried to discredit all foreign newspapermen writing against the Third Reich. 'From now on it will be attempted more and more often to plant "material" and "news" with oppositional news agencies, who by printing them will be compromised,' his secret instructions said. 'The material will be chosen in such a way that it not only leaves room for a denial but also can be refuted before public opinion.'

VI

In one instance Goebbels freely admitted that he had no idea of how to win over public opinion: this was the case of the United States. In his directives he made it clear that influencing American public opinion was of the utmost importance. 'Propaganda of the type Germany will now undertake must be based on the assumption that the American press is in open opposition to Nazi Germany,' he complained. Worse still, it was not easy to create an impression over there. 'In the US and in Canada every type of official propaganda has been developed long ago to a high level of efficiency.' Goebbels believed that it might be possible to arouse the temper of the Americans against the French by continuous mention of the fact that the latter had refused to pay their war debts. He also thought of suggesting a racial kinship between the Anglo-Saxons and the Germans. But he had few illusions as to his ultimate effectiveness.

'When we are taking up relations with North-American newspapers we must be well aware that we will have difficulty in gaining material influence, despite our strengthened financial position,' he wrote. 'It may be possible in certain cases to win over editors or correspondents. But decisive influence will be gained only by way of financial participation, a method which we have already adopted.'

Many months before his 'instructions' were sent out, he had taken a most unusual step. He had hired the best-known and highest-priced public relations man in the United States, Ivy Lee. It seems that he did not conceive the idea himself. Some sources say that Hjalmar Schacht, who knew the United States, had heard of Ivy Lee's numerous achievements—among them the near miracle of popularizing old John D. Rockefeller, who at the time he engaged Mr Lee was one of the most hated men in the United States. These sources quoted Schacht as believing that Lee alone could achieve the miracle of stopping the growing resentment of Americans against the Nazis.

According to Lee's subsequent testimony before a House investigation committee in Washington, he had been asked by some executives of I. G. Farben to 'size-up Hitler.' Early in 1933 he went to Germany and eventually worked out certain suggestions designed to create a friendlier atmosphere for Hitler abroad. Lee insisted that he submitted his ideas to I. G. Farben and entertained no relations with the German Government. His salary was to be between 25,000 dollars and 33,000 dollars a year.

At that time, as today, the profession of a public relations counsel was unknown in Europe. While large industrial concerns employed press agents and publicity experts, no government had ever felt the necessity for publicity. The nearest thing to a public relations counsel for a government was probably Goebbels himself.

There is no record to show whether Lee and Goebbels met in 1933. However, in January, 1934, Lee returned to Germany and had a number of conversations with Goebbels. No witness was present, and with both men dead now, we shall never know what actually was said between them. We know from Lee's occasional remarks that he held Goebbels in contempt for two reasons: for his inability to anticipate American reaction to some of his ideas (such as the anti-Jewish boycott) and for the very fact that Goebbels talked in high-sounding phrases about the necessity of convincing the world of the worthiness of the Nazi cause, instead of looking at his job from a purely professional point of view. Goebbels is not known to have expressed an opinion on Lee.

Lee warned Goebbels to cease propaganda in the United States, urged him to see foreign press people often and learn how to get along with them.[4] Four weeks after Lee's advice, Goebbels gave a cocktail party for diplomats and foreign correspondents. Evidently he was trying to find out whether Lee knew his business. But at a relatively early date he lost patience and began the practice of expelling foreign newspapermen from Germany. Among the first to be banned was Dorothy Thompson, at that time much more prominent as the wife of the Nobel Prize winner, Sinclair Lewis, than as a political writer in her own right. She had incurred Hitler's wrath because, having interviewed him shortly before he came to power, she had written that he lacked stature and would never get anywhere.

Other victims of Goebbels' ban were Leland Stowe, Edgar Ansel Mowrer and H. R. Knickerbocker. The latter was especially unpopular with Goebbels, who for a time nursed the fantastic idea of accusing him of murder. For days experts in the Propaganda Ministry laboured to find an angle which would allow them to play up a friend's suicide which had happened years before. Finally, they had to admit to their boss that there was not the slightest bit of evidence to support his theory, and regretfully Goebbels dropped the matter.

Every single time a foreign newspaperman was expelled the immediate consequence was a great deal of publicity for the victim. The writers were interviewed, they wrote books, they went on lecture tours. Dorothy Thompson's real career began only after she had been expelled. Leland Stowe wrote a popular book, *Hitler Means War*, Edgar Ansel Mowrer another one, *Germany Puts the Clock Back*. Ivy Lee and his successors cabled furiously from New York imploring the Propaganda Minister to stop his measures against American journalists. But Goebbels was unable to see the point. Why should he, the master of the German press, take any criticism from newsmen abroad? He continued to control their activities and reprimand them at the slightest provocation and thus lost his last chance of creating a more favourable atmosphere in the United States.

VII

Criticism against the Third Reich did not only come from abroad. Inside Germany, too, voices were raised against the Hitler regime. It was true that two-and-a-half out of seven million unemployed had found work; but wages were still exceedingly low, in fact just as low as they had been when Hitler described them as starvation wages. All the celebrations staged by Goebbels could not conceal this state of affairs.

'I see with misgiving that [Hitler's seizure of power] continues to be noisily celebrated from day to day. It were better to save our enthusiasm for a day of real and definitive results....' wrote Oswald Spengler in his book, *The Hour of Decision*, published in 1934. The philosopher, from whom Goebbels had taken some ideas about the historic mission of the Nazis, did not believe

Adolf Hitler was the new Caesar whose coming he had predicted. He was disappointed in the Nazis. During the 1933 festivals in Bayreuth he talked to the Fuehrer alone for about two hours. Later he told friends that he was horrified at the platitudes Hitler had uttered.

'I shall neither scold nor flatter,' Spengler wrote. 'I refrain from forming any estimate of those things which are only just coming into being. True valuation of an event is only possible when it has become the remote past, and the *definitive* good or bad results have long been facts: which is to say, when some decades have passed... A great event has no need of a contemporary estimate. History itself will judge when its contemporaries are no longer living... This was no victory, for opponents were lacking... It is no time or occasion for transports of triumph... Germany is in danger. My fear for Germany has not diminished... I see further than others...'

Goebbels was beside himself with fury over Spengler's unprecedented challenge of Nazi power and his scarcely concealed criticism of Hitler and himself. But he was not only angry, he was afraid. Someone in Germany had permitted himself to do his own thinking and, worst of all, the man really *could* think. Something had to be done about it.

At first Goebbels planned to answer Spengler personally. For several days and nights he worked over his reply—and then he informed his associates that he was abandoning the project. 'After all,' he said, 'a German minister cannot allow himself to be drawn into a personal argument with everybody who happens to write a book.' Instead, he ordered a number of writers to prepare a refutation of Spengler's arguments. Two pamphlets were published, but to no avail. Spengler's book was selling, while the voice of the Propaganda Ministry was ignored.

Spengler spent his remaining years in embittered silence and solitude. He died in 1936. His last words were: 'I am afraid for Germany. She is in grave danger. She may perish.'

VIII

Ever since Spengler had published his book which was so disappointing to his 'pupil' Goebbels, the Propaganda Minister joined the chorus of those who ranted against the intellectuals. Hitler had cursed the intellectuals in *Mein Kampf* as 'deadly enemies of every effective political persuasion of the masses.' Now Goebbels stated in a speech, 'Intellectualism must not be confused with national intelligence. Liberal, democratic intellectualism has confined itself to criticism, and otherwise has tended to ape western democracy.'

Unfortunately for Goebbels, he was an intellectual himself. Everything he or Hitler had said of the intellectuals fitted him perfectly. He knew it well and his hatred of the intellectuals may have been a form of self-hatred. He hated the critical aspects in himself, which he had striven to suppress ever since he met Hitler. Also, he may have been afraid of those who still permitted themselves to do their own thinking instead of thinking along the lines the Propaganda Minister prescribed. For the longer he was in charge the more he became determined that no one must be allowed to think except himself. In order to make sure of this he would go to any length.

Six years before, while attacking the Jewish Deputy Police Chief, Bernhard Weiss, Goebbels had said that Weiss committed a great error by suing him for slander and thus giving him free publicity. Now Goebbels made precisely the same mistake. Since he had become accustomed to doing things on a large scale he decided to fight criticism of the regime by a big campaign. He called it the 'Enlightenment Campaign' against 'Alarmists and Critics.' The German words he used were *miessmacher* and *kritikaster*, which are unfortunately untranslatable. *Miessmacher* had a definite anti-Semitic flavour. People who heard it visualized a sour-looking individual with a stomach ulcer who found fault with everything and spoiled whatever good things there were. *Kritikaster* was a word Goebbels himself had invented. To the average German it conveyed the idea of a crank incapable of doing anything but criticize.

The campaign lasted two months. There were more than two thousand mass meetings. After Goebbels was through, no one wanted to be considered a *miessmacher* or a *kritikaster*.

Least of all the journalists. By that time newspaper editors received what amounted more or less to tomorrow's entire paper via teletype and other news transmission media. There were directives on yellow and green paper, containing tomorrow's editorials and even tomorrow's movie reviews or book reviews. There were special instructions as to what should be put on the front page and what should be buried somewhere in the back pages.

Then something happened which Goebbels might have foreseen. All German newspapers began to look very much alike, no matter whether they were printed in Koenigsberg or in Cologne, in Hamburg or in Munich. The readers realized this and the over-all circulation of 19 millions dropped to 18 millions within one year. Goebbels was furious. More yellow and green directives followed stipulating that these official handouts must not be reprinted but rewritten. However, newspapermen had become so 'co-ordinated' that rewrites in Koenigsberg and Cologne looked exactly alike.

Goebbels assembled editors in the Propaganda Ministry and explained to them that they must not be 'afraid', that they should continue to criticize, although they must refrain from becoming *kritikaster*. They could always come to see him and discuss their problems with him, he said. Except for a notable exception, no one was foolish enough to take Goebbels literally.

But Ehm Welk, a well-known German writer and editor of one of the largest weeklies, *Gruene Post*, mustered his courage and wrote a sarcastic editorial. He explained he was deeply grateful for Goebbels' suggestion that editors should come to discuss their troubles with him personally. But, he pointed out, it was difficult to find Goebbels who was 'such a great man, living in such a big house, with so many rooms and surrounded by so many people ... I went to a house with a thousand windows,' the editorial continued, 'and I waited in a thousand antechambers to see whether I could glean any information on how to run our paper in the future.'

As soon as Goebbels learned about this, he banned that issue of the *Gruene Post*, suspended its publication for an indefinite period, had the editor's licence revoked and sent him to a concentration camp.

Eventually Ehm Welk got out, and after making the proper apologies, he was even allowed to publish his paper again. But it took the concerted efforts of many people to make Goebbels change his mind. He was completely incapable of seeing that his violent reaction was damaging his own prestige. Goebbels' friends, among them a fashion reporter to whom he was much attracted, argued with him. The lady pointed out that he should be pleased with the bit of criticism he had practically asked for. Goebbels could hardly believe his ears. After all, he was a cabinet minister, and his dignity would be impaired if he allowed others to make fun of him!

Goebbels had gone far in that one year, far down, that is. Instead of demolishing Emh Welk with a sharply ironical reply and thus putting him in his place—which this master of polemics could have done with ease—he preferred to resort to brutality rather than to an argument on the intellectual plane. He had ceased to be a writer, he was merely a dictator. He had ceased to be a fighter because he was too bad a loser.

After the case of Ehm Welk there was no one left with any desire to step out of line. The newspapers deteriorated accordingly. Therefore, in October, 1934, Goebbels issued confidential directives to all editors warning them particularly against excessive adulation of Party and state officials. 'The stigma of monotony must be removed from the German press,' he wound up.

IX

Not all *kritikaster* could be dealt with as summarily as the newspapermen. On 17 June 1934, Vice-Chancellor von Papen made a speech before the professors and students of the University of Marburg which caused a sensation. With amazing frankness he said that people were dissatisfied, that there was no sense in painting things rosier than they were; moreover, there was no reason why the Germans should be constantly told what to think and to feel.

This was a direct attack on Goebbels, although Papen mentioned no names. Half an hour afterwards, someone in the Propaganda Ministry read the speech to Goebbels over the telephone. He immediately instructed all German newspapers not to print a word of it. Then he answered Papen publicly. 'Ridiculous dwarfs!' he screamed. 'The nation has not yet forgotten the days when you, gentlemen, sitting in your armchairs, ruled the country!'

Less than a fortnight later the Gestapo appeared at the apartment of Dr Edgar Jung, Papen's private secretary, who had ghost-written the Marburg speech. He was taken away and never seen again. Nothing could be done against von Papen because Hindenburg and the army protected him.

The generals were also a bunch of *kritikaster* as far as Goebbels was concerned. They were dissatisfied with Hitler's private army and made it clear to the Fuehrer that the S.A. had to be dissolved or at least reduced to harmlessness. Their special hate was directed against Captain Ernst Roehm, Chief of Staff of the S.A., whom they wished to be removed.

Hitler eventually did remove Roehm together with hundreds of S.A. leaders in the blood purge of 30 June 1934. The background story behind this mass murder was never completely clarified. According to some rumours, Goebbels had discussed the possibility of a 'second revolution' with Roehm, with or without the knowledge of Hitler, who had long wavered whether to go along with the army or with the radical wing of his own Party.[5] Some people believed that Goebbels' participation in the 'conspiracy' was established by the fact that in the thirty-six hours of the mass murder he never left Hitler's side: he was afraid he, too, would be liquidated.

However, there is a much simpler explanation for Goebbels' nervousness. Most of the victims of the blood purge were men who only a few days before had been publicized as close friends and devoted followers of the Fuehrer. Their assassination presented a difficult propaganda problem; the matter could not be hushed up, with mechanized S.S. driving through the Reich and with wholesale killings going on.

According to Fritzsche's detailed statement, this was how Goebbels handled the problem: 'On the afternoon of 1 July, looking out of the window of my office I saw Dr Goebbels step out of the Chancellery. Soon afterwards he came to my office, something which happened only rarely. In silence, his large eyes burning, he handed me a visiting card of Adolf Hitler's. On the back there was a short paragraph which I deciphered only with the help of Dr Goebbels. It was the news of the death of Roehm. It ended with the words, "and then he was shot."

'Dr Goebbels said, "You may publish this."

'I answered, "There is a word missing."

'"What word?"

'"Court martial."

'"There was a court martial, but the word isn't there!"

'"I'm sure it was an important court martial. But to state, 'He was courtmartialled' would be a thousand times more important, and for all posterity. Let's add it."

'"I must not," Goebbels said. "The Fuehrer gave me this report as it is. He composed it himself. I must not change it."

'I nodded as though I agreed. Dr Goebbels left. I climbed the little staircase to the teletype room and dictated the news, adding "by court martial."

'I was interrupted by the telephone. "Have you put the news through?"

'"Yes", I said.

'"Without change?"

'"Yes", I said again.

'A few minutes afterwards I heard Dr Goebbels' uneven step on the stairs. When he saw what I had added, he demanded quietly but authoritatively that a rectification be made at once, and he saw to it that it was made in his presence. Then, in great agitation, he turned around to me. "Do you know that your carelessness could have cost me my head?"

'I smiled. "But I made the change against your wish. I alone would have been responsible. And you know very well that in spite of the court martial which took place there will be misunderstanding abroad—just because the word 'court martial' is not in the report."

'Goebbels almost exploded at that. And screaming something about "bourgeois qualms" and "not understanding our revolution" he left me.'

There was good reason why Goebbels should have been so alarmed. He knew as well as Fritzsche that the world would react with scepticism toward the news of Roehm's death, that not even the Germans would accept it without comment, and that it would have been better to add the word 'court martial'. But there must have been several thousand people who were well aware that there had been no court martial. And Goebbels was too good a propagandist to leave himself wide open in such a delicate question.

That night he announced the news of the 'Roehm conspiracy' and the punishment of the villains, over the radio. Hitler himself furnished what was then termed in the world press the 'inside story.' He admitted everything he had to admit, because everybody knew it anyway. And a few days later, on 11 July, Goebbels could say: 'This government ... makes no effort to conceal matters that are likely to become the subject of public criticism. It prefers to display its actions to the eyes of the people so that the people themselves may recognize the necessity of the measures taken.'

X

On 2 August, at 9 a.m., Goebbels was heard again over the German radio. He had only a short announcement to make: Reich President Hindenburg had passed away. For the next half hour all German stations remained silent. Hindenburg had left precise instructions that he wished to be buried on his estate at Neudeck. Only the next of kin were to attend his funeral. Goebbels, who filled the German press with obituary notices eulogizing Hindenburg as one of the greatest Germans who ever lived, had no intention of abiding by the Marshal's last wishes. The living propagandist superseded the dead President. Hindenburg's body was taken to Tannenberg, in East Prussia, where the deceased had won one of the major battles of the First World War. Numerous speeches were made at his grave and Goebbels had an opportunity to stage an immense spectacle, comparable only to the Party rally in Nuremberg.

The man who had died never had true greatness. He was largely responsible for the fact that Germany lost the world war and continued to fight for years after it was certain she would be defeated. He was a monarchist through and through, and no loyal servant of the Republic, although he had taken an oath on the Constitution. He was of mediocre intelligence and boasted to have read no more than six books in his life. But one thing might be said in his favour: he had always had a strong aversion towards Hitler, and when he had conquered his feelings of antipathy he was still filled with an even stronger dislike of Goebbels, which he could never overcome. Instinctively the old soldier must have recognized Goebbels for what he was, a nihilist. Hindenburg had certain convictions and beliefs—regardless of their merits—and he had felt that Goebbels had none.

Within a few hours of Hindenburg's death the army took an oath of loyalty to Hitler. Twelve days later Papen appeared at Berchtesgaden and handed Hitler the late President's testament. Immediately after its publication rumours spread that it had been faked.

There were many reasons for suspicion and doubt. The testament, when it was finally found, was described as being contained in an envelope with several large red seals. It should not have taken more than ten days to find such a document, particularly since it was impossible for Hindenburg to have composed it without the assistance of either his son or his Secretary of State, Meissner (Hindenburg could not use a typewriter). Nor could it have been 'lost', because it was drawn up in the same castle of Neudeck, which Hindenburg did not leave again before his death.

On 5 August the Propaganda Ministry had informed British correspondents that there was no testament. During the entire period between Hindenburg's death and the emergence of the testament no German paper ever mentioned that it might possibly exist. This could only mean that directives of the Propaganda Ministry had banned any mention of it.

But most indicative was the style of the document. Hindenburg was known never to have written literate German. His memoirs had to be ghosted. His testament, however, was wordy and full of expressions which he had never used in his life. He described himself as the 'Field Marshal of the World War'—the very words Goebbels had used in his last election campaign. (If Hindenburg had used the third person at all, at least he would have used the correct military term, *Generalfeldmarschall*). The testament referred to Hitler as 'My Chancellor'. This might have been said by an emperor or a king, but never by Hindenburg. There were numerous bombastic phrases such as 'flag bearer of the culture of the West' and the 'valley of extreme oppression, internal distress and self-destruction,' all of them typical Nazi clichés.

Hitler was mentioned in the testament several times, while there was no reference to Hindenburg's beloved Kaiser, and nothing about Hindenburg's deep-felt desire that Germany should again become a monarchy. And finally, although Hindenburg had been deeply religious, there was not a word about God or about religion. This alone would have been proof enough that the document was a forgery. It could have been written only by someone of the inner Nazi circle who was in every way the exact opposite of the late Hindenburg. Many believed that Hitler himself had ghosted the testament. Others, among them the French Ambassador, André François-Poncet, thought that Goebbels had rewritten it.

'Propaganda is no inflexible principle but the result of lively and deep imagination,' Goebbels declared a few days later at the Party rally in Nuremberg. He might have been unconsciously referring to the forgery of the Hindenburg testament.

XI

'Germany's present situation in the field of foreign policy resembles that of the years 1910 to 1913,' Goebbels had written in his secret directives. 'Germany's irreconcilable enemy (both of the Weimar Republic and of National Socialist Germany) is France.' This intelligence was addressed exclusively to Goebbels' agents. On the other hand, the French themselves must be persuaded that the Nazis wished for a peaceful Franco-German collaboration. It was in this spirit that Otto Abetz, a young German sincerely interested in a cultural rapprochement between the two nations approached the author Jules Romains in the autumn of 1934. Jules Remains was then president of the International PEN Club which only a few months before had come out with a strongly worded declaration against Nazi persecution of liberal Jewish and non-Jewish writers and against the burning of the books. But Monsieur Remains was also a passionate pacifist who believed, somewhat naïvely, perhaps, that peace could be secured if only enough 'men of good will' would work together to that end.

Abetz introduced himself as such a 'man of good will'. He had organized trips of young Frenchmen to Germany and now suggested that Jules Remains help him invite a group of young Germans to France—to cement cultural relations. Finally he proffered an invitation for the writer himself to go to Berlin and address German youth. Jules Romains' vanity got the better of him. In November, 1934, he accepted. When he entered Berlin University he was greeted by hundreds of S.S. men; thousands of Hitler youth were lined up for his welcome; fanfares were sounded in his honour. Never before had a private individual been accorded a similar reception in Germany. And Goebbels made a point of stressing this unusual distinction when he met the writer the following day. He pressed his hand, confided to him that the Fuehrer had been greatly impressed by the accounts of Remains' speech which filled all the newspapers (evidently on Goebbels' orders). Jules Remains was extremely pleased. He believed that he had accomplished a great deal toward bringing German and French youth together. It probably never entered his mind that he had acted as an unpaid publicity agent for Dr Joseph Goebbels.

French newspapers could be approached more easily than Goebbels had feared. An interview with Hitler was front-page news. *Paris-Soir*, the paper with the largest circulation on the Continent, sent its star reporter, Madame Titayna, to Berlin where she obtained an interview with the Fuehrer. So did Bertrand de Jouvenel for *Paris-Midi*. Apparently it never occurred to the editors that by giving these interviews such prominent display, they handed Hitler publicity worth millions. The same can be said, with some reservations, of the British press.

XII

On 16 March 1935, the Propaganda Ministry invited foreign correspondents and German newsmen to a press conference, where Dr Goebbels would make a statement 'of the utmost importance.' About a hundred journalists crowded into the small conference room and after a few minutes' delay Goebbels arrived, looking solemn and significant. He began to read a new decree saying that Hitler had restored universal military training and proclaimed the formation of a conscript army consisting of twelve army corps, altogether 36 divisions.

And then Goebbels wrote one of his most insolent articles explaining the necessity for the new measures. It was entitled, 'Clarity and Logic'. 'The German public observes with some astonishment the repercussions in the European capitals caused by the publication of the Law concerning the reconstruction of the Wehrmacht. We had believed that the world would acknowledge this fact with evident relief and a feeling of satisfaction. For the brutally frank disclosure of German intentions represents in truth a soothing element which is necessary, if not indispensable, for a logical and fruitful evaluation of the international situation.' With unsurpassed cynicism, Goebbels went on to say that for a long time 'the mystery of German rearmament' had disturbed official circles abroad, and that more than once the desire had been voiced that Germany should give an open accounting of her plans. That, Goebbels pointed out, was precisely what she had done now. 'The historic act of the Fuehrer has put an end to all vague speculations. Now the world knows where it stands.'

British, French and Italian representatives met at Stresa in Italy to protest against Hitler's unilateral action. But there the matter rested. And on 18 June 1935, the British concluded a naval treaty with Hitler's 'Ambassador-at-Large', Joachim von Ribbentrop, which permitted Germany to build up to 33 per cent of British tonnage. Goebbels was quick to point out in his first comment that the treaty was convincing proof of Germany's peaceful intentions.

By that time Mussolini's Italy had already invaded Abyssinia. The only strong voice of reproof against dictatorship and aggressive warfare came from across the Atlantic.

On 3 January 1936, Franklin D. Roosevelt told Congress: 'A point has been reached, where the people of the Americas must take cognizance of growing ill will, of marked trends towards aggression, of increasing armaments, of shortening tempers, a situation which has in it many of the elements that lead to the tragedy of general war.'

Dr Goebbels was the first to realize that here was finally an opponent who must be considered a serious threat to Hitler and his plans. Directives for comment on Roosevelt's speech were issued to the afternoon papers published on 4 January. 'Is it the business of the American President to concern himself with what happens in Europe or in Africa?'

XIII

Hitler's next coup started out like a mystery story. Around seven p.m. on 6 March 1936, several employees of the Propaganda Ministry were called back to their offices. No one knew what was in the offing. When they arrived they learned that they would not be allowed to use the telephone nor leave the building. At that time only the men next to Goebbels knew of the forthcoming announcement. During the night the leading representatives of the German press were asked to appear at eight o'clock the next morning for an important conference in the Pompeian room. A few members of the foreign press were also invited.

There was considerable speculation as to what was behind all this secrecy. Some newspapermen believed that the Propaganda Ministry was about to announce the launching of a new super-U-boat of 5,000 tons capacity. Others guessed that a new Zeppelin with as yet unknown spectacular gadgets had been built. During the night the radio announced that Hitler had called the Reichstag for the following noon to hear a declaration of the utmost importance. In the course of the night the employees of the Propaganda Ministry learned that Goebbels was making preparations for new 'elections'. Why new 'elections'? After all, there was only one party left. Slowly the news made the rounds through the offices of the Propaganda Ministry. In a few hours, units of the German Army would march into the Rhineland which, according to the Treaty of Versailles, was to remain demilitarized. Hitler was going to dissolve the Reichstag and by new 'elections' would give the German people an opportunity to approve the *fait accompli.*

The next morning at eight o'clock the expectant newspapermen were led into the Pompeian Room. Soon they, too, discovered that they were prisoners. All doors were now guarded by S.S. men. After half an hour the journalists were provided with sandwiches, loaded into buses and driven to the airport, where they boarded planes. Only after the take-off did they learn that they were *en route* to Cologne, Coblenz and Frankfurt in order to witness the march of the German Army into the Rhineland.

Three hours later Hitler announced his coup to a jubilant Reichstag. Every radio station throughout the world flashed the news. Emergency meetings of the cabinets were called in all European capitals, with the exception of London; 7 March being a Saturday, every official in Downing Street or Whitehall had departed for a weekend in the country.

Although Hitler had broken his own promises when he occupied the Rhineland, again no action was taken against him. Meanwhile Goebbels had launched a vigorous campaign, and on 29 March allegedly 99 per cent of all German voters cast their ballot, with 98.8 per cent supporting Hitler's march into the Rhineland. Hardly anyone in Germany believed these figures to be authentic. In the Zeppelin *Hindenburg* the voting had taken place while the ship was aloft. Forty people were on board, but forty-two pro-Hitler votes were counted.

XIV

At the beginning of August, 1936, Goebbels gave the biggest party of his life. It took place on his new country estate at Schwanenwerder, an island in the Wannsee lake, where some of the wealthiest and most sophisticated families in Berlin owned luxurious houses. He had bought it with the money Hitler had given him. There on the lawn surrounding the house scores of tents had been erected. A number of steam boats brought the guests to Schwanenwerder. The food served on that occasion was exquisite—which was unusual in the Goebbels household—and the champagne was gushing literally in streams. The festivities lasted until late into the night, several dance orchestras played without interruption, and there were fireworks.

Magda, in a white organdie evening gown, and Goebbels, in a white, double-breasted gabardine suit, were the smiling hosts. They could be pleased with their party: everyone with a name was there. The company had a strongly international flavour: there were Germans, Frenchmen, Englishmen, Americans, Italians... It was the time of the Olympic Games. Sport in the Third Reich was controlled by the Propaganda Ministry. Sport, as Goebbels saw it, was an excellent means of building up national enthusiasm at home and prestige abroad. Not the best man, but a German must win, was his motto. And if this was not possible, at least the winner should be an 'Aryan'.

The victory of the German prize-fighter Max Schmeling over Joe Louis in New York's Yankee Stadium in the summer of 1936 was a case in point. This victory was a great surprise to most experts, who were certain that Joe Louis would have no trouble with the ageing German boxer. In Germany, on the other hand, no one doubted that Schmeling would win. It was inconceivable that the strongest man of a nation which believed itself to be the strongest nation in the world could be beaten, of all people, by a non-Aryan, a negro. Hitler and Goebbels sent Schmeling telegrams of congratulation. Goebbels saw to it that his reception in Germany would be celebrated like the return of a triumphant general in ancient Rome.

The Olympic Games had been awarded to Germany, back in 1932, before Hitler came to power. Ever since 1933 a growing number of people all over the world had protested that the Games must not take place in a country controlled by men who believed in superior and inferior races, who so often had proclaimed their love for war. They were told, 'Sports have nothing to do with politics,' and that it was unfair and unsportsmanlike to make a last-minute change. The defenders of fairness in sports could not see that the Nazis and, in particular, Goebbels were exploiting the event to prove that Hitler's regime was universally accepted. Goebbels did his utmost to obscure the issue.

In one of his speeches he even went so far as to express hope that the Olympic Games should help to establish 'a world peace of the press.'

At the same time, the Games were a splendid opportunity for Goebbels to build up Germany's prestige abroad. Everything was done to impress the foreign visitors. For a few weeks all signs indicating that Jews were not wanted in this or that hotel or café, or could not take a swim at this or that beach were removed. Julius Streicher's anti-Semitic sheet, *Der Stuermer*, was not on display.[6]

And foreigners were impressed. They had a good time in the capital and began to doubt the reports they had read about concentration camps and Gestapo cellars. International athletes, too, were carried away by Goebbels' spectacular talents in staging the Games. There was only one hitch: far from proving the superiority of the 'Aryan' race, the Olympic Games established once more the athletic prowess of the American Negro. But this minor flaw did not detract from the magnificence of the show.

XV

On 30 October, Goebbels again stood on the platform of Berlin's Sportpalast. It seemed only a short while since he had arrived in the capital, a poor, unknown young man. Now that ten years had passed, he was one of the most powerful men in Germany, if not in Europe.

In his speech Goebbels reviewed the past ten years of his career. He told his audience how, in 1926, the Fuehrer had ordered him to go to Berlin, and how happy he had been to obey Hitler. Hitler, listening to Goebbels' speech in the Chancellery, knew full well that Goebbels was stretching the truth a little too far. Smiling, he said to his entourage: 'Let's surprise the Doctor!' And fifteen minutes later he was at Goebbels' side and made a short improvised speech. The Gauleiter had not been quite so happy to go to Berlin as he was now pretending, Hitler said; 'all the more reason to acknowledge what he had achieved:

'Never could I have conquered Berlin without you, my dear Dr Goebbels,' he continued warmly. 'Never could I have built up our propaganda machine, the hardest-hitting propaganda machine in the world, without you ... I know what you are feeling today, my dear Dr Goebbels. I am just as moved as you are by our success which is primarily your success ... Never will your name be extinguished from the history of Germany!'

On 27 December 1936, the first rationing of fats was introduced in Germany.

CHAPTER VIII

INTERLUDE

I

Before the year 1936 was up many things were going to happen. Spanish rebels under the leadership of General Francisco Franco had thrown their country into civil war. Nazi Germany was the first power formally to recognize Franco's Government, as the world learned through an interview Goebbels gave in November, 1936, just before the Fascists were stopped before Madrid.

German 'volunteers' had been sent to Spain as early as July. In later years Goebbels admitted this quite openly. In one of his articles he explained: 'As far as the authoritarian states are interfering in the struggle, they are motivated exclusively by national unselfishness, prompted only by their obligations towards Europe....' German war propaganda—similar to the Luftwaffe—was to be tested first in embattled Spain.

Goebbels had ample opportunity to show off his talents, for instance, when the German air force, ostensibly 'experimenting', destroyed the little town of Guernica on 3 May 1937. As Goebbels waited for the cry of indignation from an outraged humanity, his propaganda machine began to bombard the world with hundreds of stories about the 'Red Terror'. On 9 September 1937, he delivered a long speech on 'The Truth in Spain', in which he predicted a Communist dictatorship and inevitable chaos, unless Franco was victorious.

After one of the bitterest campaigns in American history Franklin Delano Roosevelt had been re-elected. On orders of the Propaganda Ministry the German press had adopted an attitude of 'neutrality'. The United States was a friendly power and any meddling into the internal affairs of a friendly power was to be avoided. However, Roosevelt had repeatedly voiced his unequivocal opposition to all forms of dictatorship, and this fact alone had been enough to antagonize all Nazi leaders, and Goebbels in particular. Hence the Propaganda Minister instructed the press to play down Roosevelt's victory with its accompanying outbursts of popular enthusiasm the world over. The event was to be dismissed in a few lines.

Another event which was to receive no attention whatsoever in German newspapers was the crisis of the British Crown. Goebbels was shocked beyond words by the developments. When Edward VIII renounced the throne, Goebbels said, almost dreamily, to his wife and mother-in-law: 'To think that this young man was born into the most exalted position there is in this world. Without having to move a finger, he is Emperor of India, King of England. And he, who can have any woman he wants, gives it all up—for *one* woman.'

About two years later, he was to be in the same predicament as the King of England; he was to be confronted with the same decision, and he was to make the same decision, although with a different result. But he did not know it as yet.

II

Perhaps the greatest shock Goebbels experienced in November, 1936, was the award of the Nobel Prize for Peace to the German writer, Karl von Ossietzky. His anti-militaristic views had brought him into conflict with the Army, and the courts of the Weimar Republic had sentenced him to gaol for violation of the espionage laws. During the night of the Reichstag fire he was one of the first to be arrested again.

Ever since that day he had agonized in a concentration camp. He was beaten and tortured, and finally contracted tuberculosis. But, in contrast to so many other inmates, the world had not forgotten him. Time and again there were inquiries about his fate and numerous protests were voiced in Sweden, Switzerland, Britain, and in the United States. The Nobel Prize for Ossietzky was a tribute of the civilized world against the formidable injustice done to a great pacifist.

Goebbels found himself in a strange, almost weird situation: here he was, equipped with extraordinary power, a dictator in his own right, a man against whose word there was no appeal. And there was the other man, whom he had imprisoned in a cell, condemned to silence. And yet, it was not silent about him. Soon the voices became so loud that Goebbels was forced to open the cell and to let him go—but only to make him enter the larger concentration camp that was Germany.

In Moscow the great purge before the Military Supreme Court was in full swing. Whatever truth there may have been in the charges against the defendants, the trials were absolutely unique in one respect: the defendants admitted everything the prosecution held against them, in addition to numerous other crimes which they were not called upon to disclose.

INTERLUDE

There was probably no one in the whole world who was not bewildered. Goebbels, above all, must have been shaken to his very foundations. To him, the defendants were not merely gambling away their lives—which he might have considered an heroic act of self-destruction—but they also missed the chance of making propaganda for their own philosophy, an attitude which must have seemed to him reprehensible and stupid. More than Hitler in Munich, more than Goebbels in the courts of Berlin, the Russians were in the limelight and the whole world was holding its breath to hear their testimony. This was their great chance to proclaim their philosophy of world revolution—an opportunity which, in the truest sense of the word, would never return. And yet, they remained silent.

III

On 5 October 1937, Franklin D. Roosevelt made his famous 'quarantine' speech:

'The peace, the freedom and the security of 90 per cent of the population of the world is being jeopardized by the remaining 10 per cent who are threatening a breakdown of all international order and law.... It seems to be unfortunately true that the epidemic of world lawlessness is spreading. 'When an epidemic of physical disease starts to spread the community approves and joins in a quarantine of the patients in order to protect the health of the community against the spread of the disease.... War is a contagion, whether it be declared or undeclared. It can engulf states and people remote from the original scene of hostilities.'

Goebbels was literally thunderstruck when he read the German text of the President's speech the next morning. He immediately recognized the significance of Roosevelt's words. No Frenchman, no Englishman in an official position had ever spoken so frankly, he told his assistants. The President clearly indicated that he had no faith in the peaceful assurances of German (and Japanese) propaganda. He had openly declared that he was afraid the Nazis were preparing for war. He had said exactly what Goebbels had feared someone eventually would say.

During the following weeks the German propaganda machine paid a good deal of attention to Franklin D. Roosevelt. This, according to Goebbels, was the difference between Hitler and Roosevelt: the Fuehrer's sole concern was the preservation of peace, while the American President, who had to cater to his voters, was forced to concentrate on war-mongering.

IV

About this time Goebbels had already made one of his most decisive mistakes. He had launched upon the persecution of the Catholic Church. Within the framework of a tremendous campaign—a little too big for its own good, as it developed—and acting on the biblical principle that 'Thou shalt have none other Gods but me,' he wanted to eliminate a power from which millions of Germans derived spiritual strength and comfort. For this purpose he was going to proceed above all against the Catholic monks and their alleged depravity.

The drive against the Catholics was characterized by unprecedented violence and its moral level could not have been lower. Every day the press published accounts filled with the basest accusations—stories of a type which no self-respecting newspaper ever would have printed before. On 30 April 1937, this resulted in the arrest of several thousand Catholic monks who were charged with homosexual offences. Further articles against the Catholic Church followed, all of them slanted to show that the guilt of the defendants had already been established. Suddenly, Goebbels remembered that he was a Roman Catholic; suddenly he remembered his four children, and eloquently he described the tortured imagination of a Catholic father who could not but recoil when he heard of the sexual abominations committed in Catholic seminaries.

However, despite all this noisy agitation, the enterprise was a failure. No one in Germany believed in the criminality of the monks. For the first time, perhaps, it began to dawn on millions of Germans that, in the name of the state, they were being fed with deliberate lies. Goebbels suffered a considerable loss of prestige, and people who for years had not seen the inside of a church now went there to demonstrate in whom they believed, and whom they distrusted.

'All of us working at the Propaganda Ministry could see which way things were going,' Fritzsche later said. As a matter of fact, it was so obvious that a child could have seen it. Goebbels alone stubbornly refused to be convinced of his error. None of his friends and collaborators could make him change his mind.

V

Goebbels had become a great man. It was true he was not the greatest in the land; Hitler was the one and only Fuehrer, and Goebbels knew it. Goebbels was not born to be the first, and he knew that, too. But he could be the first in his own domain—and that he was.

There he sat in his large spacious office. In the centre of the room, standing on thick red and blue rugs, was a large, pompous desk of dark mahogany, adorned with delicately-carved woodwork. In front of it was a beautiful renaissance chair with a high back. The desk was usually empty, except for a heavy bronze lamp and a bouquet of flowers in a vase. Near the window was a round conference table with low, modern arm-chairs covered with bright red silk. An over-life-size oil painting of the Fuehrer hung on the wall, flanked by a Rubens and a Rembrandt.

When Goebbels was alone he would wear glasses, for he was near-sighted. Not even his most intimate associates ever saw him wearing spectacles. His vanity would not permit it. All reports that reached his desk were written on a special typewriter, with letters three times the normal size. (Hitler used the same machines, for the same reason.) One of Goebbels' first inter-office decrees as Propaganda Minister was to prohibit the use of green ink or green pencils, which were reserved for him alone. By looking at a manuscript everyone could see at first glance what Goebbels had corrected.

There he sat. Around him were the offices of his adjutants, his private secretaries, his personal assistants, his personal stenographers. The most difficult task was assigned to the stenographers: they had to be constantly present, they had to take down his every word, because no one, including himself, knew whether and when he would refer to the things he had said.

There he sat. The Propaganda Ministry had grown to gigantic proportions in the few years that he had moved in. All the houses around the Leopold Palace had been bought up. In addition, a new, five-storied building had been erected. Its courtyard was filled with exotic trees, hot-house plants and fountains. There were five entrances, two of which were reserved exclusively for the Propaganda Minister, his under-secretaries and some exalted visitors.

The new building had about five hundred rooms. There were several larger and smaller conference rooms, a large and a small movie projection room, recording rooms and record archives. The cellar accommodated a large restaurant, where 2,000 people could be served simultaneously.

Between 300 and 500 persons a day desired to see the Propaganda Minister. But he received no one, except his collaborators, some friends and (more will be said about this later) actors and actresses. Approximately five thousand letters were arriving daily and Goebbels had given orders that every single one had to be answered within twenty-four hours, according to the Superintendent of the Propaganda Ministry, Karl Mehlis.

The staff of the Propaganda Ministry included the following top officials: three under-secretaries; four *Ministerialdirigenten*; eight *Ministerialdirektoren*; twenty-two *Oberregierungsraete*; sixty-three *Regierungsraete*; seven *Ministerialraete*. (All these titles denote various ranks in the bureaucratic hierarchy.)

Originally, Goebbels had started with 150 officials and 200 employees. At the beginning of 1936 there were 800 officials and 1,600 employees. A year later roughly three thousand people worked in the Propaganda Ministry. In April 1933 there had been five charwomen. Three years later their number had increased to 150. And the Propaganda Ministry continued to grow. Towards the end of the war, the Propaganda Ministry owned twenty-two buildings and had rented thirty-two others, and in the many hundreds of offices people wrote, took shorthand, typed, spoke into microphones, telephoned, wired—for Goebbels.

There he sat. Since his days as a Reichstag deputy and Gauleiter, when he had earned the royal sum of 900 marks per month, he had travelled a long road. From a strictly financial point of view there was still much to desire. In 1935 his income as a Cabinet Minister was 1,750 marks a month, plus a small expense account. Then Hitler arranged for an additional 3,000 marks a month. But all in all Goebbels could not have made much more than 6,000 marks a month, which is a truly ridiculous sum compared to the huge amounts which other leading Nazis pocketed in those days.

However, the Propaganda Ministry itself consumed enormous sums. Originally, the Reich Ministry of Finance had provided a budget of four to five million, but Goebbels refused even to consider such a measly amount. He approached Hitler, and when the Fuehrer had given the necessary orders the funds of the Party treasury began to flow into the Propaganda Ministry.

Beginning with 1935, sixty-seven million had been spent for ordinary expenses, in addition to sixty-five million for extraordinary expenses, but this was not all. The Reich Ministry of Finance was required to spend thirty-five million for propaganda abroad; forty million for the Transocean News Agency (which was at the same time a rallying centre for political and propaganda agents); forty-five million for the German News Agency (DNB); and forty million for film and theatre. Furthermore, a secret fund of forty-five million yearly was at Goebbels' disposal. (All figures were furnished by the superintendent of the Propaganda Ministry.)

While Goebbels' Nazi colleagues were not particular about distinguishing between official and personal funds, Goebbels himself was strict in these matters. All his fellow workers were unanimous in saying that he never spent official funds for private purposes.

There he sat, the great little man—feared, respected, flattered, cursed. He was not exactly a comfortable boss. Employees he did not like were dropped. 'Unless you were on good terms with him you lost your job,' said a courier who had worked for Goebbels for many years. His secretary, Fraeulein Inge Hildebrand, said:

'The constant change of personnel was particularly noticeable in the circle of his closest collaborators.... I don't think this can be explained merely by differences of opinion and arguments with Goebbels. I rather feel that it was due to the tremendous energy which his employees had to invest in their work. These men were not allowed to have a private life.... Whenever Goebbels was around, there was an oppressive tension in the air. And if he unexpectedly turned up, none of us knew just how to behave.... An added aggravation was the exactitude with which he insisted on having his papers arranged on his desk. He carried this little ritual to the point of absurdity. We often laughed about his maniacal sense of order: newspapers or documents had to be placed exactly in the centre of the desk; the folders must not protrude over the edge of the glass plate which covered the desk; no, the end of the folders and the glass plate must form one straight line.... In a personal conversation he, of course, would set the tone; he, of course, dominated. His repartees and phrases were often witty, more often cynical. The employees who happened to be present at such conversations, listened respectfully, smiled politely when they thought they ought to, and breathed a sigh of relief when he finally withdrew into his private office.'

VI

While Goebbels was thus enjoying his own power, his articles and speeches were becoming drab, sentimental and boring. How had this change come about? Was it not to be expected that the journalist, who hurriedly scribbled his editorials in the few minutes that remained between election meetings and administrative duties, would be able to accomplish some outstandingly good work, now that he no longer was forced to improvise?

Goebbels had been irresistible and full of drive only when he could attack. Now he represented the State, he was a Minister. Now he had to be moderate in tone and gesture, and even a certain oily solemnity was in order. But Goebbels was not made for that sort of thing.

During the years of the struggle for power the Nazi Party had fought the Reichstag, and its deputies had marched demonstratively out of the German parliament. Goebbels' articles about the Reichstag had been brilliant caricatures and he had a wonderful time when he could pour his scorn on the sleepy delegates snoring in their arm-chairs. Now Germany had left the League of Nations. What an opportunity for Goebbels! The things he could have said about the League of Nations, of its numerous commissions with their interminable and ultimately fruitless sessions; of the lack of initiative and the absence of any purposeful action among the gentlemen in Geneva! The League was almost made to order for Goebbels' satirical pen. As it was, Germany's exit took place in an atmosphere of dignified boredom, and there was not one entertaining article published on a subject which lent itself so admirably to caustic treatment.

Formerly Goebbels attacked everything, and whatever the Republic did was *a priori* no good. Now everything had to be good. He knew, of course, that this was not true; that the Party did not have the men who were equipped to rule Germany. He was indignant over the way in which Goering and Amann enriched themselves (and privately he made no bones about his feelings). But he had to cover up what he should have exposed; he had to praise what he should have criticized, although he knew that his praise was wasted on worthless individuals who should have been in gaol.

He recognized the weakness of his new position at an early date. And he did something very strange: he tried to run his newspapers and his meetings as though the Nazis were still in opposition. The Party was all-powerful in Germany, but the screaming newspaper headlines gave the impression that it was in immediate danger of being annihilated. This was not stated in so many words (on the contrary, every day the press maintained that the régime was firmly entrenched for the next thousand years), but the hysterical tone adopted by the press conveyed the tension behind this façade of bravado. Headlines such as 'Against the Jewish-Bolshevist World Danger', Jews are Inciting to World Revolution', or 'The Foreign Legionaries of the Comintern' were typical of Nazi jingoism in the papers.

Possibly the fact that Goebbels could dictate his articles at leisure, instead of rattling them off in a breath-taking tempo, was responsible for their inferior quality. Not that it made any difference to his readers. The Germans took it in their stride. Never was Goebbels more justified in his cynical contempt for the people than in the first years of the Nazi regime. On the other hand, those were the years when Germany's rearmament began to make itself felt in all spheres of the nation's economy. The layman, ignorant on the subject of economics, was happy and reassured every time he read Goebbels' marvellous statistics. Therefore, it is safe to say that in those years the German people would have backed the Hitler régime anyway, even if Goebbels and his Propaganda Ministry had not existed.

VII

Was propaganda still a means to an end? Was the ever-growing, visibly fattening-up Propaganda Ministry really no more than a public relations department in support of an idea, a government, a policy? Sometimes it looked as though the matter was reversed. Sometimes it seemed that the whole German Government had become a sub-division, as it were, of the Propaganda Ministry.

Policies were carried out or discarded, depending on their propagandistic effect. No one said: The German Government is planning this or that course of action, and how are we going to prepare the German people and the world, or how are we going to take the sting out of it? Rather, the question was: What course of action can now be taken with a minimum of international disapproval? How much will the German people accept? What would be the appropriate means to appease the world and to enthuse the Germans?

Thus propaganda had become an independent thing in itself, superimposed on reality. This new fake reality consisted largely of slogans. Goebbels had coined hundreds of slogans which his propaganda machine was hammering into the heads of the German people. It had begun with 'Germany, awake!' and it continued with 'The Jews are our Misfortune!' 'People without Space', 'Blood and Soil', and so on. And as the propagandistic slogans increased, the Germans became proportionately farther removed from reality and began to live in Dr Goebbels' own reality of total propaganda.

Towards the end of 1937, the first 1,500 miles of Reich *Autobahnen* had been completed, an event which moved Goebbels to make a speech on the 'Highways of Adolf Hitler'. It was praised everywhere as an overture to peace, although it was evident that the entire highway system had been undertaken for the speedy movement of motorized troops in the event of war.

A week before, Mussolini had walked out of the League of Nations.

VIII

Now Goebbels lived in style, although by no means as lavishly as Goering or Ribbentrop. There were cars, several house-boats, and numerous servants. He spent a great deal of money on his person. He had approximately one hundred suits and complete sets of clothes were available in each of his establishments, which enabled him to change whenever he liked.

At least twice a day he would change his shirt and underwear and, even more frequently, his shoes. According to his secretary he owned about a hundred-and-fifty pairs in all shapes and colours and made of every type of material. His favourite colour was white. In the summer he would appear, whenever possible, in a white linen suit, white shoes and white socks. This outfit set off his dark complexion to full advantage. His year-round tan was artificially produced: he spent at least one hour a day under the sun lamp and always looked as if fresh from a vacation in the mountains or at the beach. It was only in the last weeks before the end that he gave up his tanning.

Goebbels liked to surround himself with handsome people. He did not tolerate any homely secretaries. He insisted that they be smartly dressed and well groomed. He was bored with the incessant talk that woman belonged in the kitchen and must bear children. He was offended by the sight of the wives of the Gauleiters—dowdy, provincial creatures, supposedly personifying the ideal of Nazi womanhood, and finally wrote a stinging article against these and similar notions.

'Some people who either have their life behind them or else don't deserve to have it before them are moralizing night and day in the name of our revolution,' he wrote. 'Most of the time this kind of morals has nothing in common with genuine morality.... These self-styled judges of our morals have carried their prying into the very realm of privacy. They would like to establish chastity commissions all over the country to supervise the love life of the Mullers and the Schulzes. If these people had the say about it, they would turn National Socialist Germany into a moral desert, where denunciations, filthy gossip and blackmail would become the order of the day.'

Goebbels had no objection against women who used cosmetics. Nevertheless, he was rather startled to find that Magda was among them. When he surprised her one day while she was doing her face, he asked her, 'Darling, since when are you using make-up?' Whereupon she replied serenely, 'But, angel, I've always used it.'

In these matters he always remained naïve. While they were holiday-making at Bad Heiligendamm, a Baltic resort, Goebbels looked over all the women on the beach, commenting that most of them were extremely blond. And suddenly he burst out saying: 'I shall have a decree passed forbidding women to bleach their hair with peroxide.' There was a moment of embarrassed silence: Magda herself was not a natural blonde and the two film stars in their company also acquired the 'Nordic' colour of their hair at the beauty parlour. According to Magda's mother, Goebbels never learned that his wife's hair was dyed.

Magda's household economies still bordered on stinginess, although Goebbels was now free from financial worries. In her miserly way Magda economized in every direction: the children were dressed with spartan simplicity; the servants received no pay during their vacation, and above all the meals were extremely unpalatable. Several evenings a week she served nothing but fried potatoes and herring. Goebbels did not care what he ate, and he ate very little. However, the guests were less easy to please. Goebbels' house had attained a certain notoriety for serving poor and little food and many stars of the Berlin stage and screen who were invited there had dinner at home beforehand.

Magda soon realized that her parties were not particularly popular, but the food alone was not responsible for the uncongenial atmosphere. The principal trouble was that Goebbels seemed to go out of his way to make his guests uncomfortable. He invariably suggested a question-and-answer game, where he could show up everybody's ignorance. The young film stars, of course, did not exactly distinguish themselves in their knowledge of German history.

At one time one of the most popular divas, Jenny Jugo, did not even answer when she was asked whether she knew the name of a certain Prussian king. Goebbels gloated over her embarrassment, like a teacher who has caught a lazy pupil. Later Frau Jugo confessed: 'I knew that name very well but I didn't know whether he was an Aryan. So I preferred to say nothing.'

IX

Goebbels had always been devoted to the theatre. 'He was nothing but a frustrated actor,' a well-known German actress said of him.

Now he was lord and master of the legitimate stage and a few weeks after he had taken over he announced that he intended to make some far-reaching changes. 'The great beating of the drums heralding the new era must not stop at the portals of the theatre but their sound must be carried right into the auditorium and on to the stage,' he thundered. 'I reject the slogan of international art....'

Among his first 'reforms' was the dismissal of all Jewish directors and actors. This meant, in effect, that a large number of those who had built up the world-wide reputation of the German stage disappeared from the scene. Later he prohibited theatrical criticism, saying that it was pointless and destructive. 'In the future we will concentrate on the valuable, nationwide accomplishments of our theatre, but we want no further destructive reviews,' Goebbels proclaimed.

Goebbels, of all people, had banned criticism. Apparently, he had lost every trace of humour in the matter. This was particularly noticeable in his attitude toward the cabaret. The political cabaret, as it was known in Germany, was characterized by a satirical running commentary against the existing regime, against authority as such. In the Third Reich the cabarets were of course greatly handicapped because no master of ceremonies was willing to risk concentration camp or denunciation as a *kritikaster* for the sake of a good joke. Understandably enough, the handful of men who had the courage to defy the Nazis were extremely popular. Among them was a certain Werner Fink who performed nightly by standing under a suspended sword which was identified by everyone in the audience as the Sword of Damocles. At one time he appeared with his head bandaged, saying, 'The pressure from above is really terrible today.' Or else he would welcome the audience with 'Heil Hitler!' adding, 'and for the 1 per cent among you: Good evening!'

One should have thought that Goebbels could have permitted himself to laugh. But he had no talent for self-irony. From time to time he would send

Werner Fink and others to a concentration camp. Since this retaliation was anything but encouraging to actors and writers, audiences soon had nothing to laugh about. And as if any further proof was needed for Goebbels' humourless disposition, he did something truly fantastic in this precarious situation: in February, 1939, he organized a best-joke-of-the-year contest.

The result was never published.

X

From the beginning, one of the largest departments in the Propaganda Ministry was the film section. Even in the early days it had several hundred employees, concerned with every single detail of motion-picture production. Goebbels' interference began with the scenario. First of all, a brief outline of the story—from three to five pages—had to be submitted. Goebbels raised objections right there and then and most of the time the matter never got beyond that stage. Or else Goebbels had specific wishes which were communicated to the various companies with the request to observe his instructions. For instance, when the war started it was officially stated that Goebbels wished to see no further serious movies. In the following weeks suggestions for film comedies came pouring into the Propaganda Ministry. Goebbels was annoyed: who would want to produce that many comedies in such grave times? He insisted on *serious* films. There was general consternation. Not until weeks later was the misunderstanding cleared up: Goebbels' comment had not referred to serious films but to the many films about *doctors* which were made at the beginning of the war. (The pun is on the German words *ernste filme* and *Aerzte-filme*. These words which sound somewhat alike had become confused in the minds of his over-anxious colleagues.)

It continued the way it had started. Some scenarios had to be rewritten ten times, there was incessant recasting (Goebbels reserved for himself the right to reject any cast he did not like), there was constant cutting and recutting, and even then the whole work had to be scrapped in many cases because Goebbels ultimately decided against it. When a film was completed, a special screening was arranged for Goebbels; sometimes he saw it several times; usually there were scenes that had to be done over, others that he would cut out. He always found time for this sort of work.

In the early days of the Nazi movement Goebbels' understanding of motion pictures was relatively unblurred by Nazi ideology. His favourite picture, for instance, was *Battle Cruiser Potemkin*, and it did not matter to him that the film was made in Soviet Russia and directed by Eisenstein, a Jew. His favourite director was Fritz Lang, a 'non-Aryan' and violent anti-Nazi. He also had great respect for the films of Ernst Lubitsch, a German Jew; another movie which was often shown him in a private screening was *Zola*, with the Jewish actor Paul Muni in the title role. In later years he thought less and less of American films; he objected against Hollywood productions on the grounds that they were 'educationally harmful', while even in war time he continued to prefer numerous British and French films to German pictures. However, he kept such heretic opinions largely to himself and only his few intimates knew of his personal views. Publicly he declared that the German film was 'unbeatable' and would conquer the world.

Right at the beginning Goebbels made an attempt to create so-called Nazi Party films and experienced a spectacular lack of success. Despite the initial popular enthusiasm for the Nazis these propaganda pictures, such as *S. A. Man Brand*, *Hitlerjunge Quex* and *Hans Westmar*, were box-office failures.

XI

It is impossible to discuss Goebbels' attitude towards the movies without mentioning the extraordinary influence of the film on his private life. His predilection for beautiful screen stars was never a secret. He invited them to Schwanenwerder, where parties were given once or twice a week; they had tea with him alone in the privacy of his office at the Propaganda Ministry; and he would ask the one or the other for a rendezvous at his estate in Lanke, given to him by the City of Berlin on his tenth anniversary as Gauleiter. His appetite in this respect was insatiable.

The ladies who were thus favoured by him accepted his invitations with pleasure. Goebbels, who had always appealed to women, was now more attractive than ever. He was well groomed, he was charming and could be most entertaining, if he wanted. He always seemed above the situation, always a little sarcastic and aloof, a cigarette dangling at the corner of his mouth. He gave the impression that he did not take women seriously.

This impression was deceptive. In reality, his attitude toward women had not changed since the days of his early youth: he was still shy, full of romantic notions, and quite adolescent. He still kept a collection of hair tresses of the women he had loved, or believed that he had loved. Was it love? How could it be love since there were now so many women in his life? Some of his intimates believed that his excesses were due to his feeling of physical inferiority. Whatever the truth, his cheap triumphs did not make him happy.

He knew that most of the young film actresses went to bed with him to make a career. He even suspected the motives of those women who were genuinely fond of him and did not need his assistance for professional reasons. He wanted so desperately to be loved for his own sake. Time and again he told his lady friends that he could and would not do anything to further their careers. But Berlin was full of gossip about film stars who suddenly had been given this or that important role because they had slept with Goebbels. Most of these stories were invented by the ladies themselves. They had dropped so many hints that soon everyone knew what had happened, although frequently nothing at all happened. Over-anxious film producers wished to please the omnipotent Minister of Propaganda and suggested the lady in question for a particular part: and her career was made. And Goebbels had it confirmed once more that he had not been loved for his own sake.

Presumably he never held many illusions on this point. It is no accident that he never wrote a line to any of the women with whom he had affairs. To one of his mistresses he brutally explained: 'In politics you can't be careful enough. There are any number of politicians who have been ruined by a scandal. This sort of thing can't happen to me.'

Yet, it almost did.

XII

The promiscuous sex life of the Propaganda Minister, which was conducted in the broad daylight of public opinion, would have wrecked any marriage. Magda Goebbels was not the sort of woman to put up with it and things were bound to take a catastrophic turn sooner or later. The first years of their marriage passed smoothly enough. Goebbels was a devoted husband. He was considerate and attentive, and even in the most hectic days of political struggle he always found time for her.

Then, after two years of married life, she suddenly discovered that he was deceiving her. Deeply hurt and offended, she had an argument with him. He, in turn, was beside himself that she dared reproach him. He had never promised to be faithful, he reminded her.

Magda did not trust her ears. Now she demanded that he immediately end his relations with the lady (a certain Countess W.). Goebbels complied, but he was disappointed. He had hoped for an understanding mature companion and now he found a jealous woman. This was the first break. It was quickly, though superficially, mended and to an outsider the Goebbelses seemed a happily married couple.

They had six children: Helga (born 1 September 1932), Hilde (born 13 April 1934), Helmut (born 21 October 1935), Holde (born 9 February 1937), Hedda (born 5 May 1938), and Heide (born 29 October 1940).

All his children's names began with 'H'. Magda's son of her first marriage, Harald, was no exception. This curious phenomenon was never properly explained. Goebbels' favourite child was his oldest daughter, Helga, who very much resembled him. She was a precocious child, to say the least. At the tender age of eleven (that is, in 1943) she began to be interested in politics, racial questions and economic problems. Goebbels devoted much time to the little girl, he listened to her stories and her singing, and treated her like a grown-up.

Hilde was a pretty and good-natured child and very fond of animals. The three other little girls were very beautiful and quite vain for their age, but they were so young when they died that there is not much else to say about them.

To Goebbels' everlasting disappointment he had only one son, Helmut, a quiet boy and not very bright, who had trouble in keeping up with the other children at school. And it was typical of Goebbels' whole personality that he blamed this 'misfortune' on his wife. When his second daughter was born, he was so upset that he refused to visit Magda at the clinic. He would not even send her flowers, leaving it to Hitler to do so. Finally, the Fuehrer practically ordered him to go to her bedside.

When Magda's third confinement was approaching she was certain—and said so to her friends—that Goebbels would divorce her if she had another girl. Goebbels explained that she could not bear sons because she was 'too cold'. When Magda nevertheless produced a boy there was a passionate reconciliation amidst streams of tears, but a year later there was another little girl and again Hitler had to intervene to stop the couple from breaking up.

Hitler played a very special part in Goebbels' marriage. Since the Fuehrer was in power he had met innumerable new people; he had been exposed to countless new influences and Goebbels feared that Hitler might become estranged from him. He wanted to prevent this at all costs and in order to stimulate the Fuehrer's interest he worked through Magda and even his children, of whom Hitler was very fond.

But Goebbels was not alone in courting the Fuehrer: Magda herself courted Hitler. We shall never know whether she saw him only through Goebbels' eyes, or whether she succumbed to his personal magnetism. Friends who were close to the Goebbels even believed Magda was in love with Hitler. In any event, all of them agreed that Magda was completely transformed in his presence. She dropped her nonchalant pose, she became tense and exhibited a rather self-conscious charm.

She wanted to arouse his interest, she wanted to please him. One day Goebbels mentioned the case of a man who had made a derogatory remark about the Nazi regime. Hitler was unruffled and merely said that the man would have to be imprisoned. Magda, her blond hair parted in the middle, her blue eyes widened, her hands folded in her lap—the picture of a Madonna—remarked casually: 'I think he ought to be beheaded!' And serenely she smiled at the Fuehrer. As a matter of fact, so far as she was concerned, the anti-Nazis might have continued living in peace. But she thought that her ruthlessness would please Hitler.

And yet, it was Magda's fault that Hitler stayed away from Goebbels' house for almost two years. At the Nuremberg Party rally in 1934 the wives of the prominent Nazis learned for the first time that there existed a girl named Eva Braun who was Hitler's friend. None of the ladies had ever set eyes on Eva. Driven by curiosity, they started to gossip, with Magda joining in. In the end Eva Braun heard of it. She spoke to Hitler, who had a violent argument with Goebbels, in which he told him his frank opinion of Magda and the other female gossip-mongers of the Party.

Goebbels was beside himself. Not for one moment did he attempt to side with Magda. On the contrary, he covered her with reproaches and insisted that she had ruined his friendship with the Fuehrer.

XIII

Magda was very attractive to men. They were constantly courting her and—neglected as she was by her husband—she was unable to resist temptation for any length of time. Goebbels realized this and became terribly jealous. He had her telephone tapped by a special section in the Propaganda Ministry and in this way he learned of her many rendezvous and amorous conversations with a young, good-looking Norwegian.

Magda made no secret of her conduct. She told her best friend that she planned to get a divorce. She told Goebbels as well. Goebbels made a violent scene and finally threatened that he would tell Hitler 'everything', which left her unimpressed.

Now Goebbels, terrified that he might lose Magda, broke down. At three o'clock one morning he appeared at the apartment of her best friend and beseeched her to swear by the life of her child that Magda was not having an affair with the Norwegian. Eventually, moved by his frantic pleas, Magda gave up her Nordic lover, Goebbels broke with the woman who happened to be his mistress at the time, and at least outwardly their marital happiness was restored.

Their marriage had always been a far cry from the German bourgeois conception of a peaceful, pleasant life together. Although Goebbels insisted that his wife must bear children, she nevertheless had to attend all sorts of social functions with him. A week before one of her confinements she had to be present at parties which lasted until two and three o'clock in the morning, and she was obliged to go on drives at eighty miles an hour. After one week at the clinic, on her first day at home there would be another party. Once she fell out of the car when it was going at great speed, was knocked unconscious and suffered a concussion of the brain and a fractured clavicle, but three days later she could be seen in the theatre at the side of her husband.

Magda was fighting to hold Goebbels; it was like a never-ending race, always against new horses. There were parties that lasted all night, interrupted only by her brief visits to the children's room, where she would nurse her infant, then return to her guests. Sometimes she became tired and bad-tempered and collapsed, but as soon as Goebbels asked for her, she pulled herself together, made up her face and smiled. Somehow or other in this turmoil she found time for the children, whom she raised with love and patience, but she had no qualms in leaving them to third persons, such as newly-hired governesses or nurses. Magda seldom lost her composure, even when the children were sick with a high fever.

Goebbels' mother and sister who came on occasional visits did not fit at all into this crazy household. His mother had remained what she had always been—a simple, modest and God-fearing woman. Her son's overwhelming success was a source of constant surprise to her and sometimes she could be seen shaking her head and muttering to herself, 'Where on earth does he get it from?' Since she made no demands on life, she always refused the financial support Goebbels frequently offered her. But she allowed him from time to time to pay for a cure at some spa.

Goebbels' sister was a rather pretty woman who resembled him a good deal. She was quiet and reserved and made herself useful around the house. Goebbels barely noticed her presence. When Magda was at the clinic for one of her numerous confinements, and while Maria was taking care of the house, the doctor spoke very highly of her to Goebbels. He looked at his sister in surprise. This seemed to be the first time he had taken note of her existence. Magda's mother, Frau Behrendt, was often at the house, especially to take care of the children. She could not get along with her son-in-law, and their relations were strained. She never trusted him.[1] Goebbels reciprocated her feelings; he thought she talked too much, which was true, and furthermore he never forgave her for having once married a Jew.

In other words, the household offered by no means a spectacle of blissful peace when Miss X entered Goebbels' life.

XIV

Miss X was perhaps not a classic beauty but extremely attractive. She was rather small and slim and had expressive, dark eyes that dominated the pale, nervous face. Overnight she had risen to stardom at the side of a good-looking actor who may be described as the German counterpart of Gary Cooper. It was no secret that she was living with the actor and that eventually he was going to marry her.

Sometime during the summer of 1937 she met Goebbels. Ironically enough, this came about by Magda's desire to make the acquaintance of the young actor. He was invited to tea and, on the suggestion of Magda, brought Miss X along. So far as Goebbels was concerned, it was love at first sight.

For a long time no one suspected anything. Miss X would often drop in for a visit at the house of the Propaganda Minister, and she was on very friendly terms with Magda. Even her friend, the actor, had no idea how interested she had become in Goebbels himself.

He found out by accident. Late at night, returning from the studio, he discovered Miss X and Goebbels in a rather compromising position in Miss X's motor-car. Surveying the situation, he murmured, 'Now at least we know where we are, Herr Doctor,' and left.

Somehow the incident leaked out. Somehow the story spread that he had caught Miss X and Goebbels *in flagrante delicto*. Within a few days the story had been blown up to a first-rate sensation. People were whispering that the actor had slapped the Minister in the face. The actor became almost a popular hero. He was congratulated on his courage—that was how much they hated Goebbels.

There were many who had occasion to observe Goebbels and the young actress at close quarters. No one doubted that Miss X was deeply in love with the Minister. She was not concerned with her career; she was a great success anyway. She was solely concerned with the man.

Goebbels probably felt this. In any event, he loved Miss X; for him, too, it was the great consuming passion which blotted out everything else that had happened in his life. There was only one reality for him—the woman he loved. Everything else seemed to take place, as it were, behind a veil.

XV

This was at the beginning of 1938, when many things were happening in and around the Third Reich which had a definite bearing on Goebbels' own situation.

General Werner von Blomberg, Hitler's War Minister, had to resign momentarily, because he entered into a marriage which, to the German Officers Corps, was an intolerable *mésalliance*. Hitler took advantage of the resulting confusion to force the resignation of a number of generals who, in the Nazi sense, were not considered reliable. Subsequently, General Wilhelm Keitel became Chief of Staff of all the Armed Forces. Hitler was preparing the *Anschluss* with Austria. The situation had never been more favourable. In France, the cabinet of Camille Chautemps was constantly in danger of being overthrown. In Soviet Russia the purge trials followed one another in rapid succession. Thanks to a common policy in Spain there had been a rapprochement with Italy. Britain's Foreign Secretary, Anthony Eden, clearly recognized the German danger, but Prime Minister Chamberlain was reluctant to say or do anything that might antagonize Hitler. Who, then, was there to oppose the *Anschluss*?

On 13 March 1938, Goebbels announced it as an accomplished fact over the radio. On 9 April Austria was permitted to hold a plebiscite according to Goebbels' well-tested recipe, and the result surprised no one: approximately 99 per cent of the population were in favour of the annexation.

But in the succeeding events Goebbels hardly played an active part. He rarely appeared in the limelight. The great drama of his life, his love affair with Miss X, had become the core of his thinking and of all his activities. World history, which he had been so anxious to shape, had become a mere interlude.

CHAPTER IX

THE MUFFLED SOUND OF THE DRUMS

I

It was his great love.

He saw Miss X daily. No matter how busy he was, he always found time to rush to her, if only for a few minutes. He would tell his driver to stop his car one or two blocks away from her apartment. Then he would walk around the corner and up to her flat, which was situated near the Kurfuerstendamm. These furtive visits, of course, could not remain secret. Later she bought a house in a suburb, which made things somewhat easier. Goebbels joined her there almost every night.

Sometimes it was impossible for him to leave the Propaganda Ministry. Then she would drive to the Wilhelmstrasse and walk up and down the square which faced his office. He would stand near the window, where he could see her, and was happy. Sometimes he had to work at night on a long speech or an important article. Then he would call her and beg her to remain on the 'phone. He would put the receiver down and continue to work, while she sat in her room, with her ear glued to the telephone, hearing nothing but his breathing and the scratching of his pen on the paper. At least he felt that in a remote way she was with him and this, he said, gave him renewed strength.

It was his great love. And although neither of them wished it, their intimate affair was conducted, as it were, in public. Everyone in the Propaganda Ministry spoke about it. Fritzsche said, 'He staked his all.' The whole film industry talked about it. Producers and directors competed with each other to sign Miss X for a role. Neither Goebbels nor she had any part in it. The gentlemen of the German film industry were acting on their own initiative. Here was their chance to worm their way into Goebbels' good graces and unscrupulously they took advantage of the opportunity. They also tried to use Miss X for their own little schemes. Hardly a week passed without some film magnate persuading her to make this or that suggestion to the Minister. She had no personal stake in any of these projects. But as she was good-natured and liked to fancy herself in the role of an influential woman she willingly consented to her role as a messenger and in this way accomplished a great deal for those who had commissioned her. She was to experience that gratitude was not their most outstanding virtue.

Goebbels was happy, but apparently Miss X wanted more. She told her friends she wanted him to divorce his wife, she wanted to marry him. There was nothing calculating about her; she had no ambition whatsoever to become the wife of a Cabinet Minister. She wanted the man—and she could not share him with another woman.

If there had been as much as a trace of a scheming instinct in her, Goebbels, who was always suspicious, would have sensed it at once. But since she was childishly innocent about it, he became convinced that her desire was justified and he decided to speak to Magda.

All of Berlin knew the story, Magda alone was ignorant. Or had she heard rumours and simply refused to believe them? Miss X came to see her occasionally, although her visits became less frequent as time went by. Once Magda noticed a beautiful emerald ring on Miss X's finger. She asked who had given it to her. 'The man I love,' the actress was supposed to have answered. Later Magda remembered this remark.

Now Goebbels was confronting his wife, trying to explain the situation to her. Their marriage was irreparably undermined, he said, and he was in love with another woman, Miss X. He begged Magda to give him his freedom. When he asked her for a divorce she said neither 'yes' nor 'no'.

Goebbels left the house. He thought that Magda had consented and would take the necessary steps for their final separation. For a whole week he did not return, living at the Hotel Kaiserhof opposite the Propaganda Ministry. When he heard nothing from Magda, he went back to his house at Schwanenwerder. No one answered the bell, although he kept ringing. Finally Magda appeared at the door and asked him what he wanted. There was nothing for him to do here, she said. Goebbels asked whether he might see the children. Magda disappeared. A few minutes later the children came out in front of the house and here Goebbels could talk to them, every few days or so, but he was no longer permitted to enter the House. Magda had told the children, 'Father may never come home again.'

The first thing Magda did was to sell the adjacent land that belonged to the villa in Schwanenwerder. She was fully prepared to reduce her standard of living. Some of the servants were dismissed, others were told that for the time being they would receive no wages. For Magda did not dream of asking her husband for money, and he himself did not volunteer to send her any.

Then Magda had several heart-to-heart talks with Karl Hanke, under-secretary in the Propaganda Ministry, and Goebbels' closest collaborator. Hanke was tall and slender, very young, with dark and melancholy eyes. For a long time he had been in love with Magda Goebbels. She must have known about his feelings. Was she merely seeking his advice in a difficult situation, or did she yearn for an understanding soul?

She became his mistress. And, strangely enough, in his arms she not only forgot her misery but she found real happiness. To a friend she remarked, 'I suppose I can be happy with any man.' There was even talk of marriage between the two lovers. When Magda informed Goering of her intention he telephoned the Fuehrer, and the next day Magda flew to Berchtesgarden.

Magda later said that she had asked for Hitler's consent to divorce her husband. According to her, Hitler said that no doubt things would eventually straighten themselves out. Magda replied that everything between Goebbels and herself was finished.

II

Now Hitler acted. He immediately returned to Berlin and ordered Goebbels to appear before him. Then followed an extremely agitated discussion which lasted more than two hours (and which later was reported by Goebbels). Hitler acted as though he refused to take the matter seriously. After all, he had known Goebbels for such a long time and he had spent such happy hours at his home! Hitler had always believed, he said, that Goebbels' marriage was a particularly happy one, and he still believed it. Surely the whole business could be arranged to everybody's satisfaction.

Goebbels said no, it could not. The name of Miss X came up. Goebbels said he loved her and wanted to marry her.

Hitler became very excited. How did Goebbels think this could be done? He, the German Propaganda Minister, could not have a divorce. What a fine example to set for the Germans! And a foreigner, of all people. No, it was out of the question, Hitler said.

Goebbels replied: 'I have thought the matter over, my Fuehrer. I fully realize that under the circumstances I can no longer remain Propaganda Minister. Therefore, I beg you to relieve me of my duties. Please permit me to get a divorce and to marry Miss X. I shall gladly leave the country with her. The other day you said that a reliable man was needed in Tokyo. Would it be possible to make me Ambassador to Japan?'

Here it was. Here was Goebbels, ready to give up everything he had desired, for the sake of the woman he loved. Here he was willing to do what the King of England had done not so long ago. How often he had mocked the politicians who had allowed their love affairs to destroy their careers. And now he was determined to put an end to his own.

But Hitler proved a powerful stumbling-block. He went into one of his famous fits of rage. He raved like a maniac. As far as Goebbels could follow the Fuehrer's words at all in the tumultuous scene that followed, he understood that Hitler would never, never give his permission. Goebbels was asking for the impossible, he thundered. His hysterical screams culminated in the words, 'He who makes history is not allowed to have a private life!'

Goebbels was sick and tired of making history. He persisted in his argument, and finally Hitler said that Goebbels might divorce Magda, provided that after one year he would still feel the same. But in that year he would not be permitted to see or talk to Miss X. Goebbels had to give his word of honour that he would obey.

It was late in the evening when Goebbels returned to the Propaganda Ministry. He wrote a note to Miss X, explaining that on Hitler's orders he could not see her again. When she received the message she broke down. She had to be put to bed, where she spent the following weeks sobbing hysterically, refusing to take any food. All the time the house in which she lived was under surveillance by the Gestapo. Himmler believed that Goebbels would eventually try to see her and wished to prove to Hitler that the Propaganda Minister had broken his word.

Himmler went farther. During the performance of a film in which Miss X was starred there were loud sneers and catcalls from the audience. The police had been instructed beforehand not to interfere. The men responsible for this pandemonium were members of the S.S. in mufti.

Goebbels' throne was tottering. Many considered he was doomed. Not only Himmler, but also Heydrich and Goering, and many Nazis of lesser calibre were gathering 'material' against him. Hitler at that moment had no sympathy for Goebbels: a friend of Miss X, through the good offices of Eva Braun, had tried to put in a good word for the unhappy, love-sick couple, and Hitler believed that Goebbels was behind this manoeuvre. In a fit of indignation he ordered Goebbels to be kept under house arrest in the Propaganda Ministry. The news speedily made the rounds. Many among the initiated professed to know that Baldur von Schirach would be the next Propaganda Minister. Others bet on Alfred Rosenberg.

Goebbels knew that many people believed his career was finished. He also knew that rats are in the habit of leaving sinking ships. Therefore, he was genuinely surprised when a well-known Berlin actress—known for her anti-Nazi views—came to visit him. 'Your colleagues have deserted me,' he remarked wistfully. Suddenly, in a fit of despondency, he dropped his head on the desk and sobbed. He sobbed long and violently and without restraint, and then he told her of Hitler's decree.[1] Miss X's films were withdrawn and prohibited in all of Germany, on Hitler's personal orders. Miss X herself, sick in bed from the excitement, needed many weeks to recover. All this time there was not one word from Goebbels, and she could not understand his silence. Sometimes she would walk up and down near the windows of his office at the Propaganda Ministry. He would stand behind the curtain, but she did not know it. Sometimes she went to a first-night performance knowing that he would be there—she saw him but she did not know whether he had noticed her.

Her next film was cancelled—for technical reasons. The producers continued to be interested in her; there were numerous negotiations which seemed to offer chances, but then they petered out. All negotiations came to a halt in the same way, suddenly, from one day to the other, without explanation. It was always pointed out that the type of film was not desirable for the moment. It was never forbidden—it was simply not desirable.

It took Miss X a long time to understand that she was the victim of a cold, planned boycott. She refused to see it because she wanted to remain in Berlin. She still hoped that Goebbels would come back to her. Finally that hope, too, faded. By the end of 1938 she had run out of money. One day she packed her bags, loaded them into a two-seater car, and with a few thousand marks in her pocket she left Berlin, where only a year before she had been a celebrated actress. No one took any notice of her departure. Quietly she went to Prague.

Six months later, shortly before the war broke out, she returned to Berlin once more. The director of a large film company had hit upon the idea of showing her old films and even giving her a new role, now that so much time had passed, and he invited her to come to Berlin. Magda learned of her rival's contemplated comeback and dictated to her secretary an anonymous letter to herself, signed 'A Woman of the People,' in which she protested against the reappearance of the Czechoslovak star, and forwarded it to Hanke.

Hanke, accompanied by two S.S. men, drove up to the office of the film magnate, introduced himself and slapped his face. This treatment sufficed to make the magnate renounce all further plans he might have had with regard to Miss X.

Curiously enough, Hanke's action was quite unselfish, for at that time Magda was no longer his mistress: she had returned to Goebbels. At first she had resisted all pleas of Goebbels and even Hitler. She was determined to go through with the divorce and to marry Hanke. Finally Hitler lost his patience and ordered her and Goebbels to come to Berchtesgaden. There the official reconciliation took place. A picture was taken and published on the front page of the *Berliner Illustrierte Zeitung*. It showed the sulking faces of Goebbels and Magda, looking in different directions, with a beaming Hitler between them, acting as a link, so to say. If there was anyone left in Germany who did not know something was wrong in the Goebbels household—now he knew it.

Hitler, the marriage-mender, alone looked relatively pleased with himself.

Goebbels' prestige had been severely shaken. Magda knew it. 'Since the Miss X incident my husband has lost his hold over the people,' she said. 'Even the children in the street have caught on to it.' Magda, too, had become a different person; she was no longer willing to sacrifice herself for Goebbels. She wanted to 'live her own life'. She ordered a set of new dresses, she changed her hair-do, and she had her bedroom refurnished; when the furniture arrived she said she did not care for it, and had it sent back. Goebbels spent more and more of his time with other women.

On the surface everything was quiet. The nurse reported: 'To the superficial observer it was a well-organized household with healthy, well-behaved children and loving parents. Behind the scene their marriage was disintegrating, the atmosphere was oppressive and in the long run intolerable. Every day we feared a catastrophe would descend on us.'

III

In February, 1938, Ribbentrop had replaced Foreign Minister Baron Konstantin von Neurath, who was old and tired and altogether too conservative for the Nazis. Ribbentrop was younger and more dynamic, but there was much Goebbels did not like about him. Above all, he was not one of the 'old guard'. It was only a few years before the Nazis came to power that he had joined the Nazi cause and, when Hitler became Reich Chancellor, Ribbentrop was not even a member of the Party. Furthermore, he belonged to the so-called upper-class: he was of the nobility (although only through adoption), and he was rich (although only through marriage).

Once Ribbentrop had moved into the Ministry for Foreign Affairs he notified Goebbels that he could not agree with Neurath's policy to leave all propaganda abroad in the hands of the Propaganda Ministry. Foaming at the mouth with rage, Goebbels rushed to Hitler, but the Fuehrer decided against him. Ribbentrop was right, Hitler said. He was still annoyed over the Miss X incident, and furthermore told Goebbels in so many words that he had not exactly covered himself with glory with his propaganda abroad.

This marked the beginning of an open enmity between Ribbentrop and Goebbels. From that time on the two gentlemen communicated with each other exclusively in writing—to the very last days. Their letters were filled with barely concealed insults and such phrases as, 'I must insist that my instructions …' or, 'This interference with my authority …'

In order to please the foreign press Ribbentrop opened a club in the Fasanenstrasse, where the correspondents could have a decent meal; where they could have good drinks and meet pretty girls. The enraged Goebbels immediately started a competitive place, the Foreign Press Club on Leipziger Platz.

In this initial phase of intramural warfare Ribbentrop gained the upper hand. Only the propaganda attachés stationed abroad remained under Goebbels' control. The Propaganda Minister was afraid of Ribbentrop, but not merely for reasons of prestige. On the occasion of the Party rally in 1938 Ribbentrop told his ambassadors who had been called back from all parts of the world that in the future he no longer wished to see any reports stating that the western powers would oppose Hitler if he made war against Czechoslovakia or Poland.

Goebbels learned of Ribbentrop's strange order and it gave him much food for thought.

IV

For Goebbels did not want war. This does not mean that he was in any way motivated by moral considerations: He merely did not see why Germany should take unnecessary risks. He had always been of the opinion that there was no danger of war, 'unless we ourselves want it,' as he once said to Hermann Rauschning.

The easiest way to win bloodless victories was by means of propaganda. The people had to be alternately incited to the boiling point and intimidated into helpless passivity, while the rest of the world had to be insulted so long until it was only too glad to withdraw from what seemed to be an inevitable conflict. Consequently, in the end there was no conflict at all, while a whole country or a province fell into the hands of those who had conceived this propaganda.

Now it was Czechoslovakia's turn. Goebbels streamlined his propaganda machine and the German radio in particular prepared for a war of nerves. In order to underscore Germany's demands in Czechoslovakia he launched an unprecedented atrocity campaign. The headlines of all German newspapers announced, 'German Women and Children Crushed by Czech Tanks.' The next day they screamed, 'Poison Gas Attack by Czechs in Aussig!' A day later, 'The Czechs are Plundering,' 'The Czechs are Murdering,' and so on.

On 13 September 1938, Konrad Henlein, leader of the Sudeten Germans, published a proclamation to the effect that the life of Sudeten Germans under Czech rule had become unbearable. He concluded with the words, 'We want to return to the Reich!' The author of the proclamation was Goebbels. In the belief that a Cabinet Minister had to use a certain amount of restraint in his utterances he wrote articles under the pseudonym of *Sagax* whenever he wanted to make particularly blunt statements.[2]

Sagax wrote, 'It is pointless to appeal to Czechoslovakia. On the other hand, we would like to ask London and Paris: how long will Prague be permitted to abuse our patience with impunity?' Four days later: 'The cry of our Sudeten German brothers, "Back to the Reich!" will not cease until their aspirations have been fulfilled.'

Goebbels' warning was directed not so much against Prague as against the western powers. It was this type of propaganda which finally caused the aged Chamberlain to visit Hitler in Berchtesgaden and later in Godesberg. It was these journeys of the British statesman which caused Goebbels to make his propaganda still more aggressive. It was like a vicious circle, alternately threatening peace or war. Goebbels hoped to stimulate foreign tourism,[3] but he never tired of singing the praise of the fabulous German air force. He lamented over the terrible injustice done to German citizens in Czechoslovakia or to the Sudeten Germans and at the same time he conjured up the menace of German tanks.

This contradictory propaganda which nevertheless aimed at a very unequivocal goal was ultimately successful. Goebbels hypnotized the world. In Paris and London people could hear the bombs exploding and the statesmen were ready to do anything to prevent such a catastrophe. The Munich Pact, which was a betrayal of Czechoslovakia, was also the result of a war psychosis which, in turn, was precipitated by Goebbels' propaganda.

'People have asked me many times what would have happened if Chamberlain had not come to Germany,' Goebbels said in a speech at the Sportpalast, a few days after the Munich Pact. 'I can only answer them: this particular Mr. Chamberlain *had* to come.'

V

On 7 November 1938, a Polish citizen of Jewish origin, named Herschel Grynszpan, then seventeen years old, broke into the German Embassy in Paris, drew his revolver and shot the secretary of the Legation, Ernst vom Rath. No argument had preceded the assassination, and its motives were never fully explained. Grynszpan said he had wanted to revenge his parents, who had been persecuted in Germany. However, the rumours that he had become the victim of a German *agent provocateur* were never completely silenced. Others suggested that Goebbels had needed a new Reichstag fire.

He acted as though he did. 'Where was Grynszpan during the last three months? Who supported him? Who furnished him with a false passport? Who taught him how to shoot?' he screamed. 'There can be no doubt that he was hidden by a Jewish organization and systematically prepared to execute this cynical crime.'

Thus, Goebbels had established that not one Jew but Jewry as such was involved, and he continued: 'Where must we look for the men behind the scenes? For weeks and months the large Jewish newspapers abroad have been inciting the world to make war on Germany and to murder the leading representatives of the National Socialist régime.'

When Goebbels wrote these lines the German people had already reacted 'spontaneously' against the assassination of the secretary of the Legation, who was not even a National Socialist. Throughout Germany Jewish shops were looted and destroyed, Jews were beaten and killed or taken to concentration camps, synagogues burned down. It was a pogrom of unprecedented proportions and the newspapers could hardly keep up with the developments. Most of the time they confined themselves to such headlines as 'Synagogues Burning'. Thus, from various parts of the Reich ten, twenty, and fifty news items would be published, reporting the destruction of the synagogues or saying laconically that a fire had broken out in a synagogue, without further comment. This lends credence to the belief that certain editors wished to suggest to their readers that they were confronted with a series of planned crimes rather than with a spontaneous outburst of popular fury.

Goebbels, however, noted with satisfaction, 'The outburst of indignation among the population ... shows that the patience of the German people is completely exhausted....'

Ostensibly, the German Government had nothing to do with the pogrom. Goebbels commented very cynically on such 'wild' conjecture, saying: 'If I had organized the demonstrations, there would have been in the streets not a mere few thousand but 400,000 to 700,000 people, and the result would have been quite different and more thorough.'[4]

In reality, Goebbels directed and organized the events behind the scenes. Probably only a handful of people knew this, and even Fritzsche learned of it much later, through Goebbels himself. Goebbels' explanation was, 'On occasion one would just have to be radical.'[5] However, he made a serious error of judgment. To the average citizen it was one thing to read anti-Semitic articles or speeches, but quite another to stand by while one's Jewish neighbour, who had lived for years in the same apartment building and could not possibly be accused of conspiring with the Wise Men of Zion, was robbed and maltreated.

Everywhere in Germany people were horrified at the outrageous treatment of the Jews. Strangers would approach them, shake hands with them and tell them they were ashamed to be Germans. In the trolleys, in the subway, people got up and demonstratively offered their seats to Jews. In the stores they stepped back to wait until the Jews were served. And numerous so-called Aryans risked their heads to hide Jews.

Goebbels, who probably despised the Germans hardly less than the Jews— for he held only contempt for the masses of the people everywhere—had not reckoned with the fact that after five years of constant labour to influence the minds of the Germans there was anyone left to think an independent thought or to experience independent feelings. Particularly as far as the latter was concerned, he was thoroughly mistaken. However, his error was not basic; he was merely ahead of public sentiment by a few years.

When Goebbels learned of the popular reaction against his planned mass murder, he was deeply disturbed. To his assistants he made bitingly sarcastic comments about people who still regarded the Jews as human beings.

Magda thought that his tantrums were somewhat childish. Only a short while ago, with the help of a friend, she had bought a fur coat at a Jewish-owned store because it was cheaper. The travelling bag which she presented to her husband had been purchased from a Jewish firm. Now she was obliged to return some chinaware because it was found that one-fourteenth of the firm's stock was in Jewish hands. Referring to her husband's favourite daughter, she once asked Goebbels, 'And what would you do if Helga married a Jew?' He replied without a moment's hesitation, 'She would no longer be my daughter.'

His pathological hatred of the Jews almost amounted to a satire on anti-Semitism. Typical were the comments he made on 12 November during a discussion of the Jewish question in a conference, presided over by Goering.

Goebbels: 'I am of the opinion that this is our chance to dissolve the synagogues. All those not completely intact shall be razed by the Jews. The Jews shall pay for it. There in Berlin, the Jews are ready to do that ... We shall build parking lots in their places, or new buildings ... I deem it necessary to issue a decree forbidding the Jews to enter German theatres, movie houses and circuses ... I am of the opinion that it is not possible to have Jews sitting next to Germans in vaudeville shows, movies, and theatres....

'It is still possible today for a Jew to share a compartment in a sleeping-car with a German. Therefore, we need a decree by the Reich Ministry for Communications stating that separate compartments for Jews shall be available; in cases where compartments are filled up, Jews cannot claim a seat. They shall be given a separate compartment only after all Germans have secured seats. They shall not mix with Germans, and if there is no more room, they shall have to stand in the corridor.'

Goering: 'In that case, I think it would make more sense to give them separate compartments.'

Goebbels: 'Not if the train is overcrowded.'

Goering: 'Just a moment. There'll be only one Jewish coach. If that is filled up, the other Jews will have to stay at home.'

Goebbels: 'Suppose, though, there won't be many Jews going on the express train to Munich, suppose there would be two Jews in the train and the other compartments would be overcrowded. These two Jews would then have a compartment all to themselves. Therefore, Jews may claim a seat only after all Germans have secured a seat.'

Goering: 'I'd give the Jews one coach or one compartment. And should a case like you mention arise and the train be overcrowded, believe me, we won't need a law. We'll kick him out and he'll have to sit in the toilet all the way!'

Goebbels: 'I don't agree. I don't believe in this. There ought to be a law....

'Furthermore, Jews should not be allowed to sit around in German parks. I am thinking of the whispering campaign in the public gardens at Fehrbellinerplatz. They go and sit with German mothers and their children and begin to gossip and incite....

When, two years later, Grynszpan fell into the hands of the Nazis, Goebbels prepared a monster trial. Suddenly, without explanation, he stopped it before it had got started. Perhaps he was thinking of the disaster of the Reichstag-fire trial. Perhaps there were other reasons. Grynszpan was murdered in cold blood.

VI

In January, 1939—still in the period which Roosevelt had called 'peace by fear'—Hitler advised his most intimate collaborators, including Goebbels, that he was planning to start the war before the year was up.[6]

Goebbels' new propaganda campaign started on 25 February, with an article entitled 'War in Sight?' Not the Third Reich but the western democracies were inciting to war, he said. 'What do the democracies want anyway? Obviously, they lack the necessary instinct to judge the international situation.... As everyone knows, we do not want anything from the democracies.'

Britain's reply soon was forthcoming. As though defending himself against the reproach that he wanted war, Neville Chamberlain stated to a group of British and Americans at the beginning of March that the time had come to help Germany to her feet by an international loan. Chamberlain still believed Hitler wanted peace.

Goebbels had chosen this time to prepare his final propaganda campaign against the remnants of Czechoslovakia. He instructed the press[7] to play up the following themes in headlines and aggressive editorials: (1) The terrorizing of Germans in Czech territory by arrest, the shooting of Germans by state police, the destruction and damaging of German homes by Czech gangsters; (2) the concentration of Czech forces on the Sudeten frontier; (3) the kidnapping, deportation and persecution of Slovakian minorities by the Czechs; the Czechs must get out of Slovakia; (4) secret meetings of Communist functionaries in Prague.

And then, on the morning of 15 March 1939, the bewildered and disturbed citizens of Prague awoke to see German tanks rolling through their streets. In an attempt to justify the dismemberment of Czechoslovakia, Goebbels wrote on 18 March: 'The provinces of Bohemia and Moravia have now returned to the realm of the German Reich ... This ends a historical development which began in the year 1000 when the oldest Bohemian chronicler, the Slav Cosmas, said that Bohemia was a part of Germany.'

With unheard-of cynicism Goebbels acknowledged the impotent protests of the world. Germany should not have marched into Czechoslovakia because, racially, the Czechs were not Germans? It was laughable, Goebbels said. 'The call to protect the Czech people against alleged German oppression sounds really very comical when it is voiced by politicians who have squeezed together all peoples and all races of the world in their British Empire, a procedure not always accomplished by their love of mankind but more often by a good deal of violence. Apart from that, the English fail to impress us as the exponents of our own National Socialist racial principle. We had no idea that the virus of National Socialism had so infected thinking in London that all of a sudden German arguments are produced to justify their cause.'

VII

From a purely polemical point of view Goebbels had won a point; there was no answer to his cynical comments. And yet, he made a decisive error: he believed that things would go on, in fact, must go on in this fashion; he believed that the growing bitterness over Germany's ruthlessness could forever be eliminated by propagandistic means. In the future Adolf Hitler's victories could be won with the printed word alone.

It was the genuine hope to make the war superfluous, although Hitler had already decided to wage it, which was responsible for his error of judgment. Goebbels fell victim to a curious form of self-hypnosis and in the end he was so deluded that he believed he would be able to convince the others as well. 'A new war would shake our European culture to its very foundations,' he stated.

After the Nazis had marched into Prague, the relations between Britain and Germany deteriorated visibly. On 31 March, France and England guaranteed Poland's independence and pledged themselves to assist her if she were attacked by Germany. Later Chamberlain, always with an eye on a German or Italian invasion, gave similar guarantees to Rumania and Greece. Presumably he was far from delighted to commit himself in so many directions, but public opinion in his own country forced him to do so. Goebbels no doubt had impressed the British and French Governments but not the British and French people. Viewed in this light, the activities of British foreign policy was, after all, perhaps a defeat of Goebbels' methods.

Immediately after the Franco-British pact with Poland, Goebbels had written another inflammatory article, 'Who Wants War?' Of course, Germany honestly did not want war. 'If ever in a black hour of history another war should break out in Europe, the cry ought to rise around the whole globe: "The Jews are to blame!"'—two months after came Hitler's decision to wage war that same year. But Goebbels somehow still hoped that war could be avoided.

Of course, certain readjustments would have to be made. For, 'The German people belongs to the so-called have-not nations ... The British ... have a world empire of almost immeasurable proportions ... Our own territory is not large enough to feed our people.' By the end of April, again, 'We all know that there are nations who are swimming in luxury and don't know what to do with their surplus raw materials and their gold reserves; and there are other nations who hardly have the barest necessities of life.'

He never tired of this subject. On 20 May he wrote: 'Germany and Italy are the two great proletarians among the peoples of Europe. The rich nations ... are oppressing whole countries and continents and their accumulated wealth is the result of unscrupulous and immoral looting.' In an article, 'Class Struggle of the Nations?' he wrote: 'There are those who cannot possibly eat everything they produce, while the others who need that surplus must go hungry ... This is the reason for the crises and tensions which are keeping Europe in a turmoil...' Officially he was fighting the outside world, but in reality he fought just as hard against the war trend in his own country. He staked everything on his weapon of propaganda, and he hoped to terrorize the other nations so much that war would become unthinkable.

VIII

Roosevelt was convinced there would be war. As early as 14 April he addressed an appeal to the dictators: 'You realize, I am sure, that throughout the world hundreds of millions of human beings are living today in constant fear of a new war or even a series of wars.... The President then suggested that a ten-year guarantee of peace be given to all independent countries in Europe and in the Near East by Hitler and Mussolini.

Hitler's answer to Roosevelt came in an address to the Reichstag, in which he announced that Germany no longer considered herself bound by the Naval Treaty concluded with Britain in 1935, nor by the Polish Non-Aggression Pact signed in 1934. After this belligerent speech Goebbels should have realized that war was unavoidable. In fact, it seemed as though he was doing his best to make it unavoidable. When on 6 May, in a conciliatory and realistic speech, Poland's Foreign Minister, Colonel Joseph Beck, made a final appeal in favour of a peaceful settlement of the German-Polish question, Goebbels forbade German papers to publish as much as a word of it. After a delay of twenty-four hours German radio stations reported laconically that Beck had made a speech, but there was no reference to its content. Instead, the listeners heard of the crimes committed in Poland against German citizens.

During the next few days this type of propaganda was repeated over and over until it culminated in Goebbels' article 'Bayonets as Signposts', which told of (non-existent) anti-German pogroms raging in Poland.

In a conversation with Fritzsche, Goebbels revealed what was really in his mind when he unleashed this new atrocity campaign against Poland. 'All this talk about war is sheer nonsense,' he said. 'There will be a campaign against Poland, of course. However, there won't be such thing as a war against the West. England will lose her nerve and the upshot will be another Munich.'

There were a few people in England and more in France who felt that another Munich was indeed desirable, and who refused to go to war for the sake of Poland. Goebbels called them 'the voices of reason.' When the former French Minister of Aviation, Marcel Déat, published an article entitled 'Die for Danzig?' Goebbels gave him booming accolades in the press.

However, since there were not enough 'voices of reason', Goebbels came to the conclusion that Germany was in danger of being 'encircled'. The spectre of encirclement had been haunting the realms of German politics ever since the days of Edward VII; it had been heavily played up in the German press in the months preceding the First World War. Now Goebbels resurrected this term and gave it new significance. He was going to convince his own countrymen and the rest of the world that Germany was being ringed, forced to fight-defensively, of course. On 20 May he wrote an article, 'The Encirclers', followed up by another piece on 27 May, 'The Encirclers Once More'. And on 1 July he dwelt at length on the 'Terrible Word of Encirclement'.

The 'terrible word of encirclement' also occurred in all his other articles and speeches at that time. It became the all-embracing slogan, the leitmotiv of

Nazi propaganda. With the help of this word the whole world was, as it were, propagandistically encircled—by Goebbels.

Fritzsche, however, realized that foreign reaction to Goebbels' propaganda campaigns was undergoing a change. When he read the reports of monitored foreign broadcasts he became alarmed. He went to Goebbels, and putting a batch of these reports on his desk urged the Minister to find out for himself how the tone of the British had changed since the Munich Accord. It had become distinctly more aggressive. It was no easy task to convince Goebbels, but Fritzsche presented him every day with fresh evidence, until late one evening the Propaganda Minister called him to his office. 'You are right,' he said. 'The English will go to war. Something must be done to prevent this.'

Goebbels then called on Hitler. The Fuehrer listened to him but, as usual, he alone knew better: Ribbentrop had informed him the British would not march, hence they would not march.

Goebbels went back to his offices. When Fritzsche asked him about the outcome of his talk with Hitler, he merely shrugged his shoulders. Suddenly, in an outburst of despair and rage, he shouted, 'But we haven't built up everything in six years merely to lose it all in the seventh!'

Hitler was in that very hour negotiating a non-aggression pact with Stalin.

IX

Goebbels had little time to prepare the German people for this startling event. On Sunday, 20 August, there were several hints in the press to the effect that Germany and Soviet Russia were about to sign a new trade agreement, but there was no further comment. The accord seemed to be a matter of routine, without any political significance. The only thing worthy of note from this day on was the absence of all anti-Russian tirades in the newspapers. The Propaganda Ministry had given orders that the smear campaign against Bolshevism was to be stopped 'for the time being'.

On Monday, 21 August, at eleven p.m., the momentous news was suddenly broadcast over the radio. The first two paragraphs of the German-Russian Treaty read:

1. The two contracting parties undertake to refrain from any act of violence, any aggressive action, or any attack, against one another, whether individually or jointly with other powers.
2. In case one of the contracting parties should become the object of war-like acts on the part of a third power, the other contracting party will not support that third power in any form.

Most people in Germany and elsewhere were stunned. Since 1933 it had been part of the daily official curriculum to insult the Bolshevists. Newspaper supplements printed in advance still carried anti-Russian stories. For 25 August, the Munich radio had scheduled a lecture, 'I accuse Moscow—The Comintern Plan for World Dictatorship,' which had to be cancelled at the last minute and was replaced by thirty minutes of Russian music. For overnight the Russians and Germans had become comrades-in-arms. How could Goebbels explain this development to his audiences? If he had had more time, the problem would have been much simpler. But here, as many times thereafter, the real significance of the coup was its suddenness: Hitler struck without advance warning. As the Fuehrer wanted to surprise the world, Goebbels was unable to prepare the German people. Neither could he stop all anti-Russian propaganda weeks and months in advance.

Goebbels was confronted with an extraordinary dilemma. As early as spring he had attacked the western powers time and again because they would not declare war on Bolshevism. On 22 April he had complained when Lord Halifax described Bolshevism merely as 'an abstract philosophy.' On 17 June he was outraged over Chamberlain's words, saying, 'If a method can be found to guarantee the co-operation of the Soviet Union in building up a bulwark of peace, England would welcome it.'

Now he was forced to make identical statements, and he did it without batting an eyelid. On the following Tuesday afternoon he proclaimed in his newspaper, *Angriff*: 'The world stands before a towering fact: two peoples have placed themselves on the basis of a common foreign policy which during a long and traditional friendship has produced a foundation for a common understanding.'

Traditional friendship, indeed! During the following days the German press expounded its main theme, namely that the pact had diminished, if not eliminated, the danger of war. Perhaps this was what the Germans wanted to read. Without arguing, they docilely accepted the Pact and everything that was said about the 'traditional friendship' between the two countries. This may have been less Goebbels' personal accomplishment than the result of his monopoly on news. Soviet Russia too had such a monopoly, hence Foreign Commissar Molotov could say with impunity, 'Fascism is a matter of taste'. But everywhere else in the world, where the freedom of the press was still practised, the news of the Pact came as a tremendous shock.

Goebbels himself did not voice an opinion on the whole question. He only mentioned in his New Year's review of the past that 'British attempts to involve Russia in their encirclement manoeuvres have failed'.

X

But, at the time, Goebbels preferred to keep silent. Since 14 July, he had not published a single article, and he was not to publish another in the remaining months of 1939. Never before had Goebbels kept quiet for so long.

He was uneasy about the prospects of the war. He probably wondered— and mentioned his doubts to Fritzsche—whether he himself was not to blame for the turn of events. He had stepped up his propaganda in scope and aggressiveness, hoping to intimidate his opponents to such a degree that they would not dare go to war. In effect, he had scared them so much that now they were willing to risk everything. German propaganda had been too effective; and less of it would have done more good.

There he sat in his sumptuous office, outwardly as calm as ever. There would be war and he would have to make propaganda for war. This might have been avoided, but now it was too late for such speculations. What was there left to be done?

The press campaign against Poland must not be interrupted; on the contrary, its tempo had to be speeded up, if possible. 'S.S. Man Murdered!'—'Two S.A. Men Shot!'—'Innocent Family Beaten to Pulp!'—'All Poland in the Grip of War!'—'Chaos in Upper Silesia!'

What else was there to be done? The complete food rationing plan was presented to Goebbels: 700 grammes of meat per week; 280 grammes of sugar; 110 grammes of marmalade; 2 oz of coffee. Coal, soap, shoes and textiles also were to be rationed. This would be a blow to the German people and no one knew this better than Goebbels. The foreign countries would present the measure as a defeat even before the war had begun.

The last days of the month of August were hot and sultry and oppressive. From a cloudless sky the sun was blazing down on the asphalted streets of Berlin. Everywhere soldiers were on their way to the railway stations, accompanied by their wives and children. Their faces were not radiant with joy, they were serious. The Goebbels-controlled press and radio made no attempt to arouse popular enthusiasm and the Propaganda Minister seemed to think it very appropriate that the people did not look upon the war as a laughing matter.

Since 1933 there had been other momentous hours, when the square in front of Hitler's Reich Chancellery was black with crowds. Now, on 28 August, when Britain's Ambassador returned to Berlin with the final answer of his Government, there were hardly five hundred persons on the Wilhelmplatz. Everywhere in the capital and in the Reich people were opposed to the war and said so. They had no idea of what was at stake. Danzig? The Polish

Corridor? Were these aims worth fighting for? And why were they left in ignorance? Why did their Government let them grope in the dark?

And then, on 1 September 1939, Hitler told the Reichstag at the Kroll Opera House, 'Since 5.45 this morning we have replied to the gunfire of the Poles and from now on bombs will be answered by bombs.' The heat was unbearable. Most of the deputies were perspiring freely. Goering looked as if he had stepped out of a steam bath. Only Goebbels seemed cool and calm, as usual. For the first time he wore his new uniform. With his hands folded in his lap he seemed to listen intently to Hitler's speech, which in the same minute was translated into countless languages and broadcast around the globe. Hitler said: 'I have again donned the uniform which, to me, has been the dearest and the most sacred—the uniform of the soldier. And I will not take it off until victory is secured. Another end I would not wish to survive.'

Did these words have any special meaning to Goebbels' ears? Did they sound to him like a warning of fate? Did he, or could he, divine what was going to happen?

For the first time, that night Berlin was blacked out. Did Goebbels know that never again in his life would he see the lights burning in the nocturnal streets of the capital? There he sat in his enormous Propaganda Ministry and around him was darkened Berlin, a city so utterly different from the one he had known thirteen years ago, when he first arrived, when it was filled with light, colour, music, noise-filled with life.

Much work was to be done. Was it not imperative, above all, to create enthusiasm for the war? Was he not obliged to make the people happy and drunk with anticipated victory, so that they would willingly go to their death, as in 1914?

'No,' said the Propaganda Minister to Fritzsche. 'What the bourgeois calls the temper or the mood of the people is not a decisive factor in wartime. Enthusiasm is only like a straw bonfire, which is of no use to us, and there's no point in awakening it. After all, how long does it last? Let's have no illusions about it: this will be a long and tough war. For this war a firm determination which manifests itself in the daily fulfilment of duties is more necessary than the noisy celebrations of victories.'[8]

Perhaps Goebbels was the only German leader who properly estimated the length and the difficulties of the war. Now he set out to build up a propaganda machine which would be able to withstand setbacks.

This he did achieve. His machine had great strength and resilience and consequently outlasted the German Wehrmacht—and the Third Reich, too.

Two Russian cartoons
depicting Goebbels as
a rat.

PART III: ...AND THE GLORY

CHAPTER X

VICTORIES AND SILENCE

I

On 3 September 1939, the British liner *Athenia* was torpedoed and sunk in the Atlantic on her way to the United States. Hundreds of lives were lost. The passengers, mostly women and children, among them many Americans, were fleeing from war-threatened Europe.

The boat had been sent to the bottom by a German submarine, but this fact was never admitted officially. The German Admiralty kept complete silence—on advice of the Propaganda Ministry.[1]

Goebbels acted with lightning rapidity. Before Britain, the United States or any other country could comment on the incident, before it could be officially established that a British ship had been sunk by a German U-boat, Goebbels came out with the startling 'revelation' that the British themselves had sacrificed the S.S. *Athenia* in order to brand the Germans in the eyes of the world as the real culprits. This clever propagandistic manoeuvre had been engineered by the astute Winston Churchill, First Lord of the Admiralty, Goebbels claimed, but fortunately the Nazis were able to expose the dastardly trick. The headlines of the German papers and the commentators of the German radio were screaming in unison and kept up their farcical barrage for days and weeks. They declared it was absolutely impossible that the Germans were in any way connected with the sinking of the S.S. *Athenia,* for the simple reason that the Fuehrer had explicitly forbidden any and all attacks of this kind.

The Fuehrer himself was so delighted with this type of propaganda that he personally ordered a particularly aggressive article to be published in the *Voelkischer Beobachter,* accusing Churchill of mass murder in connection with the drowned victims. Goebbels, who personally directed the entire campaign, wrote only one article about the *Athenia* affair, which he did not even sign. Otherwise he remained silent until the end of the year. His self-imposed silence soon inspired all sorts of rumours. Some people said that he had been eliminated. This was true only in so far as he had no say in the wording of the German Army communiqués. The army had refused to hand over this privilege. Furthermore, there was Dr Otto Dietrich who had succeeded Walter Funk as Reich Press Chief and who was always present at Headquarters, close by Hitler's side. Hitler had charged him with issuing the so-called *Tagesparole*, a brief directive which the Propaganda Ministry passed on to the newspapers with proper annotations explaining how the war situation had to be presented to the German readers on a day-by-day basis.

Goebbels had tried to take charge of the *Tagesparole*, but Hitler had frustrated his attempts. This was a minor defeat, but certainly no serious threat to Goebbels' power.

Was there any truth in the rumours that the army had never liked Goebbels, and that the generals had suggested to Hitler that he be eliminated? And what about the reported speech Goebbels was to deliver, a warning of coming hard times and calling on every German citizen to make sacrifices, only to have Hitler allegedly veto the idea, saying, 'Do you think that you are the right man to make such a speech?'

Perhaps there was a grain of truth in all these wild tales. Perhaps some of the leading personalities even believed that Goebbels had become superfluous because the German army was winning such speedy and overwhelming victories. Nevertheless, it is extremely unlikely that Hitler ever seriously considered 'liquidating' his Propaganda Minister. Better than anyone else he knew the importance of propaganda in wartime. He himself had written: 'It was only shown during the war to what enormously important results a suitably applied propaganda may lead.'[2]

II

Hitler also knew that he owed the military victories of the first weeks (and throughout 1940) in a large measure to Goebbels' groundwork. The Poles (and later the French), confused and demoralized by the so-called 'war of nerves', were actually beaten before they went into battle. No one can say what would have happened if Goebbels' tactics in Poland and France had been as ineffective as they were with regard to Britain.

Goebbels began to size up his propaganda counterparts, and what he saw did not tend to fill him with awe or respect: the foe's propagandistic tactics were childishly amateurish. While the German armies in Poland were racing from one victory to the other, British planes appeared over Germany and dropped—leaflets, with Chamberlain's pretty-please plea that the Germans break with Hitler while there was still time.

What an incredible approach, devoid of all psychological insight! Goebbels contemptuously described the inept Britons as 'propaganda apprentices', and Fritzsche introduced the coined expression to his radio audiences. Goebbels went further. He realized with remarkable perspicacity that Allied propaganda had no ideological content: not a word was mentioned about the so-called war aims. None of the Allied propagandists seemed to know why this war was being fought. Here was where Goebbels' propaganda set in, and in hundreds of variations the question was asked the enemy: Why are you fighting this silly war?

Since the Allies did not know why they were fighting the war, they ought to stop fighting. Since they did not stop fighting, they, and they alone, were responsible for continuing the conflict. But was there any war at all? If there was, Goebbels' propaganda machine ignored it. The word war was hardly ever used in the German press. The war against Poland was a campaign or, at best, a punitive expedition, but nothing more.

The result of these underplaying tactics was that the great victories in Poland did not present themselves as such to the average German's consciousness. When the German troops were standing before Warsaw after one week's fighting the whole world was profoundly shaken, but all was quiet in the streets of the large German cities. Goebbels did not try to arouse enthusiasm where there was none. The Propaganda Ministry did nothing to embroider on the communiqués issued by Army Headquarters in plain, severe, military language. The German population was supposed to read between the lines: here are the facts, nothing but the facts, they speak for themselves; but our facts are correct and our reports alone are reliable.

Moreover, this accuracy was meant to influence public opinion abroad, and it did. Soon word got around that the German reports were more reliable than the Allied communiqués; that the Germans released information which the Allies would publish two or three days later.

On the other hand, it was true that for the time being the German reports had nothing to conceal—for they announced a string of successes. This was probably the reason why Goebbels could afford to dispense with censorship for foreign correspondents. As a matter of fact, during the first year of the war a foreign newspaperman stationed in Berlin could write as he pleased, while his colleagues in Paris and London had to cope with considerable restrictions. In Paris, the censors staged veritable orgies of stupidity. And an American correspondent in London, who asked to see one of the leaflets which were dropped over Germany by the million, was told that this could not be permitted because 'the leaflets might fall into the hands of the enemy'!

Propaganda apprentices....

Goebbels still remained silent. He was busy revamping and perfecting the machinery of his propaganda down to the last detail. He began to compose so-called training letters for his propaganda offices in the various *Gaue*. These documents of no more than 2,000 words dealt with all political questions of the day and demonstrated how they were to be handled from a propaganda point of view. In September and October, 1939, for instance, they contained these typical instructions:

'Our most dangerous and astute opponent ... was, and is, England.... England has left no stone unturned to seal off Germany with the ring of encirclement. The German people today are no longer split up into dozens of parties, but they form a unified community.... After termination of the Polish campaign it is certain that the conflict with England will be fought on one front. If the German people were leaderless, they would also be defenceless.... The idea of sinking the S.S. *Athenia* originated in Churchill's mind, for the purpose of dragging the United States into the maelstrom of the war....'

And most important of all: 'Although the German news policy still serves informational purposes, its principal design is to instruct and direct public opinion.' In other words, Goebbels did not intend whatsoever to loosen his dictatorial grip on the dissemination of news.

III

Outwardly, little had changed as far as the Propaganda Ministry was concerned. Day and night, plain-clothes men now patrolled up and down in front of the building, and Goebbels' car, like those of other cabinet members, was preceded and followed by policemen on motor-cycles. Inside the building all loudspeaker installations were closely guarded. Less important sections, such as the filing department and archives, were moved to the attics, while the radio, press and film divisions were shifted to the main building, enabling Goebbels to be in constant direct communication with them. The Propaganda Ministry was put on a round-the-clock basis and all employees were required to stay in the building for twenty-four hours at a time, after which they would take twenty-four hours off. Army cots and blankets were provided for those who spent the night there.

Very few male employees of the Ministry were inducted into the army or navy, because Goebbels was of the opinion that propagandists could do more useful work in his office than at the front. He posted a notice prohibiting voluntary enlistments. It was not until the last two years of the war that he permitted his associates to serve in the armed forces.

IV

Long before Goebbels could know that he would be excluded from editing the army communiqués, he realized that such a communiqué, regardless of whether it made drab or stimulating reading, would never do in a protracted war. He needed an instrument to bring the war to the home front, to make it fascinating and alive to the average newspaper reader. With this aim in mind he created the so-called P.K. (*Propaganda-Kompagnien*, or propaganda units).

Even before the war started a list had been compiled under Goebbels' supervision, containing the names of all newspapermen whom Goebbels considered suitable for duty as war correspondents. These reporters attended an eight-week military training course which included lectures in the specialized art of war reporting. The idea was to enable them to write with expert knowledge about a certain battalion or regiment to which they would be attached. Before they were sent to the front they had to pass an examination.[3]

Goebbels described these propaganda battalions as something entirely new and unique in the field of war reporting, which was perfectly true. (The idea was later copied by the U.S. Marines.) 'We still remember from the days of the world war that a few journalists straggling way behind the line would hang around the soldiers, pick up a word here and there, and then would write their story which would give readers at home a completely distorted and inaccurate picture of military events,' he wrote. The modern war correspondents, he said, were real soldiers, 'cold-blooded and fearless' and just as much exposed to danger as the man with the flame-thrower. 'Think of that when you read your papers, or listen to the front reports on the radio, or see the news-reel at your neighbourhood movie,' he concluded, glorifying his own propagandists.

The news-reel was particularly dear to his heart. It was made by cameramen who were inducted into the propaganda battalions. They shot whatever scenes seemed important to them, having a great deal of latitude in the choice of their subjects, for the directives they received were of a general nature. The films were taken to Berlin by special courier, censored at the Propaganda Ministry and then shown in the next news-reel. Sometimes Goebbels was dissatisfied with the reels. Then he would make a scene and scream and rage and declare that the shots were still not interesting enough, and that his cameramen had still not shown enough daring, and he would demand still better performances.

The cameramen stationed on the warships had a particularly unfortunate assignment. The ships usually were in port and there was nothing else to do but shoot scenes of the crews eating, or playing deck games. Whenever Goebbels saw such shots he lost his composure altogether. On the other hand, he was delighted with shots of diving Stuka planes, parachute jumps, air battles, truck drivers handling a load of dynamite, life in a submarine, and so on, all of which showed that the cameraman had risked his neck.

V

Despite his concern for colourful war reporting, Goebbels never lost sight of the most important point, which was his monopoly of news. In order to prevent any infraction of this monopoly he announced, on 1 September, that the Germans were no longer allowed to listen to foreign radio programmes. Whoever was caught was usually sent to jail. And if it could be proved that anyone had spread the news he had heard clandestinely, such offence called for hard labour or the death penalty.

Goebbels himself conceived this decree, which exempted virtually no one, not even the Cabinet ministers. Goebbels alone was entitled to grant a dispensation, which he did only in rare cases. Many prominent officials of the Propaganda Ministry were not allowed to listen to foreign broadcasts. They attended important functions in complete ignorance of a foreign commentary on this or that question. Only those who had to prepare the answers of the German radio to the news circulated abroad enjoyed unlimited freedom in this respect. According to stenographer Jacobs, Goebbels would permit certain ministers, for instance Rosenberg or Schwerin von Krosigk, to listen to foreign broadcasts, only to withdraw his permission later.

Although the decree became effective on the first day of the war, Goebbels had been very reluctant to take such a drastic step. He would have preferred to avoid it, if it had been possible. For it was an open admission of the existence of censorship.

For the propagandist there are two kinds of censorship: one which is admitted, the other which is not. For instance, censorship in the German-occupied territories was hidden from the readers. On Goebbels' instructions, the newspapers were not allowed to have empty spaces in their columns; for any article cut by the censor there had to be a substitute; otherwise the readers would have become suspicious.

Radio censorship, on the other hand, had to be conceded from the start. The law addressed itself not to a small group of editors but to millions of listeners, who were told which programmes were permissible, and which were not.

From the propagandist's point of view this was very dangerous, and Goebbels did everything to take the sting out of the unpleasant decree. He spent much time and ink in explaining to the docile Germans why they should not listen to foreign programmes. His principal argument was the reliability of the German radio as compared to foreign transmissions which, he claimed, consisted largely of lies. Very adroitly he established a special statistical department to record and count the lies that were circulated in the foreign press and radio. Soon Fritzsche could report 'in seven weeks' war a count of 108 cases.' It was unimportant that this figure was inaccurate. The public in general believed in the infallibility of these statistics and lent less and less credence to reports from abroad.

Other arguments were less fortunately chosen. Probably the most unsuitable of all was formulated by Goebbels in a speech after six months of war: 'Just as the soldier may not mutilate his body in order to render himself unfit for front-line service, the German citizen on the home front may not mutilate himself by listening to the lies of foreign propaganda, to lose, if only for one brief moment, the strength of his faith in our fighting forces.'

If anyone else had launched such an idea, Goebbels would have ridiculed him in his own inimitable manner. As it was, the German people themselves made fun of his solemn and untimely announcement. Goebbels, in turn, tried to make fun of those who continued to listen to foreign broadcasts, despite the penalties involved. 'We have the doubtful pleasure of listening daily to British transmissions,' he wrote. 'Their broadcasters are so miserably incompetent that it turns our stomachs.'

But no one knew better than Goebbels that all these tirades were of no avail. There was only one thing that kept the people from listening: fear. They were constantly afraid of being found out, arrested and sentenced. Not Goebbels but Himmler prevented them from listening: more than 1,500 people had already been sentenced to concentration camp, jail and hard labour for tuning in on London during the first year of the war.

However, the overwhelming majority of clandestine listeners were never caught. Goebbels' monopoly of news was shattered. Slowly but inexorably foreign news reports began to circulate in Germany, although most people were still suspicious of foreign sources. Gradually the discrepancy between official and 'unofficial' news became more and more flagrant and resulted in peculiar, sometimes hilarious, situations. For instance, there was the case of the U-boat officer who had been reported missing; according to the German Admiralty he was dead. Shortly before the funeral service began, many friends had informed the grief-stricken parents that their son was not drowned but that the British radio had just announced he had been taken prisoner. It was impossible to cancel the service without arousing the suspicions of the authorities. It had to take place all the same, although every one of the 'mourners' knew that there was no cause for sorrow.

The decree against listening to foreign broadcasts contributed a great deal to fomenting dissatisfaction among the population. Goebbels, who held his finger on the pulse of the German people, and was regularly informed of any change of its temper and mood, knew it.

He also knew that the atmosphere could not be improved by further news of German victories. The very fact that these victories were won so easily had an almost paradoxical effect on the average German: he believed that the war was a push-over and that the soldiers were having a pleasant time of it, while the home front was suffering hardships. Goebbels sent his men into the factories and always received the same information: dissatisfaction was growing. Goebbels and Labour Minister Robert Ley instructed their propagandists to make promises to the workers: after the war Hitler would build six million new houses and sumptuous hotels for workers on vacation, he would raise their wages, and so on. The workers listened, and were unimpressed.

Aware of the whispered complaints Goebbels tried to answer them. The workers were saying that Party officials dodged front-line service. '95 per cent of all Hitler Youth leaders have been drafted. 400 youth leaders alone have fallen in the Polish campaign. 68 per cent of all National Socialist S.A. men are today fighting in our ranks....' Was anyone saying that Hitler had not kept his promise to avoid a two-front war? 'Contrary to the situation in the World War we are completely safe in the East. The two-front war is a matter of the past.'

Shortly after the termination of the Polish campaign—about the time he wrote these lines—Goebbels decided to found another newspaper. He had long stopped writing for *Angriff* because its tone was too aggressive. A Cabinet Minister had to preach from a more dignified pulpit. The *Voelkischer Beobachter*, on the other hand, was too much the organ of the old Munich clique to make him feel at home in its columns.

The new publication was to be in the nature of a weekly periodical. Its back-bone would be an article by Goebbels, in which he would speak to the Germans in a more personal vein, to interpret for them the problems of the time, and to create a more intimate contact with his millions of readers. He wanted to speak to the people as a journalist, not as a Cabinet Minister, he told his colleagues.

This was the official reason for the undertaking. Unofficially, he confessed to Fritzsche that the German press was becoming more boring and monotonous every day. He said: 'The press must have more freedom. No one can write a decent article if he is hemmed in by barbed wire and gets hit over the head with a sledgehammer at the slightest provocation.'

Fritzsche replied: 'I agree with you. But you, and not I, have introduced the barbed wire and the sledgehammer.'[4] Goebbels was silent. In his new weekly he hoped to give a good example for raising the standard of the German press.

Das Reich appeared for the first time on 26 May 1940. Goebbels wrote only two leaders and then for many months he contributed nothing. It was only at the end of 1940 that he broke his silence again.

VI

Goebbels did not consider it important to smother the Allies with German propaganda, for contrary to his colleagues in Paris and London (the 'propaganda apprentices') he knew that major or minor revolts in the first war year could not be conjured up by propaganda magic, unless they were preceded by decisive military defeats. Goebbels' most important task was to succeed, where his colleague Ribbentrop had so spectacularly failed: to localize the conflict and to keep other powers out of the war.

His propaganda battle was fought on many grounds: in Zurich, Bern and Basel, in Stockholm, in Ankara and Budapest, in Lisbon and Madrid, in Washington. It was fought with every available means, from bribes and threats, whispering campaigns and films demonstrating the overpowering strength of the Wehrmacht, to statistics on German production and promises. It was waged most intensively in Switzerland and in the United States.

In the First World War the German-speaking part of Switzerland, with its key cities Zurich, Basel and Bern, had been friendly to the German cause. This time the atmosphere was definitely hostile to the Nazis. Goebbels despatched one of his most talented agents, Dr Klaus Huegel, who was also a member of the Intelligence Service, to Switzerland. He contacted a number of personalities who sympathized with the Nazis. As the Nazi Party in Switzerland had been banned, several substitute organizations were founded. It is unlikely that the Nazis intended to involve Switzerland in the war on the side of Germany. On the other hand, it was imperative for them to keep the country from joining the Allies; above all, the frank language of the Swiss press had to be restrained at all cost.

A few weeks after Huegel's journey to Switzerland 200 prominent Swiss citizens sent a petition to the Federal Government demanding censorship of the press. 'In complete ignorance of the peculiarity of our country, and dominated by the nebulous concept of an international world democracy, some spokesmen have tried to present its domestic and foreign policy as being akin to that of foreign democracies,' it said. 'Hand in hand with the insults of foreign governments, derived from the vocabulary of international emigrants, goes a planned, terroristic action which casts suspicions on many of our citizens who are advocating friendly relations ... with all neighbouring states.'

Goebbels himself could not have expressed it better. If the petition of these 200 had been accepted (it never was, although the move indirectly helped to tone down the militant attitude of the Swiss press) no Swiss paper would have been permitted to criticize Germany, and the most aggressive Swiss Nazis would have been released from jail to continue their conspiratorial activities.

Evidently the struggle for the isolation of the United States was of much greater importance, and had begun even before the outbreak of the war. The employees of the German consulates worked under the direction of the Foreign Division of the Propaganda Ministry, that is to say, under Herr von Giennanth, of the New York Consulate General, who had been sent over by Goebbels himself. These agents tried to persuade American newspapers to subscribe to the Transocean News Service; they offered tremendous bribes—in 1940 and 1941 approximately one million dollars were spent for such propaganda purposes. They launched whispering campaigns insinuating that Germany had practically won the war. Such propaganda agencies as the German Railway Information Service; the German-American Chamber of Commerce, and others worked overtime. The German radio, trying to create a friendlier atmosphere in the United States, noted with satisfaction that most Americans wished to remain neutral and that the 'warmongers' were distinctly in the minority. The American people were assured that a German victory meant no threat to their independence.

Happily for Goebbels, part of his struggle was waged by certain Americans, although they probably never realized it and were not in the pay of German propaganda.

Goebbels himself tried to win over the foreign correspondents in Berlin, but failed to impress them when he had them classified as industrial workers, which entitled them to twice the ordinary bread, meat and butter rations. The absence of any form of censorship was better suited to please them. The immediate consequence was that the Berlin correspondents began to dominate the columns of the neutral press, pushing their Paris and London colleagues to the background.

But Goebbels was too inconsistent to exploit this advantage. He was angered that the neutral papers dared to speak their mind, and he gave them his own interpretation of neutrality. 'There must not be a flagrant discrepancy between the neutrality of a state and the neutrality of its public opinion. The neutral countries would do well to remain really neutral, that is to say, their governments should not be satisfied merely with issuing timid declarations of neutrality, while their unrestrained public opinion continues to indulge in a veritable cannonade of savage insults against the Reich and its National

Socialist regime.... A physically weak person who finds himself a spectator at a boxing match had better stay in respectful distance of the two fighters.'

This was an open threat. And, indeed, Goebbels found that of all the devices he had used in his efforts to keep other powers out of the war his threats worked better than anything else. His most effective threats were his war films. Influential personalities in neutral countries were invited to see the picture of the Polish campaign. The sight of burning villages, roaring dive-bombers, bombardments of unprecedented power, of seemingly miles and miles of tanks, conveyed an eloquent message to the horror-stricken audiences: This is what will happen to you if you insist on picking a fight with us.

While the war against France was still on, he ordered a second film to be made, *Sieg im Westen* (Victory in the West). Here, too, the accent was to be on destruction.

VII

Weeks and months before the start of the Polish campaign the German press and radio had been full of atrocity stories about the fate of German citizens at the hands of their 'Polish oppressors'. But the blow in the West was to come as a surprise. Hence Goebbels had to keep quiet, and even his closest associates were completely unsuspecting when the war in the West started in earnest. During the night of the German invasion of Holland and Belgium, Goebbels notified six or eight of his colleagues, asking them to be in his office early the next morning. And on 10 May 1940, at 8 a.m., Goebbels gave Fritzsche two radio speeches which had to be broadcast at once. There was so little time that Fritzsche could not even read over his script before he stepped to the microphone.

On the other hand, a great deal of preliminary work had been accomplished. Throughout the so-called 'phony' war the French people were subject to a war of nerves which had been planned down to the last detail in the Propaganda Ministry. Its principal weapons were whispering campaigns, thousands of letters sent to private citizens and, of course, violent attacks over the radio, for which purpose Goebbels had hired several French traitors, who tried to persuade their countrymen that 'England means to fight this war to the last Frenchman.' The great writer, Jean Giraudoux, French Minister of Information, understood the nature of this propaganda war. 'For two years we have been in the middle of Hitler's war,' he declared on 14 December 1939, quoting Hitler to illustrate his point. '"Our real wars will be waged before the military operation.... Artillery preparation for attack in trench warfare will be replaced in the future by psychological decomposition of the enemy through propaganda before the armies can go into action."' And Giraudoux added: 'We are fighting this kind of war, too. We think we are gaining by doing so.' Alas, he no doubt hoped so, but at no time was he Goebbels' equal as a propagandist.

The French soldiers who manned the Maginot Line were subject to a propagandistic onslaught which climaxed everything experienced hitherto. If a Frenchman left cover, no one shot at him. German officers, with the air of tennis players who patiently wait until their opponent has gone back into position before they continue the match, allowed him to get away unharmed. Sometimes at night French soldiers were commandeered to do repair work at some point of the fortifications. Suddenly floodlights would be directed to the spot, but loudspeakers assured the startled Frenchmen that they had nothing to fear. The Germans would not shoot but only wanted to help them by providing indispensable illumination.

Then there was the propagandistic exploitation of Military Intelligence. Half an hour after the French President had arrived at a certain section of the front—a trip shrouded in secrecy and preceded by elaborate precautions—German loudspeakers would announce the President's exact whereabouts. Another time, when Churchill visited the Maginot Line and was sitting down for lunch, German amplifiers gave a detailed account of the menu he was just being served.

Goebbels had many other tricks up his sleeve; for example, leaflets with predictions which Nostradamus allegedly had made hundreds of years before, invented by Goebbels himself and predicting an early German victory. Then he had tens of thousands of copies of the Belgian periodical, *La Guerre de 1939*, reprinted, without changing a word of the text. Only the crossword puzzles were replaced, and the solution of the new puzzles was a strongly demoralizing text. The periodicals were sent to French soldiers via Switzerland. They were of course passed by the censor, since no one dreamed of investigating the crossword puzzles.

Pornographic pictures were circulated among French soldiers to arouse their fear and jealousy: photographs showing how their women were deceiving them with the British, while they themselves were immobilized in the Maginot Line. They also received letters to that effect. Such letters were written not only by Goebbels' propaganda agents but also by the French Communists, who were then opposed to the war and engaged in the same demoralizing tactics. Both Moscow and Berlin declared that the war was engineered by the British. In Moscow they were called capitalists, in Berlin plutocrats, but that was the only difference.

1. *Above left:* Goebbels as a student, *c.* 1916/1917.
2. *Above right:* Bavarian Freikorps, *c.* 1919, in somewhat celebrative national costume.
3. *Below left:* Friedrich Gundolf (1880-1931), *c.* 1916. Gundolf, professor of literature at the University of Heidelberg, was Goebbels' favourite teacher.
4. *Below right:* Freikorps, *c.* 1919, less decoratively dressed and armed with what appears to be a Schwerer 24-cm Flügelminenwerfer.

5. *Above left:* Walther Rathenau (1867-1922). Rathenau was a politician of Jewish descent and held several positions such as minister of reconstruction and foreign minister. He was assassinated in 1922.

6. *Above right:* Alfred Rosenberg, Adolf Hitler and Friedrich Weber of the Freikorps Oberland during the Munich Beer Hall Putsch, 9 November 1923.

7. *Below left:* Julius Lippert (1895-1956). Lippert participated in the assassination of Foreign Minister Walther von Rathenau.

8. *Below right:* Nazi supporters marching past Viktor Lutze, Gregor Strasser, Joseph Goebbels and Joseph Wagner at Herne, Westphalia, 1926.

9. *Above:* Front rank, from left to right: Gauleiter Joseph Wagner, Gregor Strasser, Joseph Goebbels, and Viktor Lutze. The begining of Nazi Party procession at Herne, Westphalia.

10. *Below left:* Goebbels with the first co-workers of the Berlin administrative district, 1927. He had been appointed Gauleiter of Berlin in October 1926.

11. *Below right:* A Nazi rally at Nuremberg in 1928 with a slightly slimmer Hermann Goering in the foreground.

12. *Above left*: Franz Ritter von Epp (1868-1946). He served as the head of the NSDAP's Military-Political Office from 1928 to 1945.

13. *Above right*: Horst Wessel's party membership card.

14. *Below left*: Gregor Strasser (1892-1934). On 30 June 1934, the 'Night of the Long Knives', Strasser was arrested and killed on Hitler's personal order by the Berlin Gestapo.

15. *Below right*: Party members outside the Communist Party headquarters during a ceremony in remembrance of Horst Wessel.

16. *Above left:* A studio photograph of Goebbels, *c.* 1930.
17. *Above right:* Hotel Kaiserhof in Wilhelmplatz.
18. *Below:* Goebbels with Geli Raubal and Hitler at Obersalzburg, *c.* 1929.

19. *Above:* Hitler at a rally in Westphalia, *c.* 1931. The strain is visible on his face as he hangs on hard to the *blutfahne*.

20. *Left:* The wedding of Magda and Joseph, December 1931.

21. *Below:* Goebbels meets enthusiastic *Bund Deutscher Mädel* — the League of German Girls.

22. *Above:* Magda and Joseph Goebbels electioneering, March 1932.

23. *Left:* Goebbels at Nuremberg, 1933, annotating notes for his speech.

24. *Below:* Magda and Joseph Goebbels with Hitler and other guests, a short while after they were married, *c.* 1932.

25. & 26. *Top and above left:* The night of book burning, 10 May 1933. On 6 April 1933, the Main Office for Press and Propaganda of the German Student Association proclaimed a nationwide 'Action against the Un-German Spirit', which was to climax in a literary purge or 'cleansing' (*Säuberung*) by fire. In his speech on 10 May 1933, Goebbels said: *'German men and women! The age of arrogant Jewish intellectualism is now at an end!.... You are doing the right thing at this midnight hour—to consign to the flames the unclean spirit of the past. This is a great, powerful, and symbolic act.... Out of these ashes the phoenix of a new age will arise.... Oh Century! Oh Science! It is a joy to be alive.'*

27. *Above right:* Hitler and Goering with Reichspresident Paul von Hindenburg, at a ceremony to present Hindenburg with an estate in Prussia, 6 September 1933.

28. *Right:* The Reichstag Fire, 27 February 1933. A communist, Marinus Van der Lubbe, was arrested, but he had been set up, and the main culprits were the Nazis who had primed the building with inflammables.

29. *Below:* Four Nazi thugs sing outside a Woolworth store, believing the founder was Jewish, March 1933.

30. On 1 May 1934 Hitler addressed a vast concourse of two million young Germans on the Templehof Aerodrome near Berlin. His voice was carried by 122 loudspeakers to the furthest edge of the multitude nearly a mile away.

31. Joseph Goebbels, Werner von Blomberg and the French Ambassador at the Berlin Festival, 2 March 1934.

32. Reichsbishop Muller in Nuremberg for the Nazi Congress, 8 September 1934. Although a Catholic himself, Goebbels was later to lead an assault against the Church.

33. *Above:* Goering and Goebbels at the opening of the automobile exhibition, 1935.

34. *Below:* General Karl Litzman (1850-1936) at his 85th birthday celebration, on which occasion he was given a car, 24 January 1935. Litzman became an active member of the NSDAP in his eighties.

35. & 36. *Hitlerjugend*. The Hitler Youth was first formed in 1922 for male youths between the ages of 14 to 18, and by 1933 numbered 2.3 million.

37. *Above:* Hitler and Goebbels watch a projectionist display a propaganda film.

38. *Below:* Hitler addressed 270,000 children — members of the *Hitlerjugend* — in the Lustgarten on 1 May 1935 as part of the May Day celebrations. In his speech he said that the country was experiencing troubled times, but that the future would be bright. A boy bugler is on the right sounding a fanfare.

39. Goebbels announces
the conscription order
in the Berlin Sports
Stadium, 18 March 1935.

40. Hitler saluting *Hitlerjugend* in thousands, Nuremberg, 1935.

41. A scowling Goebbels, *c.* 1935.

42. A studio photograph of Magda Goebbels, *c.* 1935.

43. Goebbels and Goering meet with firemen and others after a fire on the North-South S-Bahn subway line at Potsdamer Platz in Berlin, 28 December 1936. The fire destroyed vital equipment and the line did not become operative until 1939.

44. Goebbels, Hess and Hitler at a *Hitlerjugend* ceremony, *c.* 1936.

45. A film award ceremony, 9 June 1936. From left to right: Edda Ciano, daughter of Benito Mussolini; Joseph Goebbels; film director Leni Riefenstahl; the German ambassador in Italy, Ulrich von Hassel; Magda Goebbels; and the Italian ambassador in Berlin, Bernardo Attolico. Ulrich von Hassell was a member of the German Resistance and was executed in the aftermath of the failed 20 July 1944 plot. Helene Bertha Amalie 'Leni' Riefenstahl (1902-2003) was a film director. Her most famous film was *Triumph of the Will*, a documentary film made at the 1934 congress in Nuremberg of the Nazi Party. Riefenstahl's prominence in the Third Reich, along with her personal association with Hitler, destroyed her career following Germany's defeat. She was arrested in 1945, but released without any charges.

46. *Above*: The XIth modern
Olympiad. Germany built a
new 100,000-seat track and
field stadium, six gymnasiums,
and many other smaller arenas.
Leni Riefenstahl was
commissioned by the German
Olympic Committee to film the
Games. Her film, titled
Olympia, pioneered many of
the techniques now common
in the filming of sports. Hitler
saw the Games as an opportunity
to promote his government
and ideals of racial supremacy,
and the official Nazi party paper,
Völkischer Beobachter wrote
in the strongest terms that Jews
and Black people should not be
allowed to participate in the
Games. However, when
threatened with a boycott of the
Games by other nations, he
relented and allowed Black
people and Jews to participate.

47. The Olympic Torch, 1 August 1936.

48. Goebbels and Blomberg at a festival
in Bayreuth, July 1937.

49. The Propaganda Ministry, Wilhelmplatz, 1936. The Reich Ministry of Public Enlightenment and Propaganda (*Reichsministerium für Volksaufklärung und Propaganda* or *Propagandaministerium*) was based in the Ordenspalais in Berlin-Mitte on the Wilhelmplatz across from the Reich Chancellery. The Ordenspalais was built in 1737 and completely destroyed in 1945.

50. Goebbels in military uniform with Goering, 9 September 1936. The two men got on reasonably well until 1941 when Goebbels put the blame for the failure of the air war on Goering. From this point onwards there was open hostility.

51. Hitler with Goebbels on the balcony of the Ministry, 1 November 1936, when Hitler came to congratulate his Minister on his 39th birthday.

58. *Top*: Hitler,
Goebbels, Hess,
and Goering at the
time of Hitler's
speech at the Sport
Palace in Berlin,
Monday,
26 September 1938,
about the question
of Czechoslovakia.

59. *Middle:* Goebbels
was fascinated
by the film industry
and was an avid film
watcher. On
Thursday 28 July
1938 he was on
the set of *Prussian
Love Story*
(*Preussische
Liebesgeschichte*).
On Goebbels' left
is his first adjutant,
Karl Hanke,
standing next to a
star of the film,
Willy Fritsch who
played Prince
Wilhelm. To Fritsch's
left is Vittorio
Mussolini. The film
was made in 1938,
but was not passed
by the Nazi censors
because of
disapproval of the
star Lida Baarová,
whose affair with
Goebbels was ended
at Hitler's instigation
by the time the
film was finished.
It was released in
West Germany in
March 1950.

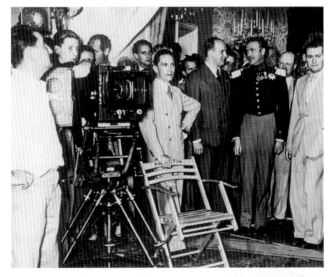

60. *Bottom*: The May
Day rally at
Lustgarten, *c.* 1938.

61. *Left:* Alfred Ernst Rosenberg (1893-1946). Rosenberg was executed on
   16 October 1946.
62. *Right:* Ulrich Friedrich Wilhelm Joachim von Ribbentrop (1893-1946).
   Ribbentrop was executed on 16 October 1946.

63. *Left:* Eva Braun (1912-1945). Eva Braun committed suicide by cyanide,
   30 April 1945.
64. *Right:* Karl Paul Immanuel von Haase (1885-1944). On 20 July 1944, after
   the failed assassination of Hitler at the Wolf's Lair in East Prussia, Haase ordered
   Major Otto Ernst Rehmer to seal off the government quarter in Berlin during the
   subsequent coup d'état attempt. Rehmer later removed the cordon and Haase was
   arrested by the Gestapo that evening whilst he was dining with Joseph Goebbels.
   He was sentenced to death and hanged later the same day at Plötzensee Prison in
   Berlin.

65. *Above:* Magda and Joseph Goebbels with the three eldest children at the Berghof, 1938.

66. *Below:* Goebbels looking at television set 'E 1' at the Radio and Televison exposition, Berlin, July 1939.

67. The Italian
consul Edoardo
(Dino) Alfieri
(1886-1966), in the
company of Goebbels
and Hitler, visits
the Great German
Art Exhibition, *Haus
der Deutsche Kunst*,
on the 'Day of
German Art', Sunday
16 July 1939. This
photograph has been
included to
demonstrate the
diminutive stature of
Goebbels.

68. The new Reich
Chancellery on
the corner of
Hermann Goering
Straße and Voßtraße,
1939.

69. An inside
view of the opulent
Reichskanzlei, 1939.

70. *Top:* Prince Paul, regent of Yugoslavia, at a visit with Goebbels at Schwanenwerder, near Potsdam. Albert Speer is to the right.

71. *Middle:* The street view of Schwanenwerder, 1942.

72. *Bottom:* A family photograph, 1942, with Harald cloned into the image. After the death of his father, Günther Quandt, in 1954, the capital belonging to Quandt Holding was divided equally between the two sons Herbert and Harald (who had been adopted by Goebbels). He served as a lieutenant in the Luftwaffe during the War. He was injured and captured in Italy in 1944; he was released in 1947. In 1959, the Quandt family acquired a majority shareholding in the Bayerische Motoren Werke (BMW).

73. *Above:* Werner Naumann (1909-1982), centre of picture. Naumann was State Secretary in Goebbels' Ministry of Public Enlightenment and Propaganda. He was present in the Führerbunker in Berlin in late April 1945.

74. *Left:* Goebbels making a speech on the steps of the Propaganda Ministry, *c.* 1940.

75. *Below:* Goebbels with a new recruit to the *Deutsches Jungvolk, c.* 1942.

76. Hitler and entourage at the reception for Japanese Foreign Minister Matsuoka, in the Reich Chancellery, April 1941.

77. *Left:* Goebbels with his children, 1943.

78. *Right:* Hans Georg Fritzsche (1900-1953) in his cell at Nuremberg. Under Goebbels' Ministry he headed the radio department before being promoted to the News Section at the Ministry. In mid-1938 he became deputy to Alfred Berndt at the German Press Division. In May 1942 Goebbels took personal control of the division, and Fritzsche returned to radio work for the Ministry as Plenipotentiary for the Political Organization of the Greater German Radio.

79. *Above:* Hitler at the Wolf's Lair, East Prussia, immediately after the failed assassination attempt, Thursday 20 July 1944.

80. *Left:* Otto-Ernst Rehmer (1912-1997). Rehmer played a decisive role in stopping the 1944 plot. He was sent to arrest Goebbels, but Goebbels managed to get through to Hitler on the telephone, and handed the handset to Rehmer sating 'do you recognise this voice?' After the War he co-founded the Sozialistische Reichspartei (SRP), advancing Holocaust denial, and is considered the 'Godfather' of the post-war Nazi underground.

81. *Below:* Rudolf Schmundt (left), Karl Friedrich Otto Wolff (centre) and Himmler. General Schmunt (1896-1944) died from wounds following the Operation Valkyrie attempt on Hitler.

82. *Above*: Goebbels greeting a committee of war volunteers, 1944.

83. *Right*: Christmas, 1944.

84. *Below*: Goebbels at an award ceremony, 16 March 1945. Sixteen-year-old Willi Hübner was awarded the *Eisernes Kreuz 2. Klasse* (Iron Cross 2nd Class) for his service as a messenger during the battle for Lauban.

85. *Left:* Otto Guensche (1917-2003). Guensche first met Hitler in 1936 and was his SS orderly officer from 1940 to 1941. Guensche was entrusted by Hitler to ensure that his body was cremated after his death on 30 April 1945. He stood guard outside the room as Hitler and Eva Braun committed suicide.

86. *Right:* Wilhelm Burgdorf (1895-1945). On 29 April 1945, Burgdorf, Krebs, Goebbels, and Bormann witnessed and signed Hitler's last will and testament. On 2 May, Burgdorf and his colleague, Chief of Staff Hans Krebs, also committed suicide by gunshot to the head.

87. *Left:* Hans Krebs (1898-1945). After a bungled attempt to surrender, Krebs committed suicide on 2 May 1945.

88. *Right:* Martin Ludwig Bormann (1900-1945). Bormann become head of the Party Chancellery in 1941. Hitler came to have complete trust in him, giving him tremendous influence. He died attempting to escape from Berlin in May 1945.

89. *Above:* A Russian soldier gives British troops a view of the Bunker, May 1945.
90. *Below:* The Goebbels' family house at Hermann Goering Straße, May 1945.

91. *Above:* The charred corpses of Goebbels and his wife.

92. *Below:* On 3 May 1945, the day after Soviet troops had discovered the burned bodies of their parents in the courtyard above, they found the bodies of the six Goebbels children in their beds in the bunker, dressed in their nightgowns, the girls wearing bows in their hair. Vice Admiral Hans Voss was brought to the Chancellery garden to identify the bodies, as was Hans Fritzsche. Their bodies were brought to the Buchau Cemetery in Berlin for autopsy and inquest by Soviet doctors. In spite of repeated attempts, even Frau Behrend, the children's grandmother, never learned what became of the bodies. After the fall of the Soviet Union it was revealed that the bodies were repeatedly buried and exhumed, along with the remains of Hitler, Eva Braun, Joseph and Magda Goebbels, General Hans Krebs and Hitler's dogs. The last burial had been at the SMERSH facility in Magdeburg on 21 February 1946. In 1970, KGB director Yuri Andropov authorised an operation to destroy the remains. On 4 April 1970, a Soviet KGB team with detailed burial charts secretly exhumed five wooden boxes. The remains from the boxes were thoroughly burned and crushed, after which the ashes were thrown into the Biederitz river, a tributary of the nearby Elbe.

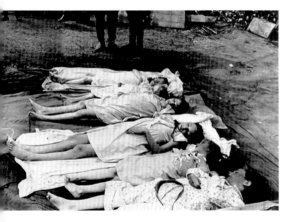

VIII

The tone of Germany's propaganda against France changed only when the war in the West broke loose, but then it changed drastically. 'Now the western offensive has descended upon the plutocracies,' Goebbels wrote.[5] 'Now their armies, trained in the pious belief that all they would have to do was to wait in the Maginot Line and to hang up their clothes on the Siegfried Line, will have to confront us in a hard and bloody battle....' In complete co-ordination with this threatening tone, the German radio blast forth about 'indescribable confusion ... annihilation ... panic ... cataclysm ... utter ruin ...', about Panzer divisions and Stukas, and, again and again, about 'thousandfold retaliation'.

Now, and only now, Goebbels endeavoured to enthuse the German people for the war. On 10 May he had forbidden the German papers to print special editions. He came out with something entirely new: he launched the so-called special radio announcements.

These special announcements interrupted whatever programme was on. A brief preliminary, 'Attention! Attention! You will hear a special announcement of the wireless service!' was followed by fanfares played by a one-hundred-men brass band. Then came the report of a new victory, followed again by fanfares. The fanfares differed, depending on the country where the victory was won, in France or later in Russia, or against England on the high seas, and the whole performance was most impressive.

The effect produced by this highly dramatic device was based on Goebbels' own calculations and was tested in countless experiments which he conducted with whatever people happened to be at hand. Before the first special announcements were ever broadcast, he called in his own family, actors and actresses, his secretaries, and they all had to listen. How long should be the interval between the preliminary 'Attention!' and the first fanfares? How many seconds would it take for the mother to rush out of the kitchen to the radio? What was to be the interval between the first fanfares and the actual announcement? How much time would pass before the mother called the father and the children? Should the fanfares be blown once, twice or three times?

Goebbels pondered and calculated and studied the effect on the living object, always with a stop-watch in his hand. And then the special announcements of German victories were pouring down on the country. Fanfares, fanfares, fanfares....

These fanfares hypnotized the whole of Germany, including Goebbels himself. About that time *Das Reich* published his article, 'The Time Without Comparison'. Why was this time without comparison? 'History does not repeat itself.' It was important to make this statement, important for the whole

German people and for Goebbels himself. Twenty-five years ago the German army had also invaded France and gone from victory to victory—only to be ultimately beaten. Were today's victories not a repetition of yesterday's history? 'History does not repeat itself.... Our situation of today cannot in any way be compared to that of 1914.'

And then French resistance collapsed, the Germans were in Paris, and Marshal Pétain asked for an armistice, just as did the German generals in 1918. Then, the Germans had to go to Marshal Foch's private railway coach in Compiègne. Now, the Nazis forced the French to go through the same humiliating procedure, and for this purpose had unearthed Foch's old coach from the museum. History was repeating itself—in reverse.

It was a brilliant propaganda idea which only Goebbels could have conceived; a parable of gigantic proportions, an over-life-sized poster announcing to the world that the tide had turned, that the Germans had won the war.[6]

Compiègne was Goebbels' big show, although he himself did not attend it. It was his principal concern that the world learn of the event as quickly and as completely as possible. This was so important that even the technical preliminaries, such as the transmission of the armistice negotiations, became newsworthy. In specially arranged broadcasts millions of radio listeners learned about the detailed technique of transmitting the historic news all over the world. This was one of the rare occasions when Goebbels permitted his audiences to take a look behind the scenes.

A few weeks later, when the victory over France was celebrated in the Reichstag, Goebbels was present. Hitler described in a long speech how this victory was accomplished. Numerous generals were promoted to field marshals. Among those singled out for distinction was 'Reichsminister Dr Goebbels, the organizer of a propaganda, the efficiency of which is best gauged by comparison with that of the World War.'

And a few moments later Hitler said: 'The course of the war during the last ten months has proved that I was right and that the opinions of our opponents were wrong.'

Rightly or wrongly, Goebbels felt that this comment was also aimed at him. Hardly a year before he had feared that a war might put an end to the Nazi régime. He had gone to Hitler to plead with him and to warn him. One hour after the speech was over, he stepped into Fritzsche's office, reminded him of that warning, pointed to Hitler's speech and said, with a lifted forefinger: 'For that I have to thank you!' Fritzsche replied, 'The war is not over yet.'

Goebbels never referred to the matter again, until March, 1945. Then he said to Fritzsche: 'Do you remember how you warned me in those days? And do you remember saying five years ago that the war was not yet over? But you never reminded me of your words. For this, I thank you.'

IX

When Hitler learned the news of the French capitulation, he went mad with joy. Astonished movie audiences the world over witnessed his strange antics in the news-reel made of Compiègne. He was certain he had won the war. When he made his Reichstag speech, he was still certain. For Goebbels, however, the spell was broken.

It did not take him long to see that Fritzsche was right. The war was not over yet. This meant that the propaganda war had to go on with ever-increasing vehemence. Victories meant advancing armies, requisitioning of buildings and food resources, rape and maltreatment. Whatever illusions had been built up by German propaganda were destroyed by the physical presence of the German troops. The more victories, the more propaganda. Goebbels realized at an early stage that it was a vicious circle.

But for the time being Goebbels had to concentrate on appeasing the home front. After the victory over France the German people had believed that there would be peace, and they were acutely disappointed when the war continued. If popular resentment accumulated it might have catastrophical consequences. Goebbels had to take immediate measures to revive their enthusiasm for the war and he transmitted at once a number of 'confidential' instructions to his propaganda offices in the Reich.

'2 August 1940... In dealing with the subject of France the speakers are requested to present emphatically the following ideas to the people: all the talk about the innocence of the French people in connection with precipitating the war ... is to be refuted categorically. The people is always responsible for its own leaders ... The mood and attitude of the French people has been decidedly anti-German... The treatment of German military and civilian prisoners in France is further proof of this hostility towards all things German ...

'Hence the speakers are to suppress any feelings of compassion about the fate of the French people... In dealing with our remaining principal enemy, England, the speakers are to point out that we do not judge the British by the same yardstick as we do any other European nation. The Englishman does not feel any common bond with the destiny of the whole of Europe... At the same time the speakers must refrain from creating the impression that the coming battle will be child's play.' Under the ruins of the Propaganda Ministry the author found the original document containing these instructions.

Contrary to the treatment of the French, 'all speeches are to culminate in the condemnation of the plutocrats, while the English people as such are to be described as the victims of their masters' brutal greed... There have been rumours saying the defeat of Britain will be followed immediately by a war with Russia. This calls for the following comment: these rumours are entirely without foundation. In explaining this point to the audiences the principal proof is to be found in the Fuehrer's speech. Furthermore, the speakers are to see to it that there will be no press reports on the subject (of a war with Russia).'

And finally: 'The speakers are requested to make no detailed, glowing promises on the subject of the European New Order after the war. All future questions in this respect are subject to the Fuehrer's decision... The solution of this task demands the leadership of the racially finest and most efficient nation in Europe ...'

This was the New Order, the New Europe—for German consumption. And while the Germans were told that they would become the masters of Europe, the peoples of the occupied countries were being given a totally different idea of the coming New Europe. Goebbels himself sounded off on the subject in a speech on 11 September 1940, to Czechoslovakian writers and musicians, painters and newspapermen. He began by saying that in a time of shrinking distances, when aeroplane and radio were transcending all frontiers, the peoples had become 'much closer to each other.' Of course, he said, 'We never ... intended to bring about this process of reorganization in Europe by force,' and 'It should not be said that if there were no National Socialists there would be peace and quiet in Europe. No, in that case others would have to act in our place.' And finally: 'Whether or not we all like each other is not necessarily under debate. This is comparatively unimportant. The principal thing is that we can offer millions of people in Europe a new basis and a new ideal in life.'

This seemed to be nothing but propaganda, but in reality it was the other way round: the Germans, and not the other nations, were fed with the propaganda, for Goebbels seriously hoped for and believed in the possibility of building a new Europe. He also knew that no time should be lost in carrying out such plans, for every day that passed made more enemies for the Germans in the occupied lands, and greatly dampened any wish of the oppressed peoples for a New Order under German tutelage.

In a rather hazy way Goebbels was thinking in terms of a Magna Charta for all of Europe, a document which would embody the general outlines of a future New Order. He discussed his idea with Fritzsche who sat down to work out the details. Goebbels read Fritzsche's final draft with great satisfaction and told him he would submit it to the Fuehrer. Hitler, on the other hand, felt that Ribbentrop should have the final say on the matter since, after all, he was Foreign Minister.

The conversation between Ribbentrop and Goebbels, as the latter described it to Fritzsche, was brief and violent. Ribbentrop read the document, shoved it aside and exclaimed: 'We don't need that sort of thing!' What he meant was that there was no reason to negotiate with the conquered peoples so long as they could be kept in line by force of arms. Goebbels rose indignantly and shouted at him: 'You will soon find out that we'll need that sort of thing very much!' Through the medium of the press he doubled his promises to introduce a New Order, but that was all he could do about it.

On another occasion he again clashed with Ribbentrop. The Foreign Minister had insisted that every interview Goebbels gave to a foreign newspaperman should be shown to him prior to its publication, and Hitler had acceded to his demand. This was absolutely intolerable for Goebbels, but, to make matters worse, Ribbentrop exploited his position in a manner at once insulting and humiliating. For instance, in April, 1940, Goebbels gave an interview to the correspondent of the *Popolo d'Italia*. He passed it on to the Foreign Office, from where it was returned to him, wildly blue-pencilled and cut down by several pages. Accompanying it was a letter (now in the author's possession) saying, 'Pages 6, 7, 8, and 14 have been deleted by the Fuehrer, with whom the *Herr Reichsminister* discussed the interview.'

Goebbels raged. In all fairness it must be stated that his constant bickering with Ribbentrop did not involve questions of prestige alone. The two men had totally different ideas on propaganda. Perhaps it would be more accurate to say that Goebbels knew something about propaganda, while Ribbentrop did not. Above all, Ribbentrop could never understand the fundamental difference between propaganda and politics.

'The face of politics changes from day to day,' Goebbels once explained to Fritzsche, while he was unburdening himself about the impossible Ribbentrop. 'Propaganda lines can only change imperceptibly. Politics can, and must, cut off corners. Propaganda cannot follow that quickly. Propaganda cannot support or explain the policy of the day, it can only support and strengthen a general political line.'

Ribbentrop would never grasp this basic truth, Goebbels argued, and he was bound to cause 'mischief'. 'If he had only stayed in his champagne business,' he often complained.

Probably Ribbentrop's greatest mistake was Lord Haw-Haw.

X

William Joyce, alias Lord Haw-Haw, the Irish fascist who had entered the service of the Propaganda Ministry a few days before the outbreak of the war, had never been one of Goebbels' favourites. He had met him briefly, studied reports about the possibilities of his broadcasts and then hired him—incidentally, for a comparatively low salary. In the first weeks of the war Joyce was hardly more than a minor player in the broadcasting section of the Propaganda Ministry, and his extraordinary success came as a surprise to everyone concerned, including himself. To what extent this success was due to the mystery which surrounded Lord Haw-Haw at the beginning of his activities (considerable time had passed before his first wife recognized his voice); whether it was due to his talent to sound like a decadent English aristocrat, or whether it was due to his inherent sense of satire, is debatable. On the other hand, it is an established fact that according to reliable estimates 50 per cent of British radio listeners tuned in on his programmes. This was true during the Polish campaign and in the first days of the war against the West. But after Dunkirk the British refused to be amused.

Here was where Lord Haw-Haw made a decisive error. He could not understand that his countrymen, who in their extreme predicament had called Churchill to the helm, no longer wanted to laugh or even to smile. Also, Lord Haw-Haw should have known that there was no point in threatening the British. But this was precisely what he did. The more desperate the situation for the English, the more gruesome the consequences which Lord Haw-Haw conjured up for them if they did not surrender to Hitler immediately. The result was that the overwhelming majority of his listeners turned their radios off.

Goebbels, according to Fritzsche, sensed the Irishman's failure even before it became glaringly evident. He realized that Lord Haw-Haw had committed an unforgivable sin as a propagandist; he had tried to follow slavishly the developments of daily politics. Goebbels decided to get rid of him. Ribbentrop went frantic with rage when he heard that the Irish propagandist had been dismissed. He called in Lord Haw-Haw and re-hired him—at an inordinately high salary. From that time on Goebbels had nothing further to do with the propaganda of the British 'Lord'. And until the end of the war that propaganda remained entirely without significance.

XI

Immediately after the collapse of France, Goebbels had advised his agents that now England was the main enemy. This was not an empty phrase. He felt the threat in his very veins. Here was a country against which his propaganda could accomplish but little. Here were statesmen and politicians who refused to be intimidated. The Churchills, Edens, Duff Coopers—how Goebbels hated them! For the time being his hatred remained largely within the realm of a personal antagonism. With the fall of France he had once more stopped writing. His last article had appeared on 16 June. Typically enough, it was concerned with the 'Resemblance of the English to God.' Since then he had written nothing of consequence, except for a few speeches to homecoming troops, on the inauguration of an art exhibition, a talk on films and youth. In July, August, September, October, November—until shortly before Christmas—not a single article.

His hatred against the English found expression in his directives to his agents and—in a film scenario which satirized a British Cabinet session. The cast consisted of Chamberlain, Churchill, Halifax, Eden, Simon and Duff Cooper, who were trying to map out a propaganda campaign against Germany. They were somewhat unhappy over the fact that as yet there had been no revolution in Germany, and utterly confused as to what to do next. Churchill had to admit to his colleagues that he had been lying about the number of German ships sunk by British U-boats. In the middle of their muddled debate all cabinet members were interrupted by an air-raid siren and rushed to take shelter.

Goebbels probably wrote the script for his own entertainment and as an outlet for his animosity. It was of course never published.[7]

British war propaganda continued to arouse his scorn. He still regarded the gentlemen who tried to compete with him as 'propaganda apprentices.' Duff Cooper, whom he had fought even before the war, meanwhile had become Minister of Information. 'The English now have a Minister of Information. To think that we have to put up with that kind of counterpart!' was Goebbels' comment. Another time he said: 'And that nincompoop is now playing a Minister in England!'

Or: 'If we had secretly planted members of the Fifth Column (so dearly beloved abroad) as associates of Duff Cooper, they could not have done a better job... It is really no fun to have to struggle every day with such abysmal incompetence.' As late as June, 1941, he said: 'There may be different opinions about the attitude of the British people and the bravery of the Empire soldiers, but one thing is certain: they have not deserved such a miserable press, such amateurish broadcasts and such a ludicrously inefficient propaganda.'

However, Goebbels recognized the real predicament of British propaganda with astonishing perspicacity. 'The British policy of news and propaganda is facing a difficult situation. To Germany, it has to present the situation in glowing colours, while to the United States it has to present it in blacker than black.'

The Battle of Britain was to bring the decision. Day after day the planes of the Luftwaffe were crossing the Channel to bring England to her knees. According to the German newspapers and the German radio the battle which had hardly started was already won. The war of nerves against Britain consisted in telling the English that Hitler would be in London by 15 August; later, this date was postponed to 15 September. On that day *Das Reich* carried an editorial (not by Goebbels) which started: 'According to the history books, Carthage burned for seventeen days. Today is the ninth day that London is burning.' German papers carried headlines such as 'England Vacillating Between Famine and Surrender.' Secret directives of the Propaganda Ministry instructed all papers to prepare articles describing Hitler's entry into London. Only the dates were omitted for the time being, to be inserted at the last minute.

The Battle of Britain was Germany's first decisive defeat and also a defeat for German propaganda. Goebbels himself was not responsible for this debacle. He had only listened to the assurances of the military, in particular to Goering—something he would never do again. He had permitted his staff to make prophecies with definite dates. The implication that London was burning for nine days, while Carthage had burned for seventeen days in all, was extremely far-reaching. It meant no more and no less that London would be destroyed within another week...

On 15 September, when the tide was turning, when Goering had to abandon his attempt to knock out England from the air, Goebbels fought a propagandist rearguard action which was so brilliant that it amounted to a propaganda victory. On the one hand, the damage suffered by the British was exaggerated beyond all proportions. In order to strengthen the idea in the minds of his listeners that London was living through hell, he was even willing to testify to the courage of the British people, including the BBC which was competing with him. 'Male and female announcers face the mike as briskly and nicely as if the air-raids were a thing they heard of in a fairy tale. I think we must respect them for this.'

German losses—158 planes on fateful 15 September alone—were never admitted. Even the defeat as such was not admitted, by the simple trick that the Battle of Britain itself was never mentioned. German propaganda only conceded that a few German planes had caused unprecedented havoc in England. Apart from that, Britain would of course be conquered, whenever the Fuehrer saw fit to give the signal.

This Goebbels promised in a speech which he made in Vienna on 26 October. He repeated his promise over the Berlin radio, saying that there could be no doubt about England's 'ultimate defeat'. Finally he assured a gathering of foreign correspondents at a press conference that 'the German war machine will smash across the Channel ... just as it has smashed through the Maginot Line.'

But never again did he commit himself to definite dates. He was convinced that this was dangerous or, as he expressed it in an interview about the 'intellectual Conduct of the War': 'There must be absolute certainty that words are followed up by corresponding events. The best policy is to build one's slogans exclusively on facts.'

XII

Christmas was approaching. The Goebbels family moved into a new house. It was an old palace, remodelled at the cost of 2,425,000 marks, situated next to the Brandenburg Gate in the Hermann Goering Strasse. The garden behind the house was adjacent to the gardens of the Ministries in the Wilhelmstrasse and to the garden of the Reich Chancellery. From his home Goebbels had only two minutes' drive to the Propaganda Ministry.

The little palace was more like a large villa and did not compare to the palaces of Goering or Ribbentrop. The switchboard operator would answer any caller, 'This is the residence'—adding no name or title. The house was furnished in tasteful, dignified style, and there was nothing pretentious about it. From the entrance the visitor passed through a large reception room. On the ground floor there were several salons, dining-room, film projection room and a small stage for theatrical performances. The first floor accommodated Goebbels' bedroom, the apartment of Magda Goebbels, the living-room of the family, the play-rooms for the children and the music-room as well as the studios of the personal assistants. They and the other personnel had their bedrooms on the second floor.

All floors of the house were covered with thick, deep rugs, the walls were lined with velvet or silk, there was only soft and indirect lighting. One could not hear a loud word, not a step, the doors closed noiselessly, the telephones (there was one instrument to every room) had been toned down from a shrill ring to a soft, purring sound. The whole atmosphere of the place breathed silence. The personnel could not be seen, it had strict orders never to get in Goebbels' way. The Minister had no other contact except with his family, his closest associates and the butler who served the meals.

Soft rugs ... quiet, noiselessness. And a few hundred feet away was the Propaganda Ministry, the German propaganda machine, buzzing with furious activity twenty-four hours a day. 240 different broadcasts were transmitted in thirty-one languages—altogether eighty-seven hours of broadcasting every twenty-four hours. Goebbels needed this machine to drown out the ever-increasing news of the atrocities and brutalities committed by the German army in Holland, Belgium, France, Norway, Poland.

However, long before the war started, he had done something much more effective to achieve this end: he had written an article on atrocity propaganda entitled, 'The Chopped-Off Children's Hands', reminding his readers how the British had succeeded in the first war in inciting the world against the Germans. 'It concerned the chopped-off hands of children, the eyes gouged out, the raping of women and the maltreatment of old men. This propaganda which was carried on for years resulted in convincing the whole world that the Germans were a nation of barbarians.' By proving over and over how much of British war propaganda had been lies, he strengthened the determination of all civilized men and women to refuse believing everything they read during a war. Now that the Germans were actually doing the very things they had been accused of in the First World War, the world simply did not believe it, and the worst the German atrocities, the less the world was ready to accept their authenticity. Goebbels had bought valuable time for the German beast—time in which it could really let go.

Christmas Eve was celebrated in the film room and the children and the personnel received many gifts. Hitler, who gave no Christmas presents during the war, sent Frau Goebbels ten pounds of coffee. There was even a regular Santa Claus, much to the delight of the children. Goebbels laughed and teased them, assuring them time and again that there really was no Santa Claus.

And then they all sang: 'Holy Night, Silent Night...'

CHAPTER XI

THE WAR OF MANY FRONTS

I

During the first few months of 1941 Goebbels devoted himself almost exclusively to the task of demolishing Winston Churchill. His hatred of Churchill was deep and bitter. His associates reported later that not a day passed without insulting and derogatory comments on the British Prime Minister. Goebbels did not care how many people listened to his invectives: the more the better. Churchill was 'the drunk who is responsible for this war.' Goebbels said unmentionable things about the private life of Churchill's daughter. Whenever Churchill's name came up, the Propaganda Minister transformed himself into the Goebbels of 1926, who could not fight unless he was hitting below the belt. He probably knew before anyone else had fully realized it that Churchill was the most inexorable, the most implacable of all enemies, the man who would not shrink from annihilating his opponent, unless he himself was annihilated.

Week after week he conducted a violent polemic against Churchill in a stream of vitriolic articles. 'Who does Churchill think he is, anyway?' 'England and her Plutocrats,' 'From Churchill's Factory of Lies,' 'Pseudo-Socialists,' 'The Old Cynic,' 'Britannia Rules the Waves,' were some of the titles. No matter what he wrote about, he always came back to Churchill, and hurled at him his hatred and impotent rage. He was beside himself when Churchill failed to admit losses allegedly inflicted upon the British Navy by German submarines. He reproached him for 'dining and wining in luxurious London restaurants' while 'British newspapers are recommending carrots and unpeeled potatoes as substitutes for meat ...'

Churchill's 'face does not have a single kind trait,' he found. 'Its contours and features are moulded by cynicism. These ice-cold eyes betray a man without feelings. To satisfy his blind and ruthless vanity he will walk over dead bodies... Exactly how England is supposed to win the war Mr Churchill does not know yet... He was just as much at a loss when he insisted that Britain declare war on the Reich...' And later: 'He does not seduce children but nations. To him, they are but a means to an end. He has the perception of a hippopotamus...' 'To gamblers like Churchill one cannot explain that it is better to go home with the remnants of their fortune rather than lose everything. All right, then, let Churchill gamble and England will pay,' so Goebbels prophesied. 'If the time comes to write the history of the collapse of the British Isles, its most decisive chapter will be entitled, "Churchill".'

In the spring of 1941, this long visualized collapse seemed imminent. 'This world order is ripe to be overthrown, more than ripe!' Goebbels shouted. The so-called 'Operation Sea Lion' which was to culminate in the invasion of Britain was preceded by a merciless air war which reached its climax on 10 May. Never before had London suffered such severe bombardments. The Houses of Parliament and the British Museum were badly damaged. Goebbels was delighted; it left him cold that historical buildings of irreplaceable cultural value were destroyed.

In fact, he still believed that the morale of the enemy could be broken by persistent air attacks.[1] But despite his own belief he was not tricked into making definite assurances to the public no matter how often Goering told him he was certain of victory. On the other hand, Goebbels gave orders to reprint a Gallup Poll of July 1940 showing that only 32 per cent of the American people believed Britain could win the war. (He carefully concealed from the Germans the result of a later Gallup Poll in the spring of 1941, which indicated that the figure had increased to 50 per cent.)

In any event, Goebbels was perturbed not only about Churchill but also about the British people, their awesome tenacity, their inability to admit defeat when, in his opinion, for all practical purposes they were defeated. 'Why does a boxer who is bleeding from his eyes, nose and mouth, reeling around the ring and with no earthly chance of victory, still continue to hammer at his opponent with careless and completely harmless blows, although he must know that all he can possibly achieve is to infuriate the other to such a degree that the final knockout blow will be all the more devastating? Why?' Goebbels cried out.

II

Every week Goebbels wrote an editorial for *Das Reich*. Through this new medium he achieved precisely what he had set out to do. His contributions were read not only in Germany but throughout Europe, and by many people who were by no means satisfied with the Party and the German Government.

These 'neutral' and sometimes 'oppositional' readers would then declare that it was merely Goebbels' style, and not the content of his articles, which impressed them. Nevertheless, the one or the other argument did not fail to leave its mark. In an article about poets and writers he commented: 'Nothing can be more deeply satisfying to contemporaries than to experience how a man of their own generation finds the right words to describe all they feel themselves in their mute helplessness.' There could be no doubt that he was referring to himself, and he was right.

Yet, it was probably first and foremost his style which left the deepest impression on his readers' minds, the style of which Goebbels himself had written that like the feeling for propaganda it could not be learned. One either had it, or one had not.

Formerly, in the days of *Angriff*, writing had been a sideline with him, to be disposed of rapidly without much thought or care. He would dictate to whoever was around, on the spur of the moment. Sometimes he would break off in the middle of other work to dictate an article because it had to be sent to the printers. While he dictated without any notes whatsoever, he would walk up and down, speaking fluently and often with pathos and gesticulation, lifting a threatening fist or hitting his desk with the palm of his hand, as though he were making a speech. He never interrupted himself until he was through, and then, without pause, he would say, 'End, end.' The stenographer was dismissed, the article was typed, seldom corrected by Goebbels, sometimes not even read over. Hence his hard-hitting, but carelessly formed sentences, slangy, aggressive and witty.

Now he approached his work differently. Weeks in advance he would start making notes; excerpts from or resumés of books were prepared for him to be studied carefully. Then, mostly late at night; he locked himself up in his office or studio and wrote his article in long-hand into a black notebook. He would edit his own text twice or three times, sometimes as much as six or seven times. When it finally was up to his expectations he would not turn it over to one of his secretaries but call up his personal stenographer to dictate the whole article over the telephone. It had to be typed at once and was then submitted to Goebbels, who made further corrections, had it retyped, then made other revisions, until the final version corresponded to his own standard of perfection.

The result was an excellent, lucid and almost austere German style, with well-constructed, rhythmic sentences, and words which conveyed the subtlest overtones. It was almost as though he were seeking to re-establish the contact with the days of his earliest youth, with the tradition of the ancient Latin and Greek masters whose works he had studied at school. Many of his articles were reminiscent of his 'Latin training' rather than of his 'Germanic origin,' as Reich Armaments Minister Albert Speer once commented appropriately. But, most of all, their content was designed to have a soothing effect on the reader. They were not written by a fighter, but seemingly by someone who had already won his battles, who stood above the situation and could speak with calm aloofness, seldom annoyed, never excited.

All other contributions in *Das Reich* were of a comparatively high standard, too. No one writing in its columns was forced to express himself in the repulsive lingo characteristic of National socialism, and the hysterical headlines found in other German papers were conspicuously lacking.

For each article Goebbels received 5,000 marks.

III

Aside from his weekly editorials Goebbels regularly wrote a number of articles which he published either anonymously or under the *nom de plume* of Sagax in the *Voelkischer Beobachter*, and in other newspapers. Furthermore, he wrote numerous speeches which he would dictate rapidly, unless they were concerned with matters of vital importance. In addition, there were his circular letters to the Gauleiters, his directives to his propagandists and speakers; there was his control over the gigantic machine of the Propaganda Ministry, the supervision of the newsreels, in fact the supervision of all motion pictures made both in Germany and Austria.

All this—his articles, speeches, circular letters, directives, the diary and the management of the Propaganda Ministry—Goebbels described as the 'Intellectual Conduct of the War.' He rightly considered himself as a kind of general, his Ministry as a kind of general staff, and he regarded his propaganda 'war' at least as important as the shooting war of the Wehrmacht.

IV

The directives for the Intellectual Conduct of the War were issued each morning at 11 o'clock in a conference over which the Minister himself presided, and subsequently in two press conferences at 1 and 5 p.m., where suggestions were channelled to the press by Fritzsche and other assistants.

In the press conferences editors were instructed on what to write, how to write it and what to omit. Attention was paid to the most insignificant detail. In discussing the reports of the official German News Agency (DNB) it was almost always indicated which stories were to be played straight and which were to be commented on.

These conferences were attended by a representative of the Propaganda Ministry (usually Hans Fritzsche), of Reich Press Chief Dr Otto Dietrich who announced the *Tagesparole*, of the Foreign Office (with whom there was often a good deal of controversy behind the scenes), and finally by a representative of the High Command.

At the 11 a.m. meeting, which was held in a conference room next to Goebbels' private office, all section heads—the chiefs of radio, German press, foreign press, theatre, literature, film, and so on—had to be present. Goebbels did most of the talking, while the others merely listened. Later they would transmit his directives to the members of the press conferences. Sometimes, but not often, the representative of the Foreign Office cautiously indicated that his chief, Ribbentrop, did not quite share the ideas of the Propaganda Minister. But most of the time the controversy between Goebbels and Ribbentrop was reflected in their correspondence. The two minor officials handling this exchange of letters were greatly amused over the fact that the Ministers were so much at odds with each other.

V

Throughout the year 1941 Goebbels tried hard to win the propaganda battle for the New European Order. The outlook became more and more hopeless until it was utterly clear that the fight would be lost, and Goebbels knew it.

From a propaganda point of view the situation was somewhat paradoxical. Through the war of nerves propaganda had helped to vanquish the armies of the enemy; in other words, it had been successful in a field where ordinarily it has no place. Now that the war on the European continent was over, propaganda was unable to convince the civilian population that it was over. It was ineffectual where, normally, it should have been successful, and this despite the fact that, for once, it was truthful. Europe's armies were beaten, but the civilian population remained unconquered, and gradually the fight against the oppressors began to get organized. Underground movements were springing up everywhere, there was passive resistance, there were attacks on the occupation troops, and Gestapo officers found it increasingly dangerous to wander unaccompanied through foreign streets at nights.

A concerted effort of the Wehrmacht, the S.S., and the Gestapo tried to stop the incipient rebellion. Hostages were arrested and shot: five Frenchmen for one German, ten Belgians for one German, fifty Poles for one German, all according to the mood and temper of the local commandant.

Goebbels tried to intensify his propaganda in the occupied territories. One of his agents declared in a lecture on propaganda abroad, 'I strongly believe that after the great successes won by our army the hour of foreign propaganda has arrived. It must help us to win the spiritual victory... In thirty or forty years all of Europe must share the opinion that the German principles alone are right. And this task can be solved.'

However, it became more insoluble from day to day, mainly due to the repressive measures adopted by the occupation troops. Goebbels strongly disapproved of all the executions, not for humanitarian reasons but because he realized that they had the opposite effect on the conquered populations: instead of being intimidated they were stirred into open resistance.

In 1941 and in the following years Goebbels made it a habit to call military commanders of the occupied territories to his office at regular intervals. He disliked the uniformed gentlemen who to him looked too rosy-checked and well fed. He tried to give them an idea of how to treat the masses in the occupied countries. According to Jacobs' notes he would say:

'Gentlemen, you are surprised about the difficulties you are experiencing in your territories, and which are caused primarily by the passive resistance of the population. Personally, I'm not in the least surprised, for the way you are handling things it will never work out. I am after all an expert in this field. I remember from my own youth how sabotage is done. I also know how it can be fought effectively. Imagine, gentlemen, that we had the enemy in our own country and that we were at his mercy. Your measures are either too lenient, or too gentle, or else they far exceed the reasonable. Apparently you know nothing of the many nuances that exist between black and white. There is such a thing as the colour grey. The occupying power in our own country would only have to compile a list with the names of former prominent men and circulate it with the following comment: If one more factory is sabotaged, if one more soldier is killed, the first twenty of the above-mentioned persons will be shot. Gentlemen, let me speak about myself for a moment. My wife, for instance, has a large circle of friends. Don't you think that she would at once go to these people—most of them are old Party members who live illegally to commit sabotage? I say, don't you think that my wife would rush to these people and would plead with them, 'For God's sake, stop this pointless resistance! Surely, you don't want them to shoot all your former leaders, do you?" I assure you, gentlemen, that every one of our wives would act in this spirit, if the situation were reversed. But now we are the ones who are in power, and therefore we can proceed accordingly.'

VI

In Fritzsche's opinion the people in the occupied territories never would have paid attention to the BBC if it had not been for the arrests and murders of hostages. For Allied propaganda was extremely ineffective, he said, at least in the beginning. This was what he told his friends in the Propaganda Ministry and this was what he said in many of his broadcasts. Time and again he ridiculed the attempts of the BBC to stir up a spirit of revolt against Hitler in the occupied countries. Occasionally he even tried to unite the oppressed nations of Europe in a fight to the finish against England, on the side of Germany.

Such attempts were of course preposterous and, furthermore, were proof of a staggering error of judgment, and it is difficult to imagine that Goebbels seriously believed his tactics would be ultimately successful. It was no secret that BBC programmes were becoming increasingly popular in all occupied countries, and it was immaterial whether this was caused by indiscriminate German reprisals or by the desire of the oppressed nations to fight for their freedom at all costs.

BBC short-wave transmitters were constantly expanding their programmes. There were seventy-eight daily news bulletins alone, altogether 300,000 words. For 150 hours the BBC broadcast in forty different languages and dialects. Listening to their German transmissions Goebbels had to admit that the British had learned a good deal from him, for instance, the trick with the phonograph record. Ten years before Goebbels had demolished Reich Chancellor Bruening by playing a record of his speech, interrupting him from time to time to make his own sarcastic marginal comments. Now the British were copying the tactic. Hitler had declared he wanted no Czechs within the realm of the Reich. The BBC announcer interrupted the record of the Fuehrer's speech, and reminded his audience that a few months after this statement German troops had marched into Prague. Hitler had declared that he would force Britain to her knees within the space of a few weeks. The announcer reminded his audience that this promise was made a year before. Hitler had promised that the war would be over by Christmas, 1940. The announcer put in a reminder that soon it would be Christmas—1941.

Goebbels was attacked by the BBC once a week in a sketch centring around two characters: Kurt Krueger, a school teacher, and Willi Schimaski, a cynical employee of the Propaganda Ministry. Throughout their conversation Kurt naïvely defended the Party line, while Willi, who was smarter but less idealistic, made it clear that it was foolish to believe everything circulated by the propaganda apparatus of his Lord and Master. 'There are many things between heaven and earth—or sky and water—which you don't know and which we propagandists keep absolutely mum about.'

Willi informed his credulous friend that England was by no means on the verge of famine, and that German U-boats were not sinking as many British ships as was generally believed.

Kurt contradicted him. 'These long summer days have been unfavourable for U-boats.'

Willi: 'And last winter the Fuehrer said that the long summer days were just the right time for U-boats.'

Kurt: 'Did he? Bless my soul! So he did! I remember. But tell me, Willi, which is the best time for U-boats?'

Willi: 'Well, no season at all, it seems.'

Kurt was beside himself about his friend's disrespectful attitude. 'It's intolerable how you speak in that highly cynical way about these matters.'

Willi: 'You are right, Kurt, it is disgusting. In fact, the only way we propagandists can keep ourselves from vomiting daily is by adopting what we call a highly cynical attitude.'

VII

Goebbels' only calculable chance of organizing a New Europe under German leadership was the total absence of any constructive ideas on the part of the Allies. During the first months of 1941 he kept attacking the Allies for the 'astonishing fact that England wages war until death without one responsible man knowing exactly why.'

In the summer of 1941, when President Roosevelt and Prime Minister Churchill created the Atlantic Charter, Goebbels' derision and scorn knew no bounds. During the morning conference he picked up the announcement about the meeting of the two statesmen and read it out loud. When he came to the passage where Roosevelt and Churchill started singing, 'Onward, Christian Soldiers...' he leaned back in his chair and said laughingly: 'I can visualize those two arch-scoundrels sitting there, their eyes turned upward to Heaven in hypocritical piety, and sanctimoniously going through their little singing routine, their voices breaking with false emotion.' And he went on in this vein, to the delight of his audience.

He had sufficient irony left for the journalists who described in detail what Roosevelt and Churchill had worn on the historic occasion. 'Imagine, gentlemen, our reporters doing that! Think of the Fuehrer viewing his troops, wearing a snowy-white tropical helmet equipped with a mosquito net, dark glasses, a white tropical suit to match—now I ask you, gentlemen, isn't that the limit? But not in England, oh, no! The British keep a straight face when they read that sort of thing.'

In an article bearing the characteristic title, 'Attack on Common Sense,' he literally tore up the Atlantic Charter in mid-air. 'Churchill and Roosevelt might have saved themselves the trouble to meet on the Atlantic merely to produce this flimsy little bit of a paper... The brains of the men who wrote this Declaration must be as dried-up as the Sahara. Not in our wildest dreams could we have imagined that the result would be so meagre, so stupid and so sterile as it now has turned out.'

Even a year later Goebbels got all upset over the fact that 'our enemies have no clear-cut conception of building up a new Europe after the war.' Here, unfortunately, his propaganda was having an easy time.

If Goebbels' propaganda in the occupied territories was handicapped by the conduct of the German troops, his attempts to win the sympathies of the foreign press for the New Europe were defeated by his own Propaganda Ministry which the correspondents viewed with ever-increasing suspicion.

They were constantly being deceived in numerous different ways. Although there was still no official censorship and correspondents could report whatever they liked, their cables were checked carefully. If they wrote something that displeased Goebbels they were invited to dinner by an official of the Propaganda Ministry, who would gently reproach them for their 'disloyal' attitude. Since it was impossible to inform them that their cables had been read, the official would assert that a German correspondent in a neutral country had seen their reports. Against recalcitrant correspondents more drastic measures were adopted. Telephone communication with foreign countries was denied them and they were forbidden to cable their despatches abroad.

In order to trick foreign correspondents the Nazis also operated through the Bureau Schwarz van Berk, which supplied them with so-called authentic features.[2] Another office for fabricating false news was the highly mysterious Boemer Auslandspresse (otherwise known as BAP), which specialized in inventing canards. After these stories had been approved by Goebbels they were planted in the foreign press via neutral countries. Amusingly enough, they sometimes duped even prominent Nazis, including Hitler himself. During one of his visits to Hitler, Goebbels found him delirious with joy over the news that a British cruiser had been sunk before Trondheim. Ribbentrop was present and reported with obvious pride that he had been the first to inform the Fuehrer. Goebbels had great trouble in convincing Hitler that the item had been faked.

Direct and indirect bribes also were used to win over the foreign press. The correspondents were given twenty cigarettes per day, they were served excellent food at the two foreign press clubs. This meant a great deal to certain correspondents from the Balkans. Some of them did a thriving business, although their monthly salary may not have exceeded 100 marks. The Propaganda Ministry gladly contributed 400 marks a month, some publicity agency for an industrial concern would pay another 300 marks, the UFA film company chipped in with 200 marks. In addition there were the food packages they were allowed to receive from Switzerland and Denmark, and which could be sold in the black market as well as the valuable birthday and Christmas presents from Goebbels.

However, Goebbels had no luck with his big and little bribes when it came to influencing the newspaper-men who really mattered. They displayed a great deal of courage, particularly those from the occupied territories, despite the fact that they were at Goebbels' mercy. In some cases their reports on conditions in Germany were more accurate than their colleagues' in the neutral countries. Strangely enough, nothing ever happened to them. Perhaps there was a remnant of respect and admiration left in Goebbels for fearless journalists.

VIII

The foreign press, however, was only one of the many problems which weighed heavily on Goebbels' mind. Once more his anti-Semitism plagued him. He told his associates that he would not rest before the last Jew was removed from Germany. 'They are the people who are poisoning the public mind because they cannot always be identified as Jews—the people who stand in line in front of the stores and try to create disaffection by seemingly harmless remarks.' When it was pointed out that this type of 'subversive activity' had been eliminated by the introduction of the Star of David—at Goebbels' own suggestion—he replied grimly: 'Now the Moses and the Levysohns are sitting at home and no longer show themselves in the streets. Instead, they are sending old mamma and old daddy to the stores, counting on the compassion of the Berliners who with their sheep-like, good-natured temperament, promptly fall for this trick. How often do I receive reports telling me that such an old Jewish mamma turns up in the subway and that two or three people immediately jump up to offer her a seat!'

What incensed Goebbels beyond anything else was the same experience he had had in 1938, when many Germans did not follow his commands but, on the contrary, found ways and means of expressing their sympathies to the Jews. Raging with anger he defended the introduction of the Star of David stigma as an 'extraordinarily humane regulation,' and to those who said that the Jews were human beings, too, he replied: 'As if we ever denied it. So are the men who steal, the men who rape children, the thieves and procurers.' In the winter of 1941, the first Jews were deported to Poland. Goebbels' associates, among them Fritzsche, asked whether there was any truth in the rumours that they would be gassed. Goebbels declared that he would have the matter checked. The next day he told Fritzsche that there was not a word of truth in the story: no Jew would be gassed, or killed in any other way.

But the Jewish problem, or rather, the problem of German reaction to the treatment of the Jews, was insignificant compared to one of the most difficult propaganda problems to be solved—and one Goebbels could not solve: the explanation of the flight of Rudolf Hess, deputy Fuehrer of the Party.

IX

Goebbels was just as surprised by Hess's flight as the rest of the world. When the news was telephoned to his house, he was speechless. Half an hour later Fritzsche looked for him at his office but did not find him there. He telephoned his home and was informed that the Minister had gone to his country residence near Lanke. It was not until two hours later that Fritzsche was able to reach him there. He urged Goebbels to give him some directives. How was the case to be commented upon? How was this flight to be explained? Goebbels was sulking: 'I'm not coming to the office today.' Fritzsche countered: 'But we have to say something!' Whereupon Goebbels answered: 'Say whatever you please. I don't know what to advise you. There are situations which even the best propagandist in the world cannot cope with.' He hung up and went to bed.

It was up to Reich Press Chief Dr Otto Dietrich to save the day, and the result was unprecedented confusion. The first news to be circulated was that Hess had become the victim of an accident during a mission over enemy territory. The leaderless Propaganda Ministry protested and argued that such a version would leave too much room for denials. Whereupon Dietrich changed the story to read that Hess had temporarily lost his mind and that, motivated by his pacifistic notions, had gone to England. Above all he was not a traitor because he had nothing to betray, it was said.

When Goebbels read this comment he had a fit. How could anyone say that Hess—after all, still the Fuehrer's deputy—had gone insane? What a ghastly impression such an announcement must make on the average German who might begin to ask himself whether all the men around Hitler were crazy! But thanks to the superbly trained staff of Goebbels' Propaganda Ministry this version of Hess's flight reached the world before the British could announce that Hess had landed in Scotland. Thus the German propaganda machine registered, at least, a scoop.

However, Goebbels himself was of the opinion that Hess had inflicted a loss of prestige on the Third Reich which could not be more devastating. He even said that the Hess affair was more serious than the desertion of an army corps.[3] Later he dictated to Jacobs notes about a conversation he had had with Hitler during a long walk in the garden of the Reich Chancellery. He said that he had asked the Fuehrer once more about the Hess case and that Hitler had confirmed that shortly before his flight to England, Hess had come to see the Fuehrer. He had asked him whether he had not changed his fundamental policy towards Britain. The Fuehrer said he had not. Thereupon Hess had decided to make his flight to England as a mediator. Goebbels added that by taking this step Hess had caused a damage to the Reich which could not be measured at this moment.

X

A few weeks after the Hess incident the German armies invaded Russia. Goebbels had known the plan long beforehand, perhaps since 10 December 1940, when Hitler had ordered secret preparations for the invasion;[4] perhaps only since 2 February 1941, when the first conference between Hitler and the General Staff took place concerning the forthcoming campaign against the Soviet Union.

None of Hitler's ministers and advisers who survived the collapse and eventually gave their testimony favoured a war against Russia. Later on, Goebbels had no opportunity to voice an opinion, but he, too, must have had his reservations. Those who worked with him have testified that he was more nervous and temperamental in the first month of 1941 than ever before. Often he would exclaim in the middle of an interview or a conference: 'If only the next few months were over!' But he never explained why he felt that way. Some observers believed that he was worried over the fight against Britain which was not proceeding according to schedule. However, it is more likely that he was thinking of Russia and was filled with scepticism. In his last book, *The Hour of Decision*, Oswald Spengler, on whom Goebbels had relied so much, had warned of a war against Russia. He had written:

> The population of this mightiest of the earth's inland areas is unassailable from the outside. Distance is a force, politically and militarily, which cannot yet be conquered. Napoleon came to know this. What good does it do the enemy to occupy areas no matter how immense?... Any idea of an offensive from the West has become senseless. It would be a thrust into empty space.

In addition, Goebbels was confronted with a particularly difficult propaganda problem. For years the Nazis had made anti-Bolshevist propaganda. Then, the bomb of the Hitler–Stalin pact had exploded on the eve of the war: from one hour to the other, the Germans were told that the Russians were pleasant and comfortable neighbours, that it was possible to live side by side with a Communist state. The cordial nature of Russian–German relations was stressed in every possible way. When Stalin embraced the German military attaché in Moscow and publicly said, 'If we stand together like brothers, then nothing can happen to us in the future,' his statement was played up in all German newspapers. After two years of this pro-Russian propaganda, how was Goebbels to effect a complete turnabout?

It was impossible to use the well-tested recipe of atrocity propaganda prior to the invasion—because the move was to come as a surprise. All Goebbels could do was to stay put and hope for the best. But even this period of comparative inactivity was full of tension because German troop concentrations in the east could not remain entirely hidden from the Russians. Something had to be done to divert their attention and Goebbels had a brilliant idea.

Suddenly all of Germany began to speak of the imminent invasion of Britain by means of gliders and parachute troops. The island of Crete had just been conquered by the Germans in that manner. On 13 June Goebbels published an article entitled, 'The Example of Crete,' in the *Voelkischer Beobachter*, saying:

> The case of Crete has proved convincingly that in so-called narrow waters the Luftwaffe is equal, if not superior to the navy, and that in a struggle between the two, even if waged under unfavourable circumstances, the sea loses its supremacy and becomes the grave of ships... If today the British are excitedly discussing the fall of Crete, all you have to do is substitute England for Crete, and then you know why they are so frantic ... The Fuehrer himself has coined the phrase that there are no more islands... If we had told Mr Churchill two months ago that we would take possession of Crete at the beginning of June he probably would have laughed, without honouring us with a reply. Today, however, Crete is in our hands, and if we told him again what would happen in the next two months, he would laugh again; and again he would be left holding the bag.

This was clear enough. People were wondering whether Goebbels had not gone too far, had talked out of turn. Soon their suspicions were to be confirmed. Two hours after the issue of the *Voelkischer Beobachter* was out Gestapo officials appeared at all news-stands and confiscated the whole edition. It was evident that the German High Command wished no one to read Goebbels' article, which revealed between the lines what had been intended as a surprise. That evening everyone in Germany believed that the invasion of Britain was imminent, and that the troop movements in the east were only a diversional manoeuvre.

Superfluous to say, Goebbels himself had ordered the confiscation of the *Voelkischer Beobachter*. It was timed so that enough people, especially foreign correspondents, would have time to read the article before it was taken off the stands. When his associates reported various rumours, he declared: 'I know that some of you gentlemen think we are going to fight Russia, but I must tell you we are going to fight England instead, for the invasion is imminent. Please arrange your work accordingly.'⁵

Nevertheless, a few people in the Propaganda Ministry had been informed of the offensive, not by Goebbels but by Hitler's adjutant, Julius Schaub, and by Alfred Rosenberg who had been chosen for an important administrative post in Russia. Among those 'in the know' was Dr Karl Boemer of the Boemer Auslandspresse. This extremely capable man had a weakness for liquor. Shortly after the publication of Goebbels' article on Crete, Boemer attended a reception at the Bulgarian Embassy. When he appeared towards 7 o'clock, he was already in an intoxicated condition. Soon he became very drunk, and told a member of the Foreign Office that he might be appointed to a new post, namely that of under-secretary in a new ministry headed by Alfred Rosenberg.

These words were enough to open the eyes of the other guests. A ministerial post would be given to Rosenberg only in connection with Soviet Russia. That same evening the Bulgarian Ambassador sent an open telegram to Sofia saying that a high official of the N.S.D.A.P. had disclosed to him that war with Russia was imminent.

Ribbentrop was notified. He got in touch with the Gestapo, and the Gestapo acted. Goebbels tried to protect his employee; he appealed to Hitler, Hitler read his letter and pencilled underneath, 'Crystal-clear investigation.'

Two days later an American newspaperman called on Boemer at the Propaganda Ministry. In the anteroom he ran into a secretary. She looked at him in surprise: 'Boemer? We've never heard this name here. Don't you think there must be a mistake?'

Thus Boemer was as good as dead before he was tried. Goebbels pleaded for him (if only to annoy Ribbentrop), and so did Rosenberg. Boemer was sentenced to three years in prison. After serving a year he was allowed to go to the front as a common soldier. Shrapnel hit him and tore open both his hips, and a few days later he died in a military hospital in Cracow. In all obituary notices he was praised as a good National Socialist.

XI

It was only a few hours before the German army invaded Russia that Goebbels broke his silence. During the night of 21 to 22 June he called a few of his section heads to Schwanenwerder and informed them of what was about to happen. From that moment on they were not allowed to leave the house nor to use the telephone until Goebbels drove back to town with them between 3 and 4 a.m. At 5 a.m. Ribbentrop called a press conference and reported the *fait accompli* of the German invasion. A few hours later Goebbels stepped before the microphone and read the Fuehrer's proclamation explaining the necessity for this move. He ended, appropriately enough, with the words: 'May God help us, especially in this fight!'

On the same day Goebbels sent his 'Confidential Information No. 13' to his propaganda agents. It was concerned with the Russian war and was entitled, 'The German Answer to the Betrayal of the Jewish-Bolshevist Rulers in the Kremlin.' The propagandists were instructed to present the war as a defensive step. 'There are to be no discussions about the importance of the Bolshevist state as a source of food and raw materials for Germany... The fight is directed not against the peoples of the Bolshevist state but against Jewish Bolshevism and its representatives.' Furthermore: 'The Jewish Bolshevist rulers have betrayed the Moscow Pact... In this connection we must point to the repeated efforts of the Fuehrer on behalf of peace, and to his tolerance with regard to Bolshevist violations of the agreement.'

Goebbels conducted this propaganda war in person. He was confronted with the difficult, if not impossible, task to accomplish in only a few days what would have required months of preparation, namely to convince the German people that this war, too, was unavoidable because it had been imposed on them by the enemy.

Four days after the war in the East had started he accused the Soviets of never having any intention 'to keep the non-aggression pact with the Reich.' But above all he noted this was not merely a question of betrayal but of a conspiracy,—'the plutocratic–Bolshevist conspiracy.'

In his endeavours to denounce the depravity of the Bolshevist régime Goebbels occasionally blundered. In directives he instructed his speakers to point out that 'the Soviet régime has succeeded in sealing off the country from the outside world,' and in an article on 6 July, he wrote: 'Listening to German broadcasts in the Russian language is punished by death. The cowardly gang of liars in the Kremlin seems to have an obscure premonition of its impending doom.' But on 17 August: 'Several traitorous characters among us, who believed that they had to quench their thirst for knowledge by listening to enemy broadcasts, have been sentenced to hard labour. It is highly symptomatic that the London radio is now pleading their cause.'

These statements succeeded each other so rapidly that the readers were bound to remember the first when they read the second. There were other minor flaws, as, for instance, the matter of the Stalin Line. The first time it popped up in German propaganda was at the beginning of July. People learned that this Maginot Line of the East had been built during the past five years. A few days later it was added that the Russians had been able to conceal this construction in a very clever way. And on 12 July came the special announcement saying that the Stalin Line had been broken.

It was true that the Russians were steadily retreating, and admitted these withdrawals in their official communiqués, but they never mentioned any Stalin Line, for the simple reason that there was no such thing. The London and Moscow radios established this fact. Goebbels was annoyed. 'In countless radio speeches and newspaper articles the propaganda offices of London and Moscow have asserted that we would never be able to smash through this fortified line,' he wrote. 'Now that the line has been broken, they maintain that there can be no question of it, that the line would never be given up. Then, when they have to admit military operations taking place east of the line, they finally come out with the ungarnished truth: there is no Stalin Line, and since it does not exist it cannot have been broken.'

There was another passage in that article which made it particularly noteworthy. In criticizing British propaganda Goebbels noted that 'only the British people would put up with it'. 'If we adopted the same method towards the German people, they would probably throw stones at us. Even the hint of a hope which cannot be fulfilled in the predictable future offends our people,' he wrote. Ostensibly these words were addressed to London. In reality, they were meant for Hitler.

Hitler had become too sure of victory, had made too many wild promises, and his unwarranted optimism was contagious. Never before had Fritzsche been led to make such boastful prophecies as in the first months of the Russian campaign; even the German army communiqué had become almost lyrical in tone. The special announcements intimated that the end of the war was near.

On 9 October it was announced that actually there were only two Russian armies in the field, both of them on the verge of being annihilated. On the same day Otto Dietrich held a conference for the foreign press. He had just left Hitler's headquarters, where he had had a long talk with the Fuehrer, and so he declared: 'The campaign ... against the Bolsheviks is over. This military decision is final.' Also, on 9 October, Hitler's Order of the Day was published. It had been communicated to the troops one week before, and read: 'Today is the beginning of the last great decisive battle of this year. It will deal devastatingly with the enemy.'

Goebbels immediately recognized the tremendous danger of a propaganda which made such reckless commitments. He was furious. He spoke of 'unbelievable irresponsibility,' and of the 'biggest propaganda blunder of the war.'[6] Fearing that the people would now harbour the illusion that the war was over he suppressed Dietrich's speech to the foreign correspondents in the

German press and radio. He even protested to Hitler although the Fuehrer shared the blame for the blunder. A day later Goebbels tried to correct this over-optimism, if it could still be corrected, by saying in a broadcast: 'The battles now going on in the central and southern sectors of the Russian front have decided the outcome of the Russian war. This, however, should not be taken to mean the end of the campaign.'

Did he know, then, that the war was lost?

XII

Be that as it may, Goebbels anxiously avoided committing himself, and in an article, 'The End of all Illusions,' published on 17 October, he indulged in so many generalities that one is tempted to believe he was describing the end of his own illusions.

Understandably enough—and of course to Goebbels' great annoyance—British propaganda seized the initiative, pointing out that Hitler had been unable to keep his schedule and had broken his promise of a speedy victory. 'The English fancy that we are conducting the war according to their own calendar,' Goebbels commented. 'They act as though they had been called to participate in the most secret conferences of our military and political leadership.' It is also possible that he was displeased with Hitler who had played this trump into the hands of Allied propaganda. Despite this fact, or perhaps because of it, he was obliged to write: 'The Fuehrer's victories are won according to his own, not the British, timetable,' adding cautiously, 'Nobody knows when this will be.'

He foresaw what would inevitably happen. The war would be long and hard and bloody, and the German people would feel let down because they had not been prepared to meet the ordeal. At the first signs of open discontent, Goebbels began to denounce them as *miessmacher und kritikaster*, as he had done in the days before the war. He singled out two fictitious characters on whom to tag his criticism: they were *Herr Bramsig* and *Frau Knoeterich* whom he scolded and admonished in numerous articles. But the situation called for more stringent measures. The members of the propaganda units were recalled and received new instructions. During these conferences Goebbels was serious, if not grim. To the newspaper-men he was a changed person for whom, it seemed, the war had just started in earnest.

He told them what he wanted from now on: tough, realistic reports which embellished nothing, and above all, no sugar-coating of the hardships experienced by the fighting troops. The home front must be made to understand what it meant to struggle through oceans of filth and blood; what it meant when a tank was destroyed in battle, when a village went up in flames, when a horse died under its rider; what it meant to suffer hunger and the murderous cold which was now setting in. He demanded from his men that their stories be free of all false heroism, that they should stick to the hard facts of a hard war...

Goebbels knew that soon hundreds of hospital trains would roll into the country, filled with soldiers without legs, arms or eyes; soldiers who had dreadful stories to tell. He had to do everything to prepare the people at home for what was in store for them.

XIII

In those weeks he lived at the Propaganda Ministry, sleeping on an army cot in a little room next to his office. He did not want to risk losing precious minutes if an important decision had to be made. He hardly saw his wife and had no time at all for his children. There were no more film screenings for him. Important conferences which had been scheduled weeks in advance were cancelled. Unless matters had a direct bearing on the war with Russia, they were relegated to the background.

He began to look tired, he lost weight, he contracted a stomach ulcer. For days he would eat nothing but oatmeal, and drink an occasional glass of milk, but he smoked countless cigarettes. Thanks to daily sun-lamp treatments he kept his tan, but the dark circles under his eyes deepened. He slept little. Sometimes, in the middle of the night, he called his masseur because a massage soothed his nerves. Then he would begin to talk about the future, about his hopes to retire from politics, to become again a private individual with private likes and dislikes, to write a book on Hitler and one on Christianity, or a book on the artistic principles of motion pictures...

Goebbels was the only one among the Nazi leaders who sensed that catastrophe loomed ahead. He, the civilian, saw farther than the generals. What could he do to prevent it, what could he do to help break Russian resistance? He flew to Hitler's headquarters, although he and all other cabinet members had been ordered not to fly in autumn and winter. He proposed to launch a large-scale propaganda campaign in occupied Russia in order to win over the population, no matter at what cost. Hitler, completely preoccupied with winning the war against Russia by his 'intuition,' referred him to Rosenberg. Rosenberg smiled condescendingly and told Goebbels he knew his Russians: with them, propaganda was a waste of time.[7]

Goebbels went back to Berlin. What else could he do to prevent a disaster? That great power, the United States, had to be kept from entering the war.

Goebbels had never abandoned his struggle for the isolation of the U.S., which he began in 1940. But in the summer of 1941 the American Government had closed his propaganda offices and arrested and expelled his agents.

XIV

On 4 December 1941, the Russians began their huge counter-offensive along the entire front. The German lines were in danger. Whose fault was it? The generals had warned Hitler of the impending winter cold and tried to persuade him to shift his troops further back. Hitler had refused. He was to blame for the consequences.

To Goebbels, the development was not surprising. In his directives he had stated grimly: 'The sacrifices of the front cannot be compensated in any way.' And in one of his articles he wrote with commendable frankness: 'Today the German nation has its biggest, but also its last chance... Just as victory would benefit all of us, defeat would annihilate us all.'

This was the first time official German propaganda conceded the possibility of defeat. It was done to shake up the home front, to clear the way for greater sacrifices in an extremely serious situation, but above all to prepare the people for a great shock.

For the events at the eastern front were indeed a great shock to the German people, and frankly incomprehensible to them. Even in case of a blitz victory several million German soldiers would have to remain in Russia. Hence the General Staff should have provided for winter uniforms, fuel, petrol that would not freeze at low temperatures, warm quarters for the troops. No such provisions had been made. The cold descended on the fighting armies, the tanks stood still because the lubricants froze in their motors, reserves were halted because the transport system broke down, the soldiers had no warm clothing, they shivered, they froze to death. Someone had made a stupendous error somewhere.

On 21 December, Goebbels published an appeal for the 'Collection of winter clothes for our Front,' and told the German people how matters stood. It was a carefully written and re-written document of great weight and brutal frankness.[8] He admitted that the competent offices of the Wehrmacht had not been able to provide all soldiers with suitable clothing. But, 'The home front ... can help protect their sons and fathers against the hardships of winter! So long as there is a single usable piece of winter clothing at home, it must be sent to the front.' He gave a list of articles that were needed: blankets, overshoes, socks, sweaters, underwear, earmuffs, headwear, knee warmers, gloves, and so on. 'Give to them whatever you have. You are helping the front to win the victory.'

Germany held its breath. Germany was rigid with shock and surprise. Was the situation as desperate as all that? Was it possible that the courageous troops, only yesterday supremely victorious, were now trapped to die in snow and ice?

Other countries were equally amazed at these announcements. In the Ministry of Information in London it was believed that Goebbels had lost his senses. Almost equally horrified were the German generals who had strongly opposed the clothes collection on the grounds that it would be a severe blow to the population at home.

But this was precisely what Goebbels had intended. 'I precipitated a shock among the people,' he later explained to his assistants, 'when I told them that we would have to face a catastrophe unless something was done at once. But I did so deliberately and consciously because I knew what the results would be. Let me give you an example to illustrate my point:

'Imagine that I would be sitting at my desk alone at night, working. Suddenly the door opens, a burglar enters my room and shouts: Hands up! It is self-evident that my first reaction is one of shock. Unconsciously I raise my hands but otherwise I sit stiffly and completely paralyzed, incapable of a clear thought. However, after a few seconds the shock begins to wear off and I begin to think what would be the most practical thing to do to get out of this dangerous situation. Maybe there is a concealed bell somewhere which I could ring without attracting attention, maybe an object within my grasp could suddenly be hurled at the attacker. In other words, my brain works feverishly to find a way out.

'The same applies to the woollens and fur collection. I produced a condition of shock in the whole people, and in view of the threatening danger it remained paralyzed for a few seconds. Then we thundered: Give us your warm clothing! And then they all produced their winter clothes, their woollens, their furs, their skis, and God knows what—and the danger was over.'

And Goebbels was right. It did not matter that the figure of 67 million pieces of clothing allegedly contributed was vastly exaggerated, as the BBC suggested. The only thing that counted was the reaction of the German home front. The Germans were shaken and frightened to death. They had listened to the accounts of the suffering of their soldiers at the front. If Goebbels ever had to fear that the home front was not up to the war, his fears were now dispelled. Goebbels had appealed to the nation's sense of honour. And those who had remained at home wanted to show that they, too, could make sacrifices for the sake of their suffering countrymen. They did not yet know that the sacrifices would become ever greater, ever more terrifying.

Deep in the heart of Russia the cold was becoming more and more intolerable. The Russians were advancing.

CHAPTER XII

WORLD WAR

I

During the night of 11-12 December a few hours after Hitler had declared war on the United States because it had 'violated all rules of neutrality'—Goebbels remained at the Propaganda Ministry. His associates were ordered to be on duty and everyone was alerted as though a major event was expected. But no one knew what was going on. There were no conferences that night, and Goebbels exchanged no personal comments with his colleagues. Every hour he read the latest news which came over the ticker. Restlessly he paced up and down in his large office. He seemed absent-minded, nervous and irritated. Something must have happened that did not fit into his scheme of things. We are left to guess what was on his mind. Many signs point to the fact that, although he must have known beforehand of Hitler's decision to declare war on the U.S., he must have secretly hoped the Fuehrer would change his mind.

Oswald Spengler had warned against any involvement with America. 'The resemblance (of the U.S.A.) to Bolshevist Russia is far greater than one imagines. There is the same breadth of landscape, which by excluding any possibility of successful attack by an invader excludes the experience of real national danger...'

Goebbels' first article after the declaration of war was published on 14 December, that is, eight days after Pearl Harbor. Entitled, 'The Great Chance,' it was full of generalities, philosophical reflections and historical comparisons, and the word 'America' was conspicuously absent. Its tone was curiously optimistic. 'The great chance has come, it is unique. The German nation will never have a similarly favourable opportunity as it has today.'

It would have been hard to say the same for Goebbels. He found himself in the most difficult situation imaginable. The war against the United States offered a propagandistic problem which, at first glance, seemed insoluble. Most Germans still remembered that America's entry into the First World War ultimately had resulted in Germany's defeat. The memory of the masses was not as poor as Goebbels would have desired. Consequently he had to act at once. In a second article he declared firmly, 'Any comparison with the third year of the World War is completely uncalled for,' and should not even be undertaken.

He quickly seized on the temporary propagandistic advantage that this time Germany, and not the U.S., had declared war. In the World War, Germany had wanted to avoid a conflict with America; this time, she was so much stronger and consequently could take the initiative. How right the Fuehrer had been to take this step! For since 7 December 'the position of the Axis powers has been strengthened in a manner which even political and military experts had believed to be altogether improbable.'

However, the reaction of the Germans was surprising. For some mysterious reason they never believed that Germany had declared war on America. Until the end, the conviction that the United States had been the aggressor could not be shaken. Thus Goebbels was clearly on the defensive. All he could do was to revive the old arguments used in the First World War, particularly the assertion that American help would either never arrive, or else arrive too late. A good deal of spade work in that respect had been done before the U.S. entered the war. As early as 30 January 1941, Hitler declared that he was not afraid of the United States, and a few days later Goebbels noted, 'The Fuehrer has left no doubt that the Reich is ready for all eventualities.' Two weeks before Pearl Harbor Goebbels had written: 'The U.S.A. has lost all terror for us...'

And how about Hitler's considered opinion that the two front war had been the cause of Germany's defeat in 1918, and that a responsible leadership would never allow a repetition of such a situation? When the Germans invaded Soviet Russia, Goebbels noted explicitly that this move was not comparable to the opening of a second front because actually England had been beaten—although she did not know it. But now the second front was here. Goebbels solved his dilemma by means of a slogan. In accordance with Hitler's dictum that 'One must never show the people more than one goal or more than one enemy,' Goebbels declared summarily that there was only one foe: the enemy was bolshevistic but also plutocratic, democratic but also imperialistic, revolutionary but also capitalistic, for the enemy was Jewish. World Jewry was the real foe. Yes, Goebbels asserted in all seriousness that the Axis and its satellites—in all about 200 million people—were threatened in their existence by approximately fifteen million people, who were widely scattered over the globe, with no state, no army, no fleet and no air force of their own. Ridiculous as his thesis was, it must nevertheless be admitted that Goebbels presented it very adroitly and carried it through with great logic.

He had begun planting the seeds for his campaign long before the Germans declared war on the United States. 'Turbulent Jewish (Bolshevist) party doctrinaires and astute Jewish capitalists are launching the most insolent coup that can be imagined... The crudest plutocracy is using Socialism in order to erect the crudest dictatorship of capital...' he wrote on 20 July 1941. A week later: 'The Jews in the City and the Jews in the Kremlin are ... in complete agreement. They dabble in Capitalism and Bolshevism, Christianity and Atheism, democracy and autocracy, Liberalism and terror, just as it suits their purposes, only to save their naked lives.'

Time and again Goebbels spoke of the 'trade alliance between Bolshevist and plutocratic Jewry', saying, 'Jewry knows two forms of maintaining its domination over the nations: that of international Capitalism and that of international Bolshevism.'

But at his morning conference Goebbels changed his tune. 'Gentlemen,' he said, 'let's not fool ourselves. There is of course no unified world Jewry—the way we present it—which will cling together in life and death. No one will seriously believe that the Jews of the City of London or the Jewish bankers in Wall Street have the same interests as the Jews sitting in Moscow's Kremlin.'[1]

Incidentally, according to Dr Taubert, Goebbels soon had occasion to regret his frankness. Someone must have reported his observation at the Fuehrer's Headquarters, for the following day Goebbels explained that his remark probably had been misunderstood: the fundamental unity of purpose of international Jewry was beyond any question of a doubt.

II

Thus Goebbels set out to prove that the United States, too, had entered the war in the service of Judaism. As early as May, 1941, he had begun to collect 'evidence' for his arguments and play it up. 'Proper attention is to be given to the findings of the *Nationalsozialistische Korrespondenz* concerning the Jewish origin of Roosevelt. Photographs of Roosevelt indicating Jewish features can be used to good advantage in that connection.'[2] Or: 'It is an open secret that the American president, Roosevelt, has surrounded himself with a large number of Jewish advisers. It is not difficult to guess what sort of advice they will whisper into his ears.'

However, all of this was mild compared to his screams about Roosevelt, now that the war with the U.S. was on. 'Seldom has there been a statesman of responsible position who has so carelessly and criminally misjudged the general world situation and the economic, moral and military strength of his opponent. Neutral observers have reported that he has become old and grey since the outbreak of the Asiatic conflict. That is only too understandable.'

Yet, Goebbels was unable to work up the type of indignation he felt over Winston Churchill. Somehow or other, the element of personal animosity was lacking. But the agitation against the United States as such was all the worse: against the press and the government, the interventionists (warmongers) and, of course, against the Jews. The cue line was that America was a country to be pitied, notwithstanding her riches. Privately Goebbels might have preferred to see certain American films or to listen to American records, but officially he stated on 18 April 1942: 'What the Americans call culture is not one in reality ... The daily bath, the motor car for father, the motor car for daughter, the higher skyscraper, the more voluminous Sunday papers...'

On 2 August: 'The same country which is warring against the oldest cultural peoples in Europe and Asia, ostensibly to save the freedom of the spirit, does not have a permanent stage nor a permanent opera. A private enterprise like the New York Metropolitan Opera lived on German and Italian operas and singers and had to close its doors at the outbreak of war, symptomatically enough, for lack of a suitable repertoire.' (Which incidentally was not true.) 'If the Americans had no money, they would probably be the most despised people on earth.'

As for the 'oldest cultural peoples in Europe and Asia,' according to Goebbels' propaganda, they were now fighting 'in defence of what they have built up over more than two thousand years.'

III

If Goebbels had been able to do it, he would have preferred to forget about the war in Russia and to make the Germans forget it, too. 'Who today still talks about the horror of the winter cold which we had to endure from January to March, 1940; who in May or June, 1942, will talk about the physical or moral burden of this winter?' the Propaganda Minister comforted his audience on 23 January 1942, realizing full well that this was poor consolation.

Despite his constant admonitions that history would not repeat itself, the people in Germany could not help thinking of another big army which had invaded Russia and had perished. What had once happened to Napoleon might now happen to Hitler. Goebbels grabbed the bull by the horns: 'A renewed reading of the literature dealing with the collapse of Napoleon's armies in the 1812 winter campaign against Russia causes us to revert once more to the battle of the German army against the Soviet Union... The comparison with Napoleon's Russian campaign limps.'

At least Goebbels hoped so. In an effort to divert public attention from the calamitous situation in Russia his propaganda apparatus concentrated with increasing vigour on—Japan. 'The beginning of winter makes it impossible to carry out large-scale operations in the East,' was Fritzsche's introduction of the new theme to his listeners. 'On the other hand, we see a war of movement in the Pacific in full swing and therefore occupy ourselves with these events...' Goebbels had already given an interview to the Japanese press in which he paid 'heartfelt tribute, in the name of the German people, to the Japanese for their work of reconstruction in East Asia.' This 'work of reconstruction' was carefully recorded through every single phase. Japanese victories became, as it were, German victories by dint of being British or American defeats.

Of equally great importance for the Propaganda Ministry were the German submarine victories. These successes were reported in special announcements introduced by fanfares. For some time in the past Goebbels had pointed out that 'the German U-boats appear in groups in the Atlantic and pick their victims among the ill-protected so-called convoys, which should be more appropriately termed funeral escorts.'

The reason for shifting the centre of gravity of German propaganda from the land war in Russia to the depths of the ocean was self-evident. The exploits of the submarine crews were surrounded by mystery, romanticism and a sense of adventure comparable perhaps to the daring feats of the pilots—and their accuracy could not be checked. When the British declared at an early date that German figures of tonnage sunk by U-boats were incorrect, Goebbels wrote in great indignation: 'It is a well-known fact that German figures in this war always corresponded to the truth. The figures we have published stem from honest German Officers and have been confirmed by countless eyewitnesses.'

This was not precisely true. The figures stemmed from Goebbels.

At an early stage of the war he had approached the Admiralty and obtained exact information as to what happened when a submarine sank a ship. The only person who could say whether a torpedo had hit its marks was the man at the periscope, usually the captain, who could tell his crew whatever he pleased, and then report it to the Admiralty. In other words, there actually was no proper control, Goebbels found, and even if all members of the crew knew that a torpedo had failed its aim, there still would be only forty witnesses who would scarcely protest if after their return they were honoured by the Admiralty for sinkings that had never taken place. Therefore, the Propaganda Ministry could operate without risk, and Goebbels exploited this situation to the fullest.

The successes of German U-boats increased to gigantic proportions while the danger of active assistance to England by the United States diminished accordingly, German propaganda claimed. 18 January 1942: 'The colossal American armament-production figures cannot suffice to terrorize the German people since that production, owing to the activity of the German submarines, will never arrive at the scene of operation...' 3 May: 'Meanwhile the enemy front is experiencing one defeat after another. Their tonnage, their most important trump in the conduct of the war, is shrinking daily at a terrifying speed.'

21 June: 'The figures of tonnage sunk by our U-boats have now reached a point which presents an acute danger for enemy naval operations, while the losses of German submarines do not correspond in any way to the boastful assertions of the British and American Admiralties.' 28 June: 'Is it to be counted for nothing that in the month of May alone England and the U.S. have lost almost one million tons of shipping space?' This propaganda continued throughout the year 1942 and into the summer of 1943. Goebbels concerned himself personally with the submarine war. He was in constant telephonic communication with the Admiralty, invented new U-boat exploits, exaggerated and dramatized whatever real results had been achieved.

IV

Still, U-boat victories were not popular. Their effect could only be measured in negative terms: if German submarines sank a sufficient number of Allied ships, the English would starve, therefore could not go on fighting and sending more planes to bomb Germany. However, the popular appeal of victory is not its negative but its positive and spectacular aspect. The popular conception of a victor is not that of a chess player who gradually manoeuvres his opponent into checkmate, but that of a daredevil conquering land, or bringing home loot and prisoners. The public is impressed by the hero of flesh and blood, not by the anonymous crew of an invisible ship operating under water.

At the beginning of the war, Goebbels had had a real, unfaked U-boat hero who, so to say, fell into his lap. As early as October, 1939, young Captain Guenther Prien was able to sink the British battleship *Royal Oak* anchored in Scapa Flow, despite all British defence measures, and afterwards he came through with a number of other successes. Prien was almost made to order for a heroic role: he was young, good-looking, talented. Unfortunately, his superiors did not cherish his popularity, which far exceeded their own, and decided to get rid of him. He was ordered to go out to sea in a submarine which needed repairs. Prien refused, was arrested and—disappeared. It was impossible to court-martial this idol of the people, so Prien vanished into a concentration camp. On 24 May 1941, the public was advised that Prien had not returned from an enemy mission. Later he was taken to the medieval cells of the military prison of Torgau, and (according to Berlin newspaper reports in February, 1946) was liquidated at the beginning of 1945.

Goebbels found no substitute for Prien. By 1942 the average length of life of a U-boat man was forty-six days.

Ever since the beginning of the war Goebbels had looked for 'heroes,' men he could build up, as he had done with Schlageter or Horst Wessel. However, the German High Command was opposed to this form of heroization, for the generals had been the stars in the First World War and did not fancy being dethroned. Even Hitler himself did not favour the idea, largely because he wanted no other gods who might temporarily obscure his fame. The Propaganda Minister had good reason for refusing to endow the generals with glamour, for most of them were not real Nazis. Often they had stood apart, reserved, a little hostile. Their victories had been military, and not Nazi victories.

But Goebbels would not give up his search for a 'hero'. Every time a war correspondent returned to Berlin, every time a cameraman delivered his cellulose strips to the Propaganda Ministry, Goebbels was notified. He talked privately to every one of them and his questions showed that he was seeking desperately for someone he could transform into a 'hero'.

There were a few fliers who might have qualified for this role. But their life, too, was short. Hardly had Goebbels made them famous when they died.

Goebbels' great chance was with Field-Marshal Erwin Rommel. This relatively-young officer did not belong to the clique of the generals, and was not an aristocrat. Furthermore, he became interested in tanks at a time when other German generals regarded them as mechanized coffins and, motorized warfare as undignified and unchivalrous. Since Hitler always was in favour of motorized weapons, he was, in a way, personally responsible for Rommel's career. After Rommel's spectacular victories in France (Abbéville), Goebbels began methodically to blow him up to heroic dimensions. Party speakers 'revealed' that Rommel was an old member of the N.S.D.A.P., and a member of the S.S. who had known Hitler in the early days of the movement. None of this was true, but it was the basis of Rommel's popularity. Time and again the war correspondents described him as a general who always fought in the front lines by the side of his troops, with supreme disregard for his personal safety.

In the winter of 1941–42 Rommel made a name for himself in North Africa. The victories of the Afrika Korps were a welcome diversion for Goebbels, for they took the attention away from the costly battles in Russia. The longer the war lasted, the more his propaganda machine concentrated on Rommel, who, although he was fighting at the front, nevertheless was not exposed to the same dangers as a U-boat officer or a flier.

The truth of the matter was that Goebbels had great sympathy for Rommel. He believed that this modest man had greater moral stature than most of the other generals, he was impressed with the almost primitive simplicity of Rommel's heroism, and he liked his straightforward and uncomplicated nature. Whenever the general came to Berlin, Goebbels would invite him to his home, where he had long talks with him and made him relate his experiences at the front. In the end he not only appreciated him as a propagandistic asset but he grew genuinely fond of him.

All the greater was Goebbels' disappointment over Rommel in July, 1944.

V

All of Goebbels' colleagues, assistants, secretaries and stenographers found that he had changed since his appeal for winter clothing for the German troops in Russia, and since the war against the U.S. had started. As far as was possible for him, he had adopted a military strictness and snappiness. He was no longer capricious and unpredictable in temper, he seldom made jokes, he would not allow himself or others to be discursive, he demanded merciless, purposeful concentration.

All those who spoke with him could feel the fundamental change in his personality. This man, whose magnificent command of the German language was equalled by no other Nazi, now confined himself to what might be called a military vocabulary, narrowed down to a minimum of cold, clear-cut words and phrases which were constantly repeated, as though there could be only one opinion on the subject under discussion.

His favourite expressions were, 'It is clear that ...', 'There can be no doubt that ...', 'I am firmly convinced that ...', 'Be that as it may ...' He always spoke 'from first-hand knowledge.' And when he criticized others, which happened with increasing frequency, he would start out by saying, dangerously calm, 'Of course, that won't do at all,' or, 'It cannot be done that way.'

The timbre of his voice changed completely whenever there was mention of Hitler. When Der Fuehrer assumed command of the eastern front at the end of 1941, Goebbels stated that now the sufferings would be more bearable, and cold and snow would no longer be 'quite so biting and torturing as before.' Later, in his radio speech on Hitler's birthday, he compared him to the greatest general Germany had ever had—Frederick the Great—and in June, 1942, he modestly described Hitler as 'the greatest military genius in our history.' Everything was bound to turn out all right, Goebbels assured the public, because 'the Goddess of History, once invoked by human beings and nations, does not stop until her work is done.'

Did Goebbels believe his own words? Did he really have unconditional faith in Hitler's mission and Hitler's greatness? We have seen that in the first months of the Russian war Goebbels caught his Fuehrer in a serious error which, from a propagandist's point of view, was inexcusable. Did he not sound a little too enthusiastic to be credible, when he now spoke of Hitler? Did it not seem that he had to make greater efforts than ever to abide by his decision never to criticize or analyze Hitler's actions and always to worship him in unquestioning loyalty?

Yes, Goebbels had to shut both eyes to keep his pledge to himself. For now that the summer was approaching, now that something had to happen in Russia, now that Hitler was planning another big offensive, Goebbels fell into an error which according to his own reasoning must be avoided at all cost: he prophesied speedy victory.

VI

The planned offensive in the south was to be camouflaged, such was Goebbels' assignment given to him by Hitler himself. Goebbels said he was 'proud' to be entrusted with this mission. 'Now we will start beating the drums,' he told his associates. 'Everyone will be led to believe that soon the central sector of the front will be mobilized for the final thrust toward Moscow. Then, when we have convinced the enemy of the reality of this campaign, we will suddenly break out in the south. In the afternoon I will send for Dr Kriegk, of the Scherl Publishing House, and tell him of our plans. I will send him to the Balkans. Kriegk is a talkative man and will see to it that everyone learns we plan another offensive against Moscow.'

There was a false ring to his enthusiasm. And what a puny assignment for a man who for the past twelve years had solved staggering propaganda problems! For a man who had camouflaged the beginning of the whole war in Russia, with a wave of his left hand, as it were, the propagandistic manoeuvre in conjunction with the southern offensive was nothing.

But during that period he had no other tasks. The war had entered a stage in which propaganda played a secondary role. There were no more blitz victories, hence there was nothing to be exploited by propaganda. The illusion of a New Europe had been buried. It was very evident that the other side had the initiative. The BBC broadcasts were able to point out daily that Hitler had not kept his promises, that Russia was not defeated, that England had not been brought to her knees. Goebbels' answers were somewhat dispirited. He would write: 'Let us consider it the greatest honour to be attacked and insulted by the enemy, and let us consider it the deepest disgrace to be praised and flattered by him. Then his mendacious propaganda will be smashed against the wall of our national discipline.'

What exactly was the state of 'national discipline' at that time? How did the Germans bear up under the war which lasted so much longer than they had been told? And, above all, what could Goebbels undertake to bolster the morale of the people?

German newspapers were more boring than ever. As head of the Press division Hans Fritzsche had tried in vain to maintain a certain level of journalistic competence. Throughout 1941 and at the beginning of 1942 he had endeavoured to eliminate the worst excesses and to keep out the most abysmal stupidities, but apparently Goebbels did not give him sufficient support. Angry and discouraged, Fritzsche resigned and, before Goebbels could interfere, volunteered for the Russian front, and thus Goebbels lost his most talented collaborator.

He now turned to his closest associate, Ministerialrat Dr Werner Naumann. Naumann had been an early Nazi, and Goebbels had met him when he was a student. He was slender and of medium height, and had finally chiselled features. He still looked extremely young, although he was in his early thirties. Goebbels had great confidence in him and gave him wider responsibility than to any other of his associates. Although Naumann was married and had five children, he was dedicated to his work, to the exclusion of everything else, and practically lived at the Propaganda Ministry, or at Schwanenwerder and Lanke with Goebbels.

Here he met Magda, who was ten years older than he. Magda again was feeling neglected. This time there was no rival, for Miss X had found no successor, and the film stars whom Goebbels would take to his place in Lanke whenever Magda was in town or in Schwanenwerder were of no consequence in his life. This time work and worries kept him away from Magda and made him a little indifferent. Magda needed comfort and understanding and Dr Naumann was the right man for an ageing woman who had managed to preserve her beauty. They took long walks in the country, talked about books, enjoyed each other's company. For him this would have been sufficient, but she was not satisfied with a platonic relationship. For the second time she deceived her husband with one of his subordinates.

VII

Since Fritzsche's departure Goebbels had more or less given up the German press as hopeless. Privately he admitted that the work of newspaper-men had become 'quite unsatisfying' because they were altogether too hampered by Goebbels' innumerable restrictions. Sometimes he was almost tempted to give them greater freedom—'after the war,' as he hastily added.

Then again he would become incensed over the stupidity of German journalists. Often he was beside himself with anger, and would shout: 'If you can't do the job, I'll go and get some of those London Jews!' And, practically on the verge of apoplexy, he would scream: 'They know how to do it!'

Finally, he concentrated more and more on his periodical, *Das Reich*. But he did try to streamline the German radio in an attempt to make broadcasts more interesting and attractive. For the radio had practically dropped to the low level of the press. Programmes consisted of speeches and music interrupted by an occasional news-show, and from five a.m. to eleven p.m. they communicated nothing but yawning boredom. All Nazi celebrations were transmitted word for word; there were interminable theoretical lectures on Nazi *weltanschauung* and racial theory to which no one cared to listen.

Goebbels rounded up his radio experts and tried to explain the fundamentals of radio broadcasts. At the start of each conference he would take out bits of paper from the pockets of his suit, filled with notes he had made while listening to the programmes. All his comments were negative, he never found anything good on the German radio.

Then Goebbels would say: 'Gentlemen, not the listeners, but *The Listener*, is important.' What he meant by *The Listener* was clear from a directive which said: 'You are not planning programmes for *Geheimrat Y.*,[3] but for the lumberjack in Bad Aibling.'

The lumberjack of Bad Aibling (a small town east of Munich) became a legendary figure. He turned up every time Goebbels lectured his radio experts. 'Do you seriously believe that this sort of thing will arouse the lumberjack of Bad Aibling?' he used to say with a mixture of irony and anger, when a programme had caused his displeasure.

There was another character who played an important part in his criticism of the radio—his chauffeur. While he was driving to Schwanenwerder or to Lanke, he always listened to the radio and then asked his driver what he thought of the programmes. The driver gave him his frank opinion: he did not seem to like the programmes. Goebbels nodded—to the voice of the people. The next day his radio experts were summoned and told of his driver's comments. Eventually even the highest executives of the German radio were living in mortal terror of Goebbels' driver. It sometimes happened that a programme which had been planned was dropped at the last minute because someone remarked during the rehearsals: 'I'm afraid the chauffeur of the Herr Minister won't like it.'

Next to the lumberjack and the chauffeur, the various Gauleiters and Martin Bormann had considerable influence in shaping the radio programmes. The Gauleiters knew the people's mood—or at least were supposed to. Often, after a conference with the Gauleiters, all previous radio plans were thrown overboard, much to the disgust of the executives. But they had given up contradicting Goebbels: for more than once Goebbels had become so irritated that he had dismissed the argumentative official and sent him to the front.

VIII

At that time Goebbels introduced several new features. First of all, there were the so-called Front Reports, recordings made at the front of the eyewitness story of the uniformed reporters, with an announcer piecing the accounts together. Then there was the Mirror of the Time, treating non-military events with the same news-reel technique. But the greatest success was Goebbels' editorial in *Das Reich*, which since November, 1941, was read over the radio every Friday night.

Here it became evident how much Goebbels' new style, calm and soothing, answered the requirements of a protracted war. Although he never made promises and always warned of over-optimism, the people responded to his articles, which gave them comfort, hope and a feeling of security. After every transmission thousands of letters poured in from all parts of the country proving that Goebbels had struck the right note. And he was able to state with satisfaction, on 8 February 1942, 'U.S. papers were writing several days ago that all hopes for the collapse of German morale have to be definitely buried.'

'Today the German people are behaving much more admirably than, for instance, during the offensive in France,' he continued. 'If the radio comes through with a special announcement every three hours, it does not take much to believe in victory. However, if the conquered territory has to be tenaciously defended, if our leadership is confronted daily with new difficulties, moral fortitude is required. And the German people have given magnificent proof of moral fortitude.'

Of course, at times their 'moral fortitude' was lacking. In an article, 'Open Talk,' Goebbels had to cheer up the Germans over reduced rations. The tenor of such announcements was worked out in advance. For instance, if the bread ration was to be reduced while the fat ration went up a few ounces to take the sting out of the measure, Goebbels would say: 'Tomorrow I don't want to read any headlines such as, "More Fat!"' Then followed an extensive lecture on the psychology of announcing unfavourable news. 'There is no point,' he would say, 'in trying to create the impression that the nutritional situation has improved. The people are much too smart not to see through such clumsy manoeuvres and it would only be to our disadvantage to start off with a favourable, but insignificant item, and then to try and brush off the negative measure which will have much graver repercussions. Therefore, it would be better if we announced with appropriate solemnity: Yes, we can very well appreciate what this means and we are in no position to tell you when this undoubtedly serious restriction will be rescinded. On the other hand, this step is absolutely indispensable because… and now follows an objective and intelligible explanation based on facts, so that every reader will say to himself: Well, I understand it, and there's nothing to be done about it.'

On the other hand, Goebbels raged against the *miessmacher und kritikaster*, who refused to make even the smallest sacrifices. 'What is so infuriating is when someone at the home front takes no notice of the war … and starts whining over the fact that there is so little tobacco, while he himself is puffing away at one cigarette after another.'

While Goebbels permitted himself such comments, he did not accord the same privilege to England or the United States. 'Enemy propaganda, intended to corrupt our national unity and morale, cannot even scratch our skin, to say nothing of piercing our hearts,' he hopefully wrote. In those days Allied propaganda was once more under heavy attack, and again Churchill was the principal villain. 'It is part of his tactics to present the past in the blackest colours and then to detect a silver lining on the dark horizon of the present… It is his strategy to paint the past darker than it was in order to make the present seem lighter than it is. He admits that things are going badly, but he adds that previously they were going still worse.' Goebbels wrote these lines on 1 March 1942, but on 22 March, he followed Churchill's recipe: 'It would be ill-fitting and tending to minimize the glorious accomplishments of our conduct of the war if we were to convey the impression, now that the worst is behind us, that our difficulties last winter had been merely child's play.'

He used his heavy guns against the United States. August W. Halfeld, a correspondent who had returned from America, had written a book entitled, *I Saw U.S.A. During the War*, which was given the widest circulation. Even judged by Goebbels' standards it was the height of bad taste. It was mainly directed against Roosevelt, who was described as a sick man on the brink of lunacy. Roosevelt's marital life was presented as scandalous, his children were delinquent, his government was incompetent, the leaders of the army were ignorant blunderers, and the heads of the fleet were ninnies. The American people were lazy, and neither young nor vigorous. The Jews played a preponderant part in all walks of life, and so did the Negroes, who were about to seize power. The United States was still a colony, Halfeld said, adding innumerable other unsavoury details in the same vein.

IX

The spring and summer offensive (which Goebbels was ordered to camouflage) had not yielded the desired results. The only one who had won a victory was Goebbels himself. For, on 6 November 1942, it turned out that Stalin had really believed in the probability of an offensive against Moscow. He said that 'the purpose of the advance to the south was ... to divert our reserves as far as possible from Moscow and to weaken the Moscow front so as to make it easier to strike at Moscow. In short, the principal objective of the German summer offensive was to surround Moscow and to end the war this year.'

This statement probably caused Goebbels to smile, but otherwise the Russians gave him little cause for mirth. They not only turned out to be formidable opponents of the German army but also witty, astute adversaries of German propaganda. Ever since August 1941 German news broadcasts transmitted over the Deutschlandsender were suddenly interrupted by an unknown voice screaming, 'Lies! Lies!' There were also derogatory comments and rectifications of the German army communiqués. The staff of the Deutschlandsender became frantic. They stopped sending news, putting on musical selections. As soon as the announcer attempted to sneak in news there was the 'voice' again cutting in when he paused for breath, speaking as clearly and as unperturbedly as ever. Finally the Deutschlandsender had to sign off and ask the public to tune in on its local stations.

German engineers who investigated the constant interruptions in the broadcasts discovered that they emanated from Moscow. Somehow a way had been found to synchronize wave length so that one station could cut in on the broadcasts of another. There seemed to be no protection against it. Later on, Goebbels' and even Hitler's voices were imitated and there were speeches that sounded completely authentic until they wound up in a maze of defeatist talk.

The man behind these propagandistic manoeuvres was Solomon Abramovich Lozovsky, Vice-Commissar for Foreign Affairs, who had a great deal of European experience. Not content with interrupting German official broadcasts or with imitating Hitler's and Goebbels' voices, his radio speakers got in direct touch with the German people, over the head of its government. This was done in the following manner:

On the body of a captured German soldier the Russians found a letter from his mother saying that father was ailing and needed nourishing food which could not be bought anywhere. This woman was named over the Russian radio, her address was given, and her neighbours were asked to convey a message if the woman could not listen in. The message said: the soldier's father should go to this or that black-market restaurant in Berlin, where the big Nazis dined and wined, and where he would be able to eat everything he needed to get well. It was mentioned, as an after-thought, that the price for such a meal far exceeded his weekly earnings.

Numerous similar items were broadcast to Germany every day. They did not have an overwhelming effect on the population, yet they made Goebbels nervous.

X

He became even more nervous by the ever-increasing demands of the Russians for a second front. This is interesting in many respects. Actually these cries were an admission of weakness and Goebbels should have noted with satisfaction that the Russians evidently feared they would not be able to carry on by themselves. But there was not a trace of satisfaction among the Nazis. The very mention of the second front caused the German General Staff to wince, and Goebbels assured his readers and listeners that all attempts to invade Europe were doomed to fail.

In order to 'prove' his point he used every shred of 'evidence'. In April, 1942, when British commandos landed at Boulogne in what was scheduled to be a brief raid he 'demonstrated' that the invasion of the Continent had failed. On 24 August, after the attempt was repeated at Dieppe on a much larger scale, Goebbels noted: 'The British Government know as well as we do ... that the attempt to make a second front can only be compared to a political and military suicide.' In an article reminiscent of his best fighting days, calling Churchill a 'prisoner of the Kremlin,' he established the thesis that the British Prime Minister had ordered the landings merely to prove to the Russians and to his own people that an invasion was not possible. In this instance Goebbels showed himself to be an excellent mind-reader. For the British did use the Dieppe raid to prove to their Russian and American allies that it would be extremely difficult in the future to establish a beach head.[4]

Goebbels never tired of proving to himself and others that an invasion was unthinkable, and it became a fixed idea in his mind. The Allies must not land in Europe, as a matter of fact, they cannot land in Europe. One of his articles was called, 'Entrance to Europe Blocked!' He asserted that 'No madness would precipitate a greater disaster for the Allies than the opening of a second front... The British have been told often enough, and with brutal frankness, that the entrance to Europe is blocked for them.' And: 'The only thing of importance are the German soldiers who are stationed everywhere and eagerly waiting for the opportunity to give Churchill's troops a hearty welcome.' Another article in the same vein was entitled, 'Even the Attempt is Punishable!' namely the attempt of an invasion, and ended with the words: 'It would be a pleasure for the German soldiers also to explain to the Yankees that for them, too, the entrance to Europe is *verboten*.'

XI

During that summer Goebbels went to Venice. It was his third trip to the city which he loved. Formerly he had used the pretext of the *Biennale*, the film festivals, to go to Venice, and he participated, as it were, in his official capacity as the master of the German film. This time he went for pleasure and relaxation and it was probably no accident that a number of young and beautiful film stars were staying there, too.

His journey was made under an unlucky star. Goebbels had planned to make a speech in Italian on the Piazza San Marco, although he could not speak Italian. He wrote his speech in Berlin, had it translated and phonetically rewritten. But when he arrived in Venice, he was given to understand that it would be better if he refrained from giving the speech.

He was beside himself over this rebuff, and equally incensed at the way he was treated during the first two official receptions.

He did not trust the Italians, and suspected them of trying to listen in on his confidential conversations. From then on he would dictate to his stenographer in a whisper, which caused a good deal of confusion. He insisted that his assistants telephoned with Berlin in an improvised code. The Luftwaffe, for instance, was referred to as 'Uncle Hermann.' This gave rise to further confusion and finally led to a kind of conspiracy between assistants and stenographers who decided to submit to him only the most important cables. Goebbels failed to see through this trick and dictated into his diary: 'The telegrams from Berlin are extremely scarce. But I am rather pleased about this momentary calm in the world. It gives me an opportunity to rest up a bit, and I certainly need it.'

After a week a gondola ride was arranged through the Canale Grande. One of the gondolas was reserved for Goebbels and three actresses as well as a tenor who, accompanied by a violin and a concertina, sang his arias to a nocturnal sky. With the exception of Goebbels all of them drank a great deal of the wine which had been stowed away in another gondola. When the tenor was silent, the two S.S. men in the fourth gondola burst into a Nazi marching song. In great indignation Goebbels commanded them to 'shut up at once with these infernal howls.'

After another hour they were all rather tipsy. Suddenly one of the actresses took off her clothes, jumped into the water and swam around, then others followed, until Goebbels, now almost by himself, was left a startled and annoyed onlooker. He finally ordered them back and the prescribed tour through the canals got under way again. Nobody opened his mouth, not even the tenor. Goebbels, too, remained silent and bad-tempered.

Several days later he gave a big party at the Palazzo del Mari. As usual he was in great form, talked to ten people at a time, and was his brilliant, witty, ironical self. Towards the end of the evening a famous magician entertained the guests with a number of tricks. He selected the Minister as his partner and amused himself by producing coins and even a rabbit from Goebbels' evening suit. Everybody was fascinated, trying to follow his movements and paying little or no attention to Goebbels, who had become merely an object of the magician's skill. After a while Goebbels remarked: 'That will be enough for tonight,' and his voice sounded unfriendly. Two days afterwards he returned to Berlin.

His tone became even more serious. He explained that the Russians should not be underestimated because 'throughout their history they have always distinguished themselves by extreme tenacity and perseverance.' 'It was never a German quality to underestimate the opponent. This is equally true in the present war,' he said.

On 26 August, Moscow reported that a battle for Stalingrad had started. One month later Goebbels stated: 'It is self-evident that for the longer duration of the war we will have to make greater sacrifices.' His propaganda compared the war to the ascent of a mountain—an image which he was to use as a leitmotif for many months to come: after the mountaineer has climbed for a long time and feels that his strength is about exhausted he suddenly notices a particularly steep stretch, which frightens him. But once he has accomplished the difficult ascent he finds to his joy and amazement that he is already at the top.

However, the other leaders of the Third Reich imagined that the final sprint would be brief. Ribbentrop declared on 27 September that Russia was lost. On 30 September Hitler spoke at the Sportpalast about the strategic significance of Stalingrad: 'The occupation of Stalingrad which will be concluded will become a gigantic success and we will deepen and strengthen this success. And you can be of the firm conviction that no human being shall ever push us away from that spot.'

Goebbels, who spoke on that same evening, was infinitely more cautious. Again he indulged in generalities, reviewed the history of the war, pointed up the propagandistic errors of the enemies, promised nothing, prophesied nothing.

His speech was the prelude to a new winter-help campaign. Since the Nazis had come to power the winter-help was organized every year. In 1933 Goebbels had inaugurated it under the motto of fighting against hunger and cold. He had been able to collect enormous sums, particularly with the aid of famous actors and actresses as well as prominent Nazis and their wives, all of whom had to participate in the collection. Especially Goering had always been a great success. He would stand with his box at the entrance of the Air Ministry and chat and joke with every passer-by who put in a coin, and people were queuing up in long lines to give Goering their money. Goebbels had not been able to shirk this duty and usually he would be stationed in front of the Hotel Adlon. Unlike Goering, he did not enjoy the performance, and when a radio reporter once came up to him for a brief interview, he motioned him away and said in a strained voice: 'Please don't. Today is the people's day.' It was very evident that the man who addressed millions from the speaker's platform found intimate contact with the masses distasteful.

But all this was quite a long while ago. Since the beginning of the war the cabinet ministers had more urgent matters to attend to than to collect coins at street corners. The wives of Goering and Goebbels, however, still busied themselves in this manner, as did the wives of less prominent Nazis. Now, in 1942, for the first time there were little unpleasant incidents. Perhaps the ladies had appeared too smartly dressed and the people probably sensed the irony that, clad in precious furs, they were supposed to fight against 'hunger and cold.' There were many derogatory comments from the public, the ladies looked wide-eyed and startled, and soon repaired to their cars.

Matters were not going well, and Goebbels knew it. His Gauleiters told it to him. He learned it from the ever-increasing number of anonymous letters arriving daily at the Propaganda Ministry. For a few weeks Dr Naumann and his secretaries seriously considered whether they should discontinue submitting to Goebbels the usual *briefuebersicht*, a survey of letters comprising six to ten typed pages with exact figures on the number of favourable and unfavourable letters, indicating the most important topics, and the percentage of letters from home and from the front. But finally Naumann decided to be honest with the Minister. Sometimes Goebbels would read the worst anonymous letters himself, his lips tightly closed, a frown on his forehead. Then he would put them aside without a word, sit down and write an article entitled, 'For Whom Does Time Work?' urging his public 'to have patience.'

For whom was time working? In the last days of October, 1942, General Montgomery defeated Hitler's darling, Rommel. The end of the Afrika Korps had begun. On 8 November the Americans landed in North Africa. On that day Hitler announced that Stalingrad had been taken.

CHAPTER XIII

THE CATASTROPHE

I

From 7 November 1942, the Propaganda Ministry was in constant telephonic communication with the army and navy supreme commands. American and British troop transports had been sighted. It was believed that the landings would take place in Sicily and in Tobruk, on the North African coast, and German submarines and part of the Luftwaffe had been rushed there to trap the Allies and annihilate their forces. Everyone in the Propaganda Ministry sat waiting breathlessly for the developments. Never before was a German victory more greatly needed than at this moment.

Instead, the Allies got off a little earlier than had been anticipated, and before Berlin could find its bearings the first landings had been accomplished. Goebbels was incensed. How was it possible that the High Command had thus been duped? He knew that it was not the fault of the Intelligence Service. Its chief, Admiral Canaris, had advised Goebbels several weeks before that he had forwarded a report to Field-Marshal Keitel and to Hitler, naming Casablanca, Oran and Algiers as the places of landing. (According to H. R. Berndorff, well-known Berlin reporter.)

The Germans had also been tipped-off from other quarters. As early as September the Grand Mufti of Jerusalem had notified Ribbentrop of the contemplated Allied invasion, and an agent of the Foreign Office had sent out warnings in August, which he followed up by exact dates of the landings.[1]

But no one had paid attention to these admonitions, and now it was too late. Instead of announcing a victory Goebbels was obliged to explain away an extremely embarrassing situation. 'Gangster methods!' screamed the Berlin press. 'A brutal assault!' shrieked the German radio. Churchill and Roosevelt were denounced as war criminals who had violated international law. The Americans were accused of grabbing military bases in the Mediterranean which they would never surrender to their rightful owners, and they were 'unmasked' as imperialists.

None of these arguments were particularly forceful, coming, as they did, from a country which for more than two years had held large parts of Europe in subjection. Goebbels knew it, but he could not think of anything better. On 18 November he made a speech, in which he barely touched on the subject of Africa, and conjectured that 'a retreat, regrettable as it may be, does not in itself represent any significant change in the military situation.'

Goebbels was not exactly inspired in those days. Nevertheless he wrote innumerable articles and made radio speeches. Most of his articles were written with almost philosophical detachment, keeping more or less to generalities; they seldom had any bearing on the prevailing war situation. The African invasion was only mentioned at a later date, and then it was presented as an attack of the Americans and British against 'their former ally, France.' The enemy's success had been won cheaply because he had 'sought and found a spot which offered only minor resistance.' As Africa was far away and the average German was not sea-minded, he gladly swallowed the argument that 'Europe is the centre in the conduct of the war, while Africa is merely on its periphery.'

Russia was farther away than Africa, but there was no sea separating the two countries, and, therefore, the people felt that the Russian front was much closer. Goebbels could still be evasive, trying to gain time, explaining his silence. 'Every report we issue is read all over the world, and it frequently happens that a news item which is useful for home consumption becomes very harmful if it is known abroad.'

This was well put and, up to a point, even correct, and hence many people bowed to the Goebbels pronouncement and resolved to be patient. But how long would their patience hold out?

II

Here is a typical day in Goebbels' life at that time.

At 6 a.m. sharp a container dropped from a chute on to a desk in room No. 24 in the Propaganda Ministry. An old man took out a sealed envelope marked 'Reports for the Minister,' went up a flight of stairs to the next floor to room No. 69, knocked, handed the envelope to a secretary on the nightshift, and left.

The secretary scanned the material—mostly news which had come in during the night—put it in a briefcase and gave it to a messenger who immediately drove to the Minister's residence (sometimes to Schwanenwerder or Lanke).

There Goebbels' personal assistant, Winfried von Oven or Dr Rudolf Semmler, who always had to be at hand, was awakened. He ascertained when the Minister would get up, gave orders to awaken him fifteen minutes beforehand, and went back to sleep. When it was time, still in his pyjamas, the assistant rushed over to the desk, briefly read the material, underlined the most important passages in red pencil, put the batch of reports in a red leather briefcase and turned it over to Goebbels' servant, who took it to his master's bedside. While Goebbels was having a cup of tea he would read the latest news.

'A few minutes before nine a.m. his black Mercedes Compressor drove up at the entrance of the Propaganda Ministry, and his adjutant—during the last years he was *S.S. Hauptsturmfuehrer* Guenther Schwaegermann—helped Goebbels out of the car. From the interior of the building emerged two officials of the Security Service, a doorman, the wife of the superintendent, and they all greeted him with 'Heil Hitler,' which Goebbels answered with his own casual version of the Hitler salute.

In the company of his personal assistant, who carried a tremendous briefcase, and followed by the adjutant and the S.D. (*Sicherheitsdienst*, or Security Service) officials he walked up the staircase covered with thick rugs and through two halls into the anteroom of his office, where two pretty secretaries welcomed him with a breezy 'Heil Hitler, Herr Minister.' 'Please let me have the latest telegrams,' Goebbels said, cleared his throat and disappeared into his office. Several minutes later he was already submerged in heaps of new material.

Meanwhile Under-secretary Dr Naumann had arrived, and rushed to Goebbels for his daily report. At ten o'clock the stenographer appeared for dictation of Goebbels' diary. He crossed the room, and stopped in front of the huge desk. Goebbels was still studying the telegrams, glanced up when his stenographer was immediately confronting him, nodded, smiled, started to dictate at once, without pause, in a rapid monotone. On his desk was a small notebook with a few entries on yesterday's developments. While he was dictating he struck out notes, the green pencil never leaving his hand, the cigarette always dangling from a corner of his mouth.

Altogether the dictation took ten minutes. Before he had said the last word, he would tear up his notes, and hand the bits of paper to the stenographer to be pulped in a special shredder.

'I want to see the latest telegrams,' Goebbels said, and they were brought in to him.

They did not improve his temper. Rommel was retreating further, and German U-boats reported but few sinkings of Allied troop transports.

The adjutant and his secretary had entered, were instructed as to who was to receive an invitation, who was to receive notes of congratulation, where and when a new trip was to be prepared. Meanwhile Dr Naumann had reappeared together with the chief of cabinet. At 11.30 a.m. the liaison officer of the Army Supreme Command dashed in, a little out of breath; he had waited to the last minute to bring the most up-to-date news. The stenographer, too, had made his entrance again. The Minister rose, shook hands with the officer, and asked, 'Well, how are things? Pretty bad, eh?'

Goebbels said the same thing every morning. The reply was just as stereotyped: 'Well, I wouldn't say *bad*, Herr Minister.' The gentlemen stepped to the large table where a number of maps were displayed. The officer began his lecture. Goebbels interrupted him frequently, asked questions which the man could not answer. In such moments Goebbels was unscrupulously honest, both with himself and others. 'Supposing the enemy should break through here, that would be terrible, wouldn't it?' The officer stammered something unintelligible, Goebbels smiled a slightly malicious smile, with just a trace of contempt, and dismissed the subject.

Actually he had learned nothing new. The military knew no more than he did himself, all they knew was what came over the ticker. Africa was being lost, Japanese victories had ceased. The situation before Stalingrad was going from bad to worse.

'This —— war,' Goebbels said, grinning. 'You've got to say that once in a while, and then you can clear your throat and go on to other things,' he added, whereupon, accompanied by his entourage, he left for his daily conference.

III

Shortly before eleven a.m. a number of cars pulled up before the Propaganda Ministry. Men in mufti and in uniform went to the first floor, where they wrote their names on a list, and then took a seat. In all about twenty men assembled around a conference table, with Goebbels presiding.

Even before he sat down he began to talk. On the basis of the telegrams just received he gave instructions to the various propaganda services. He carefully analyzed certain reports, indicating how they could be exploited to best advantage. Or, he dealt exclusively with news which had a polemical angle, suggesting the proper sarcastic commentary. On special occasions he would order a suitable cartoon to be run along with the news, although generally he did not think much of them as, for instance, in the case of Churchill, Stalin or Roosevelt. 'If we satirize these men too often,' he said, 'the effect will be negative. The people will say: Well, that Churchill, all right, he's lying, so what? But, after all, you must admit he has a certain stature. His lies have stature, you see. So don't tell me anything about public opinion, gentlemen. Isn't it true, am I not right?'

'Right!' inevitably chimed the subordinates.

If the Minister was in good humour everyone would have a roaring time at his conference, particularly when Goebbels commented on the European monarchs. 'Before I forget it,' he would say, 'here's a story on King Blank. We may publish this briefly, with an appropriately offensive comment. You know, this King Blank is a bastard. (Brief pause, while everybody laughed.) All kings are bastards! It's an occupational disease!' Prolonged laughter, while Goebbels, seized with his own hilarity, would virtually suffocate, and tears would stream down his cheeks.

His wrath could be just as noisy as his laughter. When he was angry, his voice could be heard through practically sound-proof doors. Curiously enough, in his fits of rage this little man had a habit of calling other people 'dwarfs,' even if they towered over him. 'You ridiculous dwarf!' he would thunder, limping around his unhappy victim who was thus obliged constantly to circle around in order to face his master. 'You dwarf, you! I shall throw you to the German people!' No one ever found out exactly what he meant by that enigmatic threat.

Finally, the weekly news-reel was discussed. The longer the war lasted, the more difficult it became to turn out a good news-reel. 'We cannot for ever show soldiers just advancing and retreating,' Goebbels noted. 'It looks the same anyhow.'

'Any queries or reports?' was his last question. It very seldom happened someone would ask a question. The Minister rose. By that time it was noon. He would receive some visitors—a general, a film producer, a delegation from the front, a flier who had received a high decoration.

Luncheon was served at home and was attended by Goebbels' personal assistant, his adjutant and occasional guests, and it was a brief affair. Goebbels would talk uninterruptedly about the war, about political problems, sometimes about films and literature, while the others confined themselves to a laconic 'Yes,' or 'No.' Goebbels would eat little, and then disappear for a two hours' nap. His adjutant and other close associates also tried to enjoy a siesta because the rest of the day would be strenuous and Goebbels was in the habit of working late into the night.

In the afternoon there were other visitors: propaganda speakers, Kreisleiters, Reich propaganda chiefs. Goebbels would give them an extemporaneous talk in which he endeavoured to imbue them with courage: 'You've known me long enough, gentlemen, to be certain that I have never harboured any illusions, that I have always judged the situation soberly and objectively. Here in this restricted circle I don't have to embellish anything. Therefore, I want to give you a realistic picture of the situation as it presents itself today.' And then he described it in much rosier terms than was warranted, hinted that a change for the better was imminent, that production would rise, and that new plans were about to be completed—and his visitors fell for his palaver. They were grateful for being given his confidence and so easily were comforted.

IV

They certainly needed comforting. The number of grumbling citizens increased. To tell the people that the front was remote was one thing, but to explain away Allied bombardments, in which thousands perished and whole towns were devastated, was quite another. Here was one more almost insoluble propaganda problem for Goebbels, particularly as Goering had promised the nation at the beginning of the war that no Allied planes would ever drop bombs over Germany.

The first British bombers which appeared over German cities had caused only minor damage. The population streamed to see the buildings that had been hit, acting as though they were on a sightseeing tour, and refusing to take it seriously. Goebbels, too, tried to minimize the first bombardments by limiting the news to a few lines. These were his tactics even when the air attacks increased in violence, when the damage mounted and when the people became frightened.

'The morning after a heavy air attack on large cities it is admitted that a few people also lost their lives. A week later you hear, almost parenthetically, that there had been several thousand dead.' This was written by Goebbels himself—but at the time of the German air blitz over Britain, when he ridiculed British reports. Now he used the same propaganda device. 'Every foreigner who comes to Berlin is surprised to find the city intact.' On 14 June 1942, he wrote: 'The British pretension of destroying our armament industry and our supplies by bombing ... is nonsensical... During a heavy British air raid on Cologne we lost altogether 305 dead ... but American and British papers speak of twenty thousand casualties...'

Then, suddenly, almost overnight, Goebbels changed his line. The newspapers not only were allowed to report on the bombings: they were *forced* to. The reason was that it was impossible to conceal something that was known to so many people, and Goebbels risked losing his own prestige and the confidence of the German nation.

Goebbels invented the term 'terror attack'. The average German was led to think that the Allies, without the slightest provocation, had decided to wipe out German women and children from the air and thus to terrorize a whole country. In playing up the theme of wanton Allied brutality he was counting on the forgetfulness of the masses who, he hoped, would not remember that only a little while before German planes had indiscriminately bombarded Poland, Holland, England, that they had merrily sung 'We're flying against England' and that the news of 'burning London' had been greeted with riotous enthusiasm.

His gamble was successful. The people were much too preoccupied with their own troubles, wondering from one day to the next whether they would still have a roof over their heads, to remember Germany herself had started the terror bombardments. The bombs created terrible havoc, but Goebbels noted with satisfaction that 'the British Supreme Command is making a fatal error by believing German morale can be broken by air attacks. The contrary is true.'

Goebbels followed his new propaganda line with conviction. During a conference of German newspaper publishers in September, 1942, he declared, 'It will be impossible to state in one sentence that a city like Duesseldorf lies in ruins. Special sections of press correspondents will be formed, whose duty it will be to glorify the events of night bombing in the style of battlefield reports and present them in a mystical light...'[2]

His own articles were filled with horrifying and heartrending descriptions of the bomb war. He had obtained his information first-hand: when the bombs had fallen somewhere in the provinces (Berlin at that time had hardly been touched) he would hurry to the scene, shake hands with the distressed women and children and express his condolences, arrange for sandwiches and coffee and blankets to be given to the bombed-out people. Whenever threatening shouts from the homeless crowds reached his ears, he would pretend not to hear them....

V

For Goebbels the Allied air attacks had their redeeming feature: they filled the people with anger and indignation, they strengthened their determination to continue the war. And even the small group of fearless men and women who wanted to stop the insane slaughter and were making plans to overthrow the Hitler regime were stymied in their plottings by the incessant bombardments. The lack of sleep and the permanent fear of losing all belongings dominated the people's lives and there was little energy left for conspiratorial activity.

Another blow against the so-called German underground movement or, rather, against the various little rebellious groups which operated without co-ordination or contact, was the Allied declaration of Unconditional Surrender issued at Casablanca in January, 1943. 'This means total enslavement!' Goebbels exclaimed before the radio a few hours later and there was a measure of truth in his argument. Albrecht von Kessel, one of the conspirators of 20 July 1944, stated in his diary that the announcement of unconditional surrender had destroyed six years of underground work.

Goebbels knew why he was pursuing his new theme of 'total enslavement' with such intensity. For now, at the beginning of 1943, a point had been reached which he had foreseen as early as 1933: the Germans stood no longer united behind Hitler; their enthusiasm had gone up in smoke; the glamour of their victories had been exhausted. And the fight to win over public opinion was on.

Goebbels' information about the changed mood of the people came from his propaganda chiefs, from his Gauleiters, from his Kreisleiters. He could read it in the weekly reports of the various Reich propaganda offices, and particularly in the reports of the Security Service composed by the S.S. and the Gestapo, a sort of Gallup Poll which registered and analyzed popular reaction to every event. Goebbels studied these often brutally frank accounts with the greatest care. Their contents angered him to such a degree that finally he forbade all employees of the Propaganda Ministry to read them. But they continued to be conned in secrecy and Goebbels could not dispense with them either.

If he was to keep up German morale even under the most trying circumstances, he had to work at it night and day. At the beginning of the war he could dispense with popular enthusiasm, now this was no longer possible. At first his propaganda went far to prove that the Germans had no hatred for the English, French and the other belligerents. Now he had to command the Germans, 'Don't be too fair!' Now he told the British that 'We hate you from the very depth of our souls,' thus instructing the Germans that it was their duty to hate. Now he noted angrily: 'We Germans are fanatics of objectivity. Sometimes this goes so far that, out of fear to do injustice to the opponent, we would rather inflict a wrong upon ourselves.'

He was on dangerous ground. In the fourth year of fighting, when the people had suffered a great deal and were to suffer still more, it was inadvisable to talk to them in almost scolding terms. They had to be kept in good humour. One spark might be sufficient to set off a powder keg somewhere. It so happened that it was set off right under Goebbels' nose.

The 'powder keg' was the small bridge leading from the mainland to the island of Schwanenwerder, site of Goebbels' country residence. It was meant to explode at the moment Goebbels' car was scheduled to drive across it. This, in any event, was the intention of the engineer, Dr Krumerow, who, disguised as a fisherman, had started preparations for the assassination at the beginning of December, 1942. His plan miscarried. He was arrested, tried before the People's Court, and sentenced to death.

Not a word of the incident was allowed to be published in the press, and even Goebbels' closest associates at the Propaganda Ministry were kept in ignorance. Goebbels himself was imperturbable, but Hitler was horrified when he heard of it. He sent him an enormous, bullet-proof, armoured car as a Christmas present. Goebbels was reluctant to use the vehicle, saying he would be laughed at if he drove around in Berlin in this 'armoured coffin,' but Hitler insisted.[3]

Safety measures in the Propaganda Ministry were now tightened up. Formerly, the identification passes of the employees were only examined casually; now they were subject to careful scrutiny. No visitor could get past the superintendent, at which point some official would arrive to take him through the building. The guards were equipped with steel helmets and every employee had to do guard duty at least once a week, including the women, who were required to wear slacks and steel helmets.

Goebbels' offices (the *Ministeramt*) were now completely separated from the rest of the Propaganda Ministry. One would arrive at a closed double door which was opened only upon ringing the bell and presentation of passes. The superintendent who opened it would be accompanied by two young men in Party uniform armed with pistols and shotguns. The corridor leading to Goebbels' office, laid with heavy rugs and adorned with valuable antique lamps, was constantly guarded by several men. In the anteroom to his office was a guard of five S.S. men, and again passes had to be presented. The procedure was enforced even for long-standing members of the Propaganda Ministry, who were, incidentally, searched before they were allowed to enter.

Wherever Goebbels happened to be, he was accompanied by the S.D. men, even during the recording of his speeches, although the transcription room was located inside the Propaganda Ministry.

He no longer stepped before the microphone himself. Early in 1943 the German opposition for the first time dared show its head. Overnight, the walls of houses in Munich were covered with slogans in red paint saying, 'Down with Hitler! Long live Freedom!' At the university leaflets were distributed urging the people to revolt. The Gestapo investigated, arrested two young students, Hans and Sofie Scholl, and the painter Alex Schmorel. All were tried and executed a few days later.

VI

Executions could no longer remove the danger of revolt. Himmler was probably still convinced of it, but Martin Bormann, who had succeeded Rudolf Hess after the latter's flight to Britain and who could sense popular sentiment just as well as Goebbels, no longer believed in the success of such methods. Like Goebbels, he felt that persuasion—that is, propaganda—was better than brute force. Nevertheless, the fact alone that the people were beginning to desert Hitler's cause might be construed as proof of Goebbels' failure, not necessarily as Propaganda Minister but as propaganda chief of the National Socialist Party.

At that time—December, 1942 and January, 1943—Bormann often visited the Propaganda Ministry and had private talks with Goebbels. He urged that the propaganda of the Party be stepped up; that the speakers touring the country make more speeches, more determined speeches, give more promises, and present final victory as being around the corner. Goebbels was willing to adopt these suggestions and a large part of his afternoons was now devoted to Party propaganda.

In talking to the Party speakers he tried to conjure up the good old days of the struggle for power, defining the terms of propaganda *per se* all over again. It was very evident that he considered himself more than ever the uncrowned king in that field. 'Gentlemen,' he would say, 'go to the people and ask them for the name of the British Propaganda Minister. I'll bet that not even every twentieth person will be able to tell you. But over there, I assure you, they know who we are!'

Another time: 'Propaganda means repetition. Only when the intelligent person says, "For God's sake stop it, I can't hear it any more," the moment has come for the little lumberjack of Bad Aibling to say, "Well, I never! That's the first time I heard about that. Let's find out right away what it's all about!"' Time and again he pointed to the Catholic Church: 'No one will say, "But, Father, you told us that last Sunday!" No! Day in, day out, the people listen to the same sermon, and listen patiently. The same principle applies to propaganda.'

'Propaganda is the art of simplification,' was his ever-recurrent main theme. 'Propaganda must be as simple and coarse as a woodcut. It is much easier to give a highly learned lecture before a group of scientists than to present the same topic in simple, intelligible terms, although the details may not exactly correspond to the complexities of the subject.' In other words, simplification stood for over-simplification. Here was again the small-town agitator from the Rhineland, the man who fought the battle of Berlin, who could say what he pleased because he was too obscure for his words to cause a stir or to be checked for their accuracy. Party propaganda which was made by almost anonymous Party speakers could take greater liberties than the Minister who stood in the light of publicity. This was the reason for the discrepancy between Party and state propaganda, between the instructions of the Party propaganda chief and the Reich Propaganda Minister—a discrepancy which would become more and more noticeable.

The Minister could not permit himself to make promises, but the Party speaker could promise all he wished. The Minister had to weigh every word he spoke, but the Party speaker could say whatever came into his mind. Slogans which Goebbels had banned inexorably from the vocabulary of the Propaganda Ministry were used more and more often in the Party's propaganda. In the smaller towns and villages the speakers referred to the Thousand-Year Reich as though it were an established fact. They said that Hitler was the new Messiah, that the German race was the master race, that the Fuehrer was about ready to use his secret miracle weapon, and similar things. Goebbels took care not to utter such nonsense. Occasionally Naumann would point to a particularly wild speech which was delivered somewhere in the country; then Goebbels was a little taken aback, but he quickly recovered from his first shock. 'Something is bound to stick anyway,' he muttered, adding again: 'One should think of propaganda in terms of a primitive woodcut,' whereupon the irrepressible lumberjack of Bad Aibling was cited to prove his point.

VII

Goebbels' afternoon was usually filled with receptions and the study of further telegrams, with telephone calls to the Ministry where his subordinates were holding an afternoon press conference, a radio conference and a conference for the foreign press.

Dinner took place in a small, intimate circle, with Magda almost always present. There was little to eat, as at lunch, and the unfortunate assistants of the Minister were required to surrender most of their ration points in return for the scanty food. Goebbels was very strict in these matters. He forbade Magda to buy anything whatsoever in the black market, and if an occasional food package arrived—sent, for instance, by a prominent Nazi stationed in Denmark or Holland—it was passed on to a hospital. Most of the assistants got up so hungry that they made it a rule to eat an extra meal in the canteen of the Propaganda Ministry, where, however, they had to partake of courses available without ration points.

After dinner there would be a movie. Then Goebbels retired to his office, where his real work began. Now he formulated the thoughts which had crossed his mind in the daytime, made notes on paper, conceived new ideas and plans. He used to say that they were simply crowding his brain. 'I have enough ideas for twenty Propaganda Ministries, but I haven't got the people who can carry them out', he often complained.

Ideas did not come to him spontaneously but while he was reading the news. Even at night he would read new telegrams. Arranged in big bundles, they were lying on his desk—parallel with the glass plate on it, as he had trained his office staff to do. A large part of the material was never passed on to the press or to the radio stations. Next to the so-called green and red material for the press and Reich propaganda offices there were the white, mimeographed sheets marked, 'Strictly Confidential'; news material labelled 'Class A-Special,' which was accessible only to a restricted group of political personalities; 'Class B-Special', which was still more confidential; 'Class C-Special', which was super-secret and seen by no more than five to six persons, outside of Goebbels. Here in his room, and here alone, Goebbels could read what the average citizen in the U.S. or in Britain could read every day, in addition to a good many things which neither the Allied nor the German Intelligence Services knew.

If Goebbels hit on an idea in connection with a news item or a political development—an idea for a new slogan, a poster, a movie, a speaker's campaign—he usually would ponder over it for a few days. Occasionally he would mention it to the one or the other of his associates, without asking for an opinion, merely to hear how it sounded. Then, suddenly, in the family circle, he would come out with it in a fairly digested form. 'What would you say if ...', he would start, and while he explained what it was all about he would glance around quickly from one person to the other to see the effect of it. The next morning he would present the idea at the conference. By now it had taken shape and gave the impression of being thought through in detail. His stenographer who sometimes attended all the phases of an idea was constantly surprised that Goebbels used the same words all over—it was almost primitive. 'He kept using the same clichés, without blushing,' he once said when he spoke about it.

Goebbels then elaborated on the idea, dictating exact 'Directions for Use for his associates, and insisted that all personal touches be left out in the final draft. He did not check on whether or not his orders were obeyed. Once an idea was launched it ceased to interest him, and he turned to another project.

VIII

In the late autumn of 1942, Hans Fritzsche had returned from the Russian front. That is to say, Goebbels had ordered him back because he needed him. Fritzsche, however, was reluctant to resume his former post. For, now that he had been at the front, the tone and contents of Nazi newspapers seemed more than ever pointless to him. He said to Goebbels, 'If you only knew, Herr Minister, how badly things are going at the front!'

Goebbels proposed that Fritzsche take over the direction of the entire German radio. Fritzsche countered, 'I cannot tell my listeners what I myself don't believe, namely that a victory is an absolute certainty.' Goebbels listened silently, then gave Fritzsche the job he had offered him. In the further course of their conversation they coined the term, 'pessimistic propaganda.' Goebbels also called this type of propaganda 'Strength through Fear,' punning on the 'Strength through joy' movement, but he was careful to confine such remarks to a few intimates. Actually, his new propaganda line was copied from Churchill's theme of 'Blood, Sweat and Tears.'

According to Fritzsche, Goebbels now was quite impressed with Churchill's propaganda. However, in his conferences he continued to ridicule the British Prime Minister's approach.

Goebbels agreed that people now should be told that all was not going well. In his New Year's speech he quoted the words of Frederick the Great, who inspired his soldiers in a time of stress, 'We must in such a crisis equip ourselves with guts of iron and a heart of steel and forget all our sensitivities.'

And yet, the catastrophe was only beginning. On that New Year's Day the Russian communiqué spoke of an offensive south of Stalingrad and of the consequent occupation of part of the factory area of the besieged city which, according to Hitler's previous announcement, had been conquered 'for all time.' The German army communiqué, on the other hand, vaguely mentioned minor Russian thrusts which had been repelled. And then, on 16 January 1943, the Russians launched their great counter-offensive and broke through the Nazi lines, wrecking entire Axis divisions, dispersing or capturing others, encircling with an iron band the rest and sealing them off from rescue. The German High Command still refused to admit the defeat, and even in the ensuing days there was only brief mention of 'defensive battles.'

Goebbels understood full well that the collapse at Stalingrad might mean the eventual end of the war. This was not the kind of defeat that could be brushed off. It called for a supreme effort, the same effort of which the British showed themselves capable after the disaster at Dunkirk; namely, to mobilize all forces in the country for war. This meant total war.

Totaler Krieg was a term not created by Goebbels, but by General Ludendorff. Towards the end of the First World War Ludendorff attempted to subordinate all of Germany's economy to total war, but did not succeed. Goebbels had used the term, sparingly, as early as Christmas, 1939, but only as a high-sounding phrase. Now he realized the people had to co-operate to a degree hitherto unimaginable, lest all be lost. From the middle of January, 1943, he could speak of nothing but Total War, and the idea became an obsession with him.

Goebbels rushed to Hitler and Hitler was willing to take up the idea. However, to Goebbels' great disappointment, he nominated a committee, consisting of Field-Marshal Keitel, Bormann and Hans Lammers (head of the

Chancellery), to draft the general outlines. Goebbels was to participate only in an advisory capacity. In the first conference Keitel told Goebbels that the measures to be adopted should not be too drastic because the morale of the German people would not stand it.

This, to Goebbels! What did Keitel and Lammers know of popular sentiment? What could they know of maintaining that sentiment, of strengthening it, of building it up to a will to victory? What did these gentlemen fancy they were doing? Should the German people be forever left in ignorance of the calamitous defeat at Stalingrad? How could such a defeat, which had cost 300,000 men, be kept secret? 300,000 men—this meant mourners in every city, in every village, in every street, and even the most ruthless censorship was powerless to conceal it.

All these thoughts went through Goebbels' mind, and he voiced them excitedly during luncheons and dinners and in the conferences with his staff. And then, suddenly, he had the great inspiration.

Actually, it was quite simple. History proved that a defeat must not necessarily be demoralizing, as Goebbels never tired explaining to his listeners. The Romans defeated Hannibal despite the battle of Cannae. 'And when the cry of horror—"Hannibal ad portas"—rang through the streets of Rome, the Roman senators veiled their heads with their togas. But they remained steadfast and did not capitulate, and Rome was saved. And on the site where the once so powerful Carthage had stood, peasants ploughed the land.' Defeats, Goebbels stated, were only demoralizing when they became known to the public despite shrewd government measures to keep them secret, when, added to the original shock of the defeat, the average citizen was shaken by the realization that his government was no longer telling him the truth. Starting from this premise Goebbels reasoned that nothing must be embellished or suppressed; the people must know that conditions were bad. Stalingrad was Germany's Cannae.

On 23 January, there was a remarkable conference, presided over by Goebbels. He did not even glance at the pile of telegrams on his desk. Staring straight ahead of him, he explained tensely to his listeners that the situation was desperate, and that the defeat at Stalingrad was bound to have disastrous repercussions. German newspaper readers and radio listeners must be given the truth! They should be told their alternative was Victory or Bolshevism. The fate of the Fatherland was at stake. Exact casualty lists should not be made known, true, but—and here his conferees could not believe their ears—it might be a good idea to prepare the people for the worst. The German army could not afford a second Stalingrad, he declared.

The next morning, the newspapers published melancholy accounts of the war in the East. Correspondents vied with each other in depicting the horrors of the Russian front, the suffering of the soldiers, their hopelessness and despair. In the dispatches there were sentences undoubtedly formulated by Goebbels himself, such as:

'In 1918 the weakness on the German home front forced Germany to capitulate... Rome once was in danger when threatened by Hannibal, but she triumphed. England has withstood a serious reverse, even a catastrophe. We will prove that spiritually we are stronger than the English...'

January 1943 was approaching its end. The Russians were reporting further successes near Stalingrad, while the German High Command still babbled about a successful defence.

Ten years before, on 30 January, Hitler had come to power.

IX

Again Goebbels stood in the Sportpalast. On every previous anniversary Hitler had made a speech. This time he did not appear but sent Goebbels to read his proclamation. Goebbels was nervous, fearing the multitude would resent Hitler's absence. To make matters worse, British fliers were reported overhead. Goebbels knew that if he interrupted the meeting and took shelter before the bombs fell it would be a propagandistic defeat he could not afford. Therefore, he remained on the platform and told the audience that the meeting would be postponed for an hour. Those who wished to go down to the cellars could do so, he added.

Some people left, but most of them remained and the audience was impressed that Goebbels stayed with them. For a while nothing could be heard but the faraway explosions of the missiles. Thousands of eyes were turned to Goebbels. He was aware of it and remained impassive.

Then he began to speak, and he spoke frankly. 'In this winter our soldiers are facing a new defensive battle of unparalleled severity... Who knows when and where we will be called for a final decision in this war!' He mentioned total war several times. 'In countless letters from all levels of the population, the cry for a total war effort is resounding in our ears,' Goebbels feverishly claimed. The audience in the Sportpalast, in any event, enthusiastically identified itself with these non-existent letter writers.

At home, Magda had invited a few friends, for Goebbels did not like to be alone after a big speech and had to find an outlet for his emotions. But this time, Goebbels, followed by his stenographer, immediately withdrew to his studio. The reaction of the audience at the Sportpalast had shown him he could afford to be more radical in matters of total war than he had thought. He made a telephone call and stopped the publication of one of his articles already in type and scheduled for 7 February. He concocted a new piece entitled 'The Hard Lesson,' in which he said, 'We were too well off during the war.' Reviewing the fur collection he had organized the year before, he noted, 'Today the front is not in need of fur coats but of human beings,' and he repeated, 'In countless letters from all levels of the people, the cry for a total war effort is resounding in our ears.'

The total war which Goebbels so fervently desired was more sabotaged than activated by the committee set up by Hitler. Yet, time was pressing. On 1 February, the German army communiqué admitted that the southern group of the Sixth Army had surrendered. Two days later, the overall defeat at Stalingrad had to be conceded, and a wave of horror and sadness flooded the Reich.

Now was the time to act, and Goebbels did not hesitate for a minute to carry through his strategy of gloom, and to the extreme. The terrible disaster was reported over the radio as a special announcement, just as in times of victory when momentous news was at hand. But, there were no fanfares—only the sound of muffled drums, as the orchestra played the melancholy German soldier's song, 'Ich hatt' einen Kameraden' (I Once Had a Comrade). During the remainder of the day there were only funeral marches and serious music on the radio, and all the theatres were closed.

Fritzsche was looking desperately for a military expert who could analyze the situation intelligently over the radio. Two generals came to his office, carrying the drafts of their commentary, which contained nothing but alibis and excuses. Fritzsche telephoned Goebbels who told him, 'We can't do that to the people. Throw that rubbish into the wastepaper basket.' Fritzsche himself stepped to the microphone and spoke extemporaneously for ten minutes, embellishing nothing, criticizing much.

The next day all German newspapers appeared with the black edges of mourning.

The German people were shaken and aghast.

Would Dr Goebbels' experiment succeed? In Washington and London the propagandists wondered if he had lost his mind. Press Chief Otto Dietrich had a nervous breakdown and went to bed. Heinrich Himmler temporarily toyed with the idea of taking over all censorship and suppressing all news until there was another victory to report.

Goebbels was by no means insane. His experiment was crowned with success. The people, half in a daze, pulled themselves together, and their mourning turned into a fatalistic mysticism. They were hypnotized by Goebbels' thesis that defeat and sacrifice had their 'meaning'. Goebbels screamed, 'The army of the fallen has not surrendered its arms. In reality it is marching in the ranks of the soldiers!' And the people really believed it. They gave renewed confidence in a government which obviously was telling them the truth. From now on, Goebbels could lie again.

X

Goebbels knew that after the terrifying experience of Stalingrad, the people would have been ready for anything. Now as never before they should be spurred on to the unprecedented accomplishments of total warfare.

Hitler must speak. Goebbels was fully aware that in such a moment he could not replace the Fuehrer. He said: 'There are two kinds of speakers, each fundamentally different in temperament; one speaks with the intellect, the other with the heart.' He knew he belonged to the former category. He knew (and said so himself) that 'One is limited to a mere didactic range, and, as he is cold himself, he also leaves others cold.' Hitler, on the other hand, 'probes the most secret recesses and ramifications of the soul of the masses, knows how to bare it with his masterly hand and make it respond. Just as his voice speaks from the depths of the blood, so the listener is thrilled to the depths of his blood... His art of moulding the masses is so unique that no doctrine or dogma can fit it... His speech is like a magnet, drawing whatever iron the people have in their blood from them.'

But Hitler declined to make a speech. He would speak only if a new victory was won and if the general situation had improved. Until such time he would not mount any platform and would not step before a microphone, he said.

This meant that Goebbels himself had to jump into the breach. During the following days he used every available minute to work on his address, scheduled for 18 February, in the Sportpalast—an address of vital importance. Ordinarily he dictated his speeches on the basis of a brief but detailed outline prepared by his assistants who had marked the salient points in red, blue and yellow pencil, in the order of their importance. Despite his careful editing of the finished product it was a fast method of working. This time he wrote the whole script, sentence for sentence, in long hand, then discarded most of it, rewrote it with extensive revisions. Finally at four a.m. on 18 February, his work was completed. During the last few hours he had sent it page by page to the room of his assistant, where two stenographers typed it. Fifteen minutes after the last page had been sent, he appeared in his silk lounging robe in the little office of his assistant, radiantly looked at the two secretaries and asked them: 'Well, how do you like my speech?' Everyone congratulated him on his achievement, but, without paying attention to their comments, he continued: 'Well, those ten questions, they will really strike home, don't you think? Tonight, you will see the result!' Already at the door, he added, as an afterthought: 'One thing I can assure you: as soon as this war is over, I shall be a little more economical with my strength, and get some rest.'

Goebbels had conceived his speech to be a kind of informal plebiscite on the issue of total war, and that was where the 'ten questions' came in. He was going to ask the people whether they were willing to take upon themselves the most severe sacrifices—and, he expected them to say, Ja!' In this way he wanted to bring pressure on Hitler to adopt the radical measures which so far Goebbels had demanded in vain.[4] It was a rather daring undertaking because Hitler never liked being confronted with a *fait accompli*. Perhaps this was the reason why Goebbels was so nervous and could not sleep that night. He went back to his room, read his speech out loud, made mental notes where he would have to pause, or make a special emphasis. Time and again Fritzsche, working in the room next door, saw him come out of his room, read one or two sentences, and add gleefully, 'Here they will go wild with enthusiasm.'

Then Goebbels disappeared again, posed before his mirror, stretched out his arm, gesticulated with his hands, laughed, became solemn, stared aghast at the ceiling, screamed out a sentence, whispered another—he was rehearsing the whole performance.

Fritzsche used a brief interval to ask the Minister what would happen if the people did not respond, if they rejected total war. Goebbels was dumbfounded. 'You forget that by that time I will have spoken for almost an hour. From there on I can make them climb trees if I feel like it,' he replied.

Fritzsche was silent. He also knew that Goebbels would have a few hundred men stationed as a claque, as was done during all his speeches.

Again Goebbels stood before the mirror, gesticulating, observing himself closely. As usual, he turned just a little to the left—knowing that his right profile was more attractive than the other.

XI

The Sportpalast was filled to the last seat hours before Goebbels was to make his speech. All tickets had been carefully distributed by the Nazi Party offices and the Propaganda Ministry. It would have been imprudent to take unnecessary risks and have but lukewarm sympathizers in the audience—there was too much at stake.

Despite his outward nonchalance he knew that a single speech could either save the situation, or ruin it. This was how it had been in the days of the struggle for power, this was how it was now. When he stood on the platform, with fifteen thousand people frenetically jubilant, he was filled with a great tension. Today he had to fight, today there was no time for playfulness or improvisation. During the past two weeks he had been able to neutralize the defeat at Stalingrad. That evening he had to transform it into a victory. His speech became the best he had ever made.

Amid the tumultuous enthusiasm he began to speak. Those who had heard him and knew him looked at each other in surprise: this was not the old familiar Goebbels, this was not his bright, clear and penetrating voice, these were not his clever and elegantly turned phrases. Here was a serious, troubled man who had come for an intimate, if vehement, talk with his friends and family, who was not interested in effect or applause, but who had something very important to communicate. 'Stalingrad was and is the great alarm call of fate to the German nation!' he started off. He described the situation as being more serious than anyone had realized. But, he said, he was speaking to people who had been raised in discipline, therefore, he could approach them 'with all the solemn seriousness which the situation deserves.'

He did. The Bolshevist danger was more threatening than ever, and against it the Wehrmacht was the only bulwark. If it failed, if the German people failed, then the world would go under, he said. Speedy action was necessary and not a single minute must be lost. 'Two thousand years of Occidental civilisation are at stake.' Yes, it was as serious as all that, and Goebbels admitted it, although he realized that British newspapers would note triumphantly that he had 'stretched out the first peace feelers.' But there could be no question of that. 'No one in Germany today thinks of a foul compromise, the only thing the people are concerned with is a hard war.' Yes, the war could not be hard enough for the Germans, the people were sick and tired of indulging in wishful thinking. 'We want to hear nothing more of false hopes and illusions,' he said.

The Germans had hardly begun to fight and to suffer. What had been demanded from them could not be compared to the sufferings of the Russians 'under the terror of the OGPU'. Now it was the turn of the Germans to take greater sufferings upon themselves. 'The total war is the command of the hour!' The command, not the compulsion! 'We will voluntarily relinquish our high standard of living in order to increase our war potential as rapidly and as thoroughly as possible,' he said. Did this mean Bolshevization? 'This step is not an end in itself but only a means to an end... The most radical measures are barely radical enough, and the most total measures barely total enough to achieve victory.'

He explained the measures which he considered necessary: the closing of high-class restaurants, beauty parlours, luxury shops, the dismissal of servants. 'We would rather wear patched-up clothes for a few years than bring about a state of affairs where our people would have to wear rags for centuries.' The measures for total war would release soldiers for the front and women workers for the armament industry. 'I am not disputing the fact that despite these drastic steps we will have to face a few anxious weeks, but they will help to clear the atmosphere.'

Goebbels had spoken almost an hour and his audience was in a state of delirium. He was constantly interrupted by roars of laughter whenever he was being ironical, by cries of indignation whenever he denounced the Russians or the Western Allies, by a chorus of voices when he appealed to his countrymen. For minutes at a time there was intermittent applause and shouted comments from the public. His speech had developed into a sort of duet between himself and the audience, and time and again Goebbels was obliged to lift his hands in a pleading gesture to make himself heard.

Now he had brought the people to the point where he wanted them. He had convinced them: a few more sacrifices and 'the atmosphere will be cleared.' That meant, in other terms, 'Then we will have the war behind us.' Did they want to make these sacrifices? Their answer must be, '*Ja,*' or '*Nein.*' Their answer was decisive, for 'the people who are confronting me here are a cross-section of the entire German people both at home and at the front. Am I right? Yes or No?'

'At that point,' Goebbels' stenographer noted, 'an indescribable turmoil broke loose at the Sportpalast, comparable only to the heights of enthusiasm experienced during the years of the struggle for power. The people sprang from their seats as though they had been electrified and, like a hurricane, a thousandfold "*Ja!*" thundered through the hall.'

And now Goebbels asked his Ten Questions—the real reason for the whole evening.

1. The British say that the German people have lost faith in victory. I ask you: Do you believe with the Fuehrer and with us in the final and total victory of the German people?

2. Are you willing to continue the war with wild determination and unshaken by all vicissitudes of fate and to stand behind the Fuehrer as the phalanx of the country until victory is ours?

3. Are you determined, should the Fuehrer demand it, to work ten, twelve and if necessary fourteen and even sixteen hours a day and give your last for victory?

4. Do you, if necessary, want even more total and more radical measures than we can today imagine?

5. The English claim the German people have lost confidence in the Fuehrer. I ask you: Is your confidence in the Fuehrer today greater, filled with a stronger belief and more unflinching than ever? Is your preparedness absolute and unlimited to follow the Fuehrer wherever he goes, and to do everything to bring the war to a victorious conclusion?

6. I ask you: Are you prepared to make all your efforts as from now in order to supply the Eastern front with the men and arms that it needs in order to give the fatal blow to Bolshevism?

7. Will you promise soldiers at the front that the country is behind them and will you give them all they require to achieve victory?

8. Do you, especially you women, want the government to see to it that the German women, too, give their whole strength for war effort?

9. Do you approve of the most radical measures against the small clique of shirkers and racketeers who play at peace and who exploit the nation's emergency for selfish purposes? Do you approve that anyone who commits a crime against the war effort should lose his head?

10. Do you want the people at home to be united in shouldering heavy burdens, and do you want these burdens to be equally levied upon high and humble, rich and poor? Goebbels took almost one hour to ask these ten questions—there were that many interruptions. He summarized: 'The nation is ready for everything. The Fuehrer has commanded, and we shall obey him... If ever we believed in victory faithfully and unshakenly, it is now in this hour of national rallying and inner determination. We can see it right ahead of us and all we have to do is to grasp it. And therefore, our motto is: Rise, you people, and storm, break loose!'

On the shoulders of the frenzied people Goebbels was carried triumphantly off the platform. Magda and half a dozen of his closest associates were waiting for him. He was so hoarse that he could only whisper: 'What unprecedented, nightmarish lunacy! If I had commanded them, "Go jump out of the window of your apartment," they would have done it!'

Late at night, when the guests had gone, he undressed and weighed himself on his scale. The effort of the speech had cost him seven pounds.

PART IV: GOETTERDAEMMERUNG

CHAPTER XIV

FORTRESS PROPAGANDA

I

Four weeks after his speech at the Sportpalast Goebbels held a reception for the foreign correspondents. 'Today is the tenth anniversary of the founding of the Propaganda Ministry,' was his opening statement. 'Personally I would have forgotten about it if some of you, gentlemen, had not called it to my attention....'

This was most unlikely. Goebbels, a specialist in organizing celebrations, was not the man to forget anniversaries, least of all where his Propaganda Ministry was concerned. Not only the press reception but also a subsequent question-and-answer game had been planned meticulously in advance.[1] He could adopt such procedure with impunity, for the so-called foreign press was composed largely of the representatives of satellite and occupied countries, who had no choice but to play the roles which the Propaganda Ministry assigned to them.

The purpose of the press party was self-evident: Goebbels wanted to demonstrate that he had nothing to conceal, that he was hopeful and in the best of spirits, that he was as convinced as ever of Germany's ultimate victory. The little comedy he staged was designed to correct the defeatist impression his gloomy Stalingrad address might have caused abroad. In his speech at the Sportpalast he had been solemn and gloomy; now he was easy-going, almost frivolous, and in complete control of the situation.

In such a large organization as the Propaganda Ministry occasional slip-ups were of course inevitable. When one of the radio commentators declared in a broadcast beamed overseas that Germany had not wanted the war and still deplored the necessity for it, the British interpreted his observation as a peace feeler. Goebbels learned of this from monitored broadcasts and he called for Fritzsche, made a tremendous scene and threatened, literally, to have the commentator hanged. Fritzsche had difficulty in calming the excited Minister. He could not know that real peace negotiations were taking place at that very moment. Stalin had sent a representative of the Narkomindel (Soviet Foreign Office) to Stockholm, who was authorized to conclude an armistice, providing Hitler agreed to withdraw his troops from Soviet Russia and the eastern half of Poland.[2]

It is quite likely Goebbels knew of this interlude, and tried to influence Hitler to sign an armistice pact with Russia, but there is only circumstantial evidence for this assumption. For instance, he dictated, off the record: 'All we do is talk about total war, but in reality, there is only one man who is waging total war, and that is Stalin... He is the man who lived through fifteen years of exile in Siberia and still had enough energy left to overcome all obstacles and to manoeuvre himself into the position of an authoritarian ruler.'

Roughly a year later, Goebbels himself would propose to seek an understanding with Stalin.

II

One can well imagine Goebbels' consternation when he saw that Hitler was gambling away his unique chance to end the two-front war. Apparently Hitler had not his usual control in those days. On the occasion of Memorial Day, 21 March, he addressed a select audience in the courtyard of the Berlin *zeughaus* (arsenal). Goebbels, who was among the listeners, was greatly distressed, saying that the Fuehrer had spoken too rapidly, garbled his words, had been completely incoherent and had read off his speech in the manner of a schoolboy who had failed to do his homework.

So this was the great orator whom Goebbels had always considered to be infinitely superior to himself! So this was the man who by right should have made the speech at the Sportpalast! Little imagination is needed to guess Goebbels' thoughts: not the Fuehrer, but he, Goebbels—he alone—had saved the day. That the war would continue, despite the failure of the Luftwaffe, the army and the navy, was largely his merit. He now regarded himself as the only German general who had not suffered a serious setback. In an article reviewing the wars of Frederick the Great, written at the beginning of April, 1943, he stated that 'The Prussians surely would have collapsed under the impact of the calamity, if the proud and commanding spirit of their King had not rallied them time and again. History records that at times he was the only man who faced the blows of destiny with firm manliness...'

At that moment Hitler was not displaying an attitude of 'firm manliness.' Goebbels alone had the 'proud and commanding spirit' which the situation demanded. Was he hinting, between the lines, that he regarded himself, and not Hitler, as the true successor of the great Frederick?

Although he had proclaimed total war, he exempted himself from all restrictions. With Goering, Ribbentrop, or the corrupt Gauleiters, this was a matter of course, but Goebbels had always refused to live in Byzantine style, and had been content to subsist on his scanty food rations. It was all the more astonishing, then, that he did not dismiss a single one of his servants. It was understandable that there were no cuts in the budget of the Propaganda Ministry, but when he increased his personal income from his articles in *Das Reich* from 200,000 to 300,000 marks in the year dedicated to total war, one begins to wonder about his spirit of sacrifice. In February of that year, in which he earned altogether 424,000 marks, Goebbels took steps to evade making quarterly advance payments on his taxes, but, interestingly enough, his application was turned down. He further demanded that he be allowed a 20 per cent deduction for professional expenses, although it was extremely unlikely that his overheads amounted to 60,000 marks, especially in view of the unlimited expense account to which he was entitled as a cabinet minister.

In 1942, roughly 50,000 marks were spent for miscellaneous equipment (radios, typewriters, news tickers, etc.) installed in Goebbels' household. At the beginning of March, 1943, Goebbels had a private air-raid shelter built in his backyard. While the average citizen was not allowed to have a wall painted in his apartment, workers laboured night and day, under the glow of dimmed floodlights, unloading cement, building in doors, air conditioning and a complicated lighting system which would function independently of Berlin's power stations. Architect Bartels said that 300 houses for workers could have been built with the raw materials used for Goebbels' air-raid shelter. The project, exclusive of the interior furnishings, was estimated to cost 350,000 marks, and consisted of half-a-dozen rooms, including a private bedroom and studio for Goebbels.

III

It would be difficult to prove that Goebbels was devoting himself totally to the demands of total war. Although his entire days should have been taken up with maintaining and bolstering the morale of the German people, here, at a time when conditions were steadily deteriorating, he apparently had enough leisure to concern himself with numerous extraneous matters. Even in the critical years of 1943 and 1944 the film remained his principal hobby.

Hardly an evening passed without a special screening at his home, and he continued to be interested in Hollywood productions. All films which the Germans had confiscated in the occupied territories were passed on to the Propaganda Ministry, and Goebbels saw them all. His attachés in Stockholm,

Berne and Lisbon were instructed to borrow new American films, to have reprints made or, if necessary, to steal them. These films had a soothing effect on his nerves. His associates have reported that during the last months he was often filled with thoughts of suicide; but, half an hour later, he would be heard laughing uproariously over the adventures of Donald Duck or Pluto.

But only very few actors and directors came to his house. This was due to the repercussions caused by the Gottschalk case.

Joachim Gottschalk, one of the most talented of the younger actors, had come to Berlin in the middle '30s and achieved a great career on both stage and screen. His success would have been more spectacular if he had not been married to a Jewish woman. Despite all insinuations and demands from official quarters he refused to divorce her. In the autumn of 1941 Goebbels ordered a list to be drawn up of actors and actresses who were *juedisch versippt* (who had Jewish relations) and confronted them with an ultimatum: Either they would divorce their partners or they would be forbidden to act.

None involved intended to comply with the measure. Everyone used whatever personal connections he had to appease Goebbels. The Propaganda Minister was lenient in all cases except that of Gottschalk, and there he remained inflexible. For this young man was regarded as the idol of millions of German women, and Goebbels said, 'It is intolerable to think that he is sleeping with a Jewess.' Gottschalk received a last warning: If he did not divorce his wife she and her child would be arrested and deported to Poland the next morning. That night Gottschalk and his family committed suicide by inhaling gas.

Indignation and anger swept through theatrical circles. The next morning Goebbels' pictures were spontaneously taken from the walls in the Berlin film studios. Soon afterwards Goebbels gave a party, extending invitations to the thespians, but not a single one of them appeared. They referred to him now as the 'murderer'. Goebbels tried to defend himself, ordering the artists to appear at the Propaganda Ministry, and there he told them: 'I know that artists are under a compulsion to continue play-acting even though they be off-stage. They seldom have both feet on the ground. But I want to warn everyone not to spread rumours about me that do not correspond to the truth.'

His popularity among the actors, however, was at an end. They gladly had accepted the high salaries, tax reductions and other advantages offered them under the régime, but now they were no longer happy. In the summer of 1942 Goebbels ordered the arrest of the film director, Herbert Selpin, because he had made a derogatory remark about the German army—and the next morning the man was found hanged in his cell. As Goebbels knew that most of the actors were not National Socialists and hoped eventually to go to Hollywood, he tried to compromise them as Nazis. He forced them to play in

Party propaganda films which had a strongly anti-Semitic slant, in addition to being anti-British, anti-American and, of course, anti-Russian.

It was almost impossible to reject such roles. If someone baulked, Goebbels summoned him to his office, scolded him, shouted and screamed at him until he was groggy. Admittedly, Goebbels could have done nothing but send a recalcitrant actor to a concentration camp or to the front. A courageous actor might have taken this risk, but actors as a whole are not a courageous group, and Goebbels knew it.

Goebbels was extremely consistent in dealing with these propaganda films. As late as November, 1944, he planned to make an elaborate anti-Semitic film based on *The Merchant of Venice*. But he also continued to be interested in other aspects of the motion-picture industry. For instance, he determined which young actresses should be given tryouts by the film companies; which stories should be adapted for the screen; which scenes should be cut from films already completed. As late as February, 1945, he approved the release of a film only with the proviso that certain scenes be retaken.

If one goes through the files of the film section of the Propaganda Ministry, one finds it hard to believe that Germany had been at war since 1939. There was, for instance, a project to film the life of Robert and Clara Schumann. The movie, which was to be entitled *Traeumerei*, was scheduled to be made in the middle of 1941. Right at the start, the Propaganda Ministry raised numerous objections: the actress assigned to the part of Clara Schumann was unsuitable; it seemed inadmissible that a great German composer had died insane, although that was a historical fact; that his wife had played with the Jewish violin virtuoso Joseph Joachim, although that was a historical fact; that she had performed at the Russian Imperial Court, and that the Czar was shown sympathetically, which was intolerable now that the Germans were at war with Soviet Russia, and so on.

Goebbels wished to drop the project altogether, then reversed himself. New difficulties came up. The entire cast down to the smallest role had to be approved by Goebbels. That the film was made at all and shown in November, 1944, is a miracle in itself.

IV

Despite Goebbels' Stalingrad speech, German morale was undergoing a serious crisis in the spring and summer of 1943. The Afrika Korps was defeated, North Africa was lost, and Sicily invaded. In Russia the German armies were steadily retreating, German cities were bombed, meat rations had to be reduced. Hitler was kept in ignorance on the state of German morale, and Keitel said, 'The Fuehrer is not interested in such considerations. It is his conviction that if the German people do not want to understand him and fight, they will have to perish.[3]

For Goebbels, things were not that simple. It was up to him to show initiative, as he had done in the days which preceded the Stalingrad disaster. Every day he had to explain, to calm, to encourage—the situation had deteriorated too far.

His principal argument still was the bolshevist danger—a danger not only for Germany but for the whole world. 'At the present moment we are living through one of the most critical stages of Occidental civilization,' he declared in an article entitled 'The European Crisis', obviously meant for American and British consumption—on the very day that Nazi negotiations with Stalin, much to Goebbels' regret, had broken down. Bolshevism, once it penetrated into Europe, would be like a contagious disease, he warned. No one should comfort himself with the idea that the Reds eventually would adapt themselves to European standards. 'If a fairly healthy person lies in the same bed with someone who has typhoid fever, he will not infect the typhoid patient with his health, but the patient will pass on the disease to him.' This form of argument was carried on in the following weeks, until Goebbels made an unexpected find, one that offered a unique propagandistic chance, which he intended to exploit to the fullest.

On 13 April 1943, at 9.15 p.m., the Berlin radio made the following announcement:

'From Smolensk comes news that the native population has revealed to German authorities the spot where in secret mass executions the Bolsheviks with the help of the OGPU murdered 10,000 Polish officers. German authorities ... found a pit 28 metres long and 16 metres wide in which, twelve-deep, lay the bodies of 3,000 Polish officers. In full uniform, in some cases shackled, all had wounds from pistol bullets in the back of the neck. Identification will not prove difficult since, owing to a peculiarity of the soil, the bodies are mummified, and also because the Bolsheviks neglected to remove personal documents from the clothing of the victims. It has already been established that General Smorawinski, from Lublin, is among the murdered. These officers were held first at Kozielsk, near Orlow, whence in February and March, 1940, they were shipped in cattle cars to Smolensk and thence in trucks to Kosgory, where they were murdered. Search and discovery of the other pits continue. The total number of executed officers is estimated at 10,000, which corresponds approximately to the number of Polish officers captured by the Bolsheviks.'

This broadcast, which hit the entire world like a bombshell, had been preceded by tremendous propaganda activity. Soon after the terrifying discovery in the forest of Katyn, Goebbels had sent medical specialists and chemists to the spot, had invited neutral experts as well as representatives of Bulgaria, Rumania, Croatia, Italy, Hungary and so on to participate in the investigation. Documentation was compiled, photographs were taken, the publication of a White Book by the German Foreign Office was contemplated. Peasants testified that at the time of the mass murders they remembered having heard shots, circumstantial evidence was safeguarded, such as diaries and letters found on the dead indicating that the victims had been murdered in the summer and autumn of 1940. (Smolensk did not fall into German hands until July, 1941.)

During his conference, Goebbels gave an extended lecture to the German press, telling how this matter was to be presented to the German public. 'Why did Stalin, when the head of the Polish Government-in-Exile in London, General Sikorsky, asked him of the whereabouts of the 12,000 Polish officers, reply: "They are living as peaceful citizens with us in the Soviet Union"? Why did not Stalin say right away: "We had to leave them behind and do not know where they are"? Now today, that we have uncovered the horror of the Soviet liquidation action, the Kremlin suddenly maintains we have murdered these 12,000 officers!'

Goebbels emphasized especially the importance of the newsreels. 'Foreign press representatives must be shown standing near the graves, handkerchiefs pressed to their noses, or with a burning cigarette in the mouth because they cannot stand the stench of putrefaction.' Finally he staged a solemn funeral. Priests were dispatched to Katyn, and in the presence of German and foreign correspondents and cameramen the victims were laid to rest. This offered another opportunity to go into the whole story once more, and to show the world what it could expect if Bolshevism were victorious.

All this was masterly done, and yet, somehow the entire propaganda action fizzled out. The few remaining semi-independent German papers were reluctant to play up the affair and treated it merely as another big news story. Goebbels was outraged. He declared the editors had no idea how to make a newspaper, and furthermore did not know how to take advantage of the great opportunity that had been offered them. The story should be described so often in all its gruesome details that the mere mention of the name of Katyn would make people's hair stand on end, he declared.

Presumably Goebbels did not want to admit to himself the real reason for his failure. Since the sinking of the S.S. *Athenia* the Propaganda Ministry had invented so many 'atrocities' allegedly committed by the enemy that those who knew how news was made thought that Katyn too was another canard. It may have been, although all the evidence gathered by the Poles and additional information found by the Allies after the end of the war points in the opposite direction. Whatever the case may be, the key men in Washington and London believed at once and never ceased believing that the Russians were to blame. But the public neither outside Germany nor inside accepted what Goebbels was proclaiming so loudly just because he was proclaiming it so loudly. And Goebbels noted with some bitterness and some indignation that the Katyn affair had caused no deeper rift in the coalition of our enemies ... On the contrary, in London and Washington the Poles are told quite plainly that nothing can be done for them ... British and American newspapers have dropped the Poles.'

Foreign countries had much better reasons than the Germans to distrust Goebbels, for they knew of the mass murders of Jews, which started towards the end of 1941 and continued with ever-increasing intensity. The first news of Lublin and Oswiecim, of the vans with their gassing installations, of the crematoria which burned thousands of bodies daily, of the tens of thousands of people who were forced to dig their own graves before they were executed, of the numerous other unspeakable crimes, began to seep through in Sweden, in Switzerland, in the United States, in Britain. And those who learned of them could well imagine that the same culprits also had the tragedy of Katyn on their conscience. Above all, they could not understand why Goebbels, who surely was informed of the wholesale murders of the Jews, could get so indignant about the Katyn affair.[4]

V

The failure of the Katyn affair was only one of Goebbels' frustrations. There was another important matter which proved to be a great disappointment, and that was the propaganda of retaliation.

Retaliation was, so to speak, a substitute. Goering had failed. The Luftwaffe had proved incapable of keeping enemy bombers away from German territory. What could one say to people whose houses and property were being destroyed? One could tell them: The others are just as badly off, they, too, are being bombed; and since they will get tired of it, they will automatically stop bombing Germany. Everyone in Germany knew that it simply was not true, but Goebbels could always promise that this enviable state of affairs would soon be reached. 'Day and night we are working to pay back the British terrorists in the same coin. We are certainly not watching the British air war on German territory with our arms folded,' he wrote on 6 April 1943. Two weeks later he hinted mysteriously: 'This is not the moment to disclose what is being done to give our enemies the only fitting and convincing answer to their terror attacks.' On 5 June, in a speech at the Sportpalast, he said:

'The whole German people today is imbued with but one idea—retaliation!' Goebbels' stenographer commented that in a stormy demonstration the masses expressed 'their sympathy as well as their pride over the courageous attitude of the population in the bombed districts.'

On the other hand, Goebbels carefully avoided any mention of miracle weapons. On 30 March 1941, he had explicitly stated in an article: 'In its hour of general hopelessness and confusion all there remains for propaganda is to babble about new miracle weapons...' Goebbels preferred to leave that kind of thing to his Party speakers.

The retaliation campaign was conducted with great vehemence. Goebbels of course only gave the cue line ('The voices of retaliation must wind themselves like a red thread through our entire press'), the editorial writers picked it up, the Party speakers whispered about the miracle weapon, rumours were spreading everywhere—and yet it did not strike home. The people simply no longer believed in retaliation. They said the very word was coming out of their ears.

The so-called total war developed into a total disappointment for Goebbels. As he had feared, Hitler's committee confined itself to a few resolutions but did nothing further about it. 'We have all the reserves we need,' Goebbels remarked to his entourage, 'but we don't exploit them. There are always the last 10 per cent that are lacking.'

In his morning conference he declared, 'The military believe that we can get along as we are, and others feel that the people cannot be expected to make greater sacrifices, and therefore, nothing happens. Yet, the people would be ready for anything if we only convinced them of the urgent necessity, and made it clear to them that otherwise we are heading for a catastrophe.'

As an example of total war he called the attention of the conferees to the Soviet film, *The Fighting Leningrad*. 'I can only urge you, gentlemen, to go and see that film. It will show you what total war really means. It will show you how they shovel snow before the gates of Leningrad, how old women labour with a heavy spade at forty below zero. A patrolling soldier armed with a gun walks up and down and sees to it that the work gets done. Those who collapse with cold and exhaustion drop to the ground, but no one takes any notice of them. Then again you will see how they are working in an armament factory, despite heavy bombardments. You can see the bombs falling into the workshops. No one is allowed to take shelter in the cellars—the work goes on.'

Goebbels was much upset over the fact that total war in Germany was not conducted with the same iron severity. Far from being able to carry out the drastic measures he had proposed, he was not even able to close all cafés and luxury restaurants. Horcher's, Berlin's most expensive restaurant, remained open because Goering personally had ordered it. Goebbels had Horcher's windows smashed at night and then wanted to close it in his capacity as Gauleiter, on the grounds that the people were outraged, whereupon Goering ordered guards to protect it.[5] For a full forty-five minutes Goebbels and Goering argued over the telephone about Horcher's. If the Propaganda Minister closed it down, Goering would reopen it as a club for officers of the Luftwaffe, he said.

From this moment on Goebbels put the entire blame for the failure of total war on Goering alone. In his conference he openly spoke of the boastfulness of certain people—he mentioned no names—'who, although they are incapable of accomplishing anything constructive, use every device, no matter how ruthless, to remain in the limelight, surround themselves with a tremendously blown up organization and can only set themselves in motion if accompanied by a small army of motorcars...'

This was the beginning of an open battle between Goebbels and Goering. The two men exchanged bitter letters, and Goebbels, in any event, did not care at all how many people knew of their quarrel, nor how much they knew. The more the military situation deteriorated, the more frequently Goebbels denounced his former comrade of the days of the struggle for power. At the end he blamed Goering for everything.

VI

In the meantime, the Island of Sicily had been overrun by the Allies, and Goebbels could do but little to minimize the shock for the German people. He tried to pass it off with generalities: 'So far the Allies have won no victories of any consequence. In order to do so, a little more is needed than to invade Sicily with the combined military power of two world empires.'

Since it was clear to everyone in Germany that the two world empires would not stop at Sicily, Goebbels' propaganda had to work overtime to prevent a serious break in German morale. In the face of continued Allied military victories, how could the people be convinced that there was no reason to get panicky?

It was not Goebbels but Hans Fritzsche who had proposed the slogan of 'Fortress Europe.' Obviously, if Europe was an impregnable fortress any attack against it would be smashed, no one could enter it. Goebbels shook his head when he heard these arguments. 'Most people will associate the word "fortress" with the idea of a siege,' he said. 'Besieged fortresses are usually cut off from provisions and ammunition and eventually starved out, and ultimately all that remains is capitulation. "Fortress Europe" is too defensive a term for my taste.'

Nevertheless, here and there the term popped up in the German press. And instantaneously it turned out that Goebbels had been right. For the German people, especially the Berliners, picked up the word—but used it ironically. With the almost daily bombardments in mind, they would say: 'Fortress Europe has no roof.'

However, as far as propaganda for consumption abroad was concerned, that was quite another matter. Here, Goebbels whole-heartedly approved of the term and gave orders to play it up heavily. The rest of Europe must be told that Germany was waging war not only for her own sake but for all of Europe. The Allies must be warned that an invasion was impossible. Picture series and films about German defence installations in the occupied territories were composed in the Propaganda Ministry. Goebbels instructed the German press to emphasize over and over the strength of these defences, and newspapers in the satellite and occupied countries were forced to reprint these reports. The German radio hammered away in a thousand variations on the presumable fact that 'Fortress Europe' was an unassailable bulwark of steel and stone. Foreign journalists were invited to view the fortifications and on their return they invariably stated they were much impressed.

Yet, Goebbels himself was not happy with this type of propaganda. 'It reminds me too much of the Maginot Line,' he said. In June, 1941, he had written an article ridiculing British press comment on the fall of Crete as 'Glorification of Retreats.' Yet, for quite some time now, his own articles had been nothing but just that. As the German army was fighting defensive battles, Goebbels' propaganda also became defensive, no matter how frantic his efforts to conceal it. Time and again he wrote that he was not allowed to communicate everything he knew because the enemy was to be taken by surprise. Naturally Germany's leadership had taken all possible 'counter-measures for all eventualities.'

In order to appease those who were discontented Goebbels admitted that certain plans were not going according to schedule, that mistakes had been made, but that Germany's leaders were doing all in their power to correct such errors. Goebbels again adopted an attitude of quasi-philosophical detachment which was reflected in the titles of his articles, such as, 'On Injustice in Wartime', 'On the Essence of War', 'On the Contribution of the Intellect', 'On Talk and Silence', 'On the Irreplaceability of Freedom', 'On National Duties in Wartime', and so on.

He pointed out that actually Germany had already won the war and 'must only defend her victory.' He noted that England had suffered even worse crises than Germany did now; he explained that German lines had been shortened and thereby strengthened, and as a final argument he offered the statement that Germany's collapse, which Allied propaganda had predicted for the autumn of 1943, had not materialized.

Thus the circle was completed. In the autumn of 1941, when the British press noted with satisfaction that Hitler had not kept his timetable—for instance, his prediction to march into London in September or October, 1940, had not come true—Goebbels was highly amused, rejecting, with justification, such reasoning as poor propaganda. Now Goebbels was reduced to reasoning in the same manner. The initiative had been taken from him.

VII

On 25 July 1943, the King of Italy unceremoniously dismissed Mussolini. Everyone at the Propaganda Ministry in Berlin was speechless. Finally it was decided to say that the Duce was ill. For a few days Goebbels was so upset that he failed to write his weekly editorial. What line was he to take? It was still possible that the proclamation of the King and of Marshal Badoglio to continue the war was meant seriously.

Then, on 8 September, Italy capitulated. It was Germany's greatest diplomatic defeat and could have catastrophical consequences for German morale. But once more Goebbels pulled himself together, took the reins and gave clear-cut orders. The King of Italy was 'a traitor,' the surrender was 'a stab in the back.'

Surprisingly enough, Hitler did not let Goebbels down in this emergency. Goebbels telephoned the Fuehrer and begged him to speak to the people, and Hitler complied. Two hours later he spoke over all German stations. He explained his long silence by stating that he had for months anticipated Italy's collapse and therefore would not have been able to speak to his people without mentioning such a possibility, which in turn might have precipitated the events. Hitler spoke clearly and calmly, and his words inspired confidence.

Two days later, Mussolini was spectacularly rescued by German parachutists. This was celebrated with special announcements and detailed descriptions of the event which did indeed have the aspects of a thriller movie. The German military commentator, General Kurt Dittmar, was probably justified in declaring that from the standpoint of popular morale Mussolini's rescue was comparable to a victorious battle. These favourable repercussions on German morale were due less to the action itself than to Goebbels' propaganda, which was a masterpiece in every respect. Just as six months before at the Sportpalast, Goebbels was again playing on all the chords of human emotion.

However, here, too, he remained inwardly cold. In December, when Mussolini made a speech at Milan, Fritzsche asked his boss how to handle the matter. Goebbels replied that he was not interested in Mussolini's speeches; the Duce had not been rescued for charitable reasons of friendship but exclusively for reasons of precaution and safety.

VIII

As the year 1943 advanced, the Gauleiter of Berlin became more and more restless. Berlin had already been under air attack, but the damage had been relatively slight. One month before he had visited the ruins of Cologne and had been deeply shaken by the sight he saw. Hamburg was bombed—30,000 dead. At that time Goebbels decided to evacuate Berlin's women and children. 'Men and women of Berlin!' his first proclamation read. 'The enemy is ruthlessly continuing his terror attacks against the German civilian population. It is urgently desirable and in the interest of every single individual to depart for districts which are less endangered from the air, unless for professional or other reasons he is obliged to remain in Berlin...'

'The question of whether Berlin will be attacked by British terrorist fliers is difficult to answer. In any event, it would be irresponsible on our part if we simply took it for granted that this will not happen,' he wrote a few days later. He tried to be reassuring. 'What our leadership can do will be done. Nothing will be omitted which is humanly possible.' And shortly afterwards: 'In 1940 the English conquered this ordeal under much more unfavourable political and military circumstances than ours. In 1943, it is up to us to conquer it.'

The Berliners began to pack up their valuables and send them to friends living in the country. The streets were jammed with people carrying bundles, packages, suitcases, rolled up rugs. Women and children took hasty farewells, train after train departed for the safer regions of Pomerania, Mecklenburg, Bavaria.

And then Berlin's streets, buses and subways were almost empty. The city held its breath and waited.

The first blow fell on the night of 24 August, and virtually wiped out Berlin's southern suburbs. Tens of thousands were homeless. Goebbels took immediate steps. No one was allowed to take pictures of the ruins. Newspaper reports were cautiously phrased, and, because of the immensity of the city, it was possible that the damage in the southern suburbs was dismissed as exaggerated rumours by people living in the centre, north and east. Yet, Goebbels knew that this was only the beginning; he knew it from what had happened to other cities, and furthermore, from the foreign legations and embassies located in the heart of Berlin, which had received advance warning from the British. From day to day he became more nervous. At that time he worked himself into such rage and fear that he approved of the lynching of Allied fliers by the civilian population.[6] The waiting was intolerable. It began after sunset with the approaching darkness. Every evening Goebbels asked himself and his associates whether there would be an air-raid. Between six and seven o'clock he would call his adjutant ten and fifteen times, always asking the same question: 'Any news of approaching bombers?'

The big raid occurred on the night of 22 November, shortly after 7 o'clock, during a heavy rainfall. It had become pitch dark, when suddenly the sirens screamed. Half an hour later Berlin was like a burning torch. The west end was aflame, the government district was aflame, and the tremendous heat generated by the conflagration caused a violent storm which swept through the inner city.

That evening Goebbels was addressing a meeting in the western suburb of Steglitz. He had hardly begun to speak when someone came on to the platform and handed him a piece of paper. The colour left his cheeks when he read: 'Large bomber formations heading for Berlin!' For a while he continued his speech, although he became increasingly nervous. Suddenly he asked the audience whether there was any point in going on. At that moment the alarm sounded. Everyone rushed down to the cellar. Goebbels got in touch with Gau headquarters, heard the sound of crashing bombs over the 'phone, heard someone shout that he was wanted immediately at Headquarters—another bomb hit—and the telephone had gone dead.

Goebbels decided to drive back to Wilhelmplatz. He shouted his orders at the chauffeur, who thought he had gone mad, and the car started. The night was bright red with the glow of flames, the streets were full of bricks. Houses caved in, the anti-aircraft guns were in action. At fifty miles an hour Goebbels was racing across the city—bombs were falling all around, twice his car almost plunged into bomb craters, the driver had to make countless detours because many streets were blocked; the smoke-filled atmosphere became unbreathable.

When he finally arrived at Headquarters, no one believed that he had driven through half of Berlin. He smoked cigarette after cigarette, listened to the incoming reports, aghast. 'Another two or three of such attacks, and Berlin will be no more,' he said.[7]

IX

What was there left for Goebbels to say? What could he conceal under such circumstances? Every word was too much, and every attempt to minimize the terrible calamity by propagandistic manoeuvres seemed senseless.

Among those who lost all their belongings that night were Magda's mother and Goebbels' sister, Maria (who had married the film producer, Axel Kimmich). Both the Kimmichs and Frau Behrendt now moved to Lanke. Goebbels preferred to remain in town; too much family life was hard on his nerves, but he did visit them every few days, especially to see his children. In those days Goebbels was greatly preoccupied with his children. He had decided to keep them out of the Hitler Youth. He did not hold much esteem for the youth organization of the Party, and frankly told his associates so. He firmly believed that he and Magda could give the children a better education.

In the last years of the war Goebbels' children had a private tutor. Once he hinted that he did not think much of the average teacher's qualifications. Only towards the end, in February, 1945, he said to Frau Haberzettel: 'After all, if my children went to school they would have to listen to other kids' insulting comments about their father...'

He minutely checked the books the children were given to read, and had long talks with them. The only foreign language they learned was English. Helmut studied a great deal of history and his father lectured him at length on the interrelation of historical events, although the boy was altogether too young to grasp its meaning. Goebbels also planned the daily curricula for the children, including hikes, games and movie performances. He had even found comfort in the idea that he had so many daughters. 'Daughters will bring sons into the house, sons go to the houses of their wives,' he explained.

To the very end, Goebbels' children never greeted with 'Heil Hitler.'

X

Magda had made extensive preparations for celebrating Christmas with the entire family, including her mother-in-law, her mother and the Kimmichs. After a great deal of trouble she had bought presents, and a beautifully decorated Christmas tree stood in the film projection room at Lanke. On the evening of 23 December Goebbels' adjutant arrived and reported that the Minister was about to leave for Lanke and intended to see an American movie at home. Frau Goebbels telephoned her husband that the tree had already been put up in front of the screen, hence no films could be shown. 'Is that how my wishes are respected?' Goebbels shouted back over the telephone, hung up and went alone to Schwanenwerder. Magda was not even annoyed. Later she remarked that the family had not spent such a harmonious Christmas Eve in years. At least the children were able to sing their Christmas carols without getting on their father's nerves.

Angry and sulking, Goebbels sat down and wrote his New Year's article in the solitude of Schwanenwerder. He spoke of the 'Mysterious Book of the New Year,' which 'still contains numerous riddles for us.'

Many people in Germany would have given a great deal to know what the 'Book of the New Year' was holding in store for them. The run on fortune-tellers was bigger than ever, although it was strictly forbidden to practise any forms of clairvoyance. Since the necessity for such escape was so great, Goebbels exploited it. At the beginning of the year he planted 'The Revelations of the Swedish Fortune-Teller Gruenberg' in a Norwegian paper. Gruenberg believed that for a while the war would continue to go badly for Germany but that it would end with Hitler's victory. Finally, Germany together with the western Allies would fight against Soviet Russia. The article had hardly appeared when it was clandestinely circulated throughout Germany, typed on thin paper, and passed from hand to hand. The people avidly read these prophecies and were comforted. One of those who owned a copy of the article was Magda Goebbels. However, she concealed it from her husband because she did not want him to know why she was again in such good spirits.

'Crazy times call for crazy measures,' Goebbels explained to his assistant, Dr Semmler, when he told him about his publicity trick. According to Jacobs, however, he noted in his diary that he did not know the Swedish astrologer, had nothing to do with him, but he refrained from issuing a denial. Goebbels stated that he did not mind if a large portion of the population had strong inclinations towards mysticism, provided it gave them moral support.

But not all people could be reassured by such devious manoeuvres. More and more Germans became sceptical and despaired of Nazism. Goebbels tried to explain that it was quite pointless to have any divergent opinion because the enemy did not distinguish between 'good' Germans and 'bad' Germans but wanted to destroy them all. 'No German is in a position to escape by saying: In my heart I always was a Democrat, I always hated the Nazis,' ran his argument in many articles and radio speeches. And the further course of the war seemed to justify his prediction. For the bombs were raining on all houses alike, regardless of whether they sheltered Nazis or anti-Nazis.

However, all of this was nothing but defensive propaganda, and, indeed, precisely what Goebbels had wanted to avoid. At times he felt so frustrated about it that he spoke of his desire to die—under such circumstances death might be a welcome relief, he would say. To an actress friend he confessed how difficult it was to explain the setbacks to the people. 'How much better would it be if I honestly could tell them that things are getting better! It is so terribly hard to have to distort everything.'

'Why are things made so difficult for us?' he asked in one of his articles at the beginning of 1944. 'As far as we can look back in our history, our people has always been surrounded by danger,' he noted regretfully, but at the same time with some pride. As often as he could he escaped into history which offered numerous examples showing that Germany had been saved at the last minute in many a hopeless situation. 'History is characterized by a unique and grandiose justice which overshadows all human striving and activity,' he said. This time, too, things would turn out well in the end, as they had before.

While he was preaching in this vein, he did not look on passively to see what course historical justice would eventually take but tried to take history into his own hands. Despite his constant warnings as to what would become of Europe unless Bolshevism was annihilated, he thought the only way out was to come to an understanding with Stalin. At the beginning of April he worked out a forty-page memorandum which he sent to the Fuehrer. He explained that military victory was no longer in the realm of probability, that it was impossible to reach an agreement with Churchill and Roosevelt and that, therefore, Germany would have to come to terms with Soviet Russia. Considering that Stalin was anti-American and anti-British it was feasible to combine forces with him and to turn against the West, he argued. He saw no reason why the Russians should not keep Finland, the northern part of Norway and the Balkan countries. However, he pointed out, Ribbentrop was not the right man to carry out such a policy. He himself was prepared to take the assignment.

To his associates he added he would be willing to go to Russia and talk to Stalin in person. Of course he would always carry a phial of poison in his mouth, he added—for Stalin could not be trusted.

Goebbels then waited for Hitler's reply. Three weeks later, when he visited Hitler's Headquarters, he learned that the Fuehrer had never seen the memorandum. Bormann had not passed it on to him because he felt that the war situation did not warrant such desperate measures.

Goebbels was stunned.[8]

XI

Was the situation really as desperate as all that? And what about the weapon of retaliation which Goebbels had heralded so often? It was true that Hitler planned a series of new weapons, among them jet-propelled planes which could fly 100 miles faster than Allied aircraft, and that actually only time was lacking (as would be disclosed later): time for the Nazis to put the new inventions into mass production. Hardly a day passed without Goebbels asking Reich Armament Minister Albert Speer when the matter would finally come off. In conversations with his colleagues Goebbels was unusually optimistic. 'London has, after all, a population of eight million,' he said during one of his conferences. 'Imagine the repercussions if one day London would have to be abandoned, once our reprisal weapon has started to operate.' He was firmly convinced that this would be the case, and dictated into his diary: 'There can be no defence and no warning against our new weapon. The people cannot be expected to remain in their shelters night and day. The moment comes when they simply have to emerge from their foxholes.'

He and all others with him hoped that the new weapon would frustrate all attempts to invade the European continent. For the invasion of Europe, which Allied broadcasts had predicted since 1943, remained his main obsession.

For one whole year he had been writing articles on the subject. He described in detail how the Allied troops would land—and how they would be repelled, and without using the words *Fortress Europe*, he incessantly talked about it. Time and again he gave special directives for all broadcasts beamed to Britain: 'We are only waiting until you get here! Then we shall give you a reception which you will never forget!' And his general instructions said: 'Do not betray the slightest weakness or nervousness. Be determined and sure of yourselves.'

All this was bluff. The Allies had reliable information that the Germans had no more than twelve reserve divisions stationed in northern France. But the bluff was so well executed that even Allied military experts, who had convinced themselves from aerial photographs of the coastal fortifications that there was no Fortress Europe and no Atlantic Wall, began to mutter that the fortified coastline was unassailable. British Intelligence which was kept posted daily by its agents also over-estimated the difficulties of invasion.

Apparently carried away by the optimism of his own articles, Goebbels was led to make very bold statements: the German people were more worried that the invasion might *not* take place than that it *might*, he said. And his closest associates were convinced that Goebbels' belief in the failure of any such attempt was sincere. How much Fritzsche himself who told the story was victimized by this propaganda—even one year after the end of the war—is shown by his comment, 'If the German troops had really fought hard, the invasion would have failed.'

Goebbels had ordered a utopian novel to be written which was to be published in Switzerland under the title of *Europe's Suicide*, ostensibly from the pen of a neutral author. The purpose of this fictitious account was to put the fear of God into the British and Americans by showing them what a costly undertaking in men and material the invasion would be. Even the first landings would demand twenty divisions, or roughly 400,000 casualties, while altogether five million Americans and three million British would die before the entire operation was over.

The only basis for these astronomical figures was Goebbels' fertile imagination. Particularly, the first 400,000 victims during the initial landings were propagandistically exploited in articles, radio lectures, whispering campaigns. It is doubtful whether anyone in Germany believed in the authenticity of the figures. Strangely enough, the gloomy prophecies did not fail to leave an impression at Allied Headquarters. Shortly prior to the invasion American news-men were informed from a reliable source that one ought to be prepared for 500,000 casualties. A large American magazine published a kind of invasion preview which was almost as blood-curdling in its presentation of forthcoming events as the utopian novel concocted on Goebbels' orders.

Incidentally, the book was never published. For when it was completed the invasion was over. There were 14,000 casualties. That was the end of the myth of the Atlantic Wall and of Fortress Europe.

XII

The day before the invasion Hitler called Goebbels to Obersalzberg, where the two men spent the day in intimate conversation. It was 2.30 in the morning before he finally returned to the guest house, where his entourage had waited for him. He retired immediately and gave orders to be awakened at 9 a.m. to read the latest telegrams. However, at 4 o'clock he was roused from his sleep and given the first reports on the invasion. He jumped out of bed, and said: 'Thank God, they have finally arrived! Now begins the last round!'

Hitler was optimistic all day long. Goebbels remained outwardly calm, but actually he was so tense that he was unable to close his eyes when the railroad car carried him back to Berlin that night. The next two weeks, he said, would decide the outcome of the war. But already he was experiencing an overwhelming sense of disappointment because the invasion was an accomplished fact, whereas the military had maintained it could never materialize. Once again they had failed, once again they had misinformed him, once again he had to explain the unexplainable, and to cover up their blunders.

'It is self-evident,' he said, 'that such a long coastline cannot consist of one mammoth fortification after another. Now that it is known where the enemy has landed, the real German reserves will go into action.' But when he dictated into his diary or when he spoke to the liaison officer of the German High Command, he could no longer conceal his misgivings.

Allied blows followed one another in rapid succession. Goebbels knew well that the break-through at Avranches was of decisive importance and that it meant the loss of France as a basis of operations. But he could not admit it. During a speech at an armament factory in a western German town he said: 'I don't want to dispute the fact that the enemy was able to register certain initial successes. However, I can well imagine—although I don't wish to make an outright assertion—that it might have been within the realm of our strategy to allow the enemy to penetrate into the continent in larger numbers. For only under such circumstances would it be possible to inflict a decisive defeat upon his armies.' When he was interrupted by roaring applause, he repeated, 'As I said before, I do not maintain that this is the case, but I can well imagine that it could be.'

This propaganda line was very effective. According to Allied interrogators, German prisoners of war at first believed that all the talk about the forthcoming invasion was merely a manoeuvre intended to draw German troops from the eastern front to the west. When the Allies had landed, most Germans thought that they had been deliberately tricked into the continent eventually to suffer a devastating defeat. When the Allies were steadily advancing, German soldiers believed that it would not matter if France had to be abandoned, 'because we can always get it back anyway.' 'Territories are not important,' they would say, 'the main thing is we're not fighting in Germany.'

Goebbels was indeed indignant that the invasion had succeeded beyond 'certain initial successes.' He wrote: 'As far as Europe is concerned, it must ask the invaders what they intend to liberate the continent from. Perhaps from its solidarity, or from its incipient unity? Such a liberation would be Europe's greatest misfortune.'

In other words, Fortress Europe was no more, but the 'New Europe' still existed. And what about retaliation? Yes, retaliation had materialized and was mentioned vaguely in that same article. 'Retaliation is here,' Goebbels said.

It was a tremendous anti-climax. As late as 14 June Goebbels had described to his associates the impression he had gained when he saw a technicolour film of the new weapon. 'This weapon, gentlemen, comes almost prematurely for this war. I rather believe that it will be *the* weapon of the *next* war,' he had said. The next day he learned that the German High Command, without much ceremony, had shot off the new missile. Suddenly, on the evening of 15 June 1944, they had descended on London, without advance publicity or psychological preparation. The new weapon did not even have a name.

Goebbels almost exploded with rage. He refused to have anything further to do with the whole business. One of his associates, Schwarz van Berk, proposed to call the weapon V-1, the next V-2, and so on. The letter V was to stand for *Vergeltung* (retaliation), and at the same time would serve as an antidote for the famous British 'V for Victory.' Goebbels noted: 'The Fuehrer agrees to *my* proposal to call the new weapon V-1.'

Outwardly at least this was a minor triumph for Goebbels. He had promised the weapon of retaliation until no one had any longer believed it existed. Now people knew that he had spoken the truth. However, he was fully aware that it had come too late. And, worst of all, its propagandistic effect had fizzled out.

CHAPTER XV

THE DEATH OF GOD

I

While the German High Command was burning to find out the effect caused by the new weapons, Goebbels was far more interested in the impact of his articles. He was virtually starved for foreign comment.

After each new article had been read over the radio he was in a state of feverish tension. Excitedly he would thumb through the heaps of papers on his desk, paying no attention to important reports in his frantic search for a word about himself, Goebbels. Then he would send an urgent wire to Stockholm or Lisbon requesting: 'Where are comments on Reich article?'

Derogatory criticism did not bother him. He read it all with the same consuming interest and sometimes even with satisfaction. He declared that the Russian comments, which were simply loaded with hatred, to be more objective than those of the Associated Press and United Press. If there were no remarks, he would be terribly upset. The worst that could happen to him was to be passed over in silence.

A few days after the first V-1 bombs had been dropped over England Goebbels received the frustrated author of the utopian concoction, *Europe's Suicide*. This man, a certain Dr M. Bochow, tried to defend himself by saying that he really could not be blamed for the premature invasion. As a matter of fact, his novel had been completed, he said, but someone in the Propaganda Ministry had suggested certain revisions, whereafter the manuscript had remained unduly long in their files. So the delay was not his fault, he assured Goebbels over and over.

The Propaganda Minister became a trifle impatient and finally interrupted the man's monologue. It would be easy to revise the manuscript, Goebbels said. The important angle was no longer the invasion which was a *fait accompli* anyway, but what would happen afterwards. The dreadful consequences of this event would have to be made graphically clear to the Germans, to Europe, and to the whole world.

Goebbels proposed the following rewritten version: Stalin triumphantly marches into Germany... Europe's Bolshevization proceeds at a rapid pace. England and America resist in vain. Britain, too, turns Communist. Stalin reveals his aim to Churchill during a conversation in Moscow... When England becomes a Soviet Republic, Churchill suffers a stroke and collapses, while the whole world is asking: Is that what we wanted?

Roughly these were Goebbels' orders to Dr Bochow, who then dashed off to rewrite his book and to bring it, as it were, up-to-date. Goebbels' own articles were written in more or less the same tenor. If the invasion were successful, he declared in a hundred variations, not the western powers but Stalin would be the victor. There was only one thing to do: wage total war.

'A victory of our enemies would not bring peace but an endless continuation of ever-growing misery all over the earth... This world would no longer be worth living in, it would be worse than hell,' he wrote on 16 July 1944. Four days later something happened which brought him closer to his goal of total war than all his articles and speeches.

II

On the morning of 20 July 1944, Colonel Klaus Schenk von Stauffenberg arrived at the Fuehrer's Headquarters near the little town of Rastenberg in East Prussia. He carried with him a briefcase containing a time bomb, and placed it under the table in the wooden bungalow in which the daily conference on the military situation was to take place in the presence of Hitler, Field-Marshal Keitel and a number of other prominent personages. Shortly after Stauffenberg had left the building on some pretext there was an explosion which destroyed the bungalow, killed several persons and severely wounded others. Strangely enough, Hitler himself escaped with shock and minor bruises.

Stauffenberg heard the bomb go off and assumed Hitler was dead. He rushed to his waiting plane and flew to Berlin, where a number of prominent army officers and civilians, who for more than a year had conspired against Hitler, were expecting him.

Towards 1 p.m. Goebbels received the brief and mysterious news from the Fuehrer's Headquarters that there had been an explosion. He asked for confirmation but received no answer. He decided to wait patiently but became more and more nervous, and his assistants who lunched with him noticed he was pale and absent-minded. For the time being he knew nothing of the attempted assassination.

The headquarters of the conspirators was in the Reichswehr Ministry at the Bendlerstrasse. There, everyone was firmly convinced that Hitler was dead, and the plan which had been prepared long in advance, was now being carried out. Troops under the leadership of General Erwin von Witzleben, one of the plotters, marched on Berlin and threw a cordon around the government district, where in the further course of the day all buildings were to be occupied. The most important personalities, among them Goebbels, were to be arrested. In the general rush and confusion no one thought of cutting all telephone and telegraph wires.

It so happened that a certain Lieutenant Hagen, a so-called *politischer Fuehrungsoffizier* (National Socialist political officer) gave a lecture to the officers of the Berlin guard regiment on the same afternoon. He learned that a state of emergency had been proclaimed, that Hitler was dead, and that the regiment was to occupy the government district. Hagen thought this was most peculiar, and, since he had worked at the Propaganda Ministry before he joined the army, he called up Goebbels' residence to ask him whether there was any truth to these rumours. Goebbels, who was still at home, was reluctant to come to the telephone. He had never heard of this Dr Hagen and did not want to be bothered by an unknown caller. Finally, at the man's insistence, he consented to speak to him, listened to his story, linked it up immediately with the news of the explosion, and ordered Hagen to appear before him at once.

Hagen arrived half an hour later. 'Herr Minister, this is a military revolt!' he started out. Goebbels laughed, but Hagen pointed to the window: 'Look for yourself,' he said. Down below the soldiers were marching, blocking off streets, his own house, and, in fact, the whole government district.

Goebbels telephoned Dr Naumann at the Propaganda Ministry and asked him to report to him immediately. Naumann was stopped by sentries and sent back to his offices. In the meantime a certain Major Rehmer had announced himself to Goebbels. He was accompanied by two soldiers. Goebbels who assumed that Rehmer had come to arrest him, took out a revolver from his desk drawer and received his visitor with admirable presence of mind. The first thing he did was to yell at Rehmer loud enough to make the walls tremble. He used the brief respite to tell the startled officer that Hitler was alive. As proof he put through a call on his direct line to the Fuehrer's Headquarters.

Meanwhile Goering, Himmler and Ribbentrop had arrived at Rastenburg. In the course of their excited discussion they surpassed each other in their declarations of loyalty. No one, including Himmler, realized that everything depended on what happened in Berlin. Now the decisive factor was not that the Fuehrer was alive but that the German people, and above all the army, were informed of it. If the putsch in Berlin was carried out before the news of the bungled attempt on Hitler's life reached the public the rebellious officers might still have succeeded in their designs. Everything depended on Berlin, and in Berlin there was only Goebbels.

Now he spoke with Hitler. Hitler asked to be connected with Major Rehmer, who recognized his Fuehrer's voice and pledged to place himself and his 500 men at the disposal of the Propaganda Minister. From that moment on Goebbels started out to quell the insurrection single-handed. As he put down the receiver, Hitler remained at the other end of the line, in order to be on the spot if his advice was required.

It was now 5 o'clock. Goebbels stepped out of his house into the garden, where Rehmer had his men. They were soon joined by the guards of the Propaganda Ministry now again able to leave the building although the cordon around the whole government district was still in effect. Goebbels gave the men a pep talk, told them the putsch had failed, and that they could consider themselves the saviours of the Fatherland. It was only then that most of them understood what had been at stake.

Back in his home, Goebbels divided his time between talks with Hitler and giving commands to subordinates. In the course of the next hour reliable and loyal persons from all parts of the government district came to Goebbels, carrying machine-guns and hand grenades concealed under their coats. It was planned to barricade the mansion.

Then a new visitor was announced: Lieutenant-General Paul von Haase, the Commandant of Berlin, who had come to arrest Goebbels. The Propaganda Minister received him and told Haase that he was under arrest. Although the Commandant was inside the cordon which his troops had thrown around the government district, he was also inside the protective cordon formed by Rehmer's men around Goebbels' house. Haase had not expected any resistance and completely lost his head. In his dazed condition all he asked for was some food, a bottle of red wine, and permission to telephone to his wife, and Goebbels generously granted these requests.

Encouraged by this initial success, Goebbels telephoned other suspects and invited them to his house. A good many of them accepted, were taken to various rooms, where they were treated with great courtesy, offered brandy and cigars, and thus were under arrest without even realizing it. In the meantime Rehmer had sent some of his men to the Bendlerstrasse and others to the Broadcasting House, which Goebbels considered to be particularly important. The conspirators at the Bendlerstrasse, the real leaders of the attempted putsch, upright and courageous though not very practical, behaved heroically. Some of them were shot on the spot. At the Broadcasting House an army major had arrived to occupy the building for the rebels, but since he was not clear as to the extent of his responsibilities, he telephoned Goebbels, and soon gathered he was on the wrong side. Even before Rehmer's men were on the spot the ex-rebel had taken it upon himself to defend the building against the conspirators.

Meanwhile it was 8 o'clock. Himmler flew in from Rastenburg and rushed over to Goebbels' home, where the most important prisoners were confined. Goebbels, Himmler, and Ernst Kaltenbrunner, director of the Security Service of the S.S., cross-examined the men all night. In Berlin and in the provinces the arrests continued. Goebbels realized that the putsch was not yet completely under control. The net of the conspiracy was too widely spun, there were too many ramifications, no one could predict how other generals might react, or whether another bomb might not explode somewhere. The best thing to do under the circumstances was to make the matter public.

Over the telephone Goebbels dictated an appeal to be broadcast to the people, in which he acquainted them with the facts. In this manner he was able to give indirect warnings to numerous conspirators in the provinces and occupied territories, who might have been ready to strike. On learning that the putsch had failed, many committed suicide while others pretended they had nothing to do with the matter. Thus the plotters were rendered harmless. In the course of the night hundreds of loyalty telegrams reached Goebbels' office.

After midnight Hitler spoke briefly over the radio. He was nervous and distraught and made a very poor impression. He seemed to have lost all of his former authority, he implored the Germans to disregard any orders which might be issued in his name by the conspirators. He practically pleaded with his people.

Goebbels was disgusted with Hitler's performance. He declared that Hitler should not have been allowed to broadcast in his lamentable condition. His whole personality virtually radiated a sense of panic. Why had not the Fuehrer consulted him before he decided to speak? Goebbels asked.

That night Major Rehmer, whom Goebbels had proclaimed the hero of the day, was interviewed over the radio. As a matter of precaution the interview was recorded beforehand. Goebbels had the record played back and deleted a passage saying that Rehmer had been obliged to consult his military superiors before carrying out Goebbels' orders because the Gauleiter was but a civilian official. It was typical of Goebbels to eliminate the reference, for after his accomplishments during the putsch he felt himself to be more of a soldier than a civilian. The failure of the putsch was not due to the fact that the bomb had spared Hitler; it was not due to Himmler's police organization, which should have been able to smother the plot in its initial stages; it was not due to the active interference of any of the numerous prominent men in uniform: the putsch miscarried because of the presence of mind of a crippled little civilian.

III

Goebbels left no doubt as to what he thought of his vanquished opponents for whose idealism he had no understanding. During the night he said the whole affair had been 'actually nothing but a revolution by telephone.' At the conference the next morning his contempt was supreme. 'Dilettantes, all of them dilettantes!' he cried derisively. 'I would have known how to organize that sort of thing, I can tell you! If that impossible Haase had at least drawn a revolver and liquidated me! But look what he did! Heavens, what a dilettante!' Then immediately afterwards: 'To think that these revolutionaries weren't even smart enough to cut the telephone wires—my little daughter would have thought of that!' He could not get over the fact that the others had lost their heads so completely. He never mentioned a word about his own dangerous situation, or his accomplishments on that day. Even his closest associates—excepting those who had been present—had to piece the real story together bit by bit.

Goebbels' only concern was to show the German people, if possible, the whole world, that the plotters had conducted themselves in a stupid, cowardly and miserable manner. By contrast the figure of Hitler would shine all the more radiantly. Goebbels the propagandist knew that he could not permit himself any mistakes.

Some mistakes were, of course, inevitable. Two days after the attempted assassination Dr Robert Ley made a radio speech full of the basest insults against the conspirators; it was clear the German people would be put off by his crude approach. In addition, Ley made some extraordinarily stupid comments on Count Stauffenberg's ancestors, such as 'His father was an English Countess.' Goebbels wanted to suppress the speech, but Ley assured him Hitler had read and approved it, which was untrue. The speech caused an unpleasant reaction among the Germans, as Goebbels had predicted.

In his conference of 21 July Goebbels gave precise instructions for handling the trials which were soon to take place. He personally selected journalists who were to cover the event, and ordered that only the first two days of the hearings were to be reported. Though many persons were involved in the plot—most of them had played only minor roles—the impression must be avoided that it was organized by a large group of people with infinite ramifications, rather than by 'a small clique of criminals,' as the Fuehrer had said. 'We don't want to mention all this small fry, all these bit players,' Goebbels said. 'Above all, we don't want to dignify the sons-of-bitches by giving them publicity.'

His contempt for the plotters increased as he followed the cross-examinations. Although some of the conspirators conducted themselves courageously before the People's Court, Goebbels declared: 'Now they are whining. The reason is they have no stature, not a single one of them, although it wouldn't cost them anything to show some pluck since their fate is sealed anyway. Not one of them has the miserable guts to say: Yes, this is my belief and I stick to it, and it will remain my belief as long as I live, which may not be long. And now, for God's sake, you can do with me what you like.'

There was one single exception in Goebbels' gallery of villains—that was Rommel. It must have been a great blow to Goebbels when it turned out, several months later, that this likeable officer, whom Goebbels held in such great esteem, the only one of the generals for whom he had set his propaganda machine in motion, was among the conspirators.

For when Rommel's guilt became known two high-ranking officers went to his house at Herrlingen (where he was recuperating from wounds) and confronted him with the following alternatives: either he would be arrested and have to face a dishonourable trial before the People's Court, or he could take poison and his body would be given a state funeral. In the latter case, no one would ever learn of his disgrace. Rommel did not hesitate as to which course to take. He said farewell to his wife, who could neither say nor prevent anything, but had to stand by helplessly as her husband stepped into his car, and after the engine started, put the phial of poison to his lips.

Rommel's death had almost gruesomely heroic proportions which only a Shakespeare could have invented. In this case, unless all signs deceive us, it was Goebbels who invented them. For who else among all those meting out punishment to the plotters would have wished to save Rommel's prestige, if not the man who had made him the ideal of the German people? He alone was anxious to prevent Rommel from being degraded to the scum of the earth, the same Rommel whom he had endowed with all the virtues of a German Officer and, more important, whom he really had trusted. Goebbels alone could have thought up this inhumanly cruel alternative for his former friend, and only someone who had been as fond of Rommel as Goebbels was could have known what choice the officer would make.

However, in his diary we find only the following sober entry: 'Unfortunately it has turned out that Rommel, too, was among the conspirators... All I can say is I'm grateful Rommel is dead. If he were still living, we would have been forced to inform the people of his participation in the crime... Rommel was the idol of the soldiers and such disclosure would have caused a severe shock.'

Once the trial had started Goebbels lost interest in the proceedings. Not so Hitler. Hitler was concerned with every single detail, every single bit of testimony, so much so that he ordered a film to be made of the entire affair. Cameramen were stationed behind the presiding judge, and day after day, hour after hour, yards and yards of film were shot. At night the scenes were shown to Hitler, who demanded to see them over and over. Twenty, thirty and forty miles of film had already been made, but Hitler was insatiable. Finally he sent the rolls of celluloid to Goebbels and proposed that a full-length feature be produced, which should be shown to the German people.

Goebbels, disconcerted over the idea, looked at the picture and became still more disconcerted. He was unable to understand Hitler's enthusiasm and his desire for revenge. But above all he knew that such a film would have a bad psychological effect on the people, who did not care to witness how helpless prisoners were being insulted, and fundamentally the trial was nothing but an uninterrupted insult from beginning to end. The first thing he did was to have the picture cut down roughly to eight miles, which was of course still much too long. But Goebbels had no intention of ever showing the film, and to the end he succeeded in sabotaging its performance.

Goebbels was rather disillusioned over the Fuehrer's petty narrow-mindedness. His stenographer and secretary noted—independently of each other—that a new tone had crept into his voice when he spoke of Hitler. The same was true for his diary. He took to describing the Fuehrer's appearance, his trembling hands and arms, his stoop, his sickly complexion, adding usually that these ravages were the result of the attempt on his life. The boundless admiration and enthusiasm of the former days were gone and had been replaced by something approximating pity, if not contempt.

He no longer regarded the Fuehrer as the demi-God, the incarnation of strength, the man who was always right and always successful. Hitler had failed in many respects, and even if Goebbels could not publicly admit it he nevertheless knew that Hitler himself was responsible for his failures. Hitler could be wrong. 'The Fuehrer is perhaps deluding himself a little too much,' he noted in his diary at that time. Some of his associates began to notice that he felt himself to be 'superior' to Hitler.[1]

This introduced a new era in their relations; from now on Hitler had to be influenced and, in a manner, guided, perhaps even censored. It cannot have been an accident that in those days Goebbels instructed the German press to omit all mention of the drawings and water colours which Hitler had produced in his youth.

About the same time Fritzsche came to Goebbels and wordlessly pointed to a passage in the second volume of *Mein Kampf*, Chapter IX, where Hitler lamented over the cream of German Youth being sacrificed as 'defenceless cannon fodder,' and blamed Imperial Germany's leadership for the criminal waste of human lives during the last phase of the First World War. Fritzsche said that this time Hitler was guilty of the same crime. When Goebbels said nothing Fritzsche ventured that the Fuehrer ought to abdicate. Goebbels, who would have screamed 'High treason!' only a few weeks before, remained silent.

And while Goebbels announced to the world that a miracle had happened, thanks to which Hitler had escaped unscathed, another miracle had happened to himself. For Goebbels, the bomb had struck home. The Hitler in whom he had believed all these years, because he wanted to believe, was no more. While the smoke caused by the explosion was evaporating, Goebbels' vision became clear and gradually he began to see Hitler for what he really was.

IV

In the meantime Hitler had given Goebbels full powers. On the evening of 21 July the Propaganda Minister boarded the train on his way to the Fuehrer's Headquarters, where he arrived the following morning. The guards had been increased tenfold. All who wanted to see Hitler were searched from top to toe, including Goebbels. Then he had a long conversation with the Fuehrer. The only comment he made when he took the train back to the capital was: 'If I had received these powers when I wanted them so badly, victory would be in our pockets today, and the war would probably be over. But it takes a bomb under his arse to make Hitler see reason.'

On 25 July 25 Goebbels became *Reichsbeauftragter fuer den totalen Kriegseinsatz* (Reich Director for Total Warfare). The appointment was made by Goering, but that was merely a matter of form because, for all practical purposes, Goering's role had been reduced to insignificance. Within the framework of the Propaganda Ministry a special section was formed under the name of 'Total War'. Its staff consisted only of very few officials, because Goebbels wanted the new division to be as flexible as possible. Every morning between 9 and 10 o'clock the new staff conferred with Goebbels, and submitted proposals which, if accepted, were passed on for execution. The purpose of all measures were to free men for the front and the armament industry. As the former was more important than the latter, Goebbels began to comb the factories, which were gradually being denuded of workers, regardless of their specialized skill. Goebbels commented: 'We simply must create a temporary vacuum, and the armament industry will see to it that new forces will soon fill this vacuum.' The vacuum was filled partly with slave labour recruited by the S.S. in the concentration camps.

Beginning with 28 July one decree followed the other. Mail would be delivered only once a day... Women up to the age of fifty were conscripted for labour... Trips were permitted only in the most stringent emergency... All receptions, exhibitions, and public celebrations were forbidden... The number of household servants had to be reduced... Newspapers were merged... War invalids were made available to industry... Payment of alimony to women who did not work was prohibited... Suspension of classes for all boys and girls from the age of fourteen on was decreed, which resulted in freeing 80,000 adolescents to man the anti-aircraft guns... Young screen and stage actors were to be inducted into the armament industry... The 60-hour week was introduced... All German periodicals were suspended... All theatres were closed down...

The closing of the theatres and the compulsory conscription of artists for industry was Goebbels' private revenge against those whom he had once so greatly esteemed. Not even the young ladies who had been his mistresses were exempted. Goebbels' colleague, Paul Hinkel, hit on the unfortunate idea to put the artists in a more favourable light by suggesting that they address declarations of loyalty to the Fuehrer, which would then be collected in a volume and presented to Hitler as a Christmas gift. The undertaking was pathetically unsuccessful. Many of the actors were reluctant to comply at all, others sent in colourless quotations from the German classics, and one of them had the nerve to write: 'I believe in Hitler as I believe in victory.' The irony was very transparent but there was little Goebbels could do about it.

Together with the 'Total War' section Goebbels founded another division called 'Aktion B', designed to check up on popular reaction to total war, and to give it a lift, wherever necessary. This section was organized in the same manner which had produced such spectacular success in the days of the struggle for power. One speaker and two 'brawlers' would set out on a tour, visiting restaurants and other public places, and would provoke a discussion. If the people were appropriately responsive to total war, all was well. If someone uttered a word of criticism, he would be beaten up by the indignant *Volksgenossen*, meaning the brawlers who had come along for that purpose.

The head of the new section, a certain Haegert, who took his job terribly seriously, reported to Goebbels that the mood of the people was actually very good, a comment which caused Goebbels to smile rather sardonically—he had his doubts.

Booklets were written for teachers, officials, mailmen. Every one of them proved conclusively why that particular professional group was so important for final victory. Every one of them contained a series of answers for use against the *miessmacher und kritikaster*. No one needed to think for himself, Goebbels did the thinking for them all. At the same time he encouraged the people to write to the Propaganda Ministry to submit suggestions for making the total war still more total, on how to save manpower and material, how to cause still greater damage to the enemy. Every ounce of his strength was dedicated to filling the people with the will to fight it out to the last, come what may. The great propagandist was again at work.

At that time Goebbels also rediscovered his former 'revolutionary' leanings. For total war, just like the bomb was, was a great equalizer. It wiped out all social differences. For the rich man was now obliged to work; he could no longer hire servants, he could no longer go to theatres and luxury restaurants, and he could not drive his car. 'This war is the social revolution,' Goebbels had written on 1 November 1942. 'It is destroying an old and hostile world, but behind the smoking ruins a new and better world is becoming dimly visible.'

Even Magda did voluntary factory work. She went by trolley because it would have provoked the indignation of her fellow-workers if she had arrived in her car. After all, the people were supposed to be convinced that she was motivated by idealism and a feeling of national solidarity, and wanted to set a good example for other highly-placed ladies of the Nazi hierarchy. Furthermore, every Friday she was obliged to manicure Goebbels' nails, for all beauty specialists had been drafted, yet Goebbels wanted to keep his hands in shape. If for one reason or another Magda was unable to do so, Goebbels' secretaries had to do the job. After dictation they would have to report, equipped with nail file and scissors. They rather resented the assignment and gave vent to their annoyance when they were alone among themselves.

V

The sentence which ended Goebbels' speech after the disaster of Stalingrad— 'Rise, you people, and storm, break loose!'—was a quotation from the so-called 'wars of liberation' of 1813, when the Prussians shook off the yoke of Napoleon I. That *levée en masse* was now glorified in numerous newspaper articles. Goebbels ordered a historical film to be made on the subject (*Kolberg*). The whole propaganda machine was working overtime to prove to the Germans that the defeats of their armies were in themselves not decisive so long as there were enough people left, including old men and young boys, willing to defend the Fatherland.

After this propagandistic cannonade had lasted three or four weeks it was announced that Hitler had decided on the formation of a so-called *Volkssturm* (People's Combat Unit) and once more Goebbels was charged with carrying out the assignment. He issued a decree which automatically made every man from the age of sixteen to sixty a member of the *Volkssturm*. The organization of this new unit was taken over by Party functionaries who also were ordered to institute a daily military drill for these *ersatz* soldiers. They were given, not uniforms, but merely a simple armband bearing the word *Volkssturm*.

Induction centres sprang up in every town and village. They were housed in empty stores, in city halls or court buildings, in theatres or department stores. And there they lined up—the old men, the cripples, those with stomach and kidney diseases, and the children. Everyone was accepted, everyone was duty-bound to contribute something to winning the war. Alas, the whole people had become much too fatalistic to 'rise as one man,' and there was no enthusiasm, except among the very young. Goebbels tried in vain to arouse them, issuing countless directives to his Gau propagandists, exhorting them time and again to quote Frederick the Great, Bismarck, Hitler and Goebbels. But these directives sounded dispirited, there was an undefinable air of fatigue about them: even Goebbels himself was incapable of mustering any enthusiasm—except in one or two cases.

One such occasion was the swearing in of 10,000 members of the *Volkssturm* in front of the Propaganda Ministry. Goebbels had personally attended to every detail, down to the decoration of the portals and the proper position of the microphone. He was going to speak from the balcony. At the last minute he was informed that various guests of honour would be attending the ceremony. Some of them would be standing right next to him, practically looking over his shoulder to watch him read off his prepared text. Therefore, he abruptly discarded his manuscript and began to speak extemporaneously. The longer he spoke, the more excited he became, and his excitement was genuine enough to communicate itself to the people. They were deeply moved. When Goebbels returned to his office, the guests of honour applauded him, but he stopped them with a tired gesture of his hand. Five minutes later he was back at his desk trying to cope with his never-ending work.

While Goebbels was making frantic efforts to rouse the sunken spirits of the people, a squib was published by an unknown war correspondent, which said, in essence: 'We are retreating on all fronts, half of Germany is destroyed, things cannot possibly get worse, and, by the way, we shall win the war in two months.' These words caused a tremendous sensation; they were reprinted in all German papers; it was rumoured that the government was behind it, that something special would happen, that the tide would turn.

Editors rushed to the Propaganda Ministry and demanded additional information. All they found was an alarmed minor official wringing his hands in despair. It had only been just another front report without any particular background significance, he assured them; the man who had written it knew no more than all the others, and he pleaded with them not to play up the story to such proportions. No one believed the official. They all thought there was much more to the article than the Propaganda Ministry was willing to admit, and for a whole week all of Germany was wildly optimistic—without Goebbels apparently having moved a finger.

People no longer believed what Goebbels was telling them. The propaganda of retaliation, for instance, had left a particularly bitter taste in their mouths.

THE DEATH OF GOD

What good did it do the Germans if half of London was in ruins, yet Allied fliers could not be prevented from crossing the Channel night and day to bomb German cities? Just as in the first days of the régime numerous jokes were again circulated about Goebbels, and their content strongly indicated what their inventors thought of Goebbels and his propaganda.

For instance, there was the story of Goebbels dying and wanting to go to heaven. On his way up he noticed a door with a sign, 'Hell'. Driven by his curiosity he opened it and saw many bewitchingly beautiful women. 'I had so many enemies in this world,' he said to St Peter, 'that I'd rather remain in hell.' Hardly had St Peter closed the door behind him when Goebbels found himself surrounded by ugly, grinning devils. He protested vehemently: 'Where are all the lovely girls?' Whereupon the devils replied laughingly, 'That was nothing but propaganda!'

Or another story: In Berlin there was a victory parade, with Roosevelt, Churchill and Stalin on a grandstand reviewing their victorious troops. Suddenly a manhole opened in front of the stand, Goebbels' head bobbed up, and he said, 'But we won the war all the same!' Or: Hitler, Goering and Goebbels were standing at the window of the Reich Chancellery watching the Allied troops marching into Berlin. Goebbels noted with satisfaction: 'And now comes the retaliation!' The others looked at him as though he had lost his reason, but Goebbels explained, 'After all, where are they going to live?'

The people were not content only with jokes. The Propaganda Ministry had requested the citizens to send in their suggestions for the totalization of total war. A typical proposal read: 'We would like to be enlightened about the following: When the Allies landed in Sicily you explained that this was possible only through Badoglio's betrayal. Who is now to blame for the landing in France? And where is the unassailable Atlantic Wall? The mine blockade? The giant guns, the planes, speed-boats and other defensive measures of which you have given us such glowing descriptions in the newspapers and in the newsreels? How could the Allies have carried out the landings and brought in reinforcements if our defence measures had been only half as big as your trap, Herr *Volksverdummungsminister?*[2] Instead of trying to get us out of this damned mess before we all go to hell, you continue to babble about victory. You will probably have the nerve to ask the last living German who sits naked on the ruins to make still greater contributions to final victory, you cursed, bragging megalomaniacs!'

Other letter writers recommended. 'You must go to the front, you criminals! And you, too, you clubfoot, to the front with you! To the gallows with you confounded criminals!' *Volkssturm* members threatened to break into Goebbels' bunker and to use their guns. Twice a week Goebbels read a compilation of such letters. His face remained impassive—if he was angry he

295

certainly did not show it. The guards in front of the Propaganda Minister and in the corridor leading to Goebbels' offices were reinforced.

VI

Aachen was attacked, Aachen defended itself, Aachen fell. Goebbels tried to inflame the whole population to follow the heroic example of Aachen. On the other hand, he immediately instructed the press to refrain from referring to Aachen as the 'German Stalingrad'. The mere mention of the word *Stalingrad* caused a catastrophical reaction among most Germans and, furthermore, the comparison limped: Stalingrad never fell into the hands of the enemy.

In any event, Aachen was to be the signal for Germany's scorched-earth policy, those were Goebbels' orders. Whatever territory had to be abandoned to the enemy must be stripped of anything of value. But the gentlemen of German industry, who once helped the Hitler régime into the saddle, were anything but delighted when they were asked to sacrifice their factories and coal mines. They registered despairing protests with Goering, imploring him to stop this nonsensical destruction. It was very evident that they had every intention of surviving the Nazi debacle. Also, the workers in the threatened districts refused to inundate the mines or to dynamite the factories. The Gauleiters whom Goebbels had charged with carrying out the scorched-earth policy came back reporting acts of disobedience. For the first time the lack of arms made itself felt: there was nothing with which to subdue the recalcitrant workers.

All that was left now was persuasion, persuasion and encouragement. For this purpose Goebbels undertook many trips to the fronts which had become dangerously close to the homeland. He talked to the generals, the soldiers, the propaganda speakers, the workers. Whenever possible, he travelled by train, and only in an emergency would he use a plane or a car. Unlike Goering or Himmler, he needed no special train, but merely a private coach. It consisted of a living-room about ten yards in length, equipped with table, arm chairs, a phonograph and a radio. Next to it were the somewhat smaller bedroom and the bathroom of the Minister, a tiny bedroom for Under-Secretary Naumann and a number of sleeping compartments for his entourage. During these trips Goebbels used his spare time to write his diary (even his stenographer experienced difficulties in taking dictation while the train was going at seventy miles an hour), to draft the speeches he would make the next day, and to participate in occasional parlour games. He still would exhibit a childish delight when he found that he knew all the answers and could outwit his travelling companions.

VII

On his return from these tours he would often fall into a state of despondency. He spent more and more time at his place in Lanke, where he retired to a small bungalow hidden deep in the woods. There he used his leisure hours for reading and thinking. Even at meal-time he refused to budge from his temporary hide-out to go over to the villa because he could no longer 'stand to see the people who reminded him of the war.' Sometimes he would not return to his Ministry until three or four days later.

He felt ill and fretted over getting cancer. The doctors examined him but found no trace of the disease. All that was wrong with him were his stomach ulcers, they said, attributing them to his nervous condition. They declared all his other ailments were imaginary. On another instance Goebbels conceived the notion that his nervous irritability was caused by his excessive smoking. He determined to give it up and walked around sucking Wybert tablets (a sore-throat medicant). After a few days he had had enough. Incidentally, during that brief period of abstinence his nervous tension was heightened and resulted in further outbursts of temper, so that his assistants were greatly relieved when he resumed his chain-smoking.

It is not too difficult to guess what thoughts were passing through Goebbels' mind in the solitude of Lanke. He had joined a political movement which had brought him fame and success. But he had overlooked the fact that such a dynamic movement was bound to generate opposition, counter-movements, even wars. Somewhere there was an error in the whole calculation, somewhere Hitler had gone a step too far and that step could never be retraced. One error had produced another error and finally a whole series of errors, until it was too late. Like the Sorcerer's Apprentice, Goebbels could not shake off the spirits which Hitler (and he himself) had conjured. If he had known ten years before what the fate of Germany would be in 1944, with the whole world allied against her, he might then have abandoned the Nazi cause.

But he could not admit his most intimate thoughts and fears. Neither would he permit others to express them. At the beginning of 1945 there was, for instance, the case of S.S. Gruppenfuehrer G. W. Mueller, who had been charged to investigate the situation on the western front. When Mueller submitted his first pessimistic reports, Goebbels commented that they were 'frankly defeatist'. 'Mueller isn't what he used to be. Apparently the company of the German Officers Corps didn't agree with him,' he added laconically. Later, when Mueller came to Goebbels' office to report more exhaustively on his findings, Goebbels deliberately ignored his presence, busied himself with other matters and finally cut him short when the man tried to present his opinion.

When other associates hinted at the possibility of a defeat or reported the demoralization among the people, he raged and accused them of defeatism and threatened to send them to the front. Then adjutants and assistants would try to get out of his sight as quickly as possible, for Goebbels could still shout so loud that his voice could be heard through several closed doors. 'You know, if you're mad enough to bust and a dog happens to cross your way, you kick him in the behind so that he goes flying into a corner,' he would say after he had calmed down again. His associates knew that one of them was always bound to be the dog.

The wife of one of his employees once confidentially told him that some of her officer friends were using every subterfuge possible to get away from the eastern front. Goebbels insisted that she disclose their names so that they could be properly punished. It took Magda Goebbels' personal influence to prevent the outbreak of a major scene.

Next to Goering, Ribbentrop remained Goebbels' favourite scapegoat. 'Again I spoke to the Fuehrer today, begging him to dismiss Ribbentrop, and again he refused,' Goebbels said in September, 1944. Again ... Ribbentrop's qualifications as Foreign Minister had been debunked. It turned out that his initial successes in the field of foreign policy were merely the fruits of German military victories. When he was no longer backed up by guns and tanks, no one bothered about him. According to Jacobs, Goebbels asked Hitler at one point to entrust him with the Ministry for Foreign Affairs. It is unlikely that Goebbels was motivated by personal ambition, for what glories could he reap as Germany's Foreign Minister in 1944?

Goebbels' fits of rage and attacks of melancholia were known only to his intimate associates. In their presence he let himself go. But when he was in public he continued to conduct himself with his customary serenity. He was always immaculately dressed, well groomed, unobtrusively scented. Any visitor at his home would have gained the impression that the country was at peace. The slightest bomb damage was immediately repaired, a broken window-pane replaced at once. When the plumbing was temporarily out of order, he dictated for his diary that now he, too, was as it were, bombed out. He described this minor inconvenience to the smallest detail, protesting that for the first time he had no hot water for shaving.

VIII

On 29 October, Goebbels' birthday, Hitler 'phoned, talked for a while with Goebbels and then asked to speak to Magda. When Frau Goebbels had hung up the receiver, she was almost crying with happiness. The Fuehrer had told her that soon there would be a decisive turn in the war, she said.[3] Christmas would bring a great victory.

This was the first time Goebbels learned that the German army was planning an offensive in the Ardennes.

The shock to morale caused by the invasion and the attempt on Hitler's life had worn off. Thanks to the measures of total war Hitler had acquired a new army, although it did not number one million, as Goebbels had promised. Hitler's health had been largely restored. Furthermore, weather conditions were not unfavourable to a German offensive. Allied superiority in the air was almost nullified by heavy fogs. Furthermore, the Channel ports were not yet opened, the Allies could not bring up sufficient gasoline and their tanks and planes were largely immobilized.

Hitler had gone to Bad Nauheim to direct the offensive. Goebbels, who had remained behind in Berlin, did not know very much about the plans. He was nervous and tense. An assistant inadvertently knocked a framed photograph of Hitler off Goebbels' desk and one of the glass splinters pierced the Fuehrer's left eye. Goebbels was tremendously upset and thought it was a bad omen. For the first time in his life he felt the urge to consult a fortune-teller. Once upon a time Hitler had told him of a woman who had made the most amazing prophecies to him. Goebbels tried to locate her, but she had vanished.

Since the port of Antwerp was opened sooner than he had anticipated, Hitler was forced to change his plans. Now that the Allies again were able to get all the gasoline they needed, he could not risk waiting. The Ardennes offensive started on 16 December.

In his conference of 17 December Goebbels made his first disclosure, explaining at the same time why the Fuehrer had remained silent so long: this was done to 'lull the enemy into security'. Goebbels had even gone further. 'Four weeks ago I spread the rumour abroad through German agents that Hitler was dead. By these rumours the general assumption that we could not stage a comeback was strengthened,' he said.

Nevertheless, he still remained cautious. He did not indicate the goal of the offensive, although by now he knew it. Officially it was called the Rundstedt Offensive, a precautionary measure designed to free the Fuehrer from all blame in case the move failed.

Three days later Goebbels realized that the goal would not be reached. He promptly declared in his conference that the German army had not aimed at breaking through to Paris or to the Channel coast but merely intended to tie down the enemy and force the Allies to withdraw troops from the endangered sections of the front. This aim had been fully achieved, he asserted.

However, his disappointment was so acute that he was unable to keep it to himself. He told his associates that Rundstedt had 'spoiled everything'. For

Goebbels had sincerely believed that Paris would be retaken by Christmas. He had even composed a Christmas message to the German people informing them of the new victory, and he had read several passages from it to at least two of his colleagues.

The following weeks proved that everything had indeed been 'spoiled'. The fifth and sixth German tank armies were lost and nothing had been gained.

IX

Goebbels was filled with bitterness. 'I have long cured myself of the habit of standing inwardly at attention before a general,' he said, seeing the offensive would miscarry. 'What we need is a military genius. But in this war we have neither a Moltke, nor a Schlieffen, nor a Clausewitz. What we have is, at best, good average.'

And Hitler? Had not Goebbels said of him that he was the greatest military genius of all time? Since then an eternity had passed—that is to say, almost two years. But many things had changed. In his Order of the Day at the beginning of the Ardennes offensive the Fuehrer had proclaimed: 'If the Panzer Grenadiers fail now, they will have had the last word from their Fuehrer.' The German troops had failed—but the Fuehrer did not even remotely think of doing anything about it.

Naturally Goebbels could not state such views in public. On the contrary, once more he wrote a glowing article about the Fuehrer, to be published on New Year's Day. It was always safe to write about Hitler. To him, the person of Hitler had degenerated into a mere vehicle for his propaganda.

And then once more it was Christmas. Magda decorated the tree, played Santa Claus, the children and the servants were given their presents; even the French gardener, Jean-Marie, received a small gift.

Outwardly, all was peace and harmony. Magda, plagued by doubts, was reassured by her sister-in-law Maria, who said to her: 'You can be certain that the Fuehrer has another trump card up his sleeve, otherwise all that is happening now would be sheer murder!'

Magda, however, was not convinced. Late at night, when the children were in bed and the lights on the Christmas tree were extinguished, she said to her secretary: 'Next Christmas, I'm sure, there will be peace.'

But her tone of voice betrayed her and the secretary could sense the real meaning behind her words: Magda knew that she and her children would not be there to celebrate another Christmas.

CHAPTER XVI

THE TIME BOMB

I

The Ardennes offensive developed into the Battle of the Bulge. Field-Marshal Montgomery temporarily took command of certain American divisions and, in a press interview, described the course of the battle after he took over the command from the Americans. Goebbels read the interview in the monitored radio reports, saw an opportunity, changed a few words of the text so that Montgomery appeared to claim that he had won the battle after the Americans had lost it, and then had it transmitted over the BBC wave length, ostensibly as a British broadcast.

The fraudulent manoeuvre was entirely successful. Americans who listened to the broadcast believed it to be an official British announcement and became highly indignant. By the time the BBC and the British press had revealed it as a fake the seeds of distrust had been sown. There was much inter-Allied resentment and quarrelling behind the scenes, and Goebbels had achieved what he set out to do. But the war could not be won by such propaganda tricks, no matter how ingenious.

Goebbels was seized by a sense of futility and helplessness. In the morning when he arrived at his office and scanned the latest news brought in by Frau Haberzettel, he would sometimes say: 'Where will it all end?' Next to the telegrams were piles of *Vernichtungserklaerungen*—lists of documents which had been destroyed the previous day in order to prevent them from falling into the hands of the enemy. This procedure had started as early as 10 November 1944. In January, 1945, tons of files and dossiers were thrown every day into the huge shredder to be pulped.

During the daily report on the military situation Goebbels was absent-minded, barely listening and seldom making a comment. One day, when the Battle of the Bulge was nearing its end, he interrupted the liaison officer of the High Command with the following words: 'There you sit and prattle about all sorts of trifles, while someone like myself is wondering whether the time has come to poison his wife and children!'

The officer stuttered into silence in the middle of a sentence, while the others gasped with surprise. It was the first time Goebbels had shown his despair so openly. However, he soon regained his composure and during the subsequent conference no one would have suspected the emotional upheaval within him. Later when Frau Haberzettel came in with new telegrams she found him again brooding. 'From Stockholm it is reported that we have lost more than three million dead.' He paused, and then continued: 'And the same number of wounded.' She asked him whether he believed the figures were correct, but he merely shrugged: 'Do you think I know? Do you think anyone knows?'

Turning to Fritzsche, who was entering the office, he said abruptly: 'After the war I'll go to America. There at least they will appreciate a propaganda genius, and will pay him accordingly.' Fritzsche smiled. He had heard such remarks before and knew they were not meant seriously. That day, however, Goebbels was more preoccupied than usual with the post-war period, and what he would do with himself once the fighting was over. 'In any event,' he said, 'after the war I shall live at a more leisurely pace. I will devote myself entirely to writing. All I'll have to do is to write one book a year, which will be no trouble at all. I have no doubt that I'll be able to live splendidly on my royalties, for my books will have tremendous sales.' He rambled on about writing in general and about writers in particular. In his opinion, they were all too lazy. He believed that during the last few years he had established a world record in writing—for quantity—and he voiced nothing but contempt for those who produced a measly page a day or less. He felt little inclination for work that morning. He constantly interrupted himself to chat with Frau Haberzettel, undoubtedly in an effort to take his mind off the calamitous military situation. Before lunch he had to receive a group of *Rammjaeger*. They were fighter pilots—also called suicide fliers—who had orders to ram their plane into an enemy bomber if they had been unable to shoot one down at the end of their third mission. The young men stood before him and he knew he would not see them again. 'Believe me, boys,' he commented, 'I know what it means when men like you, in the prime of their youth, go to death willingly and with open eyes, at a moment when their sacrifice might seem meaningless. I know your feelings, my brave men, and I share them. Sometimes I think of my former personal assistant, who was shot down over Crete and whose tragic death was a great blow to me because he was my friend. But now I envy him because he met his end in the face of a great and glorious victory. Today death is showing us a different countenance.'

For a minute he remained silent. Then he stepped up to the fliers, shook hands with them, looked gravely into their eyes, and gave the Hitler salute.

When they had left and the door was closed behind them, he sat down at his desk and asked one of his associates: 'Well, how was I? I suppose I found the right tone, didn't I?' Whereupon everyone hastened to assure him that he had.

II

A few days later, in the afternoon, Hitler paid a visit to the Goebbelses.

Goebbels' home was less than half a mile away from the Reich Chancellery, and the gardens of the two buildings were adjacent. Yet Hitler had not called on them for many years, and so his visit was somewhat of a sensation. Goebbels received him outside the mansion, his arm raised in the Hitler salute. The little girls, dressed in their Sunday best, curtsied before the Fuehrer, who presented Magda with a bouquet of lilies of the valley. 'Since your husband closed down all the flower shops it is difficult to find anything appropriate,' he muttered as an excuse.

All of those present—the servants, the associates, the S.S. men standing around in the lobby—were aghast at the Fuehrer's appearance. He had become an old man who was trembling all over; one of his legs was dragging and his voice sounded broken and hoarse. Behind him walked a servant with a large briefcase bearing the initial F (for Fuehrer, evidently), from which Hitler took a thermos bottle and a small package: he had brought his own tea and his own cookies. There was something ghostlike and unreal about his visit. Hitler sipped his tea and occasionally nibbled at a cookie. The conversation threatened to peter out every few minutes. Exactly an hour and a half after he had arrived he arose, shook hands with everyone, and promised to call again.

When he had gone, no one spoke a word. Undoubtedly they all had the same thought: how sick and miserable was the man to whom the whole nation looked as its saviour! As though attempting to dispel the atmosphere of gloom which had descended on all of them, Magda almost triumphantly exclaimed: 'But he wouldn't have gone to the Goerings!'

Most of the evenings were spent in the private shelter of Goebbels' home, which was directly accessible from the house. Steps covered with thick rugs led down to a depth of more than twenty yards below the ground. Members of the S.S. bodyguard were stationed on both sides of the staircase and remained at their post until Goebbels had entered the shelter. Then the heavy iron door was closed behind him. During an air-raid alarm he was usually the last to go down. He was in no particular hurry, but his family would rush down at the first warning. In the shelter all sounds were shut out. When a bomb crashed in the immediate neighbourhood the ventilators would flap on the walls, and at times the lights would go out for a few seconds.

When Goebbels worked in his office and was surprised by a day raid he would occasionally go to the basement of the Propaganda Ministry, where he had a separate apartment; consisting of two luxuriously furnished rooms. (It was typical of the Third Reich that the concrete ceilings of these two rooms were more strongly reinforced than all others in the cellar.) Here, too, were the safes containing the secret files of the Propaganda Ministry, a special switchboard and an installation equipped to supply the whole building with electricity.

But, whenever possible, Goebbels would leave his office at the first warning to go home and join his family. He would play with his children; even the children of the household personnel were included in these games. He would also have long talks with Magda. She never showed the slightest fear. As the bombardments increased in intensity and the family was obliged to spend more and more time in the shelter, Goebbels' marriage seemed to improve. The ever-present danger had forged a link between him and his wife. He often appeared to be relaxed and patient and indifferent to the constant noises and disturbances which had invaded his life. His children no longer got on his nerves.

At times the couple would sit side by side, holding hands. Or Magda would play a game of solitaire, while Goebbels, stretched out in a chair and smoking a cigarette, would gaze at her with a sort of grave satisfaction. The bitter years of their marriage, when one partner deceived the other, were forgotten. Possibly Goebbels still had occasional affairs; of Magda it is certain that she had a liaison with a painter who was then *en vogue*, but neither of them cared particularly one way or the other—they had grown older, they had become resigned. Apparently it never occurred to Magda that she might survive the approaching catastrophe—unlike the wives of other Nazi leaders, who were firmly convinced that this end did not concern them in the least and that they had no part in the whole disaster.

Towards the middle of February Magda asked Hitler's physician, Dr Theodore Morell, for a quick-acting poison and he gave it to her. She did not want to burden her husband with her sinister premonitions, but when she spoke to his associates she was amazingly frank. 'When I put my children to bed and think that in a few weeks they may no longer be alive, I could go crazy with grief,' she said. And yet it was astounding to see how firm she was in her decision to die. With her, Goebbels' propaganda had indeed been completely successful, although secretly he might have wished otherwise. Several times he had suggested that she take the children to some place in western Germany, to regions which would soon be overrun by the Americans and British. She and her children probably would not be touched, he argued. But she refused.

While sitting in the shelter during the air-raids Goebbels' only concern was the fate of the Propaganda Ministry. Every few minutes he 'phoned to find out whether the switchboard still functioned. If there was no answer he would mutter, 'Now they've probably scored a direct hit.' His joy was all the greater when he found that nothing had happened. As a matter of fact, the Propaganda Ministry was the only government building which so far had not been bombed, although the Berliners would have liked nothing better than to see Goebbels' 'Headquarters' go up in smoke—for his unpopularity was growing by leaps and bounds.

When Goebbels had convinced himself that the Propaganda Ministry was still standing, nothing else would matter to him. He hardly listened to the lecture of the liaison officer of the High Command, who reported what had happened in Berlin the previous night. 'You can keep your figures to yourself, they are not correct anyway,' he would snap. And he dictated into his diary: 'The Luftwaffe has absolutely no idea of what's going on. They are just as stupid and corrupt a bunch as their commander.'

In his conferences he expressed himself with remarkable frankness on the bombardments. 'Let's not always talk about terror attacks,' he once said. 'This is total war. And believe me, we would do exactly the same—if we only could.'

III

Such frank statements were of course confined to his inner circle. The people could not be told these truths. They must be comforted. Goebbels helped to supply bombed-out people with clothing and food. He visited maimed soldiers in the hospitals. When he heard that in certain hospitals some severely wounded men, who were too ill to be transported to air-raid shelters, were protesting against the continuation of the war, he ordered the nurses to go from bed to bed whispering, 'Keep calm, tomorrow we shall launch the V-3 to V-8, and the tide will turn'.

Goebbels also had to encourage the men who in turn were charged with encouraging others, namely the propaganda speakers and the *Kreisleiters*. Most of them were men who had grown up with the Party. Goebbels reminded them of the critical times the Nazis had faced, of the moments when all seemed lost—and then things had taken a turn for the better. He talked of the Strasser crisis, he recalled the landslide in the tiny state of Lippe. 'This little success, so insignificant in itself and out of proportion to the defeats suffered before, nevertheless showed the world that we were still there. And this is how it is today.' The others listened and nodded, they knew what it meant. All that was needed was a victory, even a little victory—and the world would know that Germany was still there.

For a year Goebbels had become increasingly certain that all was lost. All the harder he fought to strengthen the belief of others in ultimate victory. All possible arguments had been introduced in the struggle. And now the time had come for Goebbels to believe his own arguments, if only for a few moments, to be deluded by his own fake proofs. In a word, Goebbels had become the victim of his own propaganda.

This was comparable to what had happened to him when he first met Hitler. Then he determinedly stopped using his intellect and analytical powers and turned to pure and simple faith. Now again he wanted to 'believe'.

The fate of Frederick the Great, Goebbels' favourite stand-by in every desperate situation, was now invoked for his own personal salvation. In an article, 'History as Teacher,' he wrote: 'Again and again I have the experience that reading the letters and essays of Frederick the Great or the chapters in Mommsen's *Roman History* dealing with the Second Punic War has given me strength, even in the critical phases of the war.'

These were no longer propagandistic arguments. As the military situation deteriorated day by day, Goebbels believed all the more fervently that 'History must have a meaning,' that there must be a way out, for, if Germany went down, 'History would be a whore.'

More and more he began to regard himself as a historical personality. He wrote, 'Neither Alexander nor Fabius, neither Scipio nor Caesar, neither one of our great German emperors nor one of our great Prussian kings would act differently from us in our present situation and give in to the fury of destruction of the enemy.' When he first saw the film, *Kolberg*, depicting the heroic resistance of beaten Germany against Napoleon I, he told German newsmen that in a hundred years another picture would be made, a film about the heroism of Berlin—and that now was the time for each one of them to pick his part and to decide whether to be applauded or booed by the movie audience of the future. Incidentally, one of his assistants resented this remark. 'Merely to be a bit player in a picture a hundred years hence seems hardly worth dying for now,' he complained bitterly to a colleague.

In his conference Goebbels said: 'We happen to be standing on the stage of history and, therefore, according to the role which has been assigned to us, we must think in terms of greatness and act on a level of greatness. After all, that is what no one can take from us—to go down some day in the annals of history.'

To go down as what? In the first years after the Nazis came to power Goebbels once said that the world would shake in its foundations if the Nazis ever withdrew from the scene of history. Probably that was more or less a figure of speech, for then he certainly did not believe that it would ever come to that point. But was it really enough to sell one's life as dearly as possible? Was it really a satisfaction to know that half the world would go up in flames just so the Nazis could make their exit? Was it absolutely necessary to withdraw from the scene? Was there no other alternative?

It was evident that a general whose army was destroyed had to surrender. But Goebbels was not a general; he had no tanks, no planes, no concentration camps to run; his power was not physically conditioned, it could not be taken from him by occupying, destroying, overrunning, or dissolving something. His power was of the intellect, the power of persuasion, of influencing others. Was there nothing he could do to preserve that influence beyond his own destruction? Did not the world offer examples of ideas which were not backed up by guns or physical might, and nevertheless had remained alive?

Did Goebbels have to withdraw from the scene?

'He furtively looked with both eyes toward posterity,' his colleague Fritzsche would say later when speaking of these last few months. 'If you want to understand what he wrote towards the end, you have to bear this in mind.'

The final epoch saw the beginning of a propaganda which fell into two separate parts: tactical, short-range propaganda, and strategic, long-range propaganda. The former was devoted to the prolongation of the war, for every day that was won in this struggle gave providence another chance to perform a miracle. But if the miracle failed to happen, if the approaching catastrophe could not be averted, Goebbels would still be there.

Not in the flesh, to be sure, but through the effect of his propaganda. All he had to do was to create the kind of long-range propaganda which would run on its own power and require no further direction from him, who would no longer be living. He had to launch a propaganda missile which sooner or later would reach its target, perhaps years after his own death. Goebbels invented the propaganda time bomb.

IV

The obvious reflection is that this was nothing new. Every philosophy and every religion are based on the assumption that their influence will outlive the death of their founders. As for the world religions, the time factor has been vastly beneficial to their development.

But this parallel is no more than superficial.

In contrast to the founders of Christianity or Marxism—to name but two important philosophies—the originators of National Socialism (which is of course no philosophy in the strict sense of the word) attained power during their life-time. They were in a position to demonstrate the validity of their ideas, and subsequently compromised them by the complete bankruptcy of their regime. If Hitler had not come to power, Goebbels could have preached that the world eventually would realize the significance of National Socialism and embrace it. But since the Nazi rulers had sent millions of human beings to their death and brought their country to ruin, the Nazi propagandist could not point hopefully to the future. He could not even make propaganda in the pious belief that sooner or later it would sink in and produce effect, for the very fact that *he* was the one who made it was sufficient to compromise it for all times. All those associated with the collapse of the regime had disqualified themselves for posterity.

Ergo, any attempt to influence posterity could not consist merely in making Nazi propaganda, or promoting ideas which, as everyone knew, had failed. The founders of Christianity were justified in their hopes that later generations would bring hosts of zealous followers. They could speak frankly and honestly when they addressed themselves to posterity. Goebbels could not. If he wanted to perpetuate his influence at all, his future followers had to be kept in ignorance of his designs.

The characteristic of the propaganda time bomb and the *sine qua non* for its ultimate effectiveness lay in the fact that no one must know when and where it had been dropped, and when it would explode.

Hence no direct propaganda for Nazism, but rather the dissemination of ideas of which later generations might say: That man was right. Goebbels had to make prophecies. That was not too difficult. The development of the situation in Germany could easily be predicted. Here is what he foresaw in the period following the defeat: 'If this war ended with our enemies' victory, then we Germans would be condemned to be slaves and mules of the whole world for an unpredictable time... History is without mercy toward the nations who surrender... What use would un-destroyed cities be if they were populated by a nation in chains?'

On the surface, of course, such prophecies had to be disguised as warnings to continue the fighting, to avert the terrible end. But in reality Goebbels was already stating facts: he was putting himself on record. He not only knew that Germany would suffer. He also knew that the worse matters became, the more favourable the comparison with the Hitler régime. Only if the people were really desperate would they think with longing of the good old days under the Nazis. Only then would Goebbels' time bomb explode.

Après nous le déluge! So why not plan a deluge in advance? The greater the destruction caused by Allied bombers, the better it was from Goebbels' point of view. Valuable monuments, churches, castles were being wrecked. But all that people worried about was how to save their lives, and most Germans knew anyway that during a heavy bombardment it was virtually impossible for the enemy to spare historical buildings. Goebbels realized of course that the Allies intended to paralyze German war industry and communications. But that did not prevent him from declaring that they were bent on wiping out all architectural beauty and culture. Now the average German was too harassed to pay attention to these statements. Only later, when the infernal horror of the bombing nights was forgotten, his words would be remembered. People would say: 'Goebbels was right.'

The planned deluge… If Goebbels had had his say, things could not go badly enough, not only for Germany, but for all of Europe. Any later comparison would then be flattering to the Nazi régime.

Goebbels never had any illusions about the relations between the Russians and their western Allies. Churchill had always been one of the bitterest enemies of Communism. It may be assumed that the news of Churchill's attempts to persuade his American friends to invade the Balkans had penetrated into Germany via the various intelligence services; also, that the proposed Balkan invasion was designed to prevent the Russians from extending their sphere of influence further to the west. It may also be assumed that Goebbels had been informed of Churchill's hope of convincing the Americans that they should advance to Berlin.

At the Yalta Conference the Allies had conceded Berlin and the larger part of Germany to the Soviets. Whether Goebbels had any information on this point is not certain. In any event, he did know that a good deal of political dynamite had been accumulated at Yalta. In his remarkable article, 'The Year 2000', which contained a whole arsenal of time bombs, he prophesied that sooner or later the Allies would fight among themselves.

Here are a few quotations from it:

'At the Yalta Conference the three enemy war leaders, in order to carry out their programme of annihilation and extermination of the German people, have decided to keep the whole of Germany occupied until the year 2000. One cannot but admit that this project has certain grandiose aspects… How empty must be the brains of those three charlatans, or at least the brains of two of them! For the third, Stalin, has planned much farther ahead than his two partners… If the German people surrendered, the Soviets would occupy … the whole east and south-east of Europe, in addition to the larger part of Germany. In front of this enormous territory, including the Soviet Union, an iron curtain would go down… The rest of Europe would fall into political chaos which would be but a period of preparation for the coming of Bolshevism…

'Roosevelt would not be re-elected in 1948, and a Republican, that is, an isolationist, would become President of the United States. His first action would probably be to recall the American troops from the boiling cauldron of

Europe. This would be applauded by the entire American public...'

Goebbels also predicted a third world war, in which Russia would beat Great Britain. He prophesied Great Britain would go Communist, that the iron curtain would fall again, this time shutting off the whole of Europe for five more years of feverish war preparations,' and then, he wrote, 'the general attack against the United States will begin.' He continued: 'The Western hemisphere will be in its deadliest danger. The U.S. will curse the day when a long-forgotten American President in Yalta... made such a development possible...'

'Where are the days when Great Britain's word was important, even decisive in world politics? ... It seems really naïve that a British Prime Minister meddles in the arrangements for the political and social status of the Reich until the year 2000. During the years and decades to come England will be preoccupied with other worries... She will have to fight desperately to retain a small part of the position of power she once enjoyed on every continent.'

These quotations show that Goebbels was no mean prophet. However, the point is not that he knew what was coming, but that he went on record as saying what was coming, so that future generations would remember that he 'always knew what would happen.'

Even more important is the implication that things would have been different if only people had listened to Hitler. For: 'One could have imagined another development for which it is too late now. The Fuehrer proposed it in numerous memoranda and offers directed to London, the last four weeks before this war began. He suggested co-ordinating German and British foreign policy in such a way that the Reich would respect England's sea power, while Great Britain would respect German land power... That both nations ... would guarantee world peace... Bolshevism, under these circumstances, would have been restricted to its breeding place.'

He found the words in which to express the future fears of the world. It was no accident that the term of the Iron Curtain—to name but one example—was adopted in all countries; it was no accident that all over the world people began to use words Goebbels had coined. In the Russian occupied zone of Germany, for instance, the Communist Party used the Nazi slogan, 'Who is not for us, is against us!' This had been Goebbels' intention, this was why he had gone on record, so that millions of people would later repeat his words, phrases and ideas, and remember: 'That's what Goebbels said.'

In anticipation of this development he said to Frau Haberzettel: 'Only after my death people will really believe me!'

V

Due to the rationing of newsprint *Angriff* had to be suspended. Goebbels had not written in *Angriff* for years. It had become the organ of Dr Robert Ley, chief of the Labour Front, a man for whom Goebbels held no esteem. Nevertheless, the disappearance of the paper which he had laboured so hard to build up was a blow to him.

He had to go on pretending that he believed the war would be won. 'The last battle is our real chance,' he wrote, and continued: 'A nation which is determined to use the most daring means in the fight for its existence cannot possibly be beaten'. And what would that be, the most daring means? Perhaps the miracle weapon? Goebbels still could not bring himself to introduce the miracle weapon into his speeches and articles. He reluctantly had permitted the Party propagandists to announce its use for the very near future, and veritable whispering campaigns were organized to promote the idea. Once he remarked that the people had to be given some sort of moral support, and went on to say: 'No one will ever be able to reproach us for having circulated this rumour. No one will ever be able to nail us down for having made such a prediction because we never did make it.'

Yet he felt rather uncomfortable over the thought that his propaganda was gradually getting on the wrong track. When someone in his conference made a reference to the miracle weapon, he exploded: 'Let's make this perfectly clear: We have nothing left! There *are* no miracle weapons!'

Hence the last chance was not a victorious battle but a row between the Allies. Goebbels seriously believed that this would happen. To his colleagues he confided that the war could only be won 'politically,' provided, of course, that Germany was still a military factor to be reckoned with, 'provided we still exist. It does not matter if we are in bad shape, bleeding or reeling under the blows—but we must exist!'

His theory was that Britain as always was worried about the balance of power in Europe. 'Therefore one might almost say, the further Bolshevism penetrates to the west, the greater our chance to come to a political arrangement with the west, which entails the possibility to negotiate a tolerable peace. If we succeed in holding off the enemy in the west, while the Russians are further advancing, England has only two possibilities: Europe will either go Bolshevist or National Socialist—there is no other alternative. Hence, England will have to choose between two evils and there can be no question that a National Socialist Europe will be the lesser evil for her. However, all these arguments are pointless unless we are able to stop the enemy in the west.'

From the Nazi point of view this theory was quite reasonable but it could not be carried into practice because the enemy in the west was not stopped. Ironically enough, this was partly the fault of Goebbels' propaganda.

For many months German propaganda had hammered away at one theme: Don't let the Russians in! Every day the press and radio reiterated what would happen if the Russians were to overrun the country. Goebbels exploited every conceivable angle of atrocity propaganda. In his conferences he openly admitted his own forgeries and exaggerations, but went on record to explain: 'It is not important if we falsely assert that the Soviet soldier Ivan Ivanovich is murdering, plundering and raping. The only thing that counts is to drum it into the heads of the German people that they will suffer a horrible fate at the hands of the Russians. We must continue in this vein until the last German would rather perish in battle than surrender and face the enemy from the east.'

On 15 March 1945, the German press offered a striking example of this type of propaganda. It published a report saying that the entire male population of the town of Oels in Silesia had been deported by the Russian occupation authorities for compulsory labour—in Siberia. The statement was unsupported by any proof. Even if the story had been true, had not the Germans enslaved the peoples of the conquered territories? But so determined were the makers of German propaganda in their drive to spread atrocities that this obvious parallel never penetrated their consciousness.

The consequences of this campaign, which was promoted with faked photographs of whipped women and children, mutilated bodies, and so on, were quite different from what Goebbels had imagined. The population in the territories threatened by the Russians was seized with panic, millions were fleeing, blocking the highways, impeding troop movements and hindering military operations. Another reaction was even more unfortunate, as far as Goebbels was concerned: most Germans, including the soldiers, came to the conclusion that under these circumstances it would be better to cease resistance against the Americans and British and to let them into the country. Yet, the western front had to be held until the Allies would 'see sense,' because Goebbels still wanted to win the war 'politically'. All Goebbels could do in his predicament was to carry on the same atrocity propaganda against the western Allies. This about-face was accomplished from one minute to another, without any psychological preparation. The western armies, it was said, consisted mainly of gangsters, Jews and negroes, all of whom were determined to wipe out the Germans, or at the very least to sterilize them. For instance, a comparatively harmless report would be received at the Propaganda Ministry saying that 'five or six negroes had overstepped the bounds during a victory celebration in a small village.' Two hours later the German radio had blown up the item to fantastic proportions: '150 negroes of the very worst calibre assaulted a peaceful village in the Rhineland and raped most of the women. This means that the enemy in the west and the enemy in the east are using the same methods.'

All of this was too hastily improvised to be credible. As a matter of fact, the atrocity stories from the west undermined the credibility of German propaganda to such an extent that the people were beginning to dismiss the Russian atrocities as mere exaggerations. Even real assaults, supported by eyewitnesses and documents, were no longer believed. It was sufficient for the Propaganda Ministry to issue a certain statement, and it would be immediately unmasked as a lie in the eyes of most Germans. Goebbels was rapidly losing the last of his prestige.

It was an ironical twist of fate that at a moment when the healthy scepticism of the people finally came to the surface, the most fantastic lies and rumours were circulated—horror tales on the lunatic fringe which Goebbels had always kept out of his propaganda. The people whispered about bombs which would collapse human lungs by their tremendous pressure, and about explosives which would freeze everything for several miles and kill all human life within their radius.

The German people believed nothing—and everything. Propaganda had become a mere matter of chance.

VI

The war was rapidly coming closer to the homeland. A spell of unusually cold weather froze rivers and lakes and hardened the soggy highways, on which the tanks advanced virtually unchecked. Foreign names had disappeared from the German army communiqués and were replaced by German towns and villages. For the first time in more than a hundred years a war was raging on German soil. Most of the Gauleiters charged with defending their districts were running away at the mere sound of Russian guns, leaving all heroism to the people.

On 30 January—twelve years had passed since the Nazis had come to power—Hitler appointed Propaganda Minister Goebbels the 'Defender of Berlin.' This was the first indication that Berlin, this immense conglomeration of buildings and millions of people, stretching over 350 square miles, unprotected by mountains or wide rivers, was to be defended—and by a civilian.

Among the people and in so-called initiated circles the question was raised why Goebbels had been chosen for this role. The official answer was that he was the Gauleiter of Berlin, the man who had 'conquered' the city, and the logical person to defend it. In reality, however, Hitler needed someone on whom he could rely unconditionally. The generals could no longer be trusted. Goebbels, he knew, would not betray him.

Goebbels tackled his new assignment with all his available energy. He surrounded himself with a group of military advisers, among them General Reimann, whom he received every morning before his regular conference. Goebbels realized from the beginning that he had to depend largely on improvisation. Before he attended to the military details, he saw to it that the city would not be starved out. 'Steeg has arranged for all cattle in the surroundings of Berlin to be brought into the city,' he said. 'So, as far as food goes, we can hold out for roughly eleven weeks.'

He adjusted himself more and more to the role of a soldier. He did not wear a uniform—leaving this sort of privilege to Goering. But his leather coat was of military cut and he wore a German officer's cap without rank insignia. He would make frequent visits to the eastern front, which was only two or three hours' drive from the capital. Despite bombing attacks he would refuse to stop his car, even when the fliers dived steeply down to strafe the vehicles below. He would drive right to the front lines and take superfluous risks to impress the military: he wanted to show them the limping little civilian had more guts than they had.

He never let pass an opportunity to make derogatory comments on generals in his diary. 'All of them are tired out and on the verge of collapse, and all of them have given up the war. The Fuehrer stands practically alone. Again and again he is compelled to use his precious time and energy to uplift his deflated generals.' He was all the more impressed with the Russian officers. One day, after studying the background of some of the Red Army generals, he exclaimed: 'These officers are of a totally different calibre from ours. Virtually all of the Russian generals are of peasant stock, they are normal, healthy and straight-thinking men, and their successes don't surprise me in the least.' (Goebbels still identified himself with peasant stock.)

'If this war is lost, Goering will be the main culprit,' he would remark with ever-increasing bitterness. He was very unhappy that Hitler did not see his point and refused to dismiss Goering. But he did not abandon his attempts in that direction. He explained to the Fuehrer that Goering had allowed the Luftwaffe to fall into decay. Goering should not only be dismissed but arrested and beheaded, he argued. The exhausted Fuehrer could do nothing but reply that he had no substitute for his Air Minister; in the end he invoked the principle of Germanic loyalty, whatever that meant.

Another object of Goebbels' animosity was Reich Armament Minister Albert Speer. For some time he had suspected Speer of faking production figures and thus 'ridiculing me in the eyes of the German people.' But whenever the two men met, Speer succeeded in convincing Goebbels that everything humanly possible was being done. When Speer finally admitted that the situation of German production was hopeless, Goebbels was highly annoyed and called him a defeatist. 'Speer will not understand that we have no choice, that we have no possibility of withdrawing from the scene, and that we must fight this through, come what may.'

The most important question in everybody's mind was how the defence of Berlin was to be organized. Was it better to bring up all available troops and material to the Oder river to hold that front as long as possible, or should part of the forces be used to draw a defensive ring around the city itself? Goebbels was in favour of the latter, but he yielded after Hitler decided it would be too risky.

The German army—that is, the generals—were opposed to defending Berlin and suggested instead a withdrawal somewhere to the south, perhaps to the region of Berchtesgaden. Himmler, too, believed this was the only possible solution. Goebbels contradicted them. The battle which 'for many days raged over the telephone,' to quote an expression of Fritzsche, was finally decided in favour of Goebbels.

However, when the generals learned that Goebbels planned to defend the capital without the help of the army, they were literally thunderstruck. He intended to rely exclusively on the *Volkssturm*. Within a few days foreign slave workers, both men and women, dug trenches around the city, and the neighbouring fields and highways were mined. New airports were built, and *Panzersperren* (tank fortifications) were erected at the most important intersections and bridges.

Generals and cabinet members shook their heads in dismay. Ley and Speer arrived at Goebbels' home unannounced and tried to talk him out of the idea of 'saving' Berlin with the *Volkssturm*. Goebbels remained stubborn. He no longer trusted the generals who were in favour of abandoning Berlin. If it came to the worst, he said, if the enemy succeeded in penetrating into the city, he would rather fight 'to the last ditch'.

In the middle of February he announced his intentions to the German people over the radio. He denied rumours he had suffered a nervous breakdown and wanted to leave the city. On the contrary, he said, he was working night and day to prepare and to strengthen the defences of Berlin.

The suspicious Berliners had watched the proceedings of the last few weeks with some misgivings. They had inspected the trenches and the barricades and now they learned to their horror that Goebbels actually planned to carry the war right into the heart of their city. Nothing could have embittered them more than that. Goebbels was swamped with letters threatening that the guns he had distributed would be turned against him. Meanwhile life in Berlin had gradually come to a standstill. All means of transportation ceased to operate, the electric light no longer functioned with any regularity, there were rumours that the water supply would be cut off. While the defence preparations were being carried on, the city was bombarded incessantly, but often no one knew when the planes came and left, because most of the siren installations had been wrecked.

People packed their bags, grabbed a few blankets and pillows and all the food they could lay hands on, and moved down to the cellars.

On the day that Goebbels announced he would defend Berlin he had lost the last sympathies of the Berliners.

VII

Goebbels knew no more than the generals how the city could be defended effectively. The only difference was that the atmosphere of hopelessness and impotence did not make him fatalistic but intensified his rage and indignation.

Night and day he pondered over what could be done against the perpetual bombardments. After Dresden had been almost totally destroyed, he declared, according to Jacobs, that Germany should denounce the Geneva Convention. 'If it is possible to murder 100,000 civilians in two hours, the Convention has lost its meaning. We have no defence against the terror attacks of the enemy. There is only one thing we can do: we can tell the enemy that the raid on Dresden has cost us the lives of 100,000 innocent civilians, most of them women and children, and that is enough! If the enemy is capable of such inhuman cruelty, we have no further reason to be bound by the Geneva Convention. For every civilian killed in a future air attack on a German city we shall cut the throats of an equal number of British and American war prisoners. Maybe that will help.'

Goebbels underlined that these statements were strictly confidential. The next day he discussed the matter with Hitler, who agreed in principle but wished to consult some experts before making a final decision.

Four days afterwards Goebbels appeared at his conference, looking pale and furious. 'Before discussing our current problems I would like to settle another business,' he said. 'The foreign press has already been informed that Germany may consider breaking the Geneva Convention. Gentlemen! The only time this question was ever brought up was in the intimate circle of our conference.' And suddenly he yelled: 'There is a traitor among us! But I can tell you, I will find him—and then God help him! I will not have him court-martialled. No, I will strangle him here, in this room, with my own hands!'

As it happened, the traitor sat right next to Goebbels. He was his press officer, Dr Rudolf Semmler, who had hinted the story to a Swedish journalist. But Goebbels was unable to detect the culprit. Two days later he advised his associates that the indiscretion could not have been committed in the Propaganda Ministry. 'It would be impossible to imagine such a thing,' he added.

However, the immediate result was that London issued a sharp warning against any breach of the Geneva Convention, whereupon Ribbentrop lost his nerve and talked Hitler out of the plan. 'Ribbentrop was of course opposed to it,' Goebbels recounted. 'What else could one have expected from this ninny! But the Wehrmacht has also voiced its reservations and advised the Fuehrer against it.' He dictated to Jacobs that once more he presented his arguments and implored Hitler to take the indispensable step in the face of the terrible situation. However, the Fuehrer was too strongly impressed with the fact that all others were against it.

Yet despite his radicalism in the matter of reprisals Goebbels still hoped for a political solution of the war or, as he put it to his colleagues, 'to start political talks.' Hitler took a favourable view but believed that such negotiations should be based on some military victory. In other words, Hitler still had hopes, while Goebbels knew that a military victory was no longer possible. Therefore, he never stopped his efforts to make Hitler see his point of view, he even talked with members of the Foreign Office, over Ribbentrop's head.

The men in the Foreign Office were fully aware of the tensions between the Allies and tried to find ways and means of 'activating' them. Goebbels insisted this was the wrong policy. 'It would be a great mistake,' he said, 'if we were to pour oil into the fire. The delicate plants of disaffection should be left to grow entirely by themselves. They will best develop in the sunlight, not under the kerosene lamp. Some day—if we allow the situation to mature—the accumulated dynamite will spontaneously explode and then our moment will have come. Provided, of course, we are still there, still in the field, still a factor that counts.'

In the middle of February 1945 it was Goebbels' contention that the Allied coalition would break up in three or four months at the most. Would the German people be still 'on their feet' when the time came?

VIII

During the first weeks of 1945 the Propaganda Ministry received a few minor hits. A dud had fallen into a parking courtyard and several incendiary bombs had landed on the roof, but the damage was slight. Then, on 4

February, an aerial mine fell directly in front of the ramp, all windows were smashed and the front rooms reserved for Goebbels and his associates were partly wrecked. Goebbels immediately ordered foreign slave workers to repair the damage, and they were busy night and day. In the meantime the employees were not permitted to interrupt their work. Unless they had found a space in the basement they were obliged to remain at their post, wrapped in blankets and coats in offices which had neither windows nor doors, working amidst the rubble and the feverish activity of the labourers. Within two weeks the damage was restored.

Around 7 a.m. on 23 February another bomb hit the Propaganda Ministry. This time it dropped right into Goebbels' offices and destroyed the entire façade of the building. Within ten minutes Goebbels rushed to the spot, viewed the damage, silently turned around and went home.

He was very pale. 'There seems to be no point in doing anything about it,' he said. 'Too much has been destroyed. I suppose we had better confine ourselves to clearing away the debris.'

Later he decreed that the section heads, among them Fritzsche, should establish themselves in the basement, while he and his most important assistants—among them Dr Naumann, Inge Haberzettel, Otto Jacobs, Inge Hildebrand—moved to Goebbels' home so as to be in contact with him and attend to the most urgent tasks.

The news of the destruction of the Propaganda Ministry spread like wildfire. But now the people had other things to worry about. Everywhere it was whispered that Russian tanks had been sighted only thirty to thirty-five miles from Berlin. Perhaps the Russians would arrive that same night. Twilight was falling and it became very still.

During that night nothing happened. The morning papers reported that there was no immediate danger of a Russian attack. Still, barricades were built, furniture vans and street cars were overturned to block the access to important streets and bridges. It was only now that the grotesque hopelessness of their situation began to dawn on the Berliners. In the agonizing hours of fear and despair a typical Berlin joke was born. 'The storming of the barricades will take the Russians exactly one hour and one minute. For one hour they will laugh themselves sick, and in one minute they will remove the obstacles.'

With this quip the Berliners said farewell to Hitler. The régime was so discredited that it had become merely laughable. Again everything was quiet. No one seemed to be in a hurry to get anywhere. The city was waiting. Even fear had vanished. The telephone no longer functioned, the electric lighting was more off than on, and the radio was silent except for an occasional proclamation issued by Goebbels, saying always the same thing: Berlin will be defended, Berlin will not capitulate! But the Berliners were very tired of listening to his exhortations.

IX

'I would have rather lost my home and all my belongings.' Goebbels stepped to the window and gazed at the ruins of Berlin, and continued: 'Whatever may happen to Germany, the German whom we have brought up will be able to cope with anything. I am convinced that in a short while new life will spring from the ruins and cellars of the German cities. In the cellars new restaurants will be opened and theatres and symphony orchestras will start playing among the crumbled buildings.'

Some assistants came in carrying dossiers which they had rescued from the debris of their former place of work. Goebbels asked whether many people had gathered on Wilhelmplatz to look at the ruins. He was told that the streets were empty. 'Formerly they would stand for hours just to get a glimpse of me on the balcony,' Goebbels said with a sad smile. 'Formerly I would receive baskets full of fan letters. Formerly ...'

Later, when he was alone with Inge Haberzettel, he suddenly said: 'You know, I would like to be thirty years old once more, and start all over again. Then I would do everything differently.' When she asked him what he would do differently, he replied: 'No politics.'

Then he wanted to know once more the extent of the damage at the Propaganda Ministry, and how far the workers had proceeded in clearing away the rubble. Why did he not go over and see it for himself? the young woman asked. He merely shook his head.

The Propaganda Ministry was scarcely 300 yards away. He would never see it again.

CHAPTER XVII

THE BIRTH OF THE HITLER LEGEND

I

Goebbels' residence was engulfed in silence. Again everyone spoke in a hushed tone, the children tiptoed about, and to use an expression of one of Goebbels' assistants—'It was like in the good old days of the silent movies.'

Goebbels was on edge. Although he had lived through the terrific bombardments without flinching, the never-ending 'mosquito attacks' unnerved him completely. These were individual raids made by a handful of Allied planes, and, though they caused little havoc, they engendered an atmosphere of perpetual restlessness. Not a day passed without some minor damage to the house, and this proved to be a constant irritant. For instance, the electric light would go out. The sunlight could not seep into the Goebbels' home because most of the windows were covered with cardboard. The wind whistled through the apartments and the curtains fluttered wildly, and the few candles which cast a gloomy gleam would begin to flicker fitfully.

In the cellar a laboratory worker was busy transferring the diaries of the Minister to microfilm, reducing them to the size of postage stamps. Thus, in case of emergency, they could be easily stored in a safe place. From sub-basement to attic the place was overcrowded. Under-Secretary Naumann had established himself on the first floor; Fraeulein Hildebrand and Frau Haberzettel on the second, and Dr Semmler, Goebbels' adjutant, Guenther Schwaegermann, and half-a-dozen other assistants and secretaries had found temporary quarters on the third floor. In every room people typed, held conferences, gave dictation. Most of them slept on army cots and seldom got out of their clothes.

It was surprising that under these circumstances the children remained unsuspecting. Once Goebbels' press officer asked Magda, 'And what do your children think of all this?' 'They have no idea of what is happening,' she replied. 'We've told them that the enemy is coming closer but that the Fuehrer has a particularly terrible weapon which will destroy them all if the Russians, against all expectations, should penetrate into the suburbs. This weapon is so frightful that he would only use it in an extreme emergency.'

Goebbels was working harder than ever.

Each morning at 5.30 he was awakened. Emil, the servant, put the desk in order, while a secretary sorted the latest telegrams and newspapers. At 6 o'clock Goebbels would have breakfast served on his desk and begin studying the reports. At 7.30 the two press officers arrived. The daily conference was held in the film room. Usually Goebbels was in a sombre mood, while his conferees were nervous and harassed. Lunch was confined to a few minutes of gulping down some food, then Goebbels would take a short nap. His afternoon was devoted to writing articles, dictating appeals for the conduct of total war and for the defence of Berlin.

Dinner was set for 8.30 p.m. Goebbels insisted on this late hour even though the air-raids would begin earlier. In case of an alarm the meal was eaten in ten or fifteen minutes. Afterwards, unless the family gathered in the shelter, there were movies—Goebbels had resumed his favourite pastime. He smoked incessantly, drank more than usual, mostly sweet liqueurs, and the conversation would last until 2 o'clock in the morning.

It is incredible that during these last hectic weeks he still found time to work on another book. Since the beginning of the war, Goebbels had published a number of books, all of them collected articles and speeches. The one he was working on now, originally entitled, *The Virtue of Perseverance*, was another such collection. He finally called it *The Law of War*. Of the articles it contained only two had not been published previously.

Since the end of December, 1944, he had been working on the project. He would send his publisher some articles, then withdraw them, then send others. For a long time he could not make up his mind as to how they should be grouped, whether chronologically or topically. For weeks he brooded over the galley-proofs, making minor stylistic changes. He could not decide on the format of the book nor on the colour and design of the jacket. The publishers were struggling with numerous technical difficulties. There was a shortage of paper and the electric current was interrupted too often to permit rapid printing.

Goebbels had asked Field-Marshal Walter Model to write the foreword. Model, in charge of the defence of the Ruhr, finally found time to wire 700 words, which Goebbels promptly expanded to 2,000. The introduction began, modestly, with the words: 'Great words are like banners in a battle.' It was predicted the book would take its place among those classics which would be read avidly by later generations and, 'like a bronze cast,' would 'last through the centuries.'

The book was never completed because Goebbels made constant revisions to the very end.[1] Nothing is more characteristic of Goebbels than this passionate preoccupation with the book. He knew better than anyone else that the days of the Third Reich were numbered, and yet he devoted a large part of his time to minor changes in his manuscript. Once more he wanted to prove to himself that he was not only a propagandist and a statesman but, above all, a writer.

Many of the people who worked with Goebbels often speculated on the scope of his talents. Would he have been able to make propaganda for an idea other than National Socialism? One of his associates remembered that a year or two previous Goebbels had entertained a whole dinner-party by imitating a Russian commissar lecturing on propaganda. His listeners were fascinated by his gifts of identifying himself with others, and all of them were convinced that he would have been just as brilliant as a communist propagandist. However, his stenographer Jacobs remarked that this could have come about only if he had met Stalin before he met Hitler, and if he had been seized with the same enthusiasm for Communism as he had for Nazism. Much as he was a propagandist *per se*, he would have accomplished little without his initial 'faith'.

II

Goebbels found that, as a loyal National Socialist, he had to propagandize a number of things for which he had little interest or liking. In the final stages of Nazism he had to make propaganda for the Werewolves.

The idea originally stemmed from Dr Ley. This alone would have been enough to discredit it in Goebbels' eyes. Ley had gone to Hitler and suggested building up an organization composed of young boys who were to resist the enemy, particularly in those parts of Germany which had already been overrun. In this connection Goebbels noted in his diary: 'To appreciate Ley's mentality one only has to remember that he is now immersed in the subject of death rays and is experimenting with white rabbits. As was to be expected, all his experiments have failed.'

There was another reason why Goebbels was opposed to the Werewolf business. The whole idea was based on the assumption that the enemy would occupy the country, which was precisely what Goebbels' propaganda was presenting as an impossibility. Beyond that it was self-evident that a horde of youngsters was not likely to succeed where the German army had failed.

Essentially, the Werewolf scheme was to become just another partisan movement. Hitler was delighted with Ley's proposal, pointed to Russian partisan successes in 1941 and argued that there was no reason why the same should not succeed in Germany as well. What he did not see—to Goebbels it was only too clear—was that the operations of the Russian partisans were limited in time: aid was forthcoming from Britain and the United States, the Russian winter was imminent, the Russian armies were able to reorganize themselves. Now, in 1945, conditions for Germany were altogether different: there was no space for withdrawal and it was useless to play for time. Beyond the Werewolves there was nothing at all left.

However, since Hitler sincerely believed this desperate measure might yield results, since Ley seriously began to organize the Werewolves, Goebbels, equally seriously, launched a propaganda campaign.

The Werewolves have a romantic background. When they first appeared in German history they were the executive organs of the so-called Vehme courts—institutions which were created in the fourteenth century for sentencing criminals who could not be judged by ordinary courts. After the end of the First World War they appeared in the guise of German nationalists liquidating the 'traitors' who collaborated with the Allied control commissions. Many of Goebbels' former Free Corps friends in his student years in Munich, and the men around Horst Wessel and Hauenstein belonged to the Werewolves of the post-war period. Therefore, Goebbels had certain emotional sympathies for the would-be movement, although from a practical point of view he considered it worthless.

How does one make propaganda for something that does not yet exist? This was Goebbels' problem. He solved it simply by pretending that the Werewolves did exist. Overnight he created a Werewolf radio station. In all transmissions it was asserted that the station was located somewhere in occupied territory. In reality it was only a few miles from Berlin. The programmes were presented by speakers and writers whom Goebbels had personally selected. The broadcasts consisted of gay, popular music, interspersed with terse news of the exploits performed by the non-existent Werewolves.

The transmitter had only functioned for a few days when a greatly agitated high-ranking S.S. officer burst into Goebbels' office and informed the Minister that he was the actual head of the Werewolves. Goebbels then learned for the first time that a Werewolf organization had existed for a year as an integral part of the S.S., that it had been trained to operate in the greatest secrecy. Now that the Werewolves were about to strike they learned to their horror that their activities (which so far were purely in the realm of fantasy) had been announced over the radio. The officer begged Goebbels to stop all further programmes.

This was the height of confusion—musical comedy amidst, tragedy.

Goebbels dismissed the officer. Not for one moment did he consider stopping his Werewolf broadcasts. For although he did not believe that any of the Werewolves—Ley's organization or the S.S.—would be able to accomplish anything worthwhile, he saw clearly that there would be no Werewolves at all unless the German youth was convinced that they already existed and were performing heroic deeds. Every single German boy should be made to fear that he must not be the last to join the Werewolves.

Heroic deeds ... Goebbels invented them, wrote them down in a crisp, snappy style. There were stories of children who cut telephone wires, stole arms and equipment, there were stories of women who poured sugar into American gasoline tanks, thereby spoiling the fuel. Every day he would dictate between ten and twenty such brief items. To his associates he expressed himself with commendable frankness. Smacking his lips and practically savouring his own concoctions he would ask them whether this or that story appealed to them, and whether they thought it would be effective. He even went so far as to ask some of them to give him new ideas and to invent news themselves. He would walk through the offices of his assistants, ironically calling out: 'Anyone got another Werewolf item?' As most of the employees had not been out of the house for weeks, to say nothing of having left Berlin, his request boiled down to the cynical admission that the whole Werewolf business was a fantastic swindle.

Some of his assistants discreetly hinted that they saw through the bluff and ventured that the transmissions could probably no longer save the day. Goebbels countered that he was not at all sure, and that the resistance of the people would have collapsed long ago if he had not constantly spurred them on. In this connection it is interesting to note a conversation he had one evening with Inge Haberzettel. She told him openly she believed all the news about the Werewolves was faked.

Goebbels: 'Faked? What an ugly word! Let's say it's a kind of ... poetic truth.'

Frau Haberzettel: 'But... none of those things ever took place!'

Goebbels: 'But don't you see, they *should* have taken place.'

Frau Haberzettel: 'In any event, this is not news.'

Goebbels: 'Of course not! All this is news as it should be.'

Here again was the leitmotiv of Goebbels' entire propaganda: the trick to present something as a fact in order to make it a fact; to paint a reality in order to make it reality. Young people were to be told of the deeds of the Werewolves so that they would be eager to perform the deeds which were only a product of Goebbels' imagination. Up to that point Goebbels was in agreement with Hitler and Ley. The difference was that Goebbels did not believe German youth could be roused in time to bring about a decisive change in the military situation.

It was true that the Werewolf transmitter broadcast directives for day-to-day operations along with news reports. But presumably such instructions could not be judged from a short-range point of view: they, too, were time bombs. For if the Werewolves really killed a German collaborationist or assaulted a couple of Allied soldiers in ambush, as happened from time to time, this could only result in more stringent control of the German population and would constitute a strong handicap against any future Werewolf activities.

If further proof were needed to show that Goebbels' propaganda was aimed at the post-war period, it was found in the Werewolves whom Goebbels made the spokesmen for the somewhat nebulous socialistic ideas of his youth. The broadcasts stated explicitly, 'Property means nothing to us.' The Russians were rarely mentioned, while the 'gambling hyenas of the London and the New York Stock Exchange' were constantly attacked. Programmes seldom spoke of the Germans but more often of 'the German worker.'

Goebbels, eager to learn how the enemy would react to this new propaganda, could hardly wait for the first comments. When he found that no one in London believed in the existence of the Werewolves he was understandably annoyed.

It was all the more grotesque to find 'insiders', such as Dr Naumann, wallowing in incomprehensible optimism. Although these people saw with their own eyes how the news was fabricated, they would sometimes say: 'Well, maybe Germany's youth will get us out of this after all.'

III

The Berliners found it difficult to get exhilarated over the fact that German boys were pouring boiling water over the heads of enemy soldiers. It did not require much imagination to figure out how these troops would conduct themselves on their march into the city after having received such treatment at the hands of the self-styled 'partisans'.

There was little left to say to cheer the Berliners. One of the propaganda speakers tried to explain to them that the destruction was not so terrible, that in less than ten years everything would be rebuilt. That sort of glib reasoning made the people very angry. Even worse in its effect was an article by Dr Ley entitled 'With Light Baggage'. Ley informed his readers that now he, too, had been bombed out, but although he grieved about the loss of his earthly belongings, he nevertheless felt relieved. He no longer trembled in fear of air-raids. May the enemy continue to pour down his phosphorous horrors—Ley possessed nothing inflammable, and with his light baggage the marching was easier.

The population of Berlin was bitterly indignant when it read these smug words. It was known to everyone that Ley owned one of the most luxurious and largest air-raid shelters in the whole city and it was simply untrue that he had lost everything. Immediately afterwards Ley surpassed himself by writing a still more stupid article. No one who could defend himself in some form or other was completely helpless, he solemnly informed the people. He described the various forms of defence practised by all classes of animals, not forgetting the hare, which, owing to his long legs, was able to run away.

All Germany laughed. Goebbels rushed to Hitler and indignantly demanded that Ley be prohibited from writing another line. From then on Ley was under Goebbels' censorship.

However, Goebbels, too, had run out of ideas. In his inner circle he stated: 'It is impossible to believe that our enemies will be able to stand the loss of material (through their air-raids) for any length of time.' One of his associates replied ironically: 'Of course not! Just think of how much gas they must use in the long, long flight, getting from their airfields to Berlin.' Goebbels smiled, as though he had not understood the malicious hint. His articles were filled with comforting phrases of a general nature. Goebbels assured his readers that Germany would not capitulate. 'We would rather die than surrender!' One could never know when the 'turning point' would come, he said, and he spoke of the 'happy outcome of the war' which was 'almost certain.' 'Get to work! Rush to your guns!' his appeals rang out.

Rush to what guns? There were not many left, and Goebbels, the Defender of Berlin, knew it. Shortly before one of his conferences he declared: 'Of course we do not have a sufficient number of *Panzerfaeuste* (anti-tank grenades). However, we don't have to equip every single man and woman with that kind of thing. Only those who scream, "We want *Panzerfaeuste*!" will get one, and they will use it. The others will hide in their cellars anyway if ever a real tank should roll past.'

General Reimann replied: 'Herr Minister, in the last few days we have discovered a supply of 4,000 Czech pistols and guns which in my opinion should be given to the Berliners, who are so poorly armed. Of course, great care should be taken as to who receives the weapons. Preferably such persons should be mechanics who know something about the intricacies of handling them, for you see, most of them are somewhat rusty, and you never can tell…'

Such distressing details were not communicated to the Berliners, but even so, they knew enough, and they began running away.

The outer aspect of the city changed once more. The inhabitants who had stared at the approaching enemy, much like hypnotized rabbits, incapable of moving; the people who had cowered in their cellars, perhaps in the hope that the Americans and British—and not the Russians—would conquer their city, at the last minute shook off their paralysis. This happened in the first days of

April. Suddenly the railroad stations and waiting-rooms were overcrowded again, and everyone tried to squeeze into the few trains which still departed from the doomed capital, carrying his last belongings, hoping against hope to reach safety. Soldiers in uniform, evidently deserters, mingled with the civilians, but no one, including the police, paid any attention to them.

Transports with wounded returned from the front, which was only about two hours away, the bandages of the soldiers dripping with blood and pus. Berlin had become a front line city, the people panicky. Yesterday they still believed that there was a way out. Today they learned that the enemy was everywhere, that they were trapped. And yet many who could still muster enough energy ran away and there was only one thought left in their feverish brains: the worst that could happen was to be captured in Berlin.

The employees of the Propaganda Ministry had to provide their own *Volkssturm*. It was called the 'Wilhelmplatz Battalion' and was headed by Dr Naumann. Goebbels gave a speech, designed to fill his employees with fighting spirit. 'Under my leadership the Mongolian hordes will smash their skulls against the walls of Berlin!' he screamed. 'The S.S. units will hold Berlin! Two million Berliners will rise and fight! If every Berliner shoots only one enemy soldier there will be none left! If there are any defeatists among you, I will have them clubbed to death! Don't act like old women! Conduct yourselves as men!'

This strongly worded, improvised speech was greeted with an icy silence. No one applauded, no one raised his arm in the Hitler salute, no one wanted to hear the old clichés any longer.

The people thought less and less of their leaders. They saw that they had elegant air-raid shelters. They watched them disappear in their cars to the comparatively safe countryside when the alarm was sounded; they watched them cart off their hoarded possessions in big trucks for which there was always enough gasoline despite the shortage; they watched them drive off to the mountains in Bavaria or Austria. And they sensed that the gentlemen who encouraged them incessantly to hold out to the last man were unwilling to take any risks themselves. About four years before—on 30 March 1941— Goebbels had said of Churchill that 'He has, above all, the proper amount of cynicism and cruelty which are needed to bleed a people white for a hopeless cause... He cannot retreat, hence every means will be good enough for him to continue the war.'

This was precisely what the German people now thought of their leaders.

IV

In the last twenty months Hitler's New Europe had shrunk steadily, until it consisted merely of an ever-narrowing corridor between the Russians and the western Allies. The flood of bad news had left its traces on Goebbels' face. His once animated features were pale and sunken, his temples were greying. Goebbels had never been a heavy eater; now he lived almost exclusively by smoking cigarettes, drinking brandy and eating biscuits. Dr Morell prescribed various nostrums, but apparently they did not help.

While escaping into historical analogies he was led to compare the forthcoming battle of Berlin with the struggle for Moscow in the autumn of 1941, and he noted: 'General Vlassov, who then commanded the troops for the defence of Moscow [and later deserted to the Nazis] told me they had all lost their courage in those days, all except one. One single man did not lose faith—Stalin. The same is true in our own situation today. All of them have lost courage. No one any longer believes in a good outcome...'

The liaison officer of the German High Command, Lieutenant-Colonel Balzer, found himself in a particularly difficult spot. Goebbels would screech at him: 'You are a defeatist! That's what you are! And unless you change your conduct immediately, I shall have you sent to the front!' Whereupon Balzer felt duty-bound to radiate optimism during the following days. But when his information became less and less substantial, Goebbels again lost his temper and, according to Jacobs, shouted at him: 'Quit telling me all that piffle, sir! I heard every word of it last night when I was with the Fuehrer. Isn't there anything new you can tell me? I am the Defender of Berlin, sir! Do you fancy yourself that I will be satisfied with such empty phrases?'

When Balzer indicated timidly that no one had given him any further information, Goebbels made a scene: 'Sir! All you do is go to the Reichswehr Ministry in the morning, take down what they tell you and then read it back to me. My eldest daughter can do that too! You are a mere dummy, sir! I'm telling you—your 'phones should be buzzing all day long, you should get into your car and drive to the front which, after all, isn't so far away. There seems to be enough gasoline for the private little trips of Wehrmacht officers, so don't tell me you can't get to the western front.'

When Goebbels left the room the unfortunate officer muttered to himself: 'That's what he thinks. My telephones don't function any more. He still has gasoline—but I haven't.'

Owing to the lightning tempo of the military developments there was no planned, orderly evacuation of the important government offices. Every ministry organized its own evacuation as best it could. The first to leave was the Ministry of the Interior, which departed for Thuringia at the beginning of February. It was followed by the Foreign Office, which established itself on the shores of Lake Constance, while the Reichswehr Ministry shifted to Bad Gastein and to the Wolfgangsee. The General Staff moved around a good deal, but when the Russians came closer to Berlin, it returned to the capital and settled in the Reich Chancellery. However, at that time most of the staff officers had fled to Bavaria or to the west. For them the war was over.

Goebbels had nothing but contempt for his ministerial colleagues, and above all for the officers who wanted to save their lives. He categorically refused to evacuate his ministry, but he did send a whole special train filled with dossiers to Bavaria.

His associates pleaded with him. They argued that they could do a much better job elsewhere, where they would not be constantly interrupted by bombings. It seemed that he had yielded, for he demanded a special train for fifty of his most important officials to be evacuated to Bavaria. But when the train was ready he changed his mind, and it departed empty.

This dismayed his associates. Everyone was now trying to get out of Berlin. All sorts of pretexts were invented to get a leave of absence. Someone would report a case of illness in his family which had been evacuated, but Goebbels saw through the ruse. A certain Dr von Borcke hit on the idea of volunteering for the army. Before his induction he asked Goebbels for a few days' furlough. Goebbels could not refuse the request, and Dr von Borcke vanished, never to be seen again either in the army or at the office.

Goebbels was outraged and from that time on no one was allowed to have any time off, not even a few hours. One of the secretaries stayed away from the office without authorization. Goebbels sent the S.S. to her home, commandeered her to do anti-aircraft duty, and she was killed a few days later. Everyone was frightened but nevertheless all continued secretly to plan their own escape. Dr Semmler looked to the west. 'I've always admired the Americans and I have many friends among them. I will say, "Hello, boys", will shake hands with them and then try to become a German correspondent in New York,' he said.

The other press assistant, Winfried von Oven, only wished the horror would be over as soon as possible. 'I shall sleep for days and days when the shooting stops,' he said. 'And when the British and Americans come to look for me I will tell them: "I don't know anyone by that name."'

Someone else conceived a particularly original idea: 'I will disguise myself as a Rabbi and will ramble through the woods for a while.' All of them had their plans, but everyone was watching everyone else like a hawk because since Borcke's disappearance a second escape would mean that all the others would be jailed.

V

Goebbels was at the end of his rope. He had tried all possible slogans. He had promoted militarism and socialism, the New Order and European culture, he had denounced Bolshevism and the plutocrats. He had propagandized total war and the *Volkssturm*. He had planted his time bombs. What was there left for him to do?

He had to explain the defeat. He had to point out to his contemporaries and to posterity why his promises had not been realized. Therefore, he fell back on a well-tested recipe: he revived the hoary stab-in-the-back legend.

This term emerged for the first time after the First World War. It is a historical fact that the war ended because the German generals wired to Berlin that they could not hold the front for another twenty-four hours and had to ask for an armistice. Nevertheless, General Ludendorff asserted soon afterwards that the German army had been victorious but that the defeatists (Socialists and Jews) had undermined German morale, prepared the revolution and made it impossible to continue the war.

Goebbels had a whole gallery of 'culprits', who had stabbed the German people and its government in the back, at his disposal. The chief villains were of course the Italians, who had concluded a separate armistice. Then there were the German generals involved in the plot of 20 July 1944, and it could always be maintained that the entire German Officers Corps was fundamentally anti-Nazi and therefore ready for betrayal. The same was true for all the 'better class people'. (The Jews had been wiped out and consequently could not be indicted.) Goebbels' accusations ranged from deliberate misinformation of the Fuehrer on the striking power of the Red Army to such details as the failure to dynamite the Rhine bridge near Remagen.

This type of propaganda was also designed to be effective at a later date. For the future of National Socialism or any active nationalistic trend it was important to re-establish the invincibility of the German army in the minds of the German people. At the moment its vulnerability was much too obvious for any such propaganda to have an immediate effect. No one believed in the tales of the stab in the back and the betrayal, with the exception of one man: Adolf Hitler.

He who should have known better than anyone else who it was that plunged Germany into this catastrophic adventure against the advice of the most qualified German experts now was raving night and day that he was surrounded by traitors. It is not too difficult to guess Goebbels' thoughts when he witnessed these violent scenes. Little did he care what Hitler thought or believed; he was exclusively concerned with the beliefs or disbeliefs of the German people.

And the Germans must believe that the Fuehrer had been betrayed, while he himself had remained loyal to his people, fighting to the last moment for them and the great cause—and falling like a soldier in battle. Hitler must not be allowed to survive the Third Reich. Otherwise there was no chance to perpetuate the Nazi ideology. This was so clear that it needed no further proof, and Goebbels knew it.

The creation of the Hitler myth was an integral part of Goebbels' time-bomb propaganda. Towards the end of March he had persuaded the Fuehrer to stay in Berlin, come what may.[2] He reminded him of the words he had spoken on 30 January 1933—that Hitler would never leave the Reich Chancellery of his own free will. Now the moment had come to show that his vow was meant seriously, Goebbels said.

All other men around Hitler—Goering and Ribbentrop, Keitel and Jodl, Himmler and Rosenberg—pleaded with him to leave Berlin at once. They argued that from his vantage point in southern Germany the Fuehrer could view the situation in better perspective and direct his troops more effectively. None of them grasped Goebbels' point of view, or what really was at stake at that moment, and that it had become unimportant whether the war ended a week sooner or later because all was lost anyway. But for the sake of the legend a cowardly escape was impossible, and a heroic end absolutely necessary.

Then one single event caused Goebbels to waver, and filled him with new hopes, if only for a few days. Franklin D. Roosevelt died.

VI

On 12 April 1945, immediately after lunch, Goebbels left for Ninth Army Headquarters at Kuestrin. He was scheduled to speak to the staff officers there. The only person to accompany him was Dr Naumann.

This was just another of the 'pep trips' which had become part of his routine. As usual, Goebbels talked about the Seven Years' War, Frederick the Great's desperate situation, the king's decision to take poison. Then he quoted the words of Carlyle: 'Brave king! Wait yet a little while, and the days of your suffering will be over. Already the sun of your good fortune stands behind the clouds, and soon will rise upon you.' And then, Goebbels continued, Frederick's fiercest opponent, the Czarina, died unexpectedly. Her son, Peter, was an admirer of the king and made peace with him—and Frederick was saved.

The officers were frankly sceptical. One of them asked which Czarina would have to die this time to save Germany. Goebbels shrugged his shoulders. That he could not answer, he said, but he was convinced that Providence would still perform a miracle for Germany. With these words he left for Berlin.

Most of his associates had gathered in front of his home when he arrived. One hour or so before the German news agency, DNB, had called up, saying, 'Roosevelt just died.' The whole house was in a state of tremendous excitement, people were laughing and congratulating each other, and the Viennese cook shouted, 'This is the miracle that Dr Goebbels has promised us.' Dr Semmler called Ninth Army Headquarters at Kuestrin but was informed that Goebbels was on his way back. The Reich Chancellery 'phoned twice and left the message that Hitler expected Goebbels' call immediately.

It was exactly 11 o'clock when Goebbels' car pulled up in front of the entrance. Dr Semmler rushed up to him. 'Good news, Herr Minister, very good news!' Goebbels listened, stopped, was speechless. The flames of the burning nearby Hotel Adlon cast a glow on his face. He was the incarnation of astonishment. But he immediately recovered himself and walked quietly towards the house. 'This is the miracle we've been waiting for,' he murmured. Everyone followed on his trail, including the chauffeurs. Before Goebbels stepped to the telephone, he ordered a few bottles of the finest champagne from the cellar.

On the 'phone he said: 'My Fuehrer, I congratulate you. It was written in the stars that the turning point would come in the second half of April. This is the turning point.'

Goebbels became jovial and talkative. 'What do you say now?' he asked one of the drivers. 'Isn't that the finest piece of news we've had in the whole year?' The others were caught by his exultant mood. Red-faced and agitated they helped themselves to the champagne, talking rapidly and aimlessly, while Goebbels walked up and down among them hardly knowing where to begin. What would be the attitude of Roosevelt's successor? Was Truman a friend or an enemy of the Russians? In any event, sensational developments might be expected from now on.

'Only a few hours ago these officers stared at me stupidly when I told them about the Seven Years' War,' he suddenly exclaimed. He called up Ninth Army Headquarters. 'Well, who was right?' he asked triumphantly. 'Now you're stunned, eh? Didn't I tell you I was right about what I told your officers this afternoon?'

Then he gave instructions to the press. For the radio he ordered a special announcement. 'At midnight we shall broadcast it,' he commanded, 'without comment. We will communicate nothing but the fact, which speaks for itself. Then, tomorrow, we shall follow it up with our comment.'

He nervously paced up and down waiting for midnight. 'Can't you see Frau Schulze being roused by the janitor's wife saying in her best Berlin dialect, "Listen, Frau Schulze, did you hear the news?"—"No, what's up? Mosquito planes?"—"No, no, that Roosevelt is dead"—and can't you see Frau Schulze jumping out of bed, screaming "Are you kidding?"'

He became impatient. 'Isn't it twelve yet? I want to hear how the announcement sounds.' Then, finally, the news came through, he listened, turned off the radio, went upstairs to his bedroom and switched off the light.

During the following days he continued to talk about the good news and every time he commented, 'It is really quite inconceivable.' All the firmer was his belief that Roosevelt's death would bring a decisive change. He was so caught up in his own historical comparisons that he himself began to believe in them. He telephoned innumerable people, discussing the various possibilities that had suddenly opened up, and they all agreed with him. At the same time no one knew exactly what was supposed to happen, how Germany's 'great chance' was supposed to be used to the fullest. Finance Minister Count Schwerin von Krosigk wrote to Goebbels that one should persuade the Pope to use his influence to break up the east-west coalition. Goebbels made no comment on the suggestion.

VII

Nothing happened because nothing could happen. There were no negotiations because there was no basis for them. If any further proof were needed to demonstrate to the Germans that a 'political' victory as envisaged by Goebbels was an impossibility, it was Roosevelt's death. The alliance of the nations united in their struggle against Nazi Germany could not be disrupted by the death of one man—not until Germany had been brought to her knees.

Strangely enough, Robert Ley was the quickest to grasp that the situation was truly catastrophic. Two or three days after President Roosevelt's death he excitedly rushed over to Goebbels' home, passed all the security officers and finally got to the anteroom of the Minister. He could make no further progress, for Goebbels had told his secretary that he did not wish to see him, no matter what happened. He suspected that the Labour Front leader had come to ask him to lift the censorship on his articles.

Since Ley was unable to see Goebbels, he unburdened himself to his adjutant. Goebbels ought to understand that this was an extreme emergency, and that not a minute should be lost, he stammered. Goebbels must implore Hitler to use the terrible secret weapon at once, this very second, he pleaded, because in a few days it might be too late. Ley was so upset that he almost burst into tears, and the adjutant promised to convey his message to Goebbels.

Goebbels made no comment. He even refrained from ridiculing his colleague, as he was wont to do. Perhaps he secretly envied Ley for being able to believe in miracle weapons. Goebbels himself still hoped that Roosevelt's death had given Germany another chance, but he was not so certain as before. He could do nothing but sit and wait until the Americans and the Russians began to quarrel, for any interference on his part, as he had stated previously, would only alert them prematurely.

Meantime, what was he going to tell the people? How was he going to raise their hopes? He was alone. Formerly, he noted in his diary, 'when there was good news to report, the Nazi leaders would fight amongst each other in an effort to get to the microphone.' Now everyone dodged the duty of speech-making, including Hitler. Goebbels realized that the people did not understand the Fuehrer's silence. 'Can he give us no comfort, no hope?' was the ever-recurrent question in the numerous letters reaching the Propaganda Ministry. Goebbels wrote in his diary that 'the morale of the population has sunk to absolute zero.'

Hitler... Should he not act now to take advantage of the unique chance? But what could he do? For the first time Goebbels toyed with a monstrous idea: Hitler must resign. Was that a betrayal? The answer was no. The way Goebbels judged the situation, Hitler's abdication might still prevent the worst, might furnish a cause for the collapse of the great coalition, the Americans might withdraw, new possibilities might arise...

All that was needed now was time. Every day, every week might bring a new chance. It was impossible to think that Roosevelt's death had not been a sign of Providence, simply impossible.

Time, and more time, was needed. In inflammatory speeches Goebbels called upon every man, woman and child to rise. 'Our entire conduct of the war must be revolutionized. The fighting rules of former centuries have become outmoded, for our purpose they have become entirely useless. We are finding ourselves in a state of national emergency, and who cares under such circumstances about what is customary?'

Those who refused to fight were traitors and had to be punished, decreed the Defender of Berlin. The first deserters were already dangling from Berlin's lamp posts. A slip of paper attached to the bodies carried the scribbled comment, 'I am hanging here because I have neglected my duties towards my wife and children.'

However, by that time Goebbels must have realized it was all in vain. These few days, with their glimpse of hope, had ended. Before him was a vacuum.

CHAPTER XVIII

FINITA COMOEDIA

I

Goebbels had first mentioned the possibility of suicide after the Rundstedt Offensive failed, hinting that he would also poison his wife and children. This was no empty threat, nor was it meant to be a 'heroic' gesture. It was, so to speak, his private decision. He remarked to his assistants that he had no inclination to live in a Germany which would subsist on the charity of the Quakers. The man who had lived what he considered a full and fascinating life, did not wish to end his days in poverty, to say nothing of war-crime trials and prison.

However, for his public he had to maintain a heroic pose. In the final issue of *Das Reich*—the last to be distributed—he wrote an article entitled 'The Stake of One's Own Life'. He asked his readers: 'Who would even stop to consider a continued existence under such circumstances (after the defeat)?' Then he went on to say: 'The people want to see examples to fill them with inspiration... So this is the hour of decision... Let us face it with pride and integrity. It can be conquered if we use every available means. And the decisive factor in wartime is still the stake of one's own life.'

So the great cynic, who had had enough, obliquely announced that he was willing to die a hero's death. His private suicide would be an act of his own volition, but his official heroic death was not. He had manoeuvred and talked himself into this heroic position by the persuasive power of his own propaganda. It is quite possible to imagine that a man who has had everything he wanted retires, perhaps with a good book or a bottle of brandy, and quickly makes an end to it. This form of exit, however, Goebbels had blocked for himself. He had glorified so many heroes and pseudo-heroes, he had demanded so much heroism from others that he could not withdraw from the scene without fanfare. He had to do precisely what he had decided for the Fuehrer: he had to write the last scene to the whole drama, and *act it out*.

What was the most spectacular way to make an end?[3] Suicide at the last minute? Death in battle? Death in the battle of Berlin, waving the Swastika flag on the barricades? Or should he blow up his air-raid shelter?

Thus the end became his principal concern, a matter of national importance. Here, again, Goebbels 'furtively looked with both eyes toward posterity.' Throughout his life he had tried to play the part of a hero; now the play had become deadly serious—and in death alone would he become a hero.

He told his secretary that his wife and children had been evacuated to Thuringia, but had returned to Schwanenwerder. 'I shall have them come here—their presence will help me carry out my resolve,' he added. This was not entirely true. The family had never gone to Thuringia but had moved to Lanke when Goebbels' city mansion became more and more crowded with his entourage. They went to Schwanenwerder when Lanke came within range of Russian artillery. Even in his diary Goebbels did not admit the whole truth. But although he touched up some of the details, his statement was substantially correct: he had decided to stay in Berlin.

And what about Hitler? Hitler, too, decided to stay. Lately the vacillating Fuehrer had reversed a good many of his decisions and, therefore, it was not at all certain whether he would persevere in a matter which for Goebbels—and for posterity—was of such eminent importance. Goebbels had to work unceasingly to bolster the Fuehrer's determination, and this alone was reason enough to remain in the city.

On 15 April Hitler composed a proclamation of eight typewritten pages which was addressed to the soldiers on the eastern front. According to Inge Haberzettel, Goebbels cursed under his breath as he read it. He revised and deleted parts of the manuscript with his green pencil, then he threw it into the wastepaper basket, then retrieved it, and finally dictated a new proclamation culminating in the following sentences, which were extremely typical of Goebbels (but not at all of Hitler): 'This time Bolshevism will experience the ancient fate of Asia, that is to say, it will bleed to death before the gates of the Reich capital... Berlin remains German, Vienna will again become German and Europe will never be Russian. At a moment when Destiny had removed the greatest war criminal of all times (Roosevelt), the turning point of the war has been reached.'

Goebbels did not consider it necessary to submit this rewritten proclamation for Hitler's approval. This revealed how the relationship between the Fuehrer and his disciple had changed. For Goebbels, Hitler was now reduced to a puppet, to be guided by his hand according to the requirements of the moment.[4]

Hitler's birthday was approaching, and as in former years Goebbels wrote an anniversary article. However, he did not fail to commit Hitler to the heroic end he had foreseen for him. 'Germany is still the land of loyalty,' he wrote. 'In danger she will celebrate her greatest triumph. The historians of this era will never be able to record that a nation abandoned its Fuehrer, or that the Fuehrer abandoned his people.'

On 19 April—the day before the article was published—Goebbels held his last press conference. About twenty-five newspapermen and ten members of the radio division gathered in the film room. Since they were, in a way, among friends, they expected to hear some inside information. For instance, would Berlin be relieved? Was the new weapon to be used? Was there any truth to the rumours that armistice negotiations were being conducted in the west?

Goebbels arrived a few minutes late. He greeted his listeners in silence, without a smile, and began at once to speak. What he said was merely a repetition of what he had written in innumerable articles. He refused even to consider the possibility of defeat. In a defeated Germany he would not want to live and would not expect his children to live, he said. In the middle of his speech the alarm sounded, the screaming sirens drowning out most of his words, but he continued unruffled. Although he said nothing new he spoke with such warmth and conviction that even the jaded propagandists, whom nothing could arouse, were stirred against their own will. They left as uninformed as they had come, but under the ineradicable impression that they had listened to a great speaker—for the last time.

II

On that same evening, shortly after 10 o'clock, Goebbels telephoned to Schwanenwerder and asked his wife to join him in Berlin with the children. The children had already been put to bed, Magda told him, but he insisted that the whole family return at once, that very night. Together with her mother and the nurse she awakened and dressed the children. The wife of the janitor, greatly upset, came running in and thought the Russians were arriving, but Magda calmed her. 'You don't have to worry,' she said, 'the Russians will never get here. I'm only going back to town because my husband wants it.' She sounded gay and unconcerned—the children must not suspect anything. But little Helga, who was then twelve years old, said to her grandmother, when she kissed her goodbye: 'We won't live much longer.'

The car was racing along the *Autobahn* into blacked-out Berlin, down to the government district. Magda, too, realized this was the end. She was only forty-four years old, but she had become an old woman in those last six months. Unlike Goebbels, she had nothing to take her mind off her troubles, no work to keep her passionately occupied. For her, it was much harder to bear up under the ordeal which was descending on her. Above all, she could not permit herself to lose self-control, she could not relax, she had to go on pretending. Somehow she managed to play the role up to the very end.

A week before she had taken an inventory at Schwanenwerder. She and her secretary had counted all the plates and cups and saucers, the tablecloths and sheets and other household items, as though the Russians were far, far away instead of being practically at their doorstep, and blithely ignoring the fact that it might only be a question of days when these possessions would fall into the hands of the onrushing troops. The secretary asked Magda if it might not be better to get out of Berlin. Frau Goebbels was astounded at the idea. 'We will stand and fall with Berlin,' she said, thus establishing an unbreakable bond between herself and her husband.

She had considered, fleetingly, rescuing not herself, but the children. She pleaded with her husband for permission to take them to a neutral country; she promised then to return and to die with him. His answer was an unequivocal 'No!' The details of their conversation are not known as Frau Haberzettel heard only the first part. But whatever Goebbels said, his reasons must have been convincing, for from that moment on Magda was determined that her six children would die with her.

Goebbels' decision to kill the children cannot have been influenced by his flirtation with posterity, which could only be horrified at this senseless murder—a reaction he must have anticipated. The death of his children was part of his own suicide, inspired by a cynicism of almost metaphysical proportions.

Goebbels had his own notions about the significance of progeny. Through his child the father would continue to exist beyond his physical death. (That was why he wanted to have sons and was personally offended when Magda bore him one daughter after another.) By analogy, the nation assured its continued existence through its children; in a manner of speaking, children were a guarantee for its immortality. In an article, 'For the Sake of Our Children', he elaborated on this theory and stated explicitly, 'The most elementary duty of any people consists in maintaining its substance and in defending it ... against any threat.' In killing his own children he disobeyed his self-imposed laws, as he had done so often. Goebbels, the private individual, superseded Goebbels, the statesman. He extinguished his own substance because he wanted to extinguish himself. The cynic who made his exit had to make a total exit. Nothing was to remain of him.

Nothing... Goebbels was back where he had started from: he was the nihilist *par excellence*, before whom everything dissolved into nothingness because he believed in nothing. When he was young he saved himself by believing in Hitler. He clung to that faith for many years. Now that, too, was over. As a child he envied his mother for her spontaneous, simple faith. For that faith he envied her all his life and loved her all the more for it.

Now, on the evening of 19 April, he sent her away. The old woman had spent the last days with him. She was willing to stay for she was very old, suffering from a heart disease, and there was nothing life could offer her. Through all the years when he was basking in fame and success she asked nothing from her son. She was always a little disturbed over the luxury with which he surrounded himself; always a little frightened amidst the great events in which he was a central figure; always a little distressed over the evils the Nazis committed, of which, being a strict Catholic, she could not approve.

Their farewell was laden with sadness; they knew that they would never see each other again. But Goebbels did not want to include her in the final act of annihilation which was about to happen. His mother was more than merely a part of him. Her faith had lifted her beyond the realm of his nihilism. She believed and, therefore, she must live.

After his mother had left, Magda and the children arrived. And then the doors of the house closed. Goebbels' 'home' became a fortress for himself and his family—and a prison for his associates.

Two days later, on 21 April, at the end of his usual conference, once more the Minister received all the Kreisleiters of Berlin in the film room, where he made a brief speech. The general restlessness and nervousness was so widespread that his adjutant forgot to notify the stenographer. Hence only the last portion of his speech was recorded in shorthand. 'I have taken my family into the house,' Goebbels said. 'We are staying here. And I demand of you, gentlemen, that you too will remain at your posts. If necessary, we shall know how to die here.' He seemed shaken and his voice trembled and tears welled in his eyes.

That afternoon two of his secretaries vanished. They had obtained bicycles and were fleeing to their relatives somewhere in the country. Goebbels was outraged and shouted at his press assistant: 'Now I ask you, how could that ever have happened? How can there be any guarantee now of keeping regular office hours?'

From then on the doors were doubly guarded. Despite these precautions, everyone in the house was secretly packing his bags. The employees discussed the most fantastic plans of escape. One of the secretaries meant to let her hair down, put flowers in it, and hurry through the streets singing and dancing—hoping against hope she would be taken for a lunatic. One of the stenographers wanted to crawl over the wall separating Goebbels' mansion from the Swiss Legation; at least he would be on neutral soil, he thought. A few hours later nothing was left of the Swiss Legation. Lieutenant-Colonel Balzer showed the others a small brown phial. 'Do you know what that is? Prussic acid! It cost 11,000 marks, this little thing. At the Hotel Adlon they have organized a regular traffic in this commodity. After all, it is a very convenient way of dying. One drop of it on your tongue, and you flop to the ground as though you'd been struck by lightning.'

III

Here is what happened on Sunday, 22 April, in Goebbels' home:

After breakfast there were the usual discussions with his associates. Since 7 a.m. mountains of dossiers were being burned in the garden, most of them memoranda on Goebbels' regular daily conferences, and the bonfires lasted all day long.

At 10 a.m. Goebbels began to dictate his diary. Among other things, he said that he would declare Berlin a military objective unless unforeseen circumstances should favourably affect the situation. While dictating he would occasionally glance out of the window into the street. An alarm was on and a few planes were circling above the city. Goebbels smiled. 'Well, I must hand it to the Berliners for being a fine, brave bunch of people,' he said. 'They don't even go to their shelters, but stare into the sky to see what's going on.'

There followed a brief talk with his military advisers, among them General Reimann. His daily conference was cancelled, owing to the lack of transport facilities, which would prevent the conferees from appearing on time. Instead, Goebbels had his speech recorded, to be broadcast later in the day. It was a brief address in which Goebbels proclaimed Berlin to be a military objective. During the recording, enemy artillery had begun to aim at the government district. At intervals of thirty seconds the shells whizzed into the Tiergarten, exploded at the Brandenburg Gate, and suddenly there was a detonation in the immediate neighbourhood of the mansion and the resulting concussion broke the few windows left in the house. Goebbels did not move a muscle of his face. The recording was stopped, but he asked immediately, 'Well, I suppose I can go on now, can't I?' Some of the employees would have preferred to take shelter, but no one dared make such a suggestion. Goebbels finished his speech and then asked the engineer: 'What do you think? Will that noise be audible in the broadcast? It would make a nice sound effect, don't you think?'

An hour later he listened to it over the radio and the sound effect pleased him. Subsequently there were conferences with associates. He also dictated appeals to his Gauleiters. During lunch at 1 o'clock, according to the press officer, he was still in a very supercilious mood. He described Churchill as a 'little man,' spoke of Eden as a 'hoity-toity gent' and acted altogether as though he was totally unaware of the fact that the city of Berlin was in its death throes. Then he retired to the shelter for a short nap, complaining that the guns were making too much noise.

During the afternoon the artillery fire continued with increasing intensity. Added to this terrible din was the roaring of a few low-flying aircraft. A solitary anti-aircraft gun shot at them and then fell silent, presumably because it had run out of ammunition. The entire staff lounged around the lobby in the centre of the house, obviously reluctant to go to their offices, which were more exposed to the falling shells. Magda and the children divided their time between the shelter and the lobby. No one spoke a word; everything there was to say had been said a hundred times and more.

Meanwhile Goebbels had a talk with Fritzsche. He was very excited. He mentioned the latest Russian successes in the Berlin suburbs and declared the situation was hopeless. 'In the final analysis, this is what the German people wanted,' he added.[5] 'The great majority of the Germans voted in favour of our leaving the League of Nations, in other words, against a policy of appeasement and for a policy of courage and honour. It was the German people who chose war.'

Fritzsche did not trust his ears. Never before had Goebbels given Germany's exit from the League of Nations such a peculiar interpretation and, indeed, this had never been the meaning of that plebiscite. On the contrary, it had been accompanied by numerous assurances of Hitler's peaceful intentions. Goebbels was irritated and cut Fritzsche short. Only a week or so before he had searched for a means of ending the war before the whole people would be wiped out. Now he almost wished that it should perish. Brusquely he turned his back to Fritzsche and he did not even move when his most gifted collaborator walked out of the room.

At 5 o'clock in the afternoon Frau Goebbels told the nurse: 'We are now going over to the Fuehrer. Please get the children ready.' The children were happy over this visit. They wanted to know if they would get chocolate and cake from Hitler. The nurse inquired whether she ought to pack the children's nighties, but Magda replied, 'No. That is not necessary any more.' Then she turned to them with a gay smile and said: 'Each of you may take along one toy, but no more than that.'

A few minutes later Goebbels came out of his studio and went downstairs. His face looked pale and drawn and he walked more slowly than usual. Over his arm was draped a blanket, which surprised all those who saw it because he never carried anything himself. Downstairs he was helped into his coat and together with his wife and children he left the house. His chauffeur, Rach, and his adjutant, Schwaegermann, had preceded them. Two cars were waiting, the first for Goebbels, his wife and their daughter Helga, the second accommodated the other children, with Schwaegermann at the wheel. Then both cars drove away.

A few minutes later the nurse burst into Otto Jacobs' office, tears streaming down her cheeks, and crying, 'They're gone! They're gone! They won't come back!' Rapidly the news spread through the mansion. Someone had noticed that Goebbels' butler, Rohrsen, had already disappeared. A secretary had hysterics and screamed, 'We've been left in the lurch!' Suddenly the S.S. officers posted in and about the house vanished, too. Their duty had been to protect the Minister, and now they had outlived their usefulness. The women wept and tore their hair. 'Now we'll never get out of Berlin!' they wailed. 'Why wouldn't they let us go yesterday?'

It would be untruthful to say that the men conducted themselves in an exemplary manner. They were by no means the masters of the situation. No one knew exactly what had happened, all were gabbling away at the same time. Everyone wanted to get himself out of danger, but no one knew how to go about it. Strangely enough, the name of Goebbels was hardly mentioned. Whatever would happen to their former boss seemed to be a matter of indifference to them. One of the chambermaids said: 'Frau Goebbels has placed everything in the house at my disposal. She has taken along nothing.' The consensus was that the family would be dead in a matter of hours. Magda seems to have had similar ideas, otherwise she surely would have taken the children's night clothes.

Six o'clock. They all rushed to their rooms, closed their bags, in a frantic effort to get out as quickly as possible. Finally the two remaining cars in the courtyard drove off into the darkness, each crowded with nine to ten persons.

As the employees made their exit, a group of weary men marched through the garden and into the house. A voice called out: 'Whoever is not a member of the *Volkssturm* must leave immediately!'

The household personnel, the servants, the cooks, all hurriedly picked up their packed suitcases, timidly stepped out of the basement and shuffled through the meagre ranks of the *Volkssturm* out of the now deserted building. The young boys with their pinched faces stared at them with wide-open eyes...

IV

Several days before Hitler had left the Reich Chancellery and moved down to the so-called Fuehrer shelter, which had been constructed deep under the garden of the building. Strictly speaking, there were two shelters—one consisting of twelve small cubicles, the other consisting of eighteen tiny, cramped rooms. Besides Hitler, there were Eva Braun, Martin Bormann and a number of adjutants, secretaries and servants. Magda and her children were given four rooms in the smaller shelter, while Goebbels moved into the room formerly occupied by Hitler's physician, Dr Morell. He was evidently determined to stay in the Fuehrer's immediate vicinity, to prevent Hitler from changing his mind.

Two days before, on his birthday, he had been on the verge of leaving. His chauffeur, Erich Kempka, had ordered forty cars to be ready. Innumerable people came to wish him luck and all of them expected him to depart for Obersalzberg that same evening. Those who tried to persuade him to leave Berlin included Goering and Keitel, Himmler and Bormann, the Generals Hans Krebs (Chief of the Army General Staff) and Wilhelm Burgdorf (liaison officer between the German High Command and the Fuehrer's Headquarters). Hitler had said neither yes nor no. Many of the cars Kempka had assembled took important personalities to the airports. Hitler was not among them. Neither was he in the group of forty to fifty prominent Nazis who left the Reich Chancellery the following day.

On 22 April the Fuehrer staged a terrible fit of rage during his daily conference. He screamed—as so often before—that he had been betrayed, that the army was full of traitors; he shrilly cried he had been deceived on all sides, that the Third Reich was finished, and that he himself wanted to die. He would not go to Berchtesgaden, he declared.

Everyone protested vehemently. All was not lost yet, they claimed. Subsequently there were telephone conversations with Himmler, Doenitz, Ribbentrop, all of whom begged the Fuehrer not to remain in Berlin. Hitler stubbornly refused. He ordered that the population of Berlin be informed that the Fuehrer would not abandon them.

When soon after the conference Goebbels moved into the shelter, Keitel implored him to use his influence with the Fuehrer to bring him to his senses. Goebbels smiled and shook his head, saying he would not even consider such a possibility. The agitated Keitel moaned all would be lost if Hitler stayed in Berlin. Goebbels countered that all was lost anyhow.

The reasoning of the generals was incomprehensible to him. Soldiers, of all people, ought to understand that a heroic death now was more important than prolongation of a hopeless defence for a few days. But generals seemed to be incapable of changing their age-old pattern of thought. Jodl told Hitler frankly that under the prevailing circumstances he would no longer stay in the shelter. 'I shall not stay in this rat trap,' he declared defiantly. 'Here I am completely useless. I'm just sitting around. This is Headquarters only in name. With communications constantly being broken, one cannot direct a battle or give orders of any sort. I am still a soldier. Give me an army group and an order to fight, and fight I will, whenever and wherever possible. But I will not stay here one day longer.'

These were the kind of arguments Goebbels had to keep from Hitler. While the others talked of tactical considerations, he endeavoured to bewitch the Fuehrer with the mysticism of the *Nibelungen* saga. He had to hypnotize him and keep him hypnotized, until the little man from Braunau near Linz—for in the end he had again become what he had been in the beginning—would think of himself as Siegfried, going down as a glorious hero. Goebbels, who for years had thundered against defeatism, was now compelled to glorify defeat and tragic death. Defeat was not merely something negative—it was an historical event, it was Destiny. Goebbels talked of 'doomed culture,' of 'doomed Europe'. This was not entirely new: it contained a bit of Hegel, a bit of Schopenhauer, a good deal of Richard Wagner and Spengler, in addition to the whole nihilism of Goebbels' youth.

Goebbels had to keep Hitler enchained, exhorting him constantly, never letting up. This produced a paradoxical situation, with Goebbels, who actually had no official duties to perform in those last days, being busier than ever before, and having no time for anything or anyone else. Fritzsche, who was housed next door in the basement of the Propaganda Ministry, tried in vain to 'phone Goebbels. All his attempts to speak to him personally in the Fuehrer's shelter failed. It was evident that Goebbels did not want to see him again—but then, perhaps he had a bad conscience.

Goebbels' contact with the outside world was now practically non-existent. He who had been the best informed man in Europe scarcely bothered to turn on the radio. Once, however, he happened to listen in on a Moscow broadcast. He ordered an interpreter to come over from the basement of the Propaganda Ministry. When the man arrived and began to translate the programme, Goebbels waved him aside; he was no longer interested.

In the meantime, what was left of the most powerful propaganda machine in the world was disintegrating with lightning rapidity. A few transmitters were still operating but they were barely audible. Most of the newspapers either had ceased publication or else issued a single sheet. The last number of *Das Reich* was published in Leipzig because the Berlin printing works had been bombed out, and thus the edition was never distributed in Berlin.

On 22 April a new paper appeared in Berlin under the name of *Der Panzerbaer* (the Armoured Bear) and sub-titled, *Kampfblatt fuer die Verteidiger Gross-Berlins* (Paper for the Defenders of Berlin). It consisted of four measly pages, scarcely larger than book format and was crammed with sensational reports about the fighting in Berlin's subways and in the suburbs, together with impassioned appeals to the population to hold out. This was done in incredibly poor and amateurish style, worse even than the first issues of *Angriff*. Goebbels must have regarded this last journalistic product of National Socialism with more than mixed feelings. Here, too, the circle had been completed. Goebbels was again back where he had started.

And who in battered Berlin was interested in reading *Der Panzerbaer*? Who bothered about the spasmodic efforts of a dying propaganda machine? Someone conceived the idea of printing leaflets for the 'approaching' German army which was to relieve the encircled city, urging the troops to hurry. They were 'accidentally' dropped over Berlin to convey the impression that the non-existent army actually was nearing Potsdam. Was there anyone left who believed it?

Time and again Bormann, Ribbentrop and others tried to persuade Hitler to leave for Berchtesgaden. It was not until 25 April that they resigned themselves to the inevitable. By then the Russians had drawn a ring around Berlin and any attempt to escape would have entailed the gravest risks.

V

Goebbels still experienced a minor triumph, although it came too late to make him particularly happy: Goering fell into disgrace.

The creator of the Luftwaffe had gone to Berchtesgaden. From there he wired Hitler proposing to take command, inasmuch as the Fuehrer was deprived of his freedom of action. This telegram was the result of numerous misunderstandings for which Hitler himself was undoubtedly responsible. Bormann, who had intrigued against Goering for years, quickly took advantage of the confused situation and managed to convince the Fuehrer that Goering had intended to betray him. Hitler foamed at the mouth and told all those who cared to listen how deeply shaken he was by Goering's betrayal.

Goebbels played along with him. This was not particularly surprising in view of the antagonism between the two men and of Goebbels' unsuccessful attempts to have Goering discharged from office. But his enthusiasm over the fall of his colleague was only lukewarm. The man who could hate with such implacable hatred virtually had to make an effort to spew out the venomous tirades which once came to him so naturally. Much of what he said against Goering (and other 'traitors') sounded so artificial that eyewitnesses reported he had become a 'ham actor'—a charge which even his sharpest critics never before had levelled.[6] He confined his outbursts to an absolute minimum. He raised his voice only to humour the Fuehrer or, rather, to strengthen the latter's determination to commit suicide. Otherwise Goebbels remained surprisingly calm in the hysterical atmosphere of the shelter. He continued to look well-groomed, always wore clean shirts, he shaved every day and to the very end had his nails manicured.

Sometimes he would read to his children or sing folk songs with them. The children played their usual games, but there was not much space for them to move around, for they had scarcely more room than in the sleeping compartment of a train. When there was no artillery fire they were allowed to go out into the garden. On one occasion they saw a plane circling over Berlin. 'Why don't we fly away?' they exclaimed. Their mother replied: 'Don't you like it here with Uncle Fuehrer?' The children admitted that they had a fine time with Uncle Fuehrer.

Rather unexpectedly, Professor Karl Franz Gebhardt, head of the German Red Cross, appeared in the shelter. On the evening of 26 April he intended to leave the capital in several Red Cross cars. Should not the women and children be evacuated? he asked. He visited Magda in her little cubicle, but she would not hear of escape: she would stay where she was, and her children would stay with her.

With six lively children on her hands Magda was kept busy. Their clothes had to be constantly washed and ironed because she had taken no extra dresses with her. She spent many hours playing with them. Once her eldest daughter Helga, a precocious child, asked her wistfully: 'Mammy, must we die now?'

Magda managed to smile serenely, and shook her head. But as soon as Helga had gone, she burst into tears. She was paralyzed with horror at the thought of what would happen. Would she have the strength to see her own children die?[7]

Eva Braun, the other woman in the shelter, seemed to be completely reconciled to the idea of her death. As a matter of fact she was Goebbels' only ally in the little private conspiracy aiming at a hero's death for the Fuehrer.

This young woman, who had always stood in the background when Hitler was a world-wide historical figure, who was allowed to share only a few hours with him, had finally come into her own in the last stages of the Nazi regime. Now that Hitler had been abandoned by all his former comrades, except for one or two friends, he belonged almost entirely to her. Their union would be complete only in death. Eva Braun had all the romantic notions of a lovesick German housemaid.

Perhaps it was Goebbels, perhaps it was Eva Braun, who finally convinced Hitler of the necessity of dying. For on 28 April he called a meeting of all the inhabitants of the shelter. First point on the agenda: Suicide. Hitler explained that they must all kill themselves, if possible in such a manner that their bodies would not be found or identified. They all possessed poison. The mass suicide was to begin as soon as the Russians reached the Reich Chancellery. His listeners nodded in agreement and surpassed each other in their assurances that they simply yearned to die. Everyone had a special plan, they all felt like heroes. In spite of this melodramatic *mise en scène* Hitler secretly still hoped for the great miracle. As for the others, they did not even consider the idea of killing themselves. And with the exception of Goebbels' whole family and, of course, Eva Braun, no one did.

The German defeat assumed proportions unprecedented in modern history. The strip of German territory still unoccupied by the enemy became narrower and narrower. The isolated sections where there was resistance were like islands in an ocean. The Russians and the Americans already had met at the Elbe River and Germany was split into two parts.

More than half of Berlin was in Russian hands. The battle was carried on in a hundred different places. In the city itself it was no longer possible to establish contact between the various battalions. A zone which had just been the scene of heavy fighting suddenly would be transformed into an area of deepest quiet. Soldiers and *Volkssturm* members used every opportunity to sneak into the nearest house, take off their uniforms and reappear as harmless civilians.

The confusion was indescribable. The worst that could happen to a Berliner was to find troops marching into his street to defend it. Old men and women were sent to plead with the officers to move on to the next block. From hundreds of lamp posts dangled the bodies of deserters. Terrorism was the only means by which the Nazi officers could contend with the crumbling discipline. Some of them simply were shot down by mutinous troops. But such acts of open rebellion seldom occurred. German soldiers are not conspicuous for their revolutionary spirit.

The nights were bright, for the city was burning at a thousand places simultaneously, and no one made any effort to extinguish the gigantic conflagration. Berlin had been transformed into a sea of flames, and from the few planes that still got through it looked as if the world was going under.

In the Fuehrer's shelter the world did go under by the hour and by the minute. The atmosphere was altogether fantastic and unreal. The German heroes, who with a grandiose gesture had sent millions to their deaths Jews, Poles, Czechs, Yugoslavs and even Germans—were not at all resigned to die. It was true that there was a great deal of talk about death, but most of the occupants hoped something, anything, would happen to save them. Even the man whom Goebbels wanted to build up to heroic proportions, for the sake of posterity, could not give up hope.

He was afraid. Laboriously he dragged himself through the shelter, his legs and arms trembling, and the maps he touched deteriorated under his sweaty hands. He was forever forming new plans, new ideas, moving armies that no longer existed.

Then again he would tell all those who sat with him in the shelter how the end should be. Even in death he remained a dictator, who instructed the others how they were to die. 'I must insist that my body and the body of Eva Braun be destroyed before all others.' He became panicky at the idea that his body might fall into Russian hands to be placed on exhibition in Moscow.

There is no proof that Goebbels suggested this possibility to him, but it is extremely likely. Goebbels wanted Hitler's death in order to deify him. If the Russians were to get hold of the Fuehrer's body they might use it to smother the Hitler myth before it had begun to germinate. The more mysterious Hitler's death—and a death without a body was particularly mysterious—the greater the possibilities for a future Hitler legend. It is quite likely that Goebbels considered the possibility that people might ask themselves a year or two later whether Hitler had really died, or whether he had merely gone into hiding, only to reappear at the appropriate moment...

Eva Braun, Goebbels' ally in the matter of Hitler's heroic death, was duly rewarded. The Fuehrer married her. At Goebbels' marriage, Hitler was his best man. Now it was the other way round. The ceremony took place during the night of 28-29 April and lasted only a few minutes.

Then there was an informal reception, with Magda, Bormann and the secretaries participating. They sat in one of the tiny rooms of the shelter, drinking champagne and making small talk. That is to say, Goebbels monopolized the conversation. He told anecdotes of the days of the struggle for power. The others, afraid of saying something tactless, seldom dared open their mouths, for almost anything would have been tactless at such an hour. They could not even give a toast in honour of the couple and wish them a happy future. In another twenty-four hours it might all be over.

During the reception Hitler disappeared with his secretary to dictate his personal and political testaments. Goebbels signed both as a witness. The political testament was Hitler's last message to posterity: it could either destroy or build up the Hitler myth.

Was Goebbels in any way connected with the composition of Hitler's political will? This question cannot definitely be answered, but it is more than mere conjecture—in fact, it is extremely likely—that he decisively influenced the Fuehrer in the compilation of his testament. For here we find once more the classical arguments of Goebbels' propaganda. Here it was stated once more that Germany had not wanted or started the war, that the Jews alone were responsible. Here it was said that despite all setbacks the war would go down in history as the 'most gloriously brave demonstration of a people's will to live'.[8] Here Goering was given another kick in the pants (together with Himmler, who meantime had tried to negotiate an armistice with the western Allies).

Then Hitler appointed the new German government. There was to be no second Fuehrer; Admiral Karl Doenitz was to become Reich President.[9] Goebbels was chosen for the post of Reich Chancellor, that is, for the real head of the government, while Bormann as Party Minister was to take control of the Nazi Party. There followed Hitler's final pronouncement: 'Although a number of men, such as Martin Bormann, Dr Goebbels, and others, including their wives, have come to me of their own free will, and have refused to leave the capital under all circumstances, but were willing to perish here with me, I must nevertheless ask them to obey my request and, in this case, to subordinate their own feelings to the interests of the nation.'

Here was Goebbels' iron-clad excuse to dodge the suicide issue. Now, if he so wished, he could go on living and no one would be able to blame him. This was his great opportunity.

The opportunity was there, but he ignored it. He had already made his decision. He would have done away with himself even if Hitler had decided to live. It was his idea that the Fuehrer must disappear, and he did not ape him when he followed him. On the contrary, it was Hitler who followed Goebbels to his death, although he did not know it. In the end, the Leader became the one who was led.

VI

After he had signed both testaments as a witness, Goebbels withdrew to write a special amendment to Adolf Hitler's political will.

'The Fuehrer has ordered me,' he wrote, 'should the defence of the Reich capital collapse, to leave Berlin, and to take part as a leading member in a government appointed by him. 'For the first time in my life I must categorically refuse to obey an order of the Fuehrer. My wife and children join me in this refusal. Otherwise—quite apart from the fact that feelings of humanity and loyalty forbid us to abandon the Fuehrer in his hour of greatest need—I should appear for the rest of my life as a dishonourable traitor and common scoundrel, and should lose my own self-respect together with the respect of my fellow citizens; a respect I should need in any future attempt to shape the future of the German nation and State.

'In the delirium of treachery which surrounds the Fuehrer in these most critical days of the war, there must be someone at least who will stay with him unconditionally until death, even if this conflicts with the formal and (in a material sense) entirely justifiable order which he has given in his political testament.

'In doing this, I believe that I am doing the best service I can to the future of the German people. In the hard times to come, examples will be more important than men. Men will always be found to lead the nation forward into freedom; but a reconstruction of our national life would be impossible unless developed on the basis of clear and obvious examples.

'For this reason, together with my wife, and on behalf of my children, who are too young to speak for themselves, but who would unreservedly agree with this decision if they were old enough, I express an unalterable resolution not to leave the Reich capital, even if it falls, but rather, at the side of the Fuehrer, to end a life which will have no further value to me if I cannot spend it in the service of the Fuehrer, and by his side.'

Back in May, 1926, Goebbels had written: 'Then the day may come when everything will go to pieces, when the mob around you will foam and grumble and roar, "Crucify him!" Then we shall stand firmly and unshakably and we will shout and sing "Hosanna!"'

Now the moment had come to keep his vow. And Goebbels kept it. This circle, too, had been completed.

VII

About twenty-four hours later, in the early dawn of 30 April (those in the shelter no longer knew whether it was night or day) Adolf Hitler gave a farewell reception. Some twenty men and women living in the various shelters were invited. Hitler and Eva walked around, mumbling a few amiable words, shaking hands here and there. The little ceremony lasted an hour, then the newly-weds retired. Hitler called his adjutant, S.S. Sturmbannfuehrer Guensche, and explained once more: 'This is my last command. My body and the body of my wife must be burned immediately after our death—nothing must be allowed to interfere with this task.' Guensche left and the couple remained alone. Everyone in the shelter was waiting for the end.

Hours passed, strange and unreal hours. There they sat in their little rooms—Goebbels and Magda and all the others—and waited, hoping that everything would end soon.

It is difficult to visualize the weird atmosphere during those last hours, and it is equally difficult to guess the thoughts that might have passed through Goebbels' brain. Was he pleased with his achievement, was he satisfied that the Fuehrer would die the death that he, Goebbels, had urged on him? Was he content or desperate, cheerful or unhappy, calm or nervous?

He knew one thing: he had done everything so the war might be won. He had made greater efforts to achieve victory than anyone else, he had made fewer mistakes. He had maintained the people's morale despite devastating defeats. If Hitler had listened to him, total war would have started earlier, perhaps the war might have been won—who knows? But it was meaningless to ponder now over the *ifs* and *buts*. The only gesture that had any meaning was to die. Sometime in the future, perhaps, the world would understand that the war, that German resistance, had been meaningful.

He waited. Would it not have been better to leave Berlin, like Goering and Himmler, Jodl and Keitel? No, it would have only delayed the final decision for a few hours or days. 'If I were once more thirty years old...' Would he do things differently? Would he not join the Nazi Party? Would he not follow Hitler?

Hours passed, eerie hours. What was Hitler doing now? Was he still talking about German honour, Germany's future? Was he still cursing the Jews? Or was he perhaps wondering about his mistakes, in these final moments of his life? Was Hitler, too, asking himself whether he would do things differently if he were once more thirty years old?

Goebbels waited. Everyone in the shelter waited. Hours passed. Hitler was dying a hard death, harder than heroes die. Ten hours and more had passed since he had retired. And suddenly he reappeared. It was 2 o'clock in the afternoon. He wanted to have his lunch. After his meal he emerged again, accompanied by his wife. He walked through the shelter, shook hands, his eyes fixed on the others in a rigid stare, without saying a word, and disappeared. Then a shot rang out. Bormann and Guensche rushed into Eva Braun's living-room. She was lying on the couch, dead from poison. Adolf Hitler had crumpled on the floor. His head was a bloody mess. He had shot himself through the mouth.

VIII

The funeral was set for 3 o'clock. The bodies were taken upstairs and deposited on a sandy spot in the courtyard, about fifteen feet from the entrance of the shelter. Goebbels, Bormann, Sturmbannfuehrer Guensche, and the chauffeur Kempka were present. Gasoline was poured over the bodies and about to be ignited, but Russian shells fell so closely that it was too dangerous to remain in the yard. All withdrew to the entrance of the shelter. From there Bormann threw a burning rag drenched in gasoline in the direction of the bodies. He missed his aim, but succeeded the second time. The bodies began to burn. All those present raised their right arm in the Hitler salute.

There stood Goebbels. Around him the Russian shells were bursting, a few feet away from him Hitler's body was going up in flames, Berlin was burning all around. Berlin was a vast field of ruins, an ocean of hopeless misery, so totally different from the city he had come to twenty years before. A Berlin without light, colour or music—now filled with the noise of crashing bombs and shells, of crumbling buildings and the occasional bark of the anti-aircraft guns.

The bodies burned slowly; it would take a long time before they became completely unrecognizable. The men who were watching the spectacle became impatient and went down into the shelter. Was Goebbels thinking of the time when he first came to Berlin? Then the Party had only a tiny office somewhere in a basement. Ironically they called it the 'opium den'. Now this circle, too, had been completed. The Party was again back where it had started. It occupied no more than a few square yards, deep down, where the sunlight could never penetrate.

During the last meeting, which took place in the early morning hours of 1 May in the presence of Bormann, Goebbels, General Krebs and others, it was decided to attempt an escape from the Reich Chancellery. Bormann would try to join Doenitz.

General Krebs offered Goebbels and his family an armoured car. But Goebbels shook his head. 'No, thank you,' he said. 'I am no longer interested in life.'

Shortly thereafter he talked with Guensche, ordering him to set fire to Hitler's shelter as soon as the sortie began. Guensche protested, reminding him of the Fuehrer's explicit instructions to leave the shelter intact, so as to prove to the Russians that Hitler had stuck it out to the last.

Goebbels would not hear of this. 'Do as I have ordered you,' he said. He knew of course about Hitler's instructions—it was scarcely possible that such an important detail would have escaped his attention. But he believed a fire would be more spectacular. 'A fire is so popular ... it appeals to the people's imagination.' He remained a propagandist to the end.

That day, 1 May, quickly passed with preparations to break out of the shelter trap. Goebbels and Magda, who had no preparations to make, played with their children, sang with them, read to them. From time to time they would be interrupted by visitors who would debate the chances of the escape. No one any longer remembered that he had sworn to die with Hitler, and it did not enter anyone's head that Goebbels had meant his oath seriously.

Goebbels' adjutant, Guenther Schwaegermann, arrived to notify him that the exodus from the shelter was set for 9 p.m. Even he did not know that his chief would not go along. It was about 7 o'clock. He saw Frau Goebbels go into the children's room. When she emerged again, her face was ashen. Then she became aware of Schwaegermann's presence and put her head on his chest and sobbed. After a while he gathered what she was trying to say in her frantic grief: she had just killed her six children.

What had happened was that she had called in a physician, who had told the children that they must be inoculated since they would have to stay in the shelter for quite some time. Then Magda had gone from bed to bed with the doctor, watching him introduce the lethal needle into their veins.[10]

Magda was in a state of near-collapse. Schwaegermann took her to the conference room where Goebbels sat waiting. He was very pale. He did not have to be told what had happened. Time ticked away and he was silent.

Then the three went over to Goebbels' tiny room. Finally Goebbels spoke. 'Everything is over. My wife and I will commit suicide. You will burn our bodies. Can you do that?'

'Yes.'

Goebbels said, 'Here is a present for you.' And he gave him Hitler's photograph, which stood on his desk.

Magda turned to Schwaegermann. 'You see, we shall die an honourable death. If you should ever see Harald again,[11] give him our best love and tell him we died an honourable death.'

Schwaegermann left.

An honourable death.... To the last Goebbels was only concerned with how his death would look to posterity. And yet he had never been concerned with how his life looked to his contemporaries. He had lived what he considered a full life, a fascinating life, but what no one could consider a good life. From any moral standards he had been a criminal directly or indirectly responsible for the deaths of hundreds of thousands—perhaps of millions. He now intended to die an honourable death. And so far as he was concerned he did die an honourable death because he, the most prominent representative of amoral nihilism in our time, the propagandist *per se*, the high priest of a magic cult brought into existence to obscure the brains of human beings, to harden their souls, to conjure up a reality which does not exist—not necessarily for the sake of a good or bad cause, but for the sake of propaganda itself; he could not know that there can be no honour in a life which has had no goodness in it.

It was now 8.30 p.m. Goebbels and Magda went out of their room. They passed Schwaegermann and the chauffeur Rach, who had already secured the gasoline to burn the bodies. Without a word both of them went upstairs.

Schwaegermann heard a shot and raced up. They were lying on the ground. It appeared that Goebbels had shot himself, while Magda had taken poison. The S.S. man standing near the bodies said he had fired twice in order to make sure they were dead. They poured four cans of petrol over the corpses and set fire to them.[12]

It was 9 o'clock. The garden of the Reich Chancellery was bright as daylight, owing to the many fires which were burning throughout the city. The flight from the shelter had begun. Those who ran through the garden could see the bodies clearly.

IX

The fleeing group of people did not get far. Some of them died, others were taken prisoners. The Russian communiqué of the next evening read:

'Troops of the First White Russian Front commanded by Marshal Zhukov, assisted by troops of the First Ukrainian Front commanded by Marshal Koniev, after stubborn street fighting completed the rout of the Berlin group of German troops and today, 2 May, occupied the whole of the capital of Germany, the city of Berlin, centre of German imperialism and hotbed of German aggression.

'The garrison of Berlin, which defended the city, ceased resistance and laid down their arms and surrendered at 3 p.m. on 2 May. By 9 p.m. on 2 May our troops captured more than 70,000 officers and men in the city of Berlin.'

On that day, 2 May, several men were still working in the basement under the wreckage of the Propaganda Ministry. Hans Fritzsche had not left his post. When he learned of Goebbels' death he decided to make a 'peace offer' to the Russians. By the time he had instructed an interpreter, the Russians penetrated into the cellar. About the same time they discovered Goebbels' body in the garden of the Reich Chancellery.

It took quite some time before the Berliners learned that their Gauleiter and the Defender of Berlin had died, for there were no newspapers and no radio. Many who heard the news did not believe it, thinking it only a rumour, one of the many rumours which Goebbels' propaganda machine had circulated so frequently and so adeptly.

The Berliners did not care whether Goebbels was dead or alive. They were too preoccupied with their own troubles. The Russians, of whom Goebbels had warned them so often, now had descended on them. The Berliners were sitting in their cellars, trembling at what might happen to them. Fear filled their brains so completely that they had no room left for thoughts about Hitler or Goebbels. Goebbels the Propagandist had defeated himself with his own weapon.

Even later, when Goebbels' death had been confirmed a hundred and a thousand times; when the Russians showed a film of the conquest of Berlin in which Goebbels' body could be seen so clearly, so true to life that no one could doubt his identity—even then the Berliners continued to be suspicious. The people were whispering that he was in Bavaria or in Spain, that he had fled to Argentina in a submarine especially constructed for the purpose. Many believed that the body they had seen was that of his double. Some even asserted that the former Roman Catholic had withdrawn to the seclusion of a monastery, far away from all human beings.

He was considered too clever not to have taken steps to save his life. The people were so accustomed to regard him as a liar that they did not believe in his own proven death. Thus Goebbels died—in a dual sense, his own victim.

THE END

END NOTES

CHAPTER I

1. *Michael*, by Goebbels. This book will be discussed later on. There should, however, be a mention here that, according to Goebbels' mother, this book is largely autobiographical.
2. *Michael*, by Goebbels.
3. Later Goebbels used these very words in *Michael*.
4. Walther Rathenau, *Der Kaiser*.
5. Notes to *The Possessed*, by Dostoevsky.
6. *Michael*, by Goebbels.
7. *Michael*, by Goebbels.
8. 'When Hitler Speaks', 19 November 1928.

CHAPTER II

1. After the Nazis had come to power, *The Wanderer* was finally performed but for a short run. The public reacted with indifference, and Goebbels withdrew his play.
2. *Battle of Berlin*, by Goebbels.
3. The following is mainly based on the accounts of Konrad Heiden, Rudolf Olden, and Otto Strasser.
4. According to men like Konrad Heiden, Rudolf Olden and others, who have written the history of the Nazi movement, Goebbels had immediately concurred with Hitler, swung over to his side and was accused by the 'left wing' of betrayal. However, it seems more than unlikely that he would have failed to mention this sudden change of heart in the pages of his own diary.
5. *Battle of Berlin*, by Goebbels.

CHAPTER III

1. *Battle of Berlin*, by Goebbels.
2. *Battle of Berlin*.
3. *Battle of Berlin*.
4. *Battle of Berlin*.
5. *Battle of Berlin*.

CHAPTER IV

1. *World in Trance*, by Leopold Schwarzschild.
2. *World in Trance*.

3. *Goebbels*, by Willi Krause.

4. Situated only a few hundred feet from the spot where, almost thirty years later, Stalin, President Truman and Ernest Bevin were to sign the Potsdam Agreement.

5. Legend has it that Goebbels first met Magda when he was tutor to Herbert or Helmut Quandt. It was supposedly on that occasion that they fell in love. The author tried to trace the story. Both Magda's mother and her closest friend and private secretary, Ilse Freybe, said there was no truth in it. One of the former cooks of the Quandts, however, swore that Goebbels had been to the house, but when it came to proving her point it turned out she was referring to a time when she herself was no longer in their employ. All those who assured the author that Goebbels had been employed by Quandt finally had to admit that they had not proof but derived their information from some 'reliable source'. In the end, Magda's mother volunteered a more plausible explanation. It seems that a certain Dr Picht tutor of Herbert Quandt, met with an accident while skiing with his pupil in the Sudeten mountains. For some time afterwards he limped, which may have caused some people to confuse him with Goebbels. In any case, if Goebbels had met Magda in the early twenties, he surely would have mentioned her in his diary, considering that he wrote at great length about women of lesser importance in his life.

CHAPTER V

1. It is true that Goebbels' diary was full of attacks against Strasser. But it must be remembered that he published it several months after Strasser had been expelled from the Party and 'liquidated' by his former friends. Here is an example of how Goebbels touched up his diary: In the first edition Captain Roehm was mentioned several times. In later additions, after the purge, his name was omitted.

2. Later he put down his thoughts in an article of 30 January 1942.

CHAPTER VI

1. This and other revelations were found in a letter written by Karl Ernst, in the hope that fear of its publication would deter the higher-ups in the Nazi Party from purging him. However, Ernst was mistaken in his assumption. He, too, was murdered during the Roehm purge of 1934. The letter was presented at the Nuremberg trial.

2. In a speech on 20 October 1933.

3. These facts were established in the testimony of former storm-trooper Heinz Juergens after his flight to Brazil to escape the purge. Published in Brazilian papers.

4. Fritzsche himself related this conversation to the author.

CHAPTER VII

1. 2 June 1940, 'Missed Opportunities'.

2. A German newspaperman got hold of these documents and smuggled them out of the country. Later they were published by the *Petit Parisien*, a Paris newspaper, under the title, *Les Instructions Sécrèter de la Propagande Allemande*.

3. Ambassador Dodd's *Diary*.

4. Ambassador Dodd's *Diary*.

5. The rumours about Goebbels' part in the 'conspiracy' have never been substantiated. In the main they probably can be traced to the testimony of Otto Strasser.

6. Goebbels had always violently opposed the cheap, vulgar demagoguery of *Der Stuermer*, and endeavoured to have it suppressed. Later in the war, when the Nazis had to cut down on newsprint, *Der Stuermer*, on Goebbels' orders, was the first paper to be banned.

CHAPTER VIII

1. As she told the author.

END NOTES

CHAPTER IX

1. The actress in question told the author the entire story.
2. A collection of *Sagax* articles were found in the Propaganda Ministry; the file was labelled: 'Articles by Dr Goebbels.'
3. On 14 June 1938, he laid the cornerstone for the House of German Tourism in Berlin. In his speech he praised the beauties of German scenery and invited foreigners to visit the country.
4. In an article of 11 November 1938.
5. As Fritzsche testified at Nuremberg.
6. This fact has been confirmed by incontrovertible documentary evidence, since published in *Design for Aggression*, by P. de Mendelsohn.
7. As Fritzsche testified at Nuremberg.
8. He used practically the same words in a speech of 5 June 1943.

CHAPTER X

1. According to testimony presented at the Nuremberg trials.
2. *Mein Kampf*, Volume I, Chapter VI.
3. Later, these men were used to edit soldiers' newspapers abroad (*Soldat am Atlanlik, Soldat am Westwall, Adler vom Aetna, Front am Polarkreis, Lappland Kurier*, etc.).
4. Fritzsche, in making this statement to the author, may, of course, have overplayed his own courage, but according to numerous other members of the Propaganda Ministry Fritzsche was indeed one of the few persons who could, and did, criticize Goebbels.
5. *Die Verpassten Gelegenheiten* (Missed Opportunities).
6. According to Fritzsche Goebbels often boasted of the Compiègne idea.
7. The author found it in the Propaganda Ministry. The manuscript had been revised by Goebbels' own hand.

CHAPTER XI

1. According to the press referent's (Rudolf Semmler) Diary. Fritzsche added that even at that time he and other members of the Propaganda Ministry were convinced of the futility of the raids on Britain.
2. The then famous report of the parachutist dropped over Crete, written in Hemingway style and prominently published by a well-known American magazine, stemmed from that office. The author had never jumped with a parachute, to say nothing of having been to Crete; in fact, he had seen parachute jumpers only in the movies.
3. Rudolf Semmler's Diary.
4. In his Directive No. 20.
5. As Fritzsche testified at Nuremberg. Also in Semmler's Diary.
6. Rudolf Semmler's Diary.
7. According to Semmler, a captured Russian colonel said that vast numbers of the Red Army would have deserted if the Germans had promised them a free Russian state.
8. The original first draft, never published, is in the possession of the author.

CHAPTER XII

1. This corresponds to a comment he made to a 'leftist friend in one of the *National Socialist Letters* on 14 November 1925, when he said: 'It is not very likely that the capitalist and the Bolshevist Jew are one and the same thing.'
2. *What About Germany?* by Louis P. Lochner
3. Honorary title bestowed for meritorious services.
4. *Top Secret*, by Ralph Ingersoll.

CHAPTER XIII

1. From the Diary of Dr Rudolf Semmler.
2. *New York Times*, 8 June 1943.
3. Diary of Dr Rudolf Semmler.
4. Diary of Dr Rudolf Semmler.

CHAPTER XIV

1. A regular scenario was worked out by Goebbels, with deletions and revisions in his own hand.
2. The entire incident was reported with full data in the Swiss press.
3. Allen W. Dulles, *Germany's Underground*.
4. From a Nazi document now in the possession of the U.S. Army it is clear that a conference took place on 20 January 1942, in Wannsee, Berlin, headed by Reinhard Heydrich, which dealt with the extermination of European Jewry.
5. Diary of Dr Rudolf Semmler.
6. According to Fritzsche's testimony at Nuremberg.
7. This description stems from stenographer Jacobs and is essentially identical with that of Dr Rudolf Semmler in his diary.
8. Diary of Dr Rudolf Semmler.

CHAPTER XV

1. Diary of Dr Rudolf Semmler.
2. An untranslatable pun, approximating, Minister for National Stupidity.
3. Diary of Dr Rudolf Semmler.

CHAPTER XVI

1. Goebbels' last letter, dealing with paper samples, was written 12 April 1945. The galley-proofs and the file with the entire correspondence about the book were found among the wreckage of the printing works which were destroyed during the last days of the Berlin battle.
2. Diary of Dr Rudolf Semmler.
3. From Dr Semmler's Diary it is very evident that Goebbels was greatly preoccupied with such ideas.
4. This was indeed an extraordinary development. Both Fritzsche and Jacobs, with whom the author discussed this matter separately, insisted it was absolutely unthinkable that Goebbels had ever edited a manuscript by Hitler. He would have been too frightened, they said. Yet the proof for the author's contention can be found in one of Goebbels' articles, written 19 July 1942, in which he used partly identical phraseology.
5. According to Fritzsche's testimony at Nuremberg.
6. This was the account of the German flier, Hanna Reitsch. The description of the final days in the shelter is based essentially on the testimony of those witnesses who lived there and later were captured by the Allies. They also form the basis of H. R. Trevor-Roper's excellent book, *The Last Days of Hitler*, which the author also used for his documentation.
7. Magda revealed her anxieties to Hanna Reitsch.
8. Some twenty years before Goebbels had written in his novel *Michael* that the First World War 'was the great manifestation of our will to live.'
9. Again the question must be raised whether this was due to Goebbels' influence, for Doenitz was the only officer whom Goebbels trusted during the last six months and who often was mentioned with praise in his diary, according to Jacobs.
10. According to Red Cross nurse Erna Flegel, a Dr Kunz made the injections, while other witnesses assert that it was Dr Ludwig Stumpfegger, one of Hitler's physicians.
11. Magda's son from her first marriage, who had been taken prisoner by the Americans in North Africa.
12. According to Schwaegermann's testimony, Goebbels committed suicide by shooting himself. Trevor-Roper believes that he took poison.

INDEX

Aachen, conquest by Allies, 296
Abdication of King of England, 144
Abetz, Otto, 138
Abyssinia, invasion by Italy, 139
Actors and actresses, ultimatum to
  divorce Jewish partners, 266
Actresses, Goebbels' attentions to,
  155-57
Adler *vom Aetna* (soldiers'
  newspaper), 185*n*
Administration department of
  Propaganda Ministry, 114
Advertising agencies handling
  railways and air lines,
  supervisory control obtained by
  Goebbels, 113
African invasion by Allied forces,
  240*ff*
Afrika Korps, 229, 240, 268
Air attacks on Germany, Goebbels'
  handling of news concerning,
  246, 275
Air-raid shelter, Goebbels, 266
Air war against Britain, 204
Aktion B division of Propaganda
  Ministry, creation of, 293
'Alarmists and Critics,' Goebbels'
  campaign against, 132
Alhertus Magnus Catholic
  Society, scholarship granted to
  Goebbels, 19
Allied air bombardments of
  Germany, 246, 275
Allied communiqués, accuracy
  inferior to German reports in
  early stages of war, 183
Allied invasion of Europe, 281-83
Allied landing in Europe, Goebbels'
  fear of, 237
All Quiet on the Western Front

(book and movie), 82-83
Alsace-Lorraine, radio programmes
  beamed to, 125
Amann, Max, 18, 38, 43, 70, 116
  personal enrichment of, 150
American invasion landings in
  North Africa, 240*ff*
American Negro, athletic prowess
  proved in Olympic Games, 142
American public opinion, Goebbels'
  efforts to influence, 128-30
American resentment against Nazis,
  Goebbels' concern over, 129
Angriff, Der (Nazi paper founded
  by Goebbels), 57-59, 61, 75, 79,
  81, 82, 89, 99, 100,
  101, 107, 178, 188, 205, 311
Anschluss with Austria, preparation
  for, 161
Anti-Catholicism campaign, 146
Anti-Jewish decrees, 120
Anti-Nazi trend of 1932, 99-22
Anti-Nazi writers, efforts of, 121
Anti-Russian propaganda campaign,
  prior to non-aggression pact,
  177
  reversal during non-aggression
  pact, 178
  at time of German invasion of
  Russia, 214*ff*
Anti-Semitic demonstration of
  1930, Goebbels accused of
  instigation of, 81-82
Anti-Semitism, 27, 59-61, 82, 97,
  116*ff*, 169*ff*, 213, 225*ff*
Appeasement of German home
  front after French victory, 195
Archbishop of Cologne, refusal to
  chime cathedral bells, 119
Ardennes offensive, 299-301

Armistice, request by France for,
  193
Art department of Propaganda
  Ministry, 114
Articles of Goebbels, deterioration
  in years of power and peace,
  150-51
  excellence of material written for
  Das Reich, 205-6
Association of Germans Abroad,
  128
Athenia (British liner), sinking of.
  181-82
Atlantic Charter, 210
Atlantic Wall, collapse of myth, 281
Auslands-Organisation, 128
Austria, *Anschluss* with, 161
  panic of 1931, 83
  radio programmes beamed to,
  125
Austrian Hitler Youth, 74
Autobahnen, construction of, 151

Bad Heiligendamn, 153
Badoglio, Marshal, 274
Balzer, Lieutenant-Colonel, 328,
  340
Bamberg, meeting of Gaufuehrers,
  at, 1926, 43-44
B.A.P., creation to supply false news
  to neutral press, 212
Barbuuse, Henri, books burned, 118
Bartels, architect of Goebbels' air-
  raid shelter, 266
Battle Cruiser Potemkin (Russian
  movie), 155
Bavaria, Diet election of 1932, 92
Bayreuth festivals of 1933, meeting
  of Hitler and Spengler at, 131
BBC, broadcasts, increasing

JOSEPH GOEBBELS

popularity in occupied
countries, 208-09
Goebbels' praise of, 200
Beck, Joseph, Poland's Foreign
Minister, 175
Behrendt, Frau, mother of Magda
Goebbels, 13, 14, 85, 87, 160,
276
Behrendt, Herr, stepfather of Magda
Goebbels, 85
Belgium, radio programmes beamed
to, 125
Ruhr, occupation of, 30
Berchtesgaden, Hitler's home at,
41, 45
Berk, Schwarz van, 283
Berlin, Allied air bombardments
of, 276
blackout of, 179
evacuation of women and
children, 275-76
first May Day celebration, 122
Goebbels' arrival in, 47ff
Goebbels' plans for defence of,
314
last days before invasion of, 327ff
Nazi strength in 1928 and 1930,
comparison of, 80
operatic performances broadcast
to foreign countries, 125
Berlin, University of, anti-Semitic
demonstration incited by
Goebbels, 93
Goebbels' attendance at, 20
Berliner Abendzeitung (Nazi daily),
57
Berliner Boersenzeitung (daily), 118
Berliner Illustrierte Zeitung (daily),
167
Berliner Tageblatt (daily), 24, 26, 27
Berlin Gau, condition at time of
Goebbels' arrival, 50
Goebbels' first mass meeting,
52-53
removal of office to better
quarters after 1930 landslide, 81
suspension of Party, 1927-28,
54ff
Berlin Police Department,
discoveries about Reichstag
fire, 106
Berndorff, H. R., 241
Bishop of Berlin, refusal to allow
Goebbels to be married by
Catholic Church, 88
Black Reichswehr, illegal German
army, 27
Blomberg, Werner von, 160
Bloodless victory in Czechoslovakia,
Goebbels' satisfaction with, 173
Bochow, Dr M., author of book
ordered by Goebbels, 284

Boemer, Karl, 216
Boemer Auslandspresse, creation
to supply false news to neutral
press, 212, 216
Boersenkurier (Berlin paper), 84
Bohemia, 'return' to Germany, 173.
See also Czechoslovakia
Bolshevism, Goebbels'
antagonism towards, 44
Goebbels' early sympathy for, 38
Bonn, University of, Goebbels'
attendance at, 20
Book of Isidor, The (collected
articles of Goebbels), 81
Books, burning of, 118
Borcke, Dr Von, 329
Bormann, Martin, 234, 250, 254,
279, 343, 349
Boulogne, British commando raid
on, 237
Boycott of Jews, 119-42
Braun, Eva, 158, 165, 343, 347-38
Braune Haus, Goebbels' offices in
Munich at, 81
Briand, Aristide, award of Nobel
Peace Prize to, 51
Briand-Kellogg Pact, 68
Bribes, use in wartime foreign
propaganda campaigns, 189,
212
Britain, Battle of, 200;
failure of German propaganda to
intimidate, 183
Germany's all-out war effort
against, 204
Greece's independence guaranteed
by, 174
Lord Haw-Haw, unsuccessful
efforts to propagandise by,
198-99
Ministry of Information, 199,
222
naval treaty with Germany, 139,
175
Poland's independence guaranteed
by, 174
reaction to early Nazi aggression,
161
Rumania's independence
guaranteed by, 174
short-wave radio broadcasts to
occupied countries, 209
short-wave transmission from,
125
British Crown crisis, attitude of
German press, 144
British war propaganda, amateurish
quality in early part of war, 183
Goebbels' scorn for, 199
improvement in, 208-53
Broadcasting, monopoly obtained
by Goebbels, 115

Broadcasts, foreign, penalties for
tuning into, 186ff
Brueckner adjutant to Hitler, 96
Bruening, Heinrich, Reich
Chancellor, 83-84, 89, 91, 92,
94, 209
Brunswick, Duke Ernst August of,
support of Nazi Party by, 55
Buch der Lieder (book by Heine),
23
Bueckeburg, first harvest
thanksgiving celebration in, 124
Buildings owned and used by
Propaganda Ministry, 148
Bulgarian Embassy, reception at,
216
Bulge, Battle of, 301
Bullitt, William C., 128
Bureau Schwarz van Berk, creation
to supply false news to foreign
correspondents, 211
Burgdorf Wilhelm, 343
Burning of books, 118

Campaign against criticism, 131ff
Canada, efforts to propagandise,
128-50
Canaris, Admiral, chief of
Intelligence Service, 241
Capitalists, transference of money
abroad, 83
Casablanca declaration by Allies,
247
Catholic Church, persecution of,
146
Celebrations, Nazi national, 122
Censorship of foreign
correspondents in London and
Paris in early stages of war, 183
Central America, radio programmes
beamed to, 125
Central European Section of
Communist International, 107
Chamberlain, Austen, award of
Nobel Peace Prize to, 51
Chamberlain, Houston Stewart, 62
Chamberlain, Neville, reluctance to
antagonise Hitler, 161
visit to Hitler at Berchtesgaden,
169
visit to Hitler at Godesberg, 169
Proposal of loan to Germany, 173
Chauffeur, Goebbels', influence on
German wartime broadcasting,
233
Children of the Goebbelses, 157
Church, Catholic, persecution of,
146
Churchill, Winston, Atlantic
Charter, creation of, 210
Athenia sinking, accusation by
Goebbels, 181, 184

INDEX

\Goebbels' campaign against, 203, 235
appointed Prime Minister, 198
Maginot Line, visit to, 192
Civil War in France, The (book by Marx), 24
Coal Strike in Britain, 51
Cologne, Allied air bombardment of, 275
Archbishop of, refusal to chime cathedral bells, 119
Goebbels' party work in, 36
Cologne, University of, Goebbels' attendance at, 20
Commercial activities, supervisory power obtained by Goebbels, 113
Communications, Reich Ministry for, 172
Communism, Goebbels' exposure to, 24-25
Goebbels suspected of, 37
Communist International, Central European Section of, 107
Communist Party, German, 41, 47, 95, 100
dissolution of, 110
Communist press banned after Reichstag fire, 107
Communist Reichstag faction, 107
Communists, French, anti-war propaganda of, 193
Compiègne, France, World War II armistice staged at, 194
Coolidge administration in United States, 47, 68
Cooper, Alfred Duff, 199
Cosmas, Bohemian chronicler, 173
Crete, German invasion of, 215
Cultural Affairs, Goebbels' desire to be Minister of, 112
Culture interpreted by Goebbels, 118
Czechoslovakia, betrayal of by Munich Pact, 114
occupation by Germany, 173
German propaganda efforts to achieve bloodless victory over, 168
radio programmes beamed to, 125
Ribbentrop's publicity orders concerning warfare against, 161, 168

Daluege, Kurt, 47, 50, 52
Dame, Die (magazine), 23
Damned swastika Men, Those (pamphlet by Goebbels), 65
Darmstaedter und Nationalbank, 53
Dawn, Charles G., 76
award of Nobel Peace Prize to, 36

Dawes Plan, 76
Déat, Marcel, French Minister of Aviation, anti-war article by, 175
Debate, between Goebbels and recorded speech of Bruening, 92
between Goebbels and *Deutschnationale Volkspartei* men, 98
Decline of the West, The (book by Spengler), 64
De Jouvenel, Bertrand, 138
Denmark, radio programmes beamed to, 125
Deutschlandsender broadcasts interrupted by Russia, 236
Deutschnationale Volkspartei (rightist political party), 76, 98
Diary, Goebbels', 39-40, 244
'Die for Danzig?', article by French Minister of Aviation, 175
Dieppe, British commando raid on, 237
Diet election in Lippe, 102-25
Diet elections, 1932, 92
Dietrich, Otto, Reich Press Chief, 182, 207, 257
Rudolf Hess's flight to England, confusion of press releases concerning, 213
Dimitroff, Georgi, 107
Dittmar General Kurt, military commentator, 275
Divorce, Goebbels' request for, 163
DNB (German News Agency), expenditures on, 149
Doenitz, Admiral Karl, 344, 349
Dollfuss, Engelbert, Chancellor of Austria, 126
Domela, Harry, 52
Dortmund, Goebbels' party work in, 36
Dostoevsky, Goebbels influenced by, 24-27
Dresden, destruction of, 316
operatic performances broadcast to foreign Countries, 125
Dritte Reich, Das (book by Moeller van den Bruck), 63
Dusseldorf, Goebbels' early stay in, 33
Goebbels' party work in, 35
Duisburg, Goebbels' party work in, 36

East Asia, radio programmes beamed to, 125
East Prussia, Nazi strength in 1928 and 1930, comparison of, 80
Ebert, Friedrich, Reich President, 30
Eckart, Dietrich, 62, 63
Economic crisis of 1931, 83

Economics, Ministry of, forced to relinquish control of commercial activities, 113
Economy, Minister of, Funk appointed as, 118
Eden, Anthony, recognition of German danger, 161
Edward VIII, abdication from British throne, 144
Eher-Verlag, 116
Eighteenth Brumaire of Louis Bonaparte, The (book by Marx), 24
Eisenstein, Russian movie director, 155
Elberfeld, early conspiracies in, 31
Goebbels' party work in, 36
Emergency meetings of foreign cabinets following march into Rhineland, 141
Employees of Propaganda Ministry, comparative numbers, 148
'Encirclement', danger to Germany of, 175
Engels, Friedrich, 24
England, abdication of King, 144
England, Bank of, 84
Enlightenment campaign against 'Alarmists and Critics,' 132
Ernst, Karl, 106
Erntedankfest celebration, 124
Essen, Goebbels' party work in, 36
Esser, 44
Europe, Allied invasion of, 281
European New Order, 196, 207*ff*
Europe's Suicide, book ordered written by Goebbels, 280
suggested revisions after Allied invasion, 284

Fasanenstrasse press club, 168
Fascists, Spanish, recognised by Germany, 143
Feder, Gottfried, 38, 43, 63, 68
Feuchtwanger Lion, books burned, 118
Fighting Leningrad, The (Soviet film), as example of total war, 272
Films, Goebbels' personal control of, 154-55
Goebbels' principal hobby during war, 266*ff*
of Polish and French campaigns, 191
Film section of Propaganda Ministry, 114, 154
Fink, Werner 154
Fire in Reichstag, 105-06
Fischer, Hugo, 115
Flegel, Erna, 118*n*
Flisges, Richard, 24-27

Foch's private railroad car, used for armistice in World Wars I and II, 194

Food-rationing, plan at start of war, 178

Foreign Affairs, Ministry of, forced to relinquish control of foreign publicity, 113
Ribbentrop appointed to, 167

Foreign correspondents, wartime methods of deceiving, 211-12

Foreign embassies and legations, propaganda attachés in, 126-27

Foreign newspapermen, expulsion from Germany, 130

Foreign newspapers owned by German Propaganda Ministry, 128

Foreign press, Goebbels' first talk to, 128

Foreign press clubs opened by Ribbentrop and Goebbels, 168

Foreign propaganda, expenditures on, 149
results of, 129ff

Foreign publicity, control obtained by Goebbels, 113
control obtained by Ribbentrop, 168

Foreign radio programmes prohibited to German listeners, 186ff

Foreign radio propaganda, 125

Foreign tourist trade advertising, control obtained by Goebbels, 113

'Fortress Europe,' propaganda campaign on, 272, 280-45

France, efforts to propagandise, 138-59
German invasion of, 193ff
German 'war of nerves' against, 192
Poland's independence guaranteed by, 174
political difficulties of pre-war period, 161
Ruhr, occupation of, 30
short-wave transmission from, 125

Franco, Francisco, 143

Franco-British pact with Poland, 174

Franco-German collaboration, Nazi propaganda concerning, 138-39

François-Poncet, André, French Ambassador, 138

Frankfurt, short-wave radio transmission from, 125

Frankfurt, University of, Goebbels' attendance at, 20

Frankfurter Zeitung (daily paper), 118

Frankfurt on the Oder, Nazi strength in 1928 and 1930, comparison of, 80

Free Corps, 27, 30, 72

Freiburg, short-wave radio transmission from, 125

Freiburg, University of, Goebbels' attendance at, 20, 23

Fremdersrerkehr propaganda outfit, control obtained by Goebbels, 113

French Communists, anti-war propaganda of, 193

Freud, Sigmund, books burned, 118

Freybe, Ilse, 13, 87n

Frick, Wilhelm, 68, 102
appointed Minister of the Interior, 108

Friedlaender, stepfather of Magda Goebbels, 85

Fritzsche, Hans, 14, 60, 76, 111, 118, 119, 134, 147, 175, 176, 187, 189, 194, 211, 213, 218, 258, 264, 272, 280, 291, 302, 318, 341, 354
resignation as head of Press Division, 232
return to Propaganda Ministry as director of radio, 253

Front am Polarkeis (soldiers' newspaper), 185n

Funk, Walther, 118, 120, 111

Furtwaengler, Wilhelm, 118

Gallup Poll, use for propagandising by Goebbels, 204

Gebhardt, Karl Franz, 346

Geneva, Switzerland, Goebbels' visit to, 125-26

Geneva Convention, Goebbels' desire to renounce, 316-17

George Circle, poetry society, 22

German Admiralty, silence on Athenia sinking, 181

German aggression: Britain, Battle of, 200
Crete, air invasion of, 215
Czechoslovakia, occupation of, 173
France, invasion of, 193ff
Holland and Belgium, invasion of, 191
Norway, occupation of, 201
Poland, invasion of, 178-80
Rhineland, occupation of, 140-41; Russia, invasion of, 214ff
United States, declaration of war on, 223

German air force, destruction of Guernica in Spanish Civil War, 143

German-American Chamber of Commerce, propagandising in United States, 191

German Army, dissatisfaction of generals with S.A., 134
march into the Rhineland, 140-41
oath of loyalty to Hitler following Hindenburg's death, 136-37
plot against Hitler, 284ff

German Army communiqués, Goebbels denied control of, 182

German Broadcasting Company, all shares acquired by Propaganda Ministry, 115

German Communist Party, 41, 47, 95, 100
dissolution of, 110

German consulates in United States, pre-war direction in propaganda, 244-33

German General Staff, failure to prepare Army for Russian winter, 222
horror at Goebbels' clothes collection, 222

German home front, Goebbels' efforts to prepare for hardships of Russian campaign, 222-23

German National People's Party, dissolution of, 110

German Officers Corps, forced resignation of unsuitable generals, 160

German-Polish question, appeal by Beck for peaceful settlement of, 175

German Railway Information Service, propagandising in United States, 191

German underground movements against Nazis, 247

Germany: bombing by Allied planes, 246, 275
Britain, naval treaty concluded with, 139
Britain, naval treaty renounced by Hitler, 175
League of Nations, withdrawal from, 126
Poland, non-aggression pact with, Hitler's renunciation of, 175
rearming of, 139
Russia, non-aggression pact with, 176
scorched-earth policy, failure of, 296
United States, loans from, 47

Gestapo, 165, 208, 216

Giennanth, Herr von, Goebbels' agent in New York Consulate General, 191

Gilbert, Seymour Parker, 69

INDEX

Giraudoux, Jean, French Minister of Information, 192

Goebbels, Conrad, grandfather of Joseph, 18

Goebbels, Fritz, father of Joseph, 18

Goebbels, Gertrude Margaret (née Rosskamm), grandmother of Joseph, 19

Goebbels, Ham, brother of Joseph, 18

Goebbels, Hedda, daughter of Joseph, 157

Goebbels, Heide, daughter of Joseph, 157

Goebbels, Helga, daughter of Joseph, 157

Goebbels, Helmut son of Joseph, 157

Goebbels, Hilde, daughter of Joseph, 157

Goebbels, Holde, daughter of Joseph, 157

Goebbels, Konrad, brother of Joseph, 18

Goebbels, Magda (née Rietschel), wife of Joseph, 85-88
  death of self and children, plans for, 338, 353
  Hitler, personal interest in, 157
  household finances of, 96
  love affairs of, 158, 164, 233
  marital difficulties of, 157ff
  volunteer war work of, 293

Goebbels. Maria (Frau Kimmich), sister of Joseph, 13, 14, 18, 31, 159, 276, 300

Goebbels, Maria Katharina, mother of Joseph, 13, 14, 18, 159, 276

Goebbels, Paul Joseph: anti-Semitism, development of, 27
  Army plot against Hitler, quelling of, 285-52
  attempted assassination of, 248
  autobiographical novel written by, 19, 21n, 33
  birth and childhood of, 17-19
  children of, 157
  appointed Defender of Berlin, 314
  doctor's thesis of, 23
  education of, 19ff
  appointed Gauleiter of Berlin, 47
  and Goering, conflict during final phase of war, 272, 315
  household extravagances during war, 265
  lameness, reason for, 17
  League of Nations, visit to, 125-26
  love affairs of, 23, 39, 157, 160ff
  marriage of, 87-88
  appointed Minister of

Propaganda, 110
  nationalism, development of, 26-27
  as Nazi agitator, 36ff
  Nazi Party, introduction to, 28-29
  New Order, effort to create for conquered countries, 196
  premonition of catastrophe at commencement of Russian campaign, 141-42
  priesthood, ambition toward, 19
  appointed Reich Director for Total Warfare, 291
  appointed Reich propaganda chief, 69
  election to Reichstag, 67-68
  Reichstag fire, planning of, 106
  suicide, plans for, 335, 350-51
  town house of, 200-01
  war, efforts to avert, 168, 172, 175
  wartime daily schedule, 243ff

Goering, Hermann, 18, 33, 68, 78, 85, 94, 102, 108, 119, 151, 165, 172, 200, 240, 265, 270, 286. 291, 331, 343, 345
  and Goebbels, conflict during final phase of war, 272, 315
  newspapers, acquisition of, 116
  personal enrichment of, 150
  Reichstag fire, accused of, 106
  Reichstag fire trial, mishandling of, 107

Goldschmidt, Jakob, 53, 84

Gorky, Maxim, books burned, 118

Gottschalk, Joachim, 266

Graefe, Albrecht von, 39

Grand Mufti of Jerusalem, notification to Germany of contemplated Allied invasion, 241

Greece, independence guaranteed by Britain, 174

Gruene Post (weekly), 133

Grynszpan, Herschel, 169ff

Guensche, Hitler's adjutant, 350-51

Guernica, destruction of in Spanish Civil War, 143

Gundolf, Friedrich, 22, 26, 27

Gutterer, Leopold, 115

Haase, Paul von, commandant of Berlin, 286

Haberzettel, Inge, 13, 15, 277, 254, 311, 318, 319, 320

Hadamovsky, Eugen, 115, 125

Haegert, head of Aktion B, 293

Hagen, Lieutenant, discovery of Army plot against Hitler, 285

Halfeld, August, W., 236

Halifax, Lord, description of Bolshevism, 177

Hamburg, Allied air bombardment of, 275
  poison-gas deaths in 160, 69

Hanfstaengl, Putzi, 96

Hanke, Karl, 115, 164, 166-167

Hans Westmar (Nazi movie), 155

Harvest thanksgiving celebration, 124

Hauenstein, Heinz, 30, 47, 50

Haw-Haw, Lord, 198-99

Hayn, Hans, 30-31

Heidelberg, University of, Goebbels' attendance at, 20

Heiden, Konrad, 41n, 44n

Heine, Heinrich, 23

Helhorn, Anka, 23

Helldorf, Count Wolf von, 82, 96, 106

Henlein, Konrad, 168

Hess, Rudolf, 11, 33
  flight to England, 213-57

Hesse, Grand Duke of, support of, Nazi Party by, 55

Heydrich, 165

Hildebrand, Inge, £, 149, 318, 320

Himmler, Heinrich, 33, 35, 43, 118, 128, 165, 250, 257, 286, 331, 343

Hindenburg, Paul von, Reich President, 35, 83, 85, 89, 91, 100, 110
  Hitler, meetings with, 85, 94, 97 103
  refusal to prosecute Dutch Communist for setting Reichstag fire, 107
  death of, 136
  testament of, 137

Hindenburg (zeppelin), 141

Hinkel, Hans, 115

Hinkel, Paul, 292

Hitler, Adolf, 18 29
  Army plot against, 284ff
  banned as public speaker, 71
  birthday holidays, 122
  candidacy against Hindenburg for Reich presidency, 83
  Chamberlain's visits to, 169
  death of, 351
  Goebbels' early enthusiasm for, 40, 44-46
  Hindenburg, meetings with, 85, 94, 97, 103
  marriage, 348
  militarisation of Rhineland, 140-41
  putsch, beer-cellar, 33
  appointment as Reich Chancellor, 103

Hitlerjunge Quex (Nazi movie), 153

Hitler Means War (book by Leland Stowe), 130

Hitler Youth, 138-59
  Goebbels' opinion of, 277
Hoehler, Ali, 74-75
Hohenzollern, Prince August
  Wilhelm von, support of Nazi
  Party by, 55
Home Press Division, Chief of, 118
Hoover, Herbert, 83
Horcher's restaurant, Goebbels'
  efforts to close it, 272
Horst Wessel song, 75
Hour of Decision, The (book by
  Spengler), 131, 214
Huegel, Klaus, 244
Hugenberg, Alfred, 76-77, 110
  Ministry of Agriculture and
  Economics, 108

I.G. Farben, 95, 129
Industrialists, financial support of
  opposition to Ruhr occupation,
  32
  Opposition to Young Plan of
  reparations, 76
  support of Hitler, 41, 47, 103
Inflation following World War I,
  22, 30, 35
Interior, Ministry of, forced to
  relinquish control of press and
  radio, 113
International loan to Germany,
  Chamberlain's proposal of in
  16117, 173
I Saw the U.S.A. during the War
  (book by Halfeld), 236
'Isidor,' Goebbels' campaign against,
  60-61
Italian Fascists, demonstrations in
  France, 51
Italian invasion, Chamberlain's fear
  of, 174
Italy, invasion of Abyssinia by, 139
  withdrawal from League of
  Nations, 151
  under Mussolini, 69
  Mussolini dismissed by King, 274
  surrender to Allies, 274
I Was a Nazi Spy (Hollywood
  movie), 113

Jacobs, Otto, stenographer to
  Goebbels, 13, 15, 187, 208,
  278, 299, 316, 318, 322
Jaenicke, Erna, 74
Japan, commendation by Nazis for
  'reconstruction' in East Asia,
  227
  Goebbels' request to be appointed
  Ambassador to, 165
Jewry, blackmail of, 119-41
  Goebbels' accusation of guilt for
  World War II, 225

Jews, See Anti-Jewish decrees; Anti-
  Semitism
Jodl, General, 331, 344
Journalists, law controlling
  employment of, 116
Joyce, William, 198-99
Juergens, Heinz, 107n
Jugo, Jenny, 153
Jung, Dr Edgar, 134

Kaiserhof to the Reich Chancellery,
  From the (book by Goebbels),
  90
Kaltenbrunner, Ernst, 287
Kamenev, exiled to Siberia, 69
Kampfverlag, Berlin publishing
  house, 35
Katyn, mass murder of Polish
  officers at, 269
Kaufmann, Karl, 31-32
Keitel, Wilhelm, Chief of Staff, 161,
  241, 254, 268, 284. 331, 343
Kellogg, Frank Billings, 68
  award of Nobel Peace Prize to,
  68
Kempka, Erich, 343
Kessel, Albrecht von, 247
Kimmich, Alex, husband of
  Goebbels' sister Maria, 13, 276
Knickerbocker H. R., banned from
  Germany, 130
Knorke (collected articles by
  Goebbels), 65
Koch, Erich, 17, 31, 32
Koenigsberg Fair, supervisory
  control obtained by Goebbels,
  113
Kolberg (German film), 293, 307
Krebs, Hans, 343, 352
Krefeld, Goebbels' party work
  in, 36
Kreisleiters (Reich propaganda
  chiefs), 246, 306
Kriegk, Dr, 231
Kritikaster, Goebbels' campaign
  against, 132
Krosigk, Count Schwerin von,
  Finance Minister, 108, 333
Krumerow, Dr, 248
Krupp, Gustav, 32
Kuetemeyer, Hans Georg, 73
Kunz, Dr, 353n

Labour Front organised, 123
Lammers, Hans, 254
Lang, Fritz, 155
  Lanke, estate of Goebbels in, 156
Lappland Kurier (soldiers'
  newspaper), 185n
Law of War, The (Goebbels' last
  book of collected articles), 321
League of Nations, disarmament

programme of, 125
Germany's admittance to, 79
Germany's withdrawal from, 126,
  150-51
Italy's withdrawal from, 151
Lee, Ivy, 129-30
Legation secretary assassinated in
  Paris, 169
Leipzig, Nazi strength in 1928 and
  1930, comparison of, 80
  Reichstag fire trial in, 107
  Fair, supervisory control obtained
  by Goebbels, 113
Leipzigerplatz press club, 168
Leopold Palast, Propaganda
  Ministry Building, 112
  additions to, 147
Lewis, Sinclair, 130
Ley, Robert, as leader of Rheinland-
  Sued Gau, 42, 44
  as head of Labour Front, 123,
  188, 289, 311, 323, 334
Lippe, Diet election of 1993, 102-
  103
Lippert, Julius, as editor in chief of
  Der Angriff, 57
  appointed mayor of Berlin, 110
Literature department of
  Propaganda Ministry, 114
Little A B C of the National
  Socialist (pamphlet by
  Goebbels), 65
Locarno, Treaty of, 79
Louis, Joe, 141
Lozovsky, Solomon Abramovich,
  236
Lubitsch, Ernst, 155
Lublin, mass murders at, 270
Ludendorff, General, 254, 330
Luftwaffe, 200, 215, 241, 270
Lumberjack of Bad Aibling,
  Goebbels' hypothetical radio
  listener, 233

Maginot Line, propagandistic
  onslaught against, 192
Mann, Thomas, books burned, 118
Marburg, University of, von Papen's
  speech at, 134
Marx, Karl, 24, 27
May Day celebration by Nazis, 122
Mecklenburg, Grand Duke of,
  support of Nazi Party by, 55
Mehlis, Karl, 13, 148
Mein Kampf, 44, 51, 81, 131, 291
Meissner, Secretary of State to
  Hindenburg, 137
Merchant of Venice, The, planned as
  anti-Semitic film, 267
Michael (novel by Goebbels), 19,
  21n, 33, 349n
Miessmacher und Kritikaster,

Goebbels' campaign against, 132
renewal of, 219, 235
Military Intelligence, propagandistic exploitation of, 192
Military training restored in Germany, 139
Military victories, lack of enthusiasm for by German people, 183
Ministeramt (Goebbels offices), special security provisions of, 249
Ministry of Economics forced to relinquish control of commercial activities, 113
Ministry of Foreign Affairs, forced to relinquish control of foreign publicity, 113
Ribbentrop appointed to, 167
Ministry of the Interior, forced to relinquish control of press and radio, 113
Ministry for National Enlightenment and Propaganda, creation of, 110
See also Propaganda Ministry
Ministry of Propaganda. *See* Propaganda Ministry
Miss X, Goebbels great love, 166ff
Model, Walter, 322
Moeller van den Bruck, Arthur, originator of 'Third Reich,' 62
Molotov, Foreign Commissar of Soviet Union, 178
Monet, Claude, 51
Monopoly over news, commentary, and recreation established by Goebbels, 114
Montgomery, Field-Marshal, 240, 301
Moratorium on Germany's debts suggested by President Hoover, 83
Morell, Dr Theodore, 304, 328, 343
Morgan, John Pierpont, 76
Moscow, accusations of against Britain in early days of war, 193
purge of 1936, 145
Movie production, Goebbels' personal supervision of, 154
Mowrer, Edgar Ansel, 90
banned from Germany, 130
Mueller, G. W., 298
Mueller, Hermann, Reich Chancellor, 78
Muni, Paul, 155
Munich, centre of nationalist movements 27
Goebbels' first political trip to, 28
Goebbels' first speech in, 44
Hitler's beer-cellar putsch, 33

Munich, University of, Goebbels' attendance at, 20
Munich Pact, 169
Music department of Propaganda Ministry, 114
Mussolini, Benito, 66, 69
Abyssinia, invasion of, 139
dismissed by King of Italy, 274
rescue by German parachutists, 275
Myth of the Twentieth Century (book by Rosenberg), 62

National Economy, Organisation for, 111
National holidays as propaganda, 122
Nationalism, Goebbels' conversion to, 26-27
National Socialism, philosophical background of, 62
National Socialist German Workers Party, Goebbels' introduction to, 29-30.
See also Nazi Party
National Socialist Letters (newsletter), 37
National Socialist Party. *See* Nazi Party
Nationalsozialistische Briefe (newsletter), 37, 62, 115
Nationalsozialistische Korrespondenz, 225
Naumann, Werner, 232, 240, 244, 251, 286, 296, 318, 320, 327, 331
Nazi agents in foreign countries, 128-29
Nazi exploitation of Olympic Games, 141-42
Nazi meetings, ritual devised for, 71
Nazi national holidays, 122
Nazi Party, beginnings of, 29-30
films, failure of, 155
financial difficulties of, 98
mass desire to join, 111
opposition to Young Plan, 77
propaganda intensified during late years of war, 250
propaganda machine, 114
rebellion against Hitler (1925), 41-42
in Switzerland, 244
Nazi-Sozi (pamphlet by Goebbels), 65
Nazi womanhood, Goebbels' impatience with dowdiness of, 152-53
Neudeck, Hindenburg's estate at, 136-137
Neurath, Konstantin von, Foreign Minister, 108, 125, 128, 167

New Europe, 196, 207ff, 283
News, fabricated for foreign correspondents and neutral press, 211
Newspaper, drop in circulation because of government-imposed similarity, 132
Newsreels, Goebbels' use of as war propaganda, 186
News reports, German accuracy in early stages of war, 183
New York Metropolitan Opera Company, Goebbels' scorn for, 226
Nihilism, Goebbels' tendency towards, 25
Nobel Peace Prize awards, 51, 68, 130, 144
Non-aggression pact with Russia, 176-21
North Africa, American invasion landings in, 240ff
Norway, German occupation of, 201
Nostradamus, alleged predictions of, 192
Nuremberg Party Rally, of 1933, 123
of 1934, 158

Odenhausen, Johanna Maria (née Coervers), grandmother of Goebbels, 19
Odenhausen, Michael, grandfather of Goebbels, 19
Oesterreichische Kreditanstalt, 83
Olden, Rudolph, 41n, 44n
Olympic Games (1936), 141-63
Organisation for National Economy, 111
Ossietzky, Karl von, award of Nobel Peace Prize to, 144
Oswiecim, mass murders at, 270
Oven, Winfried von, 243, 330

Panzerbaer, Der (lest Nazi paper). 344
Panzersperren (tank fortifications), built for defence of Berlin, 315
Papen, Franz von, espionage in United States, 94
appointment as Reich Chancellor, 94
lack of support in Reichstag, 98
dismissal of, 100
as Vice-Chancellor under Hitler, 108
Marburg speech of, 134
presentation of Hindenburg's testament, 137
Paris Embassy, attack in, 169
Paris-Midi (daily), 138

Paris-Soir (daily), 138
'Peace by fear' period, 172
People's Freedom Party, 35
Persecution of Catholic Church, 146
Persecution of Jews. See Anti-Semitism Personnel of Propaganda Ministry, constant change in, 148
Pétain, Marshal, request for armistice, 193
Petit-Parisien (daily), 127n
Picht, Dr, 87n
P.K. (propaganda units), creation by Goebbels for war coverage, 185
Plebiscite, in Austria, 161
to expropriate ex-monarchs, 41ff
against acceptance of Young Plan, 77
Poincare, Premier, 30
Poland, appeal for peaceful settlement of German-Polish question, 175
German propaganda in preparation for war against, 175, 178
independence guaranteed by France and Britain, 174
Ribbentrop's publicity orders concerning warfare against (1938), 168
Polish Corridor, 178
Polish-German border question, 79
Polish Non-Aggression Pact, Hitler's renunciation of, 175
Pomerania, Nazi strength in 1928 and 1930, comparison of, 80
Popolo d'Italia (newspaper), 198
Popoff, Bulgarian Communist, 107
Pornographic pictures, use in propagandising French soldiers, 193
Possessed, The (book by Dostoevsky), 25, 105
Postmaster General forced to relinquish advertising of railways and air lines, 113
Prague, Nazi march into, 173
Press, supervisory power obtained by Goebbels, 113
Press clubs, foreign, opened by Ribbentrop and Goebbels, 168
Press department of Propaganda Ministry, 114
Press Division, domestic, 116
news section, 118
Press Ministry proposed for Goebbels, 112
Prien, Guenther, 229
Propaganda, campaign against Churchill, 203
Goebbels' early adventures in, 51

lecture by Goebbels on, 65-66
Poland, campaign against, 214ff, 178
Russia, campaign to explain aggression against, 214ff
slogans, Goebbels' utilisation of, 151
United States, campaign to disparage military strength of, 223
campaign to prove U.S. alliance with Judaism, 225
campaign to win U.S. wartime support, 191
to prepare for war, 172
Propaganda, Department of, speakers' section, 71
Propaganda attachés in foreign embassies and legations, 126
Propaganda instructions to agents abroad, 126
Propaganda-Kompagnien (propaganda units), creation by Goebbels for war coverage, 185
Propaganda Ministry, 110
Aktion B division, creation of, 380
bombing of, 318
expenditures of, 148
extent in 1937, 147
foreign publicity lost to Ministry of Foreign Affairs, 168
personnel, constant change of, 148
Total War section, creation of, 291
wartime routine of, 184, 201
Prophecies of Goebbels about Allied Powers, 308
Prussia, Diet election of 1932, 93
Prussian Diet, brawl between Nazis and Communists, 93
Prussian state theatres, control retained by Goering, 113
Purge of S.A. leaden, 134-56
Putsch, beer-cellar, of Hitler, 33

Quandt, Guenther first husband of Magda Goebbels, 85-86
Quandt, Harald, son of Magda Goebbels, 85, 353
Quandt, Helmut, stepson of Magda Goebbels, 85
Quandt, Herbert, stepson of Magda Goebbels, 85

Rach, Goebbels' chauffeur, 341, 354
Radek, Karl, 38
exiled to Siberia, 69
Radio, format of special announcements during war, 193
supervisory power obtained by

Goebbels, 113
African transformation by Goebbels into instrument of Nazi propaganda, 109
unavailability to Nazis in early days of Party, 109
wartime censorship of, 187
wartime features introduced by Goebbels, 234
wartime news broadcasts cut into by Russian transmitter, 236
Radio department of Propaganda Ministry, 114
Radio Division, 116
Radio personality of Hitler, development by Goebbels, 109
Radio programmes from foreign countries prohibited to German listeners, 186
Radio short-wave propaganda, 125
Railways and air lines advertising, supervisory control obtained by Goebbels, 113
Rakovsky, exiled to Siberia, 69
Rammjaeger (suicide pilots), reception by Goebbels, 303
Rastenberg, attempt on Hitler's life near, 284
Rath, Ernst vom, 169
Rathenau, Walther, 24, 26, 81
murder of, 28
Rationing, of fats, 139
of foodstuffs, 178, 268
Rauschning, Hermann, 168
Rearmament in Germany, 139
Redeverbot (ban on speechmaking), Goebbels placed under, 56
Reforms of legitimate theatre under Goebbels, 153
Rehmer, Major, 286-87
Reich, Das (weekly periodical founded by Goebbels during war), 189, 193, 200, 205, 233, 265, 335, 344
Reich, Third. See Third Reich
Reich Resident, Hitler's candidacy for, 89
Reichstag, fire, 105ff
brawl started by Nazi representatives, 93
final campaign for Nazi supremacy in, 108-31
dissolution following march into Rhineland, 140
Reimann, General, 341
Reitsch, Hanna, 346n
Remarque, Erich Maria, 82-82
Reparation, Allied demands for, 76
Retaliation, failure of propaganda of, 270-35, 279, 283
'Revelations of the Swedish Fortune-teller Gruenberg,'